HEARTS & MINDS

אוצרות

RABBI PINI DUNNER

HEARTS & MINDS

AN ORIGINAL LOOK
AT EACH PARSHA
IN THE TORAH

DEDICATED TO THE MEMORY OF

HARAV LORD JONATHAN SACKS

מוהר"ר יעקב צבי בן דוד אריה סאקס זצ"ל

אוצרות

Beverly Hills, California

HEARTS & MINDS

AN ORIGINAL LOOK
AT EACH PARSHA
IN THE TORAH

First Published 2021

Otzrot Books
Beverly Hills, California

9461 Charleville Blvd # 731
Beverly Hills, CA 90212
United States

www.otzrotbooks.com

© **Pini Dunner,** 2021

Cover Design, Layout and Printing by
Machon Sofrim 732.330.6653

ISBN 978-1-7361890-0-9, *hardcover*

A CIP catalogue record for this title is
available from the Library of Congress

Printed and bound in the State of Israel

**THIS BOOK IS DEDICATED TO
THE LIGHT OF OUR GENERATION**

HARAV LORD JONATHAN SACKS Z"L

השר מוהר"ר יעקב צבי סאקס זצוק"ל

"Good leaders create followers.
Great leaders create leaders."

YOUR LIGHT WILL NEVER BE EXTINGUISHED

ON BEHALF OF THE
OFFICERS, DIRECTORS
AND MEMBERS OF OUR SHUL

Chavi and I are honored to wish
our Rav & Mara D'Asra

Rabbi Pini Dunner

much success and hatzlacha.

May you continue to lead our congregation and our community
for many years to come.

Steve Dorfman, President
Young Israel of North Beverly Hills

Rabbi Pini Dunner

is one of the great contemporary
Rabbis of Los Angeles
And perhaps the world.
His brilliant intellect
graces and informs us.
His essays are a gift to anyone
who treasures the lessons of Torah.

Joel M. Geiderman, MD, FACEP
Beverly Hills, CA

IN MEMORY OF A SPECIAL
FATHER & GRANDFATHER

DENIS SPENCER
דוד צבי בן חיים ז"ל

Whose presence we miss
and memory we cherish.

Antony & Laurie Spencer
London, UK

———————————————⧈———————————————

Dedicated to my dear friend and "brother"

Rabbi Pini Dunner

on the outstanding achievement of
Hearts & Minds
May your wisdom and strength
continue to transcend the pages...

Celebrating with you and your beautiful family!

Bishop Robert Stearns
Israel Christian Nexus/Eagles' Wings

IN MEMORY OF OUR DEAR FATHER

HERSHEL GOLKER
ר' שלמה צבי בן ר' משה מרדכי ז"ל

Who always taught us the importance of studying Torah
and to cherish Rabbis, Talmidei Chachomim, and Yerei Shomayim.
We feel his passing every day.

**His wife, children, grandchildren,
family and acquaintances in
Israel and England**

From London to LA,

Rabbi Pini and Sabine

Lead and inspire wherever they are.
Distances don't separate our
admiration, friendship, and respect.
Proud to be their friends for decades,
and, God willing, decades to come.

Maurice and Gabriella Golker
Jerusalem, Israel

Dedicated in memory of

My beloved parents
Ted z"l and Hedy z"l Orden
and in commemoration of
Hedy Orden's first yahrzeit
חנה בת חיים ו'חוה ז"ל

Dedicated in honor of

Rabbi Pini and Sabine Dunner

in gratitude for their service

to our YINBH community

and for rising to the challenges

Presented by the Covid- 19 pandemic

Helen & Moshe Sassover and family
Beverly Hills, CA

IN HONOR OF

RABBI PINI & SABINE DUNNER

Congratulations on this wonderful book!

May you go from strength to strength.

Nadine Gerson & Robert Zeller
Beverly Hills, CA

———————⟡———————

IN LOVING MEMORY

OF MY MOTHER

RITA GERSON

רחל לאה בת ישעיהו ז"ל

July 31, 1929 – December 23, 1970

Who passed away too young,

but still lives in my heart,

mind and daily life.

Nadine Gerson

Beverly Hills, CA

With Hakarat Hatov to

Rabbi Pini Dunner

for uplifting our spirits
with words of Torah
during COVID-19.

Richard, Esther, Ari & Eliana Wood

Vancouver, Canada

DEDICATED BY

Lionel & Ruth Curry

in loving memory of
Lionel's dear father

Stanley Curry z"l

Dedicated to the memory
of our grandmother

Sonia Shooter a"h

and her sister

Gloria Lebetkin a"h

Mark & Melissa Shooter

London, UK

With immense gratitude to Hashem
for the continued רפואה שלמה of

Zvi Ryzman

צבי חיים בן הלינה שיינדיל

בתוך שאר חולי ישראל

TABLE OF CONTENTS

TABLE OF CONTENTS | 5

PREFACE

In earlier generations, it was customary to call the weekly Parsha the "*sedra,*" which means "order." Jews would date their letters by citing the day of the week of "*Seder X*" – and then refer to a verse from the weekly portion. This custom did not emerge out of nowhere, nor did it merely reflect a superficial courtesy and respect toward the Torah. Rather, the roots of this practice stem from an intrinsic Jewish belief that the weekly portion which we read in the synagogue each Shabbat directly corresponds and connects with the realities of our lives that week.

The act of learning from the weekly Parsha manifests a point of encounter between us and the word of God with reference to our everyday lives – as individuals, families, and communities, and for the Jewish People as a whole. As a direct result, Jews have always searched for signals and symbols in the Parsha to guide their lives in the present and going forward.

A classic Hasidic story describes a mother bringing her son who is very sick with influenza to visit the Rebbe's house, so that he can pray for the child. The visit takes place in the heat of the summer, and the Rebbe asks the child what he is learning at school. The boy responds that they are currently learning the portion of Vayigash. The Rebbe smiles and says, "Now I understand why you're sick with influenza. Vayigash is a winter Parsha, which explains why you are suffering from the cold weather. You need to learn something from the Book of

Bamidbar, which we read in the summer, and you will soon recover."

This story might strike us as odd, but it embodies a sincere faith that there is a link between the seasonal cycle and the associated Torah's portions – and this idea transcends the fact that the Rebbe's advice does not seem logical to us, as obviously one can suffer from influenza and "winter illnesses" at any time of the year. Indeed, many sermons have been written throughout Jewish history connecting the Parsha of the week to the time of the year, such as Parshat Mikeitz and Chanukah, Parshat Nitzavim and Rosh Hashanah, among others.

The Torah tells us: תורה צוה לנו משה מורשה קהילת יעקב – "Moses commanded us Torah, a heritage for the community of Jacob" (Deut. 23:4). The Talmud comments on this verse (Pes. 49b): אל תקרי מורשה אלא מאורסה – "do not read it as *morasha* (heritage), rather read it as *me'orasa* (betrothed)."

One way to relate to the Torah is as an inheritance, which we maintain and respect by virtue of its ancient sanctity. But our Sages are teaching us that we must also relate to the Torah as our "betrothed" lover – as if it is new, fresh, fascinating, and relevant.

But to do this effectively is no simple challenge, especially when we must overcome barriers of language and style, cultural differences, and so much more. And this mission is made even more difficult in this day and age, with flickering screens constantly ambushing us from every angle, and levels of attention dwindling significantly. The ability to read longer written texts, and to absorb the information they contain, is becoming more challenging with each passing day.

Not many rabbis know how to turn Torah into a "betrothed," and not many rabbis know how to find an audience for their creative thoughts in today's generation. Rabbi Dunner is one of them. Like an *haute-couture* tailor, he artistically weaves his original ideas into the verses of the Torah and various commentaries, finding a connection between them and a dazzling variety of diverse contemporary topics that engage our generation. His familiarity with the modern world, Western culture, and the challenges of present-day society, coupled with his superb Torah scholarship, as well as his ability to convey messages in language that is easily understood, transform his sermons and articles into something that is meaningful and compelling for everyone.

As the rabbi of Young Israel of North Beverly Hills, one of the most unique communities on the West Coast of the United States, Rabbi Dunner knows how to introduce the world of Torah concepts to different audiences – whether they are familiar with Torah Judaism or are more remote from their heritage – by fusing those treasured concepts with contemporary ideas and challenges. For me personally, and for Tzohar as an organization, it is a great privilege to have a close and meaningful relationship with Rabbi Dunner. We share the same notions and dreams of a Judaism that is accessible and inviting in a world that is so alienated and detached.

On a personal note, one of the great rabbinic heroes of my youth as a yeshiva student was the great scholar, Rabbi Josef Hirsch Dünner of Amsterdam (1833-1911), the late esteemed Chief Rabbi of Holland. I was deeply drawn to his Talmudic writings, and adored every aspect and detail. As a Talmud lecturer and Rosh Yeshiva, I would never teach a passage of Talmud without first checking what the great Rabbi Dünner had to say, so that I could include his novel ideas in my presentation.

When I first visited Rabbi Pini Dunner at his home, I inquired if there was any connection between him and the great Rabbi Dünner of Amsterdam. Imagine my amazement when he responded that yes, there was a connection – Rabbi Josef Hirsch Dünner of Amsterdam was his grandfather's great-uncle, and his grandfather, Rabbi Yosef Tzvi Dunner of London, was the first member of the Dunner family to be named after this illustrious forebear. From then on my soul has been linked with his. It is clear to me that Torah always returns to its home.

We are lucky to live at a time when there is an increasing number of our brothers and sisters whose interest in what the Torah has to say is deepening. Many people, young and old, want their lives to be reinvigorated through Torah. Rabbi Dunner's book will offer these Torah seekers the opportunity to have their lives refreshed, enabling them to quench their thirst for Torah with the living waters of his wonderful words.

Rabbi David Stav
TZOHAR Organization
Shoham, Israel

FOREWORD

I n our digital age, the dissemination of knowledge is speedier and reaches further afield than ever in human history. Until two decades ago, the major problem in research was the seeking of information. It was the chase, which could often take months of sending letters and waiting for replies, laboriously going through card indexes, and suchlike, until a sufficient database was available for the critical stage of analysis.

Today, all that has changed. Searching for information in an era of Google and other cyber search engines enables us to collect vast amounts of information within minutes, and to store it all on a disk which fits into our pocketbooks and can go with us anywhere in the world. The problem in research today is our ability to sort out and select those parts of the data which are relevant, and which enable us to do something meaningful.

This applies as much to our desire to reach deeper understandings of philosophical and ethical teachings, a task which does not always lend itself to research norms of the world of social scientists, or those attempting to create a synthesis between questions of belief with the behavioral norms of the society within which we live and interact on a daily basis.

How much more so is this problem relevant when we try to apply the teachings of Torah to the realities of our existence in a technological, often spiritual-less, world. Few are the teachers and rabbis who have succeeded in merging the two into a meaningful synthesis, drawing on the teachings of Torah and its diverse commentaries to assist us in understanding more clearly how to face the challenges of our contemporary society – a society which, at first glance, seems so far removed from the prophets of old.

Making Torah relevant to people's everyday lives is what makes the Torah into a "tree of life," as contrasted with an ancient text to be explored, and this requires our rabbis and teachers to be fully conversant with the technologies and challenges of the real world. These challenges have changed over time as the Jewish people have moved beyond the pre-technological era of a poverty-stricken Eastern Europe, irrespective of its deep learning tradition, to one in which every syllable or murmur diffuses so rapidly that mistakes can never be corrected and where messages have to be concise and leave an indelible imprint on the psyche.

But there are a few teachers and writers in the world who are able to combine the two in a way that does not require retreating into the sealed ghettos of a fundamentalist society where the outside world is perceived as a threat, or alternatively a total break with tradition and religion as constituting an outdated and irrelevant way of looking at the world.

The world has just recently mourned the passing of one of the true masters of bringing the Torah to life, the late Rabbi Lord Jonathan Sacks, who attained global recognition and esteem for the masterful way in which he made Torah meaningful to hundreds of thousands of people, and not just those of the Jewish faith. His was a deeply intellectual approach which, over time, and increasingly through the sophisticated use of the new forms of social media, alongside his many books, succeeded in finding its way into the hearts and minds of a generation who are more turned on by a populist culture which seeks short sharp headlines and instant gratification.

I am reminded of another Rabbi Professor I knew thirty years ago when I first moved to the south of Israel and started working at Ben-Gurion University. Rabbi Professor Avraham Kushelevsky was a member of a renowned eastern European rabbinical family who, unlike most of his close relatives, opted for the world of science (in the field of nuclear engineering), but a world of science which was instructed by his deep religious learning and knowledge, which was vast.

In the community in which I reside in Metar in the south of Israel, and where I cherished Rabbi Professor Kushelevsky as a neighbor and as the unofficial rabbi of our small Ashkenazic community (which he helped found), he was renowned for his weekly talks on Parshat Hashavua, which, without effort, brought the religious, the historical and the contemporary together in such a way that it seemed obvious and logical. What he managed to get over in a short, sharp, intellectually cutting message was far more than many preachers and teachers manage to do in a much longer time frame. No one ever returned home from listening to him without something deep to ponder over during their Shabbat meal.

This is the style which is successfully taken on by my friend Rabbi Pini Dunner in this collection of short essays on Parshat Hashavua which he has written over the course of several years, during his tenure as rabbi of the Orthodox community in Beverly Hills.

Drawing from his own personal history, bringing together the Orthodox world of his famous rabbinical family, merging it with his real world experiences as a Modern Orthodox rabbi, the founder of a yuppie community (The Saatchi Synagogue) in London, his rich and deep knowledge of Jewish commentaries and texts (of all sorts, from the Lithuanian teachers to the Hassidic masters), he successfully remolds the ancient teachings into a series of short and memorable messages which his readers and listeners can take home with them to mull over during the coming week.

He is also able to draw on his own impressive collection of original Jewish texts and manuscripts of which he has become a leading collector in his own right.

Each of the essays in this collection contain a clear structure. A contemporary issue in world affairs is mentioned, this is linked to the Parshat Hashavua – the weekly Torah portion – and is analyzed through the eyes and the writings of specific Torah commentators who have grappled with similar problems during their own lifetime. His views on contemporary problems facing the Jewish world, Israel and society as a whole, are highlighted. He draws together such seeming contrasts as the respective leadership traits of Joseph with those of former Israeli president Shimon Peres; an understanding of the concept of *tohu va'vohu* ("chaos and disorder") in a world in which we seek order; the contemporary importance of prayer as understood through the experience of the Biblical figure of Isaac; impeachment and the judicial process as understood through the story of Joseph and his brothers and mediated through the teachings of the Netziv (Rabbi Naftali Zvi Yehuda Berlin); the need for a balanced education as seen through the eyes of Jacob – and the list is endless.

Rabbi Dunner's expertise draws on his cognizance with the Jewish worlds of the UK (where he grew up), the USA (where he has lived and practiced as a rabbi for the past decade), and Israel (which he visits frequently). His life encounters and friendships with such diverse personalities as Lord Sacks, his father Aba Dunner (who was one of Europe's major Jewish *askanim* during the post WWII era), and Rabbi Shlomo Carlebach (with whom he shared a deep relationship) has stood him in good stead to make his own contribution at bringing the different strands together in an attempt to make sense of the contemporary challenges he faces as a rabbi and teacher in today's Western world.

The specific views expressed by Rabbi Dunner will not necessarily find favor with each and every reader in each and every circumstance. I would beg to differ with him on some of these views, not least concerning Israel or his take on the pros and cons of multiculturalism and its impact on a democratic and egalitarian society. But what Rabbi Dunner does is to demonstrate how these issues can be meaningfully interpreted through the texts he brings. He challenges us to think along with him, to raise questions as and where necessary, and to go with him along the path of bringing the Torah in all of its glory into the modern world, rather than throwing it overboard or leaving it to the exclusivity of small self-enclosed groups for whom the real world and its complexities are not part of their daily experience.

For me, it is ironic to think that for a short time as a young rabbi in the 1990's, when his career was just beginning, Rabbi Dunner was the rabbi of a small community in the Notting Hill neighborhood of West London (yes, the same Notting Hill which most people identify with the Hugh Grant movie) where my own grandfather had been the rabbi during the 1920s and 1930s.

It is interesting to compare the sort of people and the sort of messages which would have been relevant then, with those that are required today. It was a poor neighborhood, with many first- and second-generation immigrants from Eastern Europe. This small community produced some famous people – Harry Tabor, the father of Israeli solar energy; Rabbi Kopul Rosen, a Torah giant who later founded Carmel College and could potentially have been a Chief Rabbi of Britain had he not passed away at a relatively young age; and Abe Harman, later to be Israel's ambassador to the United States – three lives which combined the worlds of science, Torah and politics.

But for most of the congregants, it was a life of toil, as they worked hard to make a living, had limited time for study (but always found the time), and whatever resources they did have they invested in the education of their children and grandchildren. The third and fourth generations became successful in all walks of life, often (but not always) at the cost of forsaking tradition and the Torah understandings of contemporary life. In the UK, as in the USA, many of this generation now seek a meaningful merging of the two and it is to this generation that Rabbi Dunner's collection of essays resonates.

Hopefully this will be but the first volume of an ongoing series of essays, covering the entire Torah, one to be used not just for self-gratification but for sharing, around the dinner table, with family members and children in particular.

Professor David Newman
Ben-Gurion University
Erev Chanukah, December 2020

INTRODUCTION

C ould you envisage living your life without ever speaking your mind, or – imagine this! – without ever speaking at all? The Order of Cistercians of the Strict Observance, a Catholic monastic order better known as Trappists, is best known for its strict code of silence. This stringently observed regulation originates in the fact that Trappists, as a branch of the Benedictines, closely observe the "Rule of Saint Benedict," which includes, among other things, the requirement to reduce all conversation to an absolute minimum.

Truthfully, "absolute minimum" could mean at least some verbal communication, but in reality Trappists don't talk at all. In spite of the fact that they do not take an absolute vow of silence, their belief is that speech distracts monks and nuns from a religiously desired state of tranquility and receptivity – after all, speech might lead them to fulfil personal desires rather than being fully absorbed with the will of God – and so in practice, their code of "almost" silence means that ordinary conversation is virtually non-existent in a Trappist monastery. Although, rather curiously, the order has developed a highly sophisticated sign language to enable communication – which, to be perfectly frank, I have always thought rather defeats the purpose.

And while I'm being frank, let me say this – not only do I think it would be impossible to establish an equivalent sect or religious order within Judaism, I also happen to think it would be distinctly un-Jewish. The reason for this is really quite simple – all forms of extreme abstention are considered antithetical to Jewish thought. While other religions revel in absolute restrictions as an ultimate realization of spiritual fulfillment, in the belief that by denying the human body of what it craves physically one can purge it of its base materialism, thereby allowing the vacuum to be filled with spirituality and Godliness, Judaism – particularly after the Jewish mysticism renaissance of the sixteenth century – embraces the material world as the primary medium by which we can serve God as human beings.

As Jews, our task in life is to harness God's creation and use it in every way possible, so that each and every divine spark contained in the material world can be united with its ultimate purpose. Of course, some aspects of the material world are elevated through use while others serve God via the medium of rejection. For example, the same spiritual goal is achieved by eating kosher meat as can be achieved by not eating bacon. But the crucial point is this – to forbid meat completely would be an ungodly denial of the spiritual value and potential of meat. Similarly, physical relations within marriage have a spiritual value that is on-par with abstention from illicit sexual contact, represented in the Torah by the prohibitions against incest and adultery.

The use of words in speech and verbal communication is no different. A human being's use of words and speech to communicate ideas, feelings, observations, and so much more, is what truly separates us from all other sentient creatures on earth. And yet, our most powerful tool for the good can so easily become a weapon wielded for bad. Harnessing our power of speech so that we can enhance our spiritual status is probably the most difficult challenge we face as human beings throughout the course of our lives.

Think about it. Out of the many thousands of words we say every day, how many of them are devoted to a spiritually elevating agenda? It was for precisely this reason that our sages set prayers for us to say and recite at regular intervals, so that we can routinely focus our power of speech for a spiritual purpose.

But prayers are not enough. Trappist monks and nuns also pray, and they also regularly listen to readings from the scriptures – portions read out aloud for them by one of their fellow monastics, who must obviously use his or her power of speech to do that. Articulating other people's words – even if they are in the form of prayers, or are words taken from scripture – just cannot be compared to the freedom to express yourself using your own words. Self-generated words are a window into our thoughts, demonstrating how we have processed the world around us, a show of how we are able to exercise control over our intellect to improve our understanding of reality. Denying ourselves this ability means locking up the most unique human ability of all – the gift from God of individual human autonomy, that enigmatic illusion that allows space for free choice.

Indeed, is there anything that we say that is actually original? We have a principle in Judaism, enshrined in Ecclesiastes (1:9): וְאֵין כָּל חָדָשׁ תַּחַת הַשָּׁמֶשׁ – "there is nothing new under the sun." The sages of the Talmud interpreted this verse to mean that anything meaningful said or written throughout the course of history has a source in the Torah, namely the first five books of the Hebrew Scriptures. It is a truly amazing idea, namely that the answer to everything – all of the world's wisdom and every "eureka" moment – can be found in the Divine text of the Torah, the ultimate source of God's life-force in creation.

The Talmud (Taanit 9a) records that the great sage Rabbi Yoḥanan was stumped by his precocious nephew, the son of his most frequent interlocutor, Rabbi Shimon ben Lakish, regarding exactly this point:

> **Rabbi Yoḥanan once encountered the young son of Reish Lakish as he was sitting and studying. He was reciting the verse: "The foolishness of man perverts his way, and his heart frets against the Lord" (Prov. 19:3).**

The young man cited this verse as a test for his uncle, challenging him to find a source in the Torah for the idea expressed by the verse that when someone sins and then terrible things happen to him, he will likely try to work out what it is that he did wrong which would have resulted in the awful things he is experiencing now.

Rabbi Yoḥanan was baffled by the boy's challenge, and blurted out in amazement, "is there really anything that is written elsewhere in the scriptures that is not alluded to somewhere in the Torah?" But as hard as he tried, Rabbi Yoḥanan was unable to come up with a corresponding Torah reference, and eventually he gave up.

Whereupon the boy smiled at him and said: "How could you miss it? This idea is mentioned clearly with regard to Joseph's brothers, when it says: 'And their heart failed them and they turned trembling to one to another, saying: What is this that God has done to us?'" (Gen. 42:28). This verse exemplifies the idea that when a sincere person sins and encounters problems later on, he will consider his past actions to see if he can work out why it is that he is going through such a bad patch.

Rabbi Yoḥanan was so impressed by the boy's suggestion, that despite his old age and poor eyesight he made a special effort to look at him, as he wanted to focus on the features of this gifted young man who had taught him something new and so meaningful.

On the basis of this idea, one must conclude that any code of silence is pointless, as whatever we say, and whatever thoughts come into our heads that we may wish to articulate, as long as we are devoted to God, the words that emerge will always somehow trace themselves back to the Torah, the true mouthpiece of all wisdom. Ironically, rather than being a limitation, it is exactly this idea that gives Jewish scholarship its most fundamental freedom – the right to be *meḥadesh*, which means the right to come up with novel ideas and new interpretations.

The great rabbinic luminary Naḥmanides ("*Ramban*"; 1194-1270), in his seminal work *Milḥamot Hashem* – a vigorous defense of the halakhic codifier Rabbi Isaac Alfasi (1013-1103) against the criticisms of Rabbi Zeraḥiah ha-Levi of Girona (1115-1186) – takes this idea even further, informing us that there is an "obligation ... to search through the subjects of the Torah ... and bring to light their hidden contents." In other words, being a *meḥadesh* is not a passive opportunity, but an active and ongoing obligation. Each and every one of us must look to the Torah for direction regarding our own day-to-day lives, as well as the life of the world around us, and then we must convey those ideas to our family, friends, acquaintances, and work colleagues – in short, the widest possible audience available to us.

The Torah is not an ancient work containing narratives and precepts timebound to the early period of Jewish national and religious history. On the contrary, it is a living, breathing fount of Divine wisdom that can offer meaningful clues to help us understand and unravel contemporary events, and to get to the bottom of every aspect of human existence, including technology, medicine, psychology, politics, business, and relationships – just to name a few.

Some years ago, when I first began to write a regular column on the Torah portion, I would use my weekly articles as an opportunity to offer generic ethical advice, or to present a solution to some textual or narrative anomaly that cropped up in a particular *parsha*. But after just a few weeks of doing this, I received a call from my good friend, George Schaeffer, a stalwart of our community in Beverly Hills and a devoted supporter of countless good causes.

He was very blunt, as he always is. "Would you mind if I gave you some constructive criticism?"

"Not at all," I replied, not sure where he was going with this.

"You're a great writer, and I love reading the way you write things, but…" ("oh gosh, here it comes," I thought to myself – and took a deep breath) "…although the way you write is great, forgive me for saying so – your content is bland. It doesn't have much in it that is relevant to my life, and I also don't like to be lectured. Come on, Pini, make it more relevant. I know you can do it, because I've heard you speak from the pulpit, and also whenever we chat privately – you really know how to connect Judaism to real life. All you need to do is to put that skill into your writing."

I thanked him then for his advice, and I thank him again now. In fact, even more so now. I can truly say that as a direct result of that conversation with George, I sat down and came up with a formula for my weekly column that has since proven to be extremely successful. I decided that from then on, whatever I wrote would somehow have to be relevant, informative, contemporary, and interesting – and that it should always have a connection with the weekly portion. As King Solomon said in Ecclesiastes: "there is nothing new under the sun," and as Rabbi Yoḥanan exclaimed to his nephew: "everything is alluded to in the Torah." And Naḥmanides challenges us to find these hidden nuggets, and to demonstrate that even the greatest *hiddush* is actually "a tale as old as time."

In reading this selection from my weekly articles, you will discover that no topic is off-limits, no information is too obscure, and no idea is too remote that I won't write about it and connect it to the Torah portion. I delight in embracing the widest possible range of knowledge, reveling in both breadth and depth, and I only do it so that I can demonstrate that whatever the topic or idea may be, it can always be found somewhere in the Torah, or at least the solution to the puzzle or problem it presents can be sourced in the Torah.

There is no such thing as a "code of silence" in Judaism. Just comb through a page of Talmud to see what I mean. Indeed, I have taken my lead from the sages of the Talmud, who acted and continue to act as the foundation of Judaism and Jewish life some 2,000 years after their thoughts were recorded in the Mishna and Gemara. I have taken their example by leaping head-first into any subject that comes my way, devouring it in every vivid detail, and

I then take the utmost pleasure in seeing it reflected in our foundational text, the Torah itself.

If silence prevailed, there would be no wisdom in the world. Even the partial or selective silence of rabbis and Torah teachers is antithetical to the glorious Jewish heritage that has seen us survive thousands of years against the odds, in a sea of mistrust, suppression and hatred. It is the power of words that has enabled us to get to this point, and it will be the power of words that will propel us to our ultimate future, the Messianic age of redemption and salvation, that we all hope to live to see, speedily in our days.

I would like to take this opportunity to thank my dear friend of many years, Menachem Butler, executive director of the Julis-Rabinowitz Program on Jewish and Israeli Law at the Harvard Law School, for being the impetus behind this publication. He is a fellow traveler in the quest for knowledge, and in the desire to share that knowledge with the widest possible audience. He has also acted as an invaluable resource and networker for countless academics and rabbis active in the field of Jewish and Hebrew Studies, for which he has received scant public recognition, and for which he deserves to be showered with accolades and honors.

How many books have been written and papers been presented only as a result of Menachem's indefatigability and tireless efforts? And yet, the byline will have the academic's name or the rabbi's name, and not Menachem's name – a lacuna that has for far too long been overlooked. I am proud to have co-written some articles with Menachem over the years, but there are many others published in my name that could neither have been written nor published without his generous help. So – even though I know he deserves much more than this! – let me say: thank you, thank you, thank you!

One of the great inspirations of my rabbinic career was the former Chief Rabbi of the United Kingdom, Rabbi Lord Jonathan Sacks z"l (1948-2020), whose recent untimely passing has devastated us all, and to whom this unworthy volume of my articles is dedicated. In 1978 he was appointed to be the rabbi at Golders Green Synagogue on Dunstan Road, just around the corner from my childhood home on Hodford Road, and that was when I first got to meet him and his wonderful wife Elaine. I distinctly recall the close relationship that Rabbi Sacks soon formed with my late father, Rabbi Aba Dunner z"l (1937-2011), a relationship that endured until my father passed away.

During the latter years of my father's life the relationship between these two great men took on a whole new dimension, after Rabbi Sacks was elevated to the presidency of the Conference of European Rabbis, an extraordinary organization that federates rabbis across Europe, from Kazakhstan to Portugal, and everywhere in between. My father was the CER's untiring executive director, and together with Rabbi Sacks he determinedly worked to protect the rights of Jews in Europe, at the exact moment in time when antisemitism had begun to creep back into the political mainstream, and started to threaten the equilibrium that had endured since the end of the Second World War.

When I began my stint as rabbi of London's Saatchi Synagogue in 1998, one of the first people to call and congratulate me was Chief Rabbi Sacks. He generously agreed to attend and address our fledgling community on a number of occasions, all of them memorable and meaningful. I am delighted that we continued to remain in touch after my family moved to Los Angeles, with Rabbi Sacks attending the opening of the new building for Young

Israel of North Beverly Hills, and also addressing our community on his various visits to the West Coast. Most importantly, I continued to benefit from Rabbi Sacks' incredible scholarship via his website, where I could read his articles and listen to his podcasts.

Rabbi Sacks was truly the "rabbi's rabbi," combining intellect and acumen, content and exposition, and most importantly – scholarship and "*menshlichkeit.*" Our generation was privileged to have profited from close contact with such greatness, and it is so desperately sad that his passing denies us the many more years we could have had of his stimulating erudition and matchless presentation. Mercifully, he has left behind a true legacy of peerless material for us to benefit from, a timeless gift to Jewish life that will endure for decades and beyond.

Rabbi Sacks' predecessor was the extraordinary rabbinic scholar, Rabbi Lord Immanuel Jakobovits z"l (1921-1999). The Jakobovits family and the Dunner family share a remarkable joint history. Rabbi Jakobovits' father was a rabbi in Königsberg, East Prussia, where Rabbi Jakobovits was born in 1921. A few years later the Jakobovits family moved to Berlin, where my late grandfather, Rabbi Joseph H. Dunner z"l (1913-2007), studied at the rabbinical seminary and was a youth counselor at the Ezra youth group attended by the young Immanuel, with whom he formed a close relationship.

In 1936, during the period of prewar Nazi Germany's oppression of Jewish life, my grandfather was appointed chief rabbi of East Prussia, and moved to Konigsberg, where my late father was born in 1937. Later on, the two families reconnected in London, and particularly after 1966, when Rabbi Jakobovits was appointed as the new Chief Rabbi of the United Kingdom and Commonwealth countries.

My father's warm personal friendship with Rabbi Jakobovits extended well beyond professional interactions, and on one notorious occasion, my father – who was an inveterate prankster – inveigled himself into Buckingham Palace to act as Rabbi Jakobovits' "kosher wine butler" at the recently appointed chief rabbi's first state banquet with Queen Elizabeth II.

I heard the story numerous times from both of them over the years, and while I have no doubt that it had been embellished and enhanced over time, what was utterly clear is that the last person on the planet Rabbi Jakobovits expected to see as he conversed with Her Majesty in the state dining room at Buckingham Palace was my father, and the shock of seeing him there, hovering over him as he poured kosher wine, rendered him utterly speechless. I fear that the shock never quite left Rabbi Jakobovits – as he readily admitted every time he was reminded of the incident.

When Rabbi Jakobovits retired from the chief rabbinate in 1991, his extraordinary wife, Rebbetzen Amelie (1928-2010), known universally as "Lady J," called me to see if I would help them pack up her husband's library at their grace-and-favor home at 85 Hamilton Terrace in St John's Wood, for their move to Hendon. Of course I immediately agreed, and told her I would do it with the greatest of pleasure. We spent a number of days packing up decades of wonderful memories – thousands of books and dozens of boxes of papers charting a life of scholarship and public service in equal measure. Imagine my delight when I realized a couple of years later, after marrying Sabine, that our new home was just one block away from the Jakobovits' home, and that I would have the opportunity of spending time with this incredible couple on a regular basis.

We were particularly delighted to include Rabbi Lord Jakobovits as one of those honored to participate at the Brit Milah of our first son, Shlomo, who was born in December 1996. I noted in the introduction to my speech at the celebratory breakfast which followed that it was a rare occasion indeed to have the heads of all the London *Batei Din* attend an event, together with both a current chief rabbi and a former chief rabbi. In attendance were Emeritus Chief Rabbi Lord Jakobovits; Chief Rabbi Lord Sacks; Dayan Chanoch Ehrentreu (b.1932), *Rosh Beit Din* of the London Beth Din (also known as "The Court of the Chief Rabbi"); Rabbi Michoel Fisher z"l (1910-2004), a student of the Chofetz Chaim and Emeritus *Rosh Beit Din* of the Federation of Synagogues (he gave a typically iconoclastic speech); Dayan Yaakov Yisrael Lichtenstein, Rabbi Fisher's successor as *Rosh Beit Din* of the Federation of Synagogues; and of course my dear grandfather, Rabbi Joseph H. Dunner, *Rav Av Beit Din* of the Union of Orthodox Hebrew Congregations in London. It wasn't a bad lineup for a freezing cold winter morning!

Thinking of that day, and of all of my formative years, I cannot fail to recall the incredible parenting I was privileged to receive from my dear wonderful parents, Rabbi Aba and Miriam Dunner z"l, two of the most incredible people anybody could ever meet or know.

My father was always helping people and he seemed to have time for everybody. He also had an incredible sense of humor and could turn the most awkward atmosphere into a feast of joy, just with a comment or even a change of expression. My mother, Miriam Chana Tikva Cohen of Rotterdam (1941-2006), was a hidden child of the Holocaust. She was the warmest most caring mother one could wish for, who took care of house and home to a level that was the envy of all, without ever stressing herself or others – or giving up on her afternoon nap. She was also a remarkable intellect, well-read and incredibly intuitive, educated in diverse areas of knowledge, and she often surprised us with the range and depth of information she was familiar with.

Both of my parents were also incredible grandparents, and they both died far too young, depriving my children of very special grandparents, who could have continued to enhance their lives immeasurably. The impression they left on my own life is beyond expression – indelible and valuable in ways I cannot even articulate. No day goes past without me thinking of them, and I am constantly conscious of the influence they had on me. I cannot begin to imagine what they would have thought of the path my life took after their passing, but I know that they would have been there every step of the way, encouraging me and advising me, and so proud of every achievement.

Thankfully, we are still privileged to have our lives enhanced by my dear in-laws, Josl and Esther Ackerman, pillars of the North-West London Jewish community, both of them incredible role-models to our children, their family, and anyone who knows them. Josl miraculously survived the Holocaust years, escaping with his mother and siblings to London in 1941 via Budapest and multiple other stops across Europe, even as the Nazis closed in on the Jewish community, and indeed, much of his family succumbed to the Nazi murder machine. I must admit, I have never met a more upbeat person in my life – nothing, and I mean nothing, gets him down, and he only sees the good in any and every situation. Josl is now in his late 80s, and notwithstanding every setback he has experienced he continues to be an inspiration, as positive as ever, and so encouraging, never, not even for a moment, depressed or negative.

Esther is an institution in our family and across her community. She is the daughter of the former chief rabbi of Belgium, Grand Rabbin Robert Dreyfus z"l (1913-2002), and is always regal and striking. At the same time, she remains accessible and available, constantly there for family and friends alike, offering advice and care, an affectionate matriarch to her ever-growing family. We look forward to enjoying many more years from them both.

Since moving to Los Angeles in 2011, with the great physical distance this has put between our close family unit and the wider family, we have come to appreciate these family connections to an even greater extent, but we have also come together as a family unit, and I particularly want to pay tribute to my wife Sabine, whose amazing efforts to maintain a wonderful family life while keeping us all connected to our family members across the globe has been a remarkable feat, and not always easy. Indeed, the hardest part is keeping me connected, as I am always lost in a book or involved in obscure research, or distracted by some communal project.

Keeping me grounded so that I remain conscious of immediate family obligations is nothing short of a herculean feat worthy not just of praise, but of an Olympic gold medal. As I said in introducing my previous book, *Mavericks, Mystics & False Messiahs*, all of my intellectual and published products are equally Sabine's, as without her none of it could happen, nor would it. If you are reading this book and you enjoy it, make sure to thank

Sabine, who is the engine of all my output, and the shining light of my life.

Our children, whose input into our lives cannot be overstated, are all an inspiration. Shoshana (and Zion), Dalia (and Jonathan), Shlomo, Eli, Meir, and Uri – each of them is different, but all of them an integral and vital part of the unit we call our family. They must be thanked and acknowledged for their incredible forbearance – and I thank them from the bottom of my heart.

Senators, congressmen, international politicians, rabbis, chief rabbis, Hollywood actors, bishops, pastors, professors of every discipline, industrialists, successful businessmen, top physicians and lawyers, judges, diplomats, and so many more – our children have literally seen and met every kind of person imaginable, most often around our Shabbat table, but truthfully in every kind of setting.

Despite it all, they don't ever bat an eyelid – it's all just another day with their parents, as far as they are concerned. And that has been a true blessing. Meanwhile, each of them has developed so well on their own trajectory, making us incredibly proud, and they are a pride to our community, to the Jewish people, and the world-at-large. Our love for them is immeasurable, and our pride is infinite. And now that we have grandchildren, we have experienced the ultimate *nachas*. May we merit many more years of joy, as we watch the future develop, and our family grow.

There are many other people to thank, too many for me to name each of them individually, but all of whom have helped me reach important milestones in my life and to achieve so much. I do, however, wish to individually thank those who have had a direct hand in getting this book published, first and foremost those who have combed through the manuscript to check for errors or inconsistencies. Pini's "Baker Street Irregulars" for this particular project are my brother Zev, Allan Engel, my sister-in-law Chava Wulwick, Diana Rosenfelder, and Gaby Hirsch. Thank you for the time you put into checking everything, and I particularly enjoyed Allan's acerbic observational comments, highlighted in blue in his return document. Some of the comments I took on the chin, while others I deflected outright – but most importantly, all of them made me smile. And I especially need to thank Carly Einfeld and Madeline Kramer at the YINBH office, whose invaluable help has been incredible.

And needless to say, Maurice and Gabriella Golker deserve deepest appreciation, not just for their support of all my literary projects and for carefully vetting the text to help iron out errors while offering useful suggestions, but also because they are so generously acting as surrogate parents to our *chayal boded*, Meir, whose IDF army experience has been exponentially improved by being part of the Golker family in Jerusalem (which includes Meir's Golker "sisters," Lily and Grace!).

I would also like to thank Professor David Newman of Ben Gurion University for his wonderful foreword. We both share a passion for Anglo-Jewish history and have the experience of rabbinic forebears and wider family in the British rabbinate. Even though his field of expertise is geopolitics and political geography, for which he is internationally recognized and acclaimed, his intimate familiarity with Jewish texts combined with his knowledge of modern Jewish history makes him uniquely suitable to judge the writings of a rabbi with a love of both history and rabbinics. The inclusion of his foreword enhances this book, and I am truly grateful.

Let me also thank Rabbi Eliezer Ralbag of Lakewood NJ, who has assisted me with the launch of a new publishing house which we have called *Machon Otzrot*, and I am truly delighted that this book is *Machon Otzrot*'s first publication. The main purpose of *Machon Otzrot* will be to publish English and Hebrew works relating to rabbinic scholarship and modern Jewish history, focusing principally on primary texts and reissuing previously published materials, with scholarly annotations, illustrations, and introductions composed and peer-reviewed by a range of contemporary experts.

Machon Otzrot publications will include works that showcase original research into Hasidic, Mitnaggedic, yeshiva world, and Sephardic materials, all drawn from public and private collections of rare books and manuscripts. The scholars and experts on *Machon Otzrot*'s publishing board will prioritize high quality scholarship, and *Machon Otzrot* will spare no expense to ensure that all of its publications are of the highest quality. Rabbi Ralbag, with his expansive and experienced team of scholars and publishing professionals, along with his relentless enthusiasm and deep appreciation for the material we intend to publish, is an invaluable partner in this endeavor and I truly appreciate his partnership.

Thank you to all the generous sponsors who have made the publication of *Hearts & Minds* possible, and to the readers – please understand that without their support you would not be able to read this book. The book publishing world has gone through turmoil over the past few years, and without the generosity of those who appreciate how important books are and remain, the publication of niche books such as this one would simply not be possible.

I would like to single one of the sponsors for a special mention, only because he wished to remain anonymous, which means that you won't find his name among the sponsorship messages. I will honor his request for anonymity – but he knows who he is, and he knows that at critical moments in my life he was there to support me, with the kind of kindness and friendship that is a very rare commodity. We spent time in Israel together over thirty years ago, during our yeshiva days, and at that time neither of us could have ever imagined the trajectory our lives would take. And yet here we are, so many years later, still connected, and always ready to acknowledge that every day is a precious gift from God. And as we always like to remind each other, never ever take even one day for granted.

Finally, let me thank you, the reader, for taking the time to wade through what I fondly refer to as my "ramblings," but what is in reality the literary product of my endlessly curious mind and boundless thirst for knowledge. Hopefully, I have been able to present and share everything I have discovered in such a way that it teaches you something – or many things – that you didn't know, while also reformulating for you those things you did know in a way that truly enhances them. And if you leave this book better informed and more connected to God and His Torah than when you began it, I will have achieved my objective – and for the opportunity to do that, I would like to thank you from the bottom of my heart.

With warmest blessings and all good wishes,

> Pini Dunner
> Beverly Hills, California
> December 2020

BEREISHIT

BEREISHIT

TRY AND TRY AGAIN

first published October 24th, 2019

The name Thomas Haig Palmer (1782-1861) will mean nothing to you unless you are a keen aficionado of early and mid-nineteenth-century United States history, and even then, it is highly unlikely you will have stumbled across him. Born in 1782 in Kelso – an obscure Scottish Borders market town most famous for its twelfth-century abbey – Palmer, together with two sisters and two brothers, immigrated to the United States in 1804, and initially settled in Philadelphia. The sisters soon got married, while the three brothers busied themselves setting up a print shop and publishing house, a business their late father had succeeded at in Scotland.

After Palmer's two brothers had moved off separately to New Orleans and Louisville to try their hand at running printing and publishing outfits elsewhere in the United States, Palmer met and married Joanne Fenton in 1822, and soon afterward moved to the tiny town of Pittsford, Vermont, where his wife's family lived. Palmer, a sophisticated urbanite, found rural life in Vermont incredibly unstimulating and backward, but instead of spending the rest of his life complaining, he decided to devote the remainder of his years to improving life in his new home state, and particularly in the realm of education.

He was appointed state superintendent of education, and used the position to ensure local children were educated to the standard he had benefited from at his schools in Scotland, and, in particular, he strongly stressed the need to examine teachers to ensure they met basic standards, a pioneering idea at the time. Palmer also personally wrote and published educational primers, including *The Palmer Arithmetic*, and also *The Moral Instructor*, both of which became national bestsellers, used in schools across the country. In his later years, Palmer dabbled in politics and proposed a world peace plan that mandated arbitration between warring parties, which some later argued could have prevented the Civil War. But the proposal was dismissed in Congress by Henry Stuart Foote (1804-1880), a senator from Mississippi who was chairman of the United States Senate Committee on Foreign Relations.

Palmer died in 1861 in more-or-less complete obscurity, and was buried in Pittsford, along with his immediate family. His house, a refined revivalist architectural residence that must have seemed quite out-of-place in its rural setting when it was built in 1832, is now a bed-and-breakfast hotel on Route 7 in Vermont.

You are probably wondering about my detailed interest in a footnote individual like Thomas Palmer, even bearing in mind my insatiable curiosity for historical oddities. The truth is I am consumed by the fact that Palmer has been the victim of one of the most egregious literary misattributions of modern times. In 1840 Palmer published an educational guide for teachers, titled *The Teacher's Manual*, which he described as "an exposition of an efficient and economical system of education suited to the wants of a free people."

In the chapter titled "Moral Education," Palmer included a remarkable motivational poem that most modern reference works mistakenly attribute to a contemporary British educator called William Hickson (1803-1870). But what is most remarkable about this poem is not its misattribution, nor even the fact that no one has ever heard of the original author. It is that despite these facts, the poem's refrain has become a staple motivational mantra which continues to be widely used across the English-speaking world.

Here is the poem in full:

'Tis a lesson you should heed,
If at first you don't succeed,
Try, try again;
Then your courage should appear,
For if you will persevere,
You will conquer, never fear
Try, try again;
Once or twice, though you should fail,
If you would at last prevail,
Try, try again;
If we strive, 'tis no disgrace
Though we do not win the race;
What should you do in the case?
Try, try again;
If you find your task is hard,
Time will bring you your reward,
Try, try again;

> *All that other folks can do,*
> *Why, with patience, should not you?*
> *Only keep this rule in view:*
> *Try, try again.*

Palmer's timeless poem came to mind when I chanced upon a *Sefat Emet* interpretation of the second verse in Genesis, in which he offers a stunning explanation for the way pre-creation is presented in the Torah, which also offers an insight into a particularly confounding Midrash – although the *Sefat Emet* makes no direct reference to this.

In describing the situation before the point of creation, the Torah says (Gen. 1:2): וְהָאָרֶץ הָיְתָה תֹהוּ וָבֹהוּ – "the earth was unformed and completely void," usually understood to mean that there was total nothingness. But *Midrash Rabba* (3:7) quotes Rabbi Abahu as saying that "God first created other worlds and destroyed them," deriving it from the verse, "and God saw all that He had made, and behold it was very good." This sounds like it's saying, "this world pleases me, those others did not please me." In other words, the concept of *tohu va'vohu* is not a description of pre-creation nothingness; rather it is a reference to previous abortive attempts by God to fashion a physical world – attempts that failed to satisfy Him and were therefore abandoned.

The theological conundrum this presents is clear and obvious. How are we meant to understand the idea that God tried and failed, having created chaos and disorder at first, and then that He was only happy with the version of creation with which we are familiar?

The *Sefat Emet* cuts to the chase by contrasting the disorder and chaos of the initial attempts with the order and stability that marked the final version. Even before time had begun, God wanted to embed a crucial lesson of life into the creation narrative. Although we may be discouraged by a lack of success during the initial stages of a project, with none of the elements coming together as they should to produce a coherent whole, ultimately we need to know that success awaits those who persevere – a rule that even applies to God! Or, to borrow a line from Palmer, "once or twice, though you should fail, if you would at last prevail – try, try again."

BEING A PRACTICAL DREAMER

first published November 29th, 2018

T his week I attended the benefactor screening of *Never Stop Dreaming*, a new movie about the life of Shimon Peres (1923-2016) produced by Moriah Films, a division of the Simon Wiesenthal Center.

Peres was born in a nondescript *shtetl* in Poland, today Belarus, called Vishneva – into a traditional Eastern European Jewish family. His unlikely life story, that saw him evolve from an anonymous immigrant to workaholic Zionist pioneer, to builder of Israel's robust defense infrastructure, to political top dog, and finally into one the world's most recognized statesmen, is nothing short of remarkable.

In his final years, as he reflected on his more than seventy years of public service, he concluded that all of his achievements were the result of an irrepressible optimism, which was fueled by dreams of a better future. In his memoirs, suitably titled *No Room for Small Dreams*, published in 2017 – a year after his passing at the age of 94 – Peres wrote extensively about his many dreams for Israel, both past and present, adding poignantly that his "only regret is not having dreamed more."

What struck me most during the movie was that Peres the dreamer was heavily augmented by Peres the pragmatist, always ready to act decisively and with practical insight so that an unachievable dream could become a reality. This was most notable in his campaign to turn Israel into a nuclear power, which resulted from Peres's unrelenting pursuit of a strategic relationship with France during the 1950s.

Israel and France had common interests in the Middle East. Both were enemies of the Egyptian populist leader Gamal Abdel Nasser (1918-1970), who actively sought the destruction of Israel and the ejection of the French from Algeria. Soon after the humiliating Suez Crisis debacle, France began to aggressively pursue an independent defense strategy that would not rely on the United States, consequently reversing its non-nuclear policy so that it could build its own nuclear deterrent. Peres used the opportunity to cash-in on his warm relationship with high-level French politicians painstakingly built up over several years, and he lobbied the French government to help Israel get its own nuclear project off the ground.

But at the last minute, before an official letter approving the cooperation could be signed by the French prime minister – Peres's close friend Maurice Bourgès-Maunoury (1914-1993) – the French government collapsed and Bourgès-Maunoury was no longer prime minister. Undeterred by this cruel twist of fate – one that appeared to kill off any hope of an Israeli nuclear program – Peres the dreamer immediately morphed into Peres the pragmatist, and he urged his friend to sign a backdated letter so that France would be obligated to honor it. Inexplicably, Bourgès-Maunoury agreed, and the rest, as they say, is history. It was this very letter that resulted in the creation of Israel's nuclear deterrent, and in historical terms it is arguably as important as the Balfour Declaration in terms of the existence of the State of Israel.

Dreaming partnered with proactivity did not begin with modern Zionism and Theodore Herzl's famous declaration, "if you will it, it is no dream." It is a phenomenon deeply embedded in the Jewish psyche, beginning with the life of Joseph, son of the patriarch Jacob and his wife Rachel. There is no greater dreamer in the Torah than Joseph, who infuriated his brothers and bewildered his father with his grandiose dreams of an elevated future in which his own family would pay homage to him. And despite numerous and seemingly irreversible setbacks, he continued to dream, reaching for the stars even as his life was mired by tragedy and disaster.

Thrown into jail following a false accusation of sexual assault against his master's wife, and after languishing there for nine years, he is joined by two senior members of Pharaoh's palace staff. Both of them experience dreams that seemed to hold information about their situation, and Joseph the dream expert offered his interpretation. One of the two, Pharaoh's butler, was destined for freedom and reinstatement, so Joseph the dreamer quickly turned into Joseph the practical, and he asked the butler to seek his release when the opportunity presented itself.

Although Joseph is criticized for this by the Midrash, which sees his request as a dereliction of absolute faith in the divine plan, Joseph clearly did not get the message. Two years later, when he was extracted from jail at the suggestion of the butler, to interpret a pair of dreams that had confounded Pharaoh, without solicitation he proposed a practical solution to the crisis for Egypt predicted by those dreams, as a result of which he was appointed viceroy of Egypt. This stunning reversal of fortune resulted not only in the salvation of his starving family in Canaan, but the elevated position about which he had dreamed all those years earlier and which saw his family pay homage to him.

No dream can ever rely on faith alone. Armchair dreamers are nothing more than timewasting fantasists. When we recite the words of *kiddush* on Shabbat, which describe God's purpose in creating a world that included the Sabbath, we say (Gen. 2:3): כִּי בוֹ שָׁבַת מִכָּל מְלַאכְתּוֹ אֲשֶׁר בָּרָא אֱלֹקִים לַעֲשׂוֹת, normally translated "as on [the Sabbath] God ceased from all the work of creation that He had done." In Kabbalah and Hasidic thought, however, the final word of the verse – *la'asot* – is not translated as "that he had done," but more literally as "to do," and rather than referring to God, it refers to us proactively engaging with the world around us to achieve the objectives of our dreams and aspirations.

Creation wasn't an end, it was only the beginning; it is up to us to finish the story. God's creation is a platform, but while faith and dreams are a motivator, only action can turn these ingredients into an improved reality. Joseph's dreams only seemed fantasy to his brothers because they failed to detect his determination and willingness to pursue them. Shimon Peres was often portrayed in his lifetime as an impractical dreamer, and in some instances his dreams were indeed impractical. Nevertheless, without his dreams and the unrelenting practical pursuit that accompanied them, the Israel we all cherish and take pride in might very well not have thrived, or even survived.

IT'S NOT ABOUT HIM, IT'S ABOUT YOU

first published October 26th, 2016

There is an old rabbinic refrain, based on a discussion in the Talmud (Kidd. 70a): כָּל הַפּוֹסֵל בְּמוּמוֹ פּוֹסֵל. Roughly translated, this means that those who criticize others usually hone-in on faults they themselves possess. Modern psychology has a word for this phenomenon – "projection." Sigmund Freud (1856-1939) included projection as one of the six "ego defense mechanisms," defining it as the impulse to attribute one's own unacceptable thoughts, feelings, motives and behaviors onto somebody else or a group of others.

Projection seems to be in vogue these days, particularly at the United Nations Educational, Scientific and Cultural Organization, better known as UNESCO. In a move that raised the ante even for this discredited body, UNESCO has just ratified yet another preposterous resolution deliberately ignoring the Jewish heritage of Jerusalem, identifying Jerusalem's holy sites using Arabic names. Of the 21 countries eligible to vote, 2 opposed the resolution, 8 abstained, 1 was absent at the time the vote was taken, and 10 voted in favor. These 10 countries need to be closely examined in light of their eagerness to target Israel on the groundless charge that it has no respect for the holy sites of other faiths.

Despite robust attempts to subvert the closed ballot electoral procedure by those who were supporting the resolution, in the hope that an open vote would embarrass more countries on the committee to vote in favor, the vote was eventually taken in a secret ballot. Notwithstanding this, diplomatic sources named the countries who voted for the resolution as Lebanon, Cuba, Kuwait, Tunisia, Turkey, Azerbaijan, Kazakhstan, Indonesia, Vietnam and Angola. Not one of these countries has a human rights record or a cultural heritage record that meets even the most basic international standard.

Lebanon, Cuba and Kuwait are countries where to have an independent voice is to run the risk of arrest, torture, imprisonment, and even death, at the hands of government authorities. In Tunisia – one of the only Arab countries still home to a small community of Jews – antisemitism is rife. One of its most prominent imams, Sheikh Ahmad Al-Suhayli, has frequently incited hatred against Jews, in 2012 proclaiming that "God wants to destroy this [Tunisian] sprinkling of Jews and is sterilizing the wombs of Jewish women." Meanwhile, Turkey is one of the most oppressive countries in the world, tolerated by the West only because of its willingness to cooperate on military matters, as a result of which Western countries turn a blind eye towards the country's ongoing overt discrimination against its Kurdish minority, and more recently towards the Turkish government's heavy-handed reaction to the attempted coup this past summer.

Azerbaijan and Kazakhstan are no better. The media in these countries have been intimidated into complete submission, and non-governmental agencies operating in them studiously desist from making any comments or observations on human rights abuses, for fear of being targeted or expelled. Indonesia is a country where to be anything but a Muslim is highly dangerous. Hundreds of Christian churches have been destroyed since Indonesia's independence in 1945, and Judaism is not even a recognized religion. Vietnam's human rights record is one of the worst on the planet, and although ethnic minorities make up just 15% of the population, they account for 40% of those below the poverty line. Most farcical of all is Angola, where Islam was officially banned in 2013, with the government shutting down every mosque in the country, although the Angolan Ministry of Culture later denied this.

That this ragtag collection of retrograde states has the power to determine the attitude of an international body towards Jerusalem, the beating heart and soul of Judaism for more than 3,000 years, and also the birthplace of the world's most populous monotheistic faith, Christianity, just demonstrates how destructive a force projection can be. Those who oppress see everyone else as oppressors; those who hate claim to be hated by everyone else; and those who disrespect history accuse others of having no respect for history.

But instead of allowing these countries the liberty of pointing fingers at others, responsible countries of the world need to force them, and others like them, to face up to their own dismal record of rights violations of every definition and permutation.

In Bereishit, God responds to Cain's frustration and dejection by telling him (Gen. 4:7): הֲלוֹא אִם תֵּיטִיב שְׂאֵת וְאִם לֹא תֵיטִיב לַפֶּתַח חַטָּאת רֹבֵץ וְאֵלֶיךָ תְּשׁוּקָתוֹ – "if you do the right thing you will overcome your negative drive; if, however, you do wrong, in the end it will catch up with you." This statement is puzzling and seemingly pointless. Surely Cain didn't need God to tell him this in order to know it. Isn't this a statement of the obvious?

But perhaps what God was telling Cain was that in the final analysis, it would all boil down to him, and no one else. "If you do the right thing, you will overcome." By projecting your weaknesses and faults onto your brother, Abel, you are distracting yourself from the task at hand. It was not because Abel's offering was superior that yours was rejected; your offering was rejected because it could have been better and should have been better.

We never want to be judged by being compared to others, but this can paradoxically lead to an obsession with those others, and a total loss of focus on our own shortcomings. Cain needed to focus on the Cain scale, not the Abel scale. If he scored an 'A' on his own scale, his 'A' would be have been equal and equivalent to Abel's 'A'.

The United Nations needs to stop telling countries to see themselves as comparable parties in a large international partnership. This has only led to every failed and rogue state finding fault in every other country of the world, rather than focusing on their own faults and improving themselves without reference to others. The ridiculous UNESCO vote regarding Jerusalem should add new impetus to reforming the UN root and branch, so that such a farce can never happen again.

NOACH

LESSON OF THE ARAB SWORDSMAN

first published October 31st, 2019

I was 11 years old when the movie blockbuster *Raiders of the Lost Ark* was released in theaters. My parents debated whether I could join a group of my friends to see the movie; they thought that maybe the search for the biblical ark-of-the-covenant theme was inappropriate for a *frum* kid studying in a yeshiva elementary school, trivializing a very serious subject and Judaism's holiest object.

In the end they relented, and I went to see the movie with my friends. We were absolutely mesmerized, not just by the action sequences, but by the fact that film producers in Hollywood were interested in something our Jewish faith considered so sacred. The idea that a storyline featuring modern-day gentiles risking their lives to get their hands on the *Aron HaBerit* ("Ark of the Covenant"), the centerpiece of the Holy of Holies as described in our Torah, was truly exhilarating.

I remember we walked out of the cinema with an extra bounce in our step, a bounce no doubt boosted by the climax sequence during which the Nazi villains were incinerated. After all, most of us were children or grandchildren of Holocaust survivors, and seeing evil Nazis suffer was quite a change from the whispered narrative we were rather more familiar with. And, of course, we were delighted that the Holy Ark had not fallen into the hands of the Nazis!

One particular scene in the movie had everyone in the cinema laughing. At a certain point, Marion Ravenwood, an associate of the movie's hero, Indiana Jones, is kidnapped in Cairo by a gang of thugs hired by the Nazis to stop Jones and his group from hindering their attempts to locate the Ark. The leader of the gang is an Arab swordsman, a well-known and feared bandit in the city's underworld. As Jones frantically searches for Ravenwood in Cairo's bustling streets, the crowd suddenly parts and the Arab swordsman is standing there facing him, just a few paces away, grinning evilly, with an oversized scimitar in his hands.

As the crowd goes quiet, and Jones stands seemingly helpless in the face of his imminent death, the swordsman flamboyantly shows off his skills with the fearsome weapon, presumably to intimidate Jones before finishing him off. Completely unfazed, Jones takes out his revolver and shoots him dead. The street crowd cheers, and Jones heads off to continue his search for Ravenwood.

Theater audiences across the world loved this scene, and it is considered one of the most memorable moments in the movie, recently reemerging as a popular gif. But as it turns out the entire sequence was an accident. Jones was actually meant to have a spectacular fight with the swordsman, using his bullwhip to get the better of him, but on the day the scene was going to be filmed, the actor, Harrison Ford, was suffering from dysentery, which meant, as he said later in an interview, that "he found it inconvenient to be out of my trailer for more than 10 minutes at a time." Production could not possibly delay the shoot until he recovered, as they had to leave for the next filming location in just a couple of days, so the director decided to change the scene and shorten the filming time to accommodate Ford's unfortunate situation.

But nothing happens for nothing. The scene is powerful – as well as funny – because it points to the classic miscalculation made by those who are used to supremacy, and who never imagine that their dominance will be challenged, or their power will be diminished. Think of the doomed cavalry charges of the First World War, mounted soldiers galloping towards certain death as machine guns ripped them and their horses to pieces. Cavalry divisions had been the ultimate symbol of military power for centuries, but by the 1920s frontline cavalry had more-or-less completely disappeared from the military lineup of world powers. And those who were slow to do away with their cavalry were vulnerable, and suffered the consequences in future military confrontations.

Doing things in exactly the same way they were always done is not a holy goal; if anything, it is an unholy trap that can be both self-deluding and destructive. To be clear, this powerful but important idea is not only drawn from an amusing moment in a popular movie. There is a much more powerful source at the heart of one of the most puzzling episodes in Parshat Noach.

The *Sefat Emet* offers a startling explanation as to why Noah became inebriated after emerging from the Ark after the Great Flood. Surely he knew his drinking limits, and, if he was a righteous man, would have taken care not to drink too much so that he become embarrassingly drunk. The *Sefat Emet* therefore suggests that Noah's drunkenness was due to biological changes he had experienced as a result of the new post-flood conditions. This physiological transformation meant his alcohol tolerance was lower, and a small amount of wine which would previously not have affected him now caused his intoxication.

Rabbi Yitzchak Menachem Weinberg, the Tolna Rebbe of Jerusalem, is highly regarded as an expert in finding common ground between modern methods of education and ensuring the continuity of Jewish traditional values for the emerging generation. He suggests that the *Sefat Emet*'s explanation has far broader implications, bringing to our attention an urgent need to be aware of differences between different eras. The methods that were effective in a previous generation can end up "intoxicating" the next.

Forcing our children to be educated in the style of times gone by, just like Noah's wine, can end up doing more harm than good. The blind assumption that what was done in the past was good then, so must be good now, poses a great danger, particularly if we want to maintain the values and traditions of that past. Adapting to the realities of the present has to be a constant consideration, even as we struggle to retain the identity of previous generations. Nobody wants to be the Arab swordsman, displaying stunning swordsmanship, only to die with a bullet in the chest.

THESE RELIGIOUS FANATICS ARE LIKE NOAH, NOT ABRAHAM

first published October 11th, 2018

During the intermediate days of Sukkot 2018, several hundred ultra-orthodox anti-Zionists demonstrated outside the United Nations while Israeli Prime Minister Benjamin Netanyahu addressed the U.N. General Assembly. The gathering of Hasidic Jews in traditional clothing, which included numerous young children, held up signs and chanted slogans such as "Israeli Nazis" and "Jews Worldwide Condemn Israeli Brutality."

The most disturbing aspect of this outpouring of animosity was not the hostile anti-Israel rhetoric, which supporters of Israel are sadly used to. Rather it is the devout religiosity of these bile-spewing Israel-haters. How is it possible for God-believing Jews to be in such denial about the miracle of the ingathering of the exiles, and of Jewish autonomy in our ancestral homeland? And make no mistake, these demonstrators are devoutly observant Jews who would never desecrate a Shabbat prohibition, nor eat food that is not strictly-kosher. Moreover, there were no women or girls at their demonstration, as mixed gatherings are forbidden, and all of them had no doubt attended synagogue that morning, praying fervently with their *Arba Minim* in honor of the festival.

The zealous devotion that marks the Judaism of these Israel-haters surpasses the Jewish observance of many Jews who support Israel, and both Jews and non-Jews find it bewildering to see overtly religious Jews display such hostility towards Israel. How does it make any sense?

At the beginning of Parshat Noach the medieval commentator Rashi offers a rather disturbing observation, regarding the reference to Noah as a "perfectly righteous man in his generation."

According to Rashi, "some interpret this as praise, while others interpret it as criticism." Those who consider it criticism question whether Noah would have been considered righteous in the generation of Abraham, believing that the founding patriarch of the Jewish nation would surely have eclipsed Noah. The implication of the conditional adjunctive "in his generation" is that Noah would not have matched up to Abraham's superlative perfection and was only able to shine because he lived in an era of miscreants.

But later commentaries query this interpretation. After all, the Torah calls Noah a *tzaddik tamim* – "perfectly righteous" – a phrase only used to describe the most pious of individuals. How can Noah's critics be so cynical about his righteousness if the Torah showers him with such praise?

A little later on we are told that Noah did exactly as he was expected to. After God had told him about the destructive flood, and the need for him to build an ark, we are informed (Gen. 6:22): וַיַּעַשׂ נֹחַ כְּכֹל אֲשֶׁר צִוָּה אֹתוֹ אֱלֹקִים כֵּן עָשָׂה – "Noah did everything God asked him to do, so he did." One commentary suggests that the extra phrase "so he did" implies that in the same way Noah did everything expected of him in relation to the Ark, "so he did" all the other things God expected of him, referring to the laws of morality and society, later codified as the Seven Noahide Laws.

Although this may sound like effusive praise, it is the epitome of a backhanded compliment. Everyone human being was expected to behave morally and justly, but only Noah was given the special mission to build an Ark. This was Noah's fifteen minutes of spiritual fame – he was the man chosen by God to save humanity – but instead of rising to the occasion, Noah's reaction was tepid. He treated this task just the same as all the other tasks he was obligated to perform. He could have been Abraham. He could have been Moses. He could have been King David. But he was quite happy being plain old Noah.

The revered Hasidic master, Rabbi Elimelech of Lizhensk (1717-1787), proposes an idea that adds a further dimension to this remarkable insight. Just as Noah had a unique task that only concerned his generation, each period in our history has a specific mitzvah that requires a concerted effort by the Jews of that era. If one treats this mitzvah just the same as any other, or if one disparages it, even if one is righteous in every other way, the historic opportunity has been missed, and one is just like Noah – a perfectly righteous failure.

The great Maimonides ("*Rambam*"; 1138-1204) feared for the future of Judaism during his lifetime due to the insidious inroads made by Greek philosophy. In response he wrote a masterful work called *Moreh Nevukhim* ("Guide for the Perplexed"), in which he offered a compelling philosophical backdrop to the Jewish faith. Reading it today, most of us would consider *Moreh Nevukhim* long on content and short on relevance. If we believe in God and the Torah, we believe; if not, this book won't change our minds. The fact is, however, that this was not a book written for our generation. Maimonides wrote *Moreh Nevukhim* for his era; and like an Abraham, rose to the occasion to perform a mitzva uniquely relevant to his day.

Rabbi Moses of Coucy, who lived a century after Maimonides, was horrified by the fact that the Jews of his time – all of them devoutly Torah-observant – did not wear *tefillin*. He decided to launch a campaign to correct this omission, and single-handedly ensured that the mitzva of *tefillin* was reinstated. Nowadays such a campaign would be an utter waste of time; all Torah-observant Jews own and wear *tefillin*. But Rabbi Moses of Coucy's *tefillin* campaign was a mitzva uniquely relevant to his day, and he responded like Abraham.

In the twenty-first century, our unique mitzva is to ensure the security and viability of the State of Israel, home to more than six-and-a-half million Jews and to the most thriving and vibrant Jewish life of any period in our history since the destruction of Jerusalem in 70 C.E. To treat Israel as if it is just like any other mitzva would be to miss an exclusive opportunity given to us by God. And as to those who denigrate Israel, and visibly flaunt their hatred of this modern-day miracle, even if in every other respect they are devout Jews, in reality they are just like Noah – perfectly righteous perhaps, but ultimately losers confined to their limited world, destined to be sidelined in favor of the Abrahams whose love and support for Israel will be their defining mitzva.

THE BRUTAL MURDER OF MY PENPAL, EITAM HENKIN

first published October 15th, 2015

I
n November 2014, my friend Menachem Butler sent me a recent article published by a young rabbinic scholar from Israel called Rabbi Eitam Henkin. The subject of the article was an obscure rabbinic eccentric, Rabbi Joseph Shapotshnick, the protagonist of a book I have been working on for many years, which Menachem was aware of.

Menachem is undoubtedly the Jewish world's most indefatigable networker of Jewish academics, and he gave me Eitam's email address so that we could be in touch. I reached out to him, and we engaged in a brief exchange of emails. I sent him some of the material I have written on Shapotshnick, and we commented on each other's research. In his final email – written on December 4, 2014 – Eitam informed me of the recent birth of his fourth child.

In October 2015, Eitam and his wife Naama were brutally murdered by Arab terrorists while driving with their four children towards their home in Neria. Their murder was utterly senseless, and most likely random – part of a wave of terrorism perpetrated against Jews in Israel by Islamic Jew-haters.

Tragically the Henkins' cold-blooded killing quickly receded into the background as news of many other similar killings and attempted killings emerged, dominating our attention, and clogging up our social media. But the face of the man I corresponded with but never met, as seen in the many photos that appeared on the internet after his slaying, continues to haunt me. I can't get it out of my head. He and I shared a common interest in the eclectic side of Jewish religious history, and I felt an automatic affinity with him.

Eitam was younger than me, and now he will never reach my age. He won't be there to celebrate the barmitzvas or weddings of his children. He will never write another article, nor research another topic. He and his wife, both flowers in full bloom, have been ripped away from their families, and prevented from making their full, lifelong contribution to the Jewish people. Their violent death sickens me to my stomach.

But what sickens me more is the reaction of the world, and particularly some of those within the liberal progressive Jewish world. There is a quote often misattributed to Albert Einstein (1879-1955): "the definition of insanity is doing the same thing over and over again and expecting different results." In this situation it is not even "doing" the same thing, it is "saying" the same thing – again and again, like some sort of tantric mantra, almost as if by saying these things they become true.

"Israel's occupation of the West Bank is to blame."

"Those crazy fanatical Jews who insist on Temple Mount rights are provoking these attacks."

"We need a two-state solution so that the root of the hostility against Israel is addressed."

What a load of codswallop!

Has it not dawned on those who say these things that there is no "solution" short of Messianic redemption? There is not a two-state solution, not a one-state solution, not an expulsion solution, not a theocracy solution, not a democracy solution. The uncomfortable status-quo, in spite of its horrible downside, is preferable to every other "solution."

You cannot make peace with people who see or at least present Jews as the illegitimate invaders and occupiers of "their" territory, falsely kept in place by the United States. That this narrative is a lie wrapped in layers of lies seems to no longer be relevant. The Palestinian Arabs have slowly but surely convinced the world to believe it. No wonder no one protests as Jews are randomly stabbed and killed going about their daily lives in Israel. Instead Israel is enjoined to act with restraint against these murderers.

How about encouraging Arabs not to leave their homes with kitchen knives to stab Jews for the crime of being Jewish? How about encouraging Palestinian Arab leaders to insist publicly and convincingly that their people should immediately desist from trying to kill Jews? But of course nobody does that. Because if the narrative is that Jews are guilty of illegal occupation, and guilty of incitement by wanting to visit Temple Mount, then Jews have it coming to them, and are lucky that only a few of them are getting killed. It is sickening, just utterly sickening.

It is also extremely dangerous, although not for Jews. The Torah portion Noach begins with a strange verse explaining the cause of the devastating flood (Gen. 6:11): וַתִּשָּׁחֵת הָאָרֶץ לִפְנֵי הָאֱלֹקִים וַתִּמָּלֵא הָאָרֶץ חָמָס – "the world was corrupted before God; the world was filled with thievery." The following two verses present thievery as the cause for the flood, not the corruption before God.

Defying God by worshipping pagan effigies and engaging in sexual immorality was somehow more tolerable than the fact that the world was full of cheats and thieves. The Talmudic sages depict a society where even those who were appointed to secure justice fostered corruption, robbery and fraud by legalizing it.

Western civilization has evolved into a society that celebrates God denial and sexual immorality, but until recently all of that could be excused in light of the free world's overall sense of justice and fair play, both domestically and internationally. Wrong was wrong, right was right, and right was always worth defending against wrong. So, despite the awful threat, the Western world did everything it could to oppose Soviet Russia, and indeed refused to tolerate any evil, wherever it reared its ugly head.

Sadly, in recent years, this fundamental structure has been undermined. The free world's attitude towards Israel is just a symptom of that change, as is the tolerance for Iran's nuclear program, or Russia's invasion of Crimea. Democracies that pride themselves as bastions of justice and rectitude inexplicably support as well as defend lies and corruption. The world needs to turn a corner, and to head back to where it once was. If not, the direction we are heading in spells devastation and disaster.

LECH LECHA

DON'T CONFUSE ME WITH FACTS

first published November 6th, 2019

In his seminal 1869 essay, *The Subjection of Women*, the celebrated nineteenth-century British social philosopher John Stuart Mill (1806-1873) wrote, "So long as an opinion is strongly rooted in the feelings, it gains rather than loses in stability by having a preponderating weight of argument against it." One cannot fail to wonder whether Mill prophetically foresaw all those who rage on the internet and social media, for whom facts are summarily dismissed as fake news while only opinion and strong feelings matter.

In November 1945, the advertising industry journal *Advertising & Selling* published an article that described a meeting between a group of ad agency executives and one of their clients.

Having presented a market survey which clearly showed how the promotional policies their client was following were disastrous for his company, the client nonetheless told them he wanted to continue with the current strategy. "But how can you say that in the face of all this evidence?" they asked him. Undeterred, he replied simply: "Don't confuse me with facts!"

This remarkable line somehow entered popular consciousness as the ultimate example of self-defeating irony, most famously as the desk sign: "My mind is made up – don't confuse me with the facts!" Shockingly, this bizarre riposte has now made the return journey from the sphere of humor, and lodged itself firmly back in the real world – or as real as one considers the social media world to be.

Some years ago, as an avid collector of Jewish polemical publications, the difference between a thesis and a polemic suddenly dawned on me. A thesis is the attempt to draw conclusive information out of all the available evidence, while a polemic is trying to deliberately use carefully selected evidence to support a predetermined conclusion. What has become notable in recent years is that much of the discourse on all matters of public concern – particularly but not exclusively on social media – is self-evidently colored by a polemical handicap, despite being presented as utterly factual and impartial. And all of this without so much as a hint of irony.

I was not yet an adult at the time of the Watergate hearings, but I have read numerous books and articles on the subject of Richard Nixon's impeachment, although none of them more jarring than the 2004 interview with G. Gordon Liddy, chief operative of the so-called "White House Plumbers" unit, who was convicted of conspiracy, burglary, and illegal wiretapping for his role in the Watergate break-in, and served almost five years in jail.

"The official version of Watergate is as wrong as a Flat Earth Society pamphlet," Liddy snapped at journalist Johann Hari after she gingerly broached the subject of his infamous role in the affair. He went on to tell her that the Watergate burglary was never about Nixon winning the '72 election, but was actually the brainchild of White House Counsel John Dean's efforts to find and destroy evidence of his fiancée's involvement in criminal activities.

The most remarkable aspect of this ludicrous claim is not its outrageousness – although it is indubitably outrageous – rather it is that the claim was made in the heat of anger well over thirty years after the events took place. The danger of involving feelings when it comes to disagreements and disputes is that they turn what is possibly legitimate into something rancid and destructive, leading to smoldering hatreds that long outlast any meaningful aspect of the matter at hand.

Leaders and opinion formers have a sacred duty to all of those whom they influence to temper their public utterances, so that any harm done by the fray is short-lived, mitigated by their dignity, rather than aggravated by a public display of emotion. The inevitable alternative is that the argument will long outlive the issues that caused it in the first place.

One of the notable quarrels recorded in Genesis is the territorial dispute between the shepherds of Abraham and those of his nephew Lot. It would appear from the text that they found it difficult to occupy shared land, ultimately resulting in a firm parting of ways arbitrated by Abraham.

The verse recording the breakdown includes a curious repetition (Gen. 13:6): וְלֹא נָשָׂא אֹתָם הָאָרֶץ לָשֶׁבֶת יַחְדָּו כִּי הָיָה רְכוּשָׁם רָב וְלֹא יָכְלוּ לָשֶׁבֶת יַחְדָּו – "the land could not support them staying together, for their possessions were so numerous; and they could not remain together." At first we are told the facts – Abraham and Lot's shepherds could not live alongside each other as there was not enough land for all of their flocks to graze. But then the verse repeats itself, adding yet again that they could not remain together.

In his commentary on Lech Lecha, Rabbi Simcha Bunim Sofer of Pressburg (1842-1906) notes that this is the classic, if tragic, trajectory of all arguments. Initially there is a valid reason for the disagreement, one that could be resolved without rancor if cool heads prevailed. The shepherds of Abraham and Lot certainly had legitimate concerns; they were rightfully worried about how the land they lived on could comfortably support their owners' ever-increasing flocks. With sensitivity and finesse this problem could certainly have been resolved amicably. But what began as a valid dispute soon degenerated into wanton hatred – it no longer had anything to do with the facts, rather it was a matter of "they could not remain together." And at that point the only available option was complete separation – an unbridgeable gulf that led to a pointless rift between two close family members, and resulted in one of them descending into the degenerate world of Sodom and Gomorrah.

I have no doubt that had social media existed when Abraham lived, Lot's self-righteous shepherds would have blasted their "facts" all over Twitter and Facebook, feeling entitled to prove their point-of-view, enraged by their adversaries' audacious refusal to see things their way. Antonio, the title character of William Shakespeare's *Merchant of Venice*, declares that "the devil can cite Scripture for his purpose." (Act 1, Scene 3). It is so true. The shepherds on both sides of this dispute could have tweeted: "even the Torah says we cannot remain together." But I fear they would have been missing the point entirely.

LEARNING TO SPEAK THE LANGUAGE OF GOD

first published October 18th, 2018

I n the summer of 1725, a group of hunters near Hamelin, Lower Saxony, spotted a strange looking creature, unlike any animal they had ever seen before. Rather than kill it, they decided to trap it, only to discover that the animal they had caught was actually a human boy. The feral child was aged roughly ten or eleven years old, wore no clothes, and was unable to speak. He appeared to have been living wild for years, feeding on berries and other vegetation, and he moved around on all fours, just like a monkey.

The news of this unusual discovery soon found its way to George I of Great Britain (1660-1727), who had a summer palace close by, near his former hometown of Hanover. The curious king sent for the boy and named him Peter, after formally including him as a member of the royal household. Within a year, "Peter the Wild Boy" was brought to London, where he was introduced to the royal court on April 7, 1726. The event was a sensation. Peter, who had been dressed up in a green velvet suit, scampered around the room on his hands and knees, even bounding up to the king, as delighted courtiers gasped in amazement and applauded.

Reports of Peter's antics at the royal court in London were the subject of numerous articles and pamphlets, and his fame spread across England. Soon afterwards, the celebrated architect and painter, William Kent (1685-1748) – who was in the midst of decorating the Grand Staircase at Kensington Palace with portraits of the king's favorite servants – was instructed to include Peter in the mural, and Peter's likeness can still be found there today.

Peter was not the first feral child to be discovered, neither was he the first to draw such widespread attention. Nevertheless, he was the first to be subjected to this kind of intense scrutiny in the period of history we now call the Age of Enlightenment. Modern science and modern philosophy were still very much in their infancy, as was political satire. But all of them eagerly piled into the debate over the meaning of Peter's strange persona, the result of his having been disconnected from civilization throughout his formative years, and everyone tried to unravel what this phenomenon contributed, if anything, to the understanding of humanity and the human condition.

Eventually King George grew tired of Peter and had him entrusted to the care of the former court physician, John Arbuthnot (1667-1735), who attempted to teach Peter to speak, with no success. Peter was ultimately given over to the care of a farmer in Hertfordshire, and granted an annuity so that his needs would be met. He disappeared from public view, living out his life in simplicity and tranquility, and he died in 1785.

Over the centuries since Peter's discovery, a motley range of similarly feral children have been discovered across the world, inspiring literary character's such as Rudyard Kipling's Mowgli and Edgar Rice Burrough's Tarzan. While scientists initially embraced the idea of learning from feral children, more recently they have become rather more skeptical of advancing sociological or anthropological theories based on any study involving a feral child. In the "nature vs. nurture" debate, feral children are considered an unscientific distraction, with the causes of their behavior ascribed to a range of mental health issues that have nothing to do with their time in the wild. (Interestingly, in 2011 Peter the Wild Boy was given a post-mortem diagnosis of Pitt-Hopkins Syndrome, although this widely disseminated theory has very dubious foundations.)

The one aspect of living in a retrograde environment during formative years that everyone agrees will have an irreversible effect is in the area of linguistics. If a child does not spend time with other humans who speak a language, beyond a certain age that child will never learn to speak, even if he or she can learn to walk upright, wear clothes, and eat with a knife and fork. Interestingly, long before Peter appeared on the scene, the latent primeval dialect of humanity was the object of fascination for sophisticates and resulted in several celebrated language deprivation experiments. The most famous of these was carried out by James IV of Scotland (1473-1513), who arranged for two babies to be raised by a deaf woman on the isolated island of Inchkeith. According to one version of the story the children ended up speaking to each other in Hebrew.

The Critical Period Hypothesis argues that human beings have a limited time during their earliest years to acquire language skills in a linguistically rich environment, after which it becomes very difficult, and in many cases impossible. While this theory remains controversial, in the case of feral children who grow up with no human vernacular, the language vacuum during the "Critical Period" has a permanent and irreparable effect.

This may explain both the purpose and the timing of the first test directed at Abraham by God at the beginning of Lech Lecha (Gen. 12:1): וַיֹּאמֶר ה' אֶל אַבְרָם לֶךְ לְךָ מֵאַרְצְךָ וּמִמּוֹלַדְתְּךָ וּמִבֵּית אָבִיךָ אֶל הָאָרֶץ אֲשֶׁר אַרְאֶךָּ – "God said to Abram, 'Go forth from your land, from your birthplace, and from your father's house, to the land that I will show you.'" The commentaries puzzle over the inclusion of three separate points of origin, as well as the vague destination description. It is also odd that Abraham would need to remove himself from any particular place in order to become the great patriarch. Surely a superior person is great wherever he is.

However, it appears that for Abraham to emerge as the progenitor of monotheism, and as founder of the nation that would become the ambassador of monotheism for all time, he needed to learn the vernacular of God before it was too late. This was unachievable in an environment drowning in pagan beliefs and idol worship. Abraham needed to extract himself totally and thoroughly from this spiritually feral setting so that he could arrive at his destination – namely, "the land that I will show you." This was not merely a geographic location, but a place where meaningful conversations with God could take place.

Our own interactions with God are often marred by our location, and the longer we wait to extract ourselves from a potentially damaging environment, the harder it will be to learn the language of God when we do. Peter the Wild Boy never learned to speak. Abraham not only learned to speak, but his language, our language, continues to be spoken to this day.

DIVERGENT THINKING IS CRITICAL TO JUDAISM

first published October 26th, 2017

O ver the past week, all of us have been shocked by images of yeshiva students and their rabbinic mentors disrupting traffic and causing mayhem in Israel, as they protest the recent arrest of two young men who refused to register for the Israeli army, a prerequisite for any yeshiva student who wants an exemption from army duty to allow him to study. While we instinctively know that these protests are wrong, the organizers justify them by claiming it is their religious duty to resist the Israeli government, even as their actions have been condemned as a "Torah desecration" by ultra-orthodoxy's most elevated authority, Rabbi Chaim Kanievsky of Bnei Brak.

Even so, they have dismissed Rabbi Kanievsky, and every other critical voice, claiming that Judaism is based on centuries of tradition and Jewish law, which will be endangered by any compromise with modernity, epitomized by any association with the modern-day State of Israel.

So how are we to prove them wrong?

In 1967, the celebrated American psychologist J. P. Guilford (1897-1987) came up with a psychometric model, which quickly became widely accepted as a definitive tool to characterize different individuals. People's approach to life, said Guilford, can broadly be divided into two separate categories. There are those who are "convergent" thinkers, and there are others who are "divergent" thinkers. A convergent thinker will only ever see a limited number of options in any situation, all of them predictable and predetermined by experience. Any decision they make will have had a precedent or comparable experience in their past, or in the normative experience of their culture or society. A divergent thinker is very different. He or she is never satisfied with the most obvious solutions, and will always look to do things differently, seeking options that are not immediately apparent.

The advantage of divergent thinkers is that they are "creative" – they think "outside the box" – while the downside is that they don't follow rules as a default, and their creativity can often add unnecessary complexity and risk to their lives. As a result, society generally tends towards convergent thinking, in the belief that sticking to the rules and what one knows is always going to be the safer option. But while this is true to a degree, convergent thinking can often lead to self-destructive complacency, as people continue to follow a set pattern of behavior, even though it isn't really working. Or, as Albert Einstein (1879-1955) put it, "we cannot solve our problems with the same thinking we used when we created them."

Organized religion is seen as the ultimate form of convergent thinking, and Judaism is no exception. After all, being a normative Jew is all about embracing tradition, and being committed to a continuum based on history and precedent. Any attempt to question tradition or to venture into new territory is immediately portrayed as heresy and rebellion. But does this really mean there is no room for creativity and divergent thinking as a religious Jew? Personally, I can never reconcile myself to the limitation of a binary option. As one of my teachers once remarked, "there are two types of people in this world – those who think there are two types of people, and those who don't." I fall firmly into the latter category.

Despite the very convergent nature of a religious framework, I believe that in order to be dynamic, a convergent system must be combined and augmented with a divergent element that is creative and original. The proof for this can be found in the contrast made by the Talmud between our founding patriarch, Abraham, and Noah, whose righteousness is characterized as having been confined to his own time and place, while Abraham is celebrated as the progenitor of monotheism, whose influence has outlived him by millennia.

In describing Noah, the Torah tells us that "he walked with God" (Gen. 6:9), while Abraham is described as having "walked before God" (Gen. 17:1). The medieval commentator Rashi observes that Noah constantly needed God's support in order to stay the course, while Abraham was ahead of the game, an innovator in an age of pagan stagnation. Although Noah never challenged God regarding the decision to destroy his generation, nor made any attempt to rectify the iniquities of his day, Abraham was ready to go to war against a superior military force when his nephew was captured, challenged God over the destruction of Sodom and Gomorrah, and even questioned God regarding the promise that his descendants would inherit the Land of Canaan, in light of the fact that he had no children.

Strikingly, our first direct encounter with Abraham is when God instructs him (Gen. 12:1): לֶךְ לְךָ מֵאַרְצְךָ וּמִמּוֹלַדְתְּךָ וּמִבֵּית אָבִיךְ – "go from your land, your birthplace, and the house of your father, to land that I will show you." Abraham would never have succeeded as the pioneer of God's plan for an elevated humanity if he had simply remained righteous in the heart of his comfort zone. He needed to move beyond his familiar surroundings, and prove that his remarkable piety would endure and thrive in unexpected places and unforeseen circumstances.

The Midrash presents Abraham as the model of ultimate obedience to God's will. Remarkably, this seems to have been the result of his divergent thinking while behaving convergently. Noah, who was limited by his tunnel-vision convergence, and was seemingly unable to take risks for his faith, is disparaged by comparison, remembered only as the conduit between Creation and Abraham.

Judaism may rely on the bedrock of convergent thinking to ensure a consistent religious society, upheld by norms and requirements that guarantee its survival. But without divergent thinking to supplement it, our faith becomes a moribund prison, and results in the kinds of scenes we have witnessed in Israel these past weeks. To remain faithful Jews in the security of an ivory tower is the inferior Noah option. It is high time for these yeshiva student protesters to remember that they are the spiritual descendants of Abraham, not Noah.

VAYERA

THE THREAT OF SODOM

first published November 14th, 2019

Unsurprisingly, the recent release of Donald Trump Jr.'s debut book, *Triggered*, immediately unleashed an avalanche of reaction across the political spectrum, much of it negative. Alex Nichols in *The Outline* called *Triggered* "Fox News you can read on the toilet," adding that "this book sucks," while late-night TV-host mockery has been rife. "Basically, for $18, you get to read his father's *Twitter* account," was Jimmy Kimmel's verdict. Don Jr.'s appearance on *The View* alongside a panel of high-profile celebrities and pundits was an unmitigated disaster, quickly descending into an exchange of withering personal attacks.

Some of those who have reviewed *Triggered*, even as they disparage the content, are prescient enough to note that President Trump's eponymous son has the makings of a right-wing political contender of the future. Writing in *The Guardian*, Lloyd Green, a middle-of-the-road Republican who worked for the late President George H. W. Bush (1924-2018), dismisses Don Jr.'s book as "one-eyed, loose with the facts and a crude attack on the left," but nevertheless acknowledges the obvious fact that the younger Trump "truly connects with the party's base," adding that "come 2024 Don Jr. could well be on the ticket."

Meanwhile, *Triggered* immediately hit "#1" on *The New York Times* bestseller list, and the book is rated "#3" on Amazon. It would appear that Don Jr.'s lengthy presentation of "all the tricks that the left uses to smear conservatives and push them out of the public square" is of great interest to a very significant group – a group that clearly does not view *Triggered* as "one-eyed," "loose with the facts," or "crude." Which makes it all the more surprising that Don Jr.'s visit to UCLA this past Sunday night ended up with him being booed off the stage – ironically not by liberal opponents of the Trump presidency who are the bogeymen focus of *Triggered*, but rather by far-right activists annoyed at the refusal of event organizers to allow a Q&A.

Turning Point USA, the nonprofit which arranged Don Jr.'s visit to UCLA, subsequently issued a statement to explain their reluctance to allow audience involvement – "we were made aware of a preplanned effort to disrupt the event." Although their statement failed to mention that the main instigator behind the planned disturbance was a right-wing agitator by the name of Nick Fuentes, a 22-year-old YouTuber neo-fascist conservative who openly supported the 2017 racist "Unite The Right" rally in Charlottesville, and has regularly criticized US support for Israel.

Fuentes and his many thousands of acolytes, alongside other similar groups, are working feverishly to dominate the Trump-era Republican movement, and their ugly agenda has escalated to the extent that they are ready and willing to humiliate the president's son just to score political points. Sometimes referred to as alt-right, or "America Firsters," the views of these fringe extremists, whose racism and antisemitism is endemic and unreconstructed, are insidiously seeping into the mainstream, changing the political landscape in ways that cannot be minimized or ignored.

Not that things are different on the left. In September, Trenton NJ City Council president Kathy McBride used an antisemitic slur while referring to negotiations between Jewish city attorney Peter Cohen and a local woman, saying he was "able to wait her out and Jew her down." And we are all familiar with Rep. Ilhan Omar's infamous tweet "it's all about the Benjamins, baby," using a classic antisemitic trope to articulate her view that the predominantly Jewish pro-Israel lobbying organization AIPAC pays politicians to support Israel.

Most shockingly, many liberal-leaning Jews rushed to Omar's support, claiming "it's not inherently antisemitic to criticize Israeli government policies or AIPAC" – demonstrating that they had either missed the point entirely, or preferred to remain blind to the increasing number of voices in their camp that are worryingly comfortable with tropes and prejudices which we had all thought were dead-and-buried in mainstream politics. On the right, too, many are reluctant to call out the ever-increasing extremist belligerence that is steadily becoming mainstream.

One of the most disturbing stories in Genesis is the story of the two visitors who came to rescue Abraham's nephew Lot and his family from the destruction of Sodom. After Lot insists on inviting them to be guests in his home, a mob gathers outside demanding that Lot deliver the two visitors to them "so that we may be intimate with them" (Gen. 19:5). All the commentaries agree that the mob's intent was to rape the visitors, but Naḥmanides ("*Ramban*"; 1194-1270) explains that the motive was humiliation not sexual, underpinned by a hatred of outsiders and those different to them, who they imagined planned to undermine their established identity by stealing what was theirs and contaminating their perfect existence.

Shockingly, Lot offers his own daughters in exchange for the two visitors, and although his proposal is rejected by the mob, after which the mob was neutralized by blindness, the question remains – how could Lot, brought up in the home of Abraham, the Torah's paragon of kindness and humanity, have even thought to offer his daughters to a violent mob intent on grievous sexual assault? Clearly Lot was not an evil man – on the contrary, he had welcomed the visitors to his home as treasured guests. But he had fallen into the trap of those who try to reconcile the irreconcilable.

Lot mistakenly believed he could withstand the temptations of Sodom, but over time he allowed himself to fall prey to its ways, even as he imagined he had remained true to his roots. The truth is, however, that you cannot live in Sodom and remain unchanged. Although Lot is a wonderful host, he is nonetheless willing to do something heinous and unthinkable to be that perfect host – sacrifice his own daughters. Is this Abraham's way? Or is it the way of Sodom? Lot was trying to be both, but evidently his proximity to Sodom had eclipsed any trace of Abraham, even though he was oblivious to this devastating truth.

Those among us who profess to represent the mainstream political and ideological values that have underpinned democracy for so long need to take a long hard look at the sinister rise of fringe extremism, and the effect it is having on the mainstream. The road from Abraham to Sodom is much shorter than we think.

WHEN DOING NOTHING PREVENTS THE TRIUMPH OF EVIL

first published October 25th, 2018

"The only thing necessary for the triumph of evil is for good men to do nothing."

We've all heard that quote dozens, if not hundreds of times. More often than not it is attributed to the eighteenth-century Irish-born British statesman Edmund Burke (1729-1797) – as it was by President Kennedy in a famous speech he gave to the Canadian Parliament in 1961. But Burke never said it; rather it was the nineteenth-century British philosopher and political theorist John Stuart Mill (1806-1873) in 1867:

> *"Let no one pacify his conscience by the delusion that he can do no harm if he takes no part, and forms no opinion. Bad men need nothing more to compass their ends, than that good men should look on and do nothing."*

Mill's aphorism has since become an axiom of political thinking in the western world. We have been trained to believe that it is the duty of responsible human beings to take a principled stand when bad things are happening, or even if they might happen. Not to do so would be nothing less than a callous dereliction of our duty.

Mill's elevated ideal has consequently been used as an argument in favor of preemptive military campaigns, and to promote a wide variety of drastic political measures aimed at righting perceived societal ills, causes that have been brought to the public's attention via the medium of relentless lobbying. Sadly, these interventions are often championed by unscrupulous individuals or groups, who have perfected the art of manipulating public opinion in favor of dubious ideals and ideologies, urging courses of action they claim will prevent a heinous evil.

But such special interest interventions seldom make things better; indeed, they frequently mask insidious aims or prejudices that are far more destructive than the evil they purport to be fighting.

One such cause is the longstanding campaign for a "two-state solution" as the resolution for Israel and the Palestinians. This longstanding political mantra insists that the two-state solution is the only way to resolve the fraught situation of Arab antagonism towards the existence of the State of Israel that has resulted in interminable terrorism and wars.

Supporters of this dogma believe there must be a "State of Palestine" alongside the State of Israel, in territory Israel captured from Jordan during the 1967 Six-Day War. Decades of evidence that this idea is a fallacy has not brought people to their senses, and the United Nations along with every Western democratic country, all of whom should know better, continue to actively pursue this cause without ever pausing to reflect how their activism might be producing more harm than good. Even Israel's supporters have joined in the endless calls for this endgame, and as recently as last week the Washington D.C. based pro-Israel lobbying organization AIPAC tweeted that it "remains fully supportive of direct negotiations leading to a two-state solution," albeit with the rider that AIPAC is only for a "Jewish state of Israel living in peace with a demilitarized Palestinian state."

Nevertheless, any activism that gives oxygen to this destructive fire poses a grave danger to Israel. As it turns out, it can actually be better to do and say nothing so that good people who know what they are doing – in this case Prime Minister Netanyahu and his government, along with the majority of the Israeli electorate who have ensured that Netanyahu is the longest-serving Israeli prime minister in its 70-year history – can do what they need to do, even if what they are doing is not the paradigm of perfection. Any voice that interferes with the way Israelis run their affairs and insists on a two-state solution that involves the formal creation of terrorist-run state is not a voice that prevents the triumph of evil, rather it is a voice that enables the triumph of evil – an evil that will ultimately lead to the kind of devastation no true democrat would ever want to see, certainly not the original author of the aforementioned quote.

After the destruction of Sodom and Gomorrah in Vayera, the Torah reminds us why Lot was saved (Gen. 19:29): וַיִּזְכֹּר אֱלֹקִים אֶת אַבְרָהָם וַיְשַׁלַּח אֶת לוֹט מִתּוֹךְ הַהֲפֵכָה – "God remembered Abraham, so He sent Lot from amidst the upheaval." The simple interpretation of this verse is that Lot was saved in Abraham's merit, as his own merits were not sufficient. But the medieval commentator Rashi offers quite a different understanding of the verse. He proposes that Lot was saved on the basis of a great service he had done for Abraham many years earlier. After encountering the famine in Canaan when they first arrived, Abraham and his family, including his nephew Lot, traveled to Egypt, where Abraham decided to hide the fact that he was Sarah's husband in order to remain alive. Lot, who had nothing to fear if he exposed Abraham's misrepresentation, did not reveal his uncle's identity, as a result of which he was later saved from certain death when Sodom and Gomorrah were destroyed.

The rabbinic commentator, Rabbi Elijah Mizraḥi (1455-1525), is quite puzzled by this idea. Surely, he asks, even a person's worst enemy would not divulge information that would result in their certain death, unless they were compelled to do so for some self-serving reason. In which case, why was Lot's silence rewarded? He didn't do anything so special that it warranted such a glorious reward.

Rabbi Mizraḥi suggests that although we tend to view everything in our lives through the rubric of "action-reaction," with benefits only accruing to those who do a worthy act, what Rashi reveals is that there is another equally important model at play. It is not just what you do that matters; effects are of equivalent and perhaps greater importance. And if not doing something produces a greater long-term benefit, then that is the option one should take. Moreover, if the positive consequences are indeed far-reaching and meaningful, the reward will be significant, as Lot later discovered.

Sometimes, the only thing necessary for the triumph of good is for people to do nothing.

LOT'S WIFE AND THE MANNEQUIN CHALLENGE

first published November 17th, 2016

I was recently made aware of a viral Internet phenomenon known as the "Mannequin Challenge." People pose for a video, staying perfectly still while a video is taken by someone moving around the static subjects, and the video is then posted online. This curious fad began in early October and has since turned viral. Thousands of Mannequin Challenge YouTube videos have been viewed many millions of times over the past month. Notably, Hillary Clinton, together with her husband Bill and singer Bon Jovi, along with at least a dozen other people, posed for a Mannequin Challenge aboard their plane while airborne on Election Day last week. Watching that video, and any Mannequin Challenge videos, feels like being walked through a 3-dimensional photograph, actively observing a moment frozen in time.

The idea of a mannequin frozen in time is reminiscent of an episode in Parshat Vayera. As Lot and his family flee Sodom, the Torah informs us that Lot's wife defied the instructions of her saviors (Gen. 19:26): וַתַּבֵּט אִשְׁתּוֹ מֵאַחֲרָיו וַתְּהִי נְצִיב מֶלַח - she looked behind her in the direction of Sodom in the midst of its destruction, despite having been told not to, and was transformed into a mannequin-like pillar of salt. The sages of the Talmud (Ber. 54a; *Yalkut Esther* 1054) inform us that the pillar of salt remains visible to this day, as a reminder of what Lot's wife did, and to warn us not to try and imitate her. But while I'm sure local tourist guides have a lot of fun with that, confidently identifying some random pillar of salt on the shores of the Dead Sea as Lot's wife, so that hapless tourists can take selfies with it, I must admit this facet of Sodom's destruction leaves me puzzled, as does the rabbinic reference to the pillar of salt acting as a reminder. What exactly are we to be reminded of?

Incidentally, earlier this week twenty-six swimmers completed an extraordinary feat – they swam across the Dead Sea from Jordan to Israel. The salinity of Dead Sea water is ten times higher than that of normal seawater, and it is physically impossible for anything to sink below its surface. Nevertheless, even though staying afloat is not an issue, propelling oneself through highly salinized water is extremely challenging, and long-term exposure to Dead Sea water is also dangerous, even life threatening, making the challenge of swimming the just under eleven miles across the salty lake all the more difficult.

The seven-hour swim was organized to raise awareness of the fragile state of the Dead Sea, the lowest body of water on earth, which is receding at the alarming rate of one meter a year. I know it sounds kind of crazy, but the Dead Sea is dying. It is an environmental disaster unfolding in real time, with all suggested solutions for its reverse either unviable, or unsatisfactory. It seems a lone pillar of salt is no longer enough to act as a reminder to humanity. Our generation apparently needs a salinized landscape that looks like something out of a sci-fi movie to get the message across. But what is the message?

Lot's wife is intricately bound up with what is referred to in rabbinic literature as the "character trait of Sodom." The Midrash tells us that when she served a meal to her visitors – the two angels who were there to save her family from obliteration – she claimed to have run out of salt and went next door to borrow salt from her neighbors. The ruse masked her real intent – to bring attention to the visitors so that they would be dragged out of her house and killed. The Midrash cites a number of wicked practices that were common in Sodom, including the giving of marked coins to indigent travelers, then refusing to sell them any food in exchange for the coins. Once the beggars had starved to death the owners of the marked currency would retrieve their money.

Perhaps the sin of Sodom was not the malicious nature of its actions; rather it was the duplicity that accompanied them. Behind the mask of bonhomie was an underhanded immorality. The city of Sodom was not unique in its evil; evil abounded at the time it existed and has flourished ever since. Instead, Sodom's egregious sin was that it epitomized evil dressed up as good, thus posing a danger of immeasurably greater magnitude than evident evil. Lot's wife didn't protest when her husband invited the guests; she welcomed them in and then used subterfuge to try and have them murdered. Later on, she joined her husband in his escape, playing along with his quest to abandon Sodom – but it was all a ploy. Her heart and mind were stuck in Sodom, inextricably bound up with its iniquity.

Much of the evil in contemporary times is presented to us as good – trendy causes dressed up as human rights, or ugly prejudices and intolerances presented to us as political dogma. One primary target of modern Sodom is organized religion. Another one is the State of Israel. In the name of human rights and concern for human suffering, the right of both Jews and Christians to practice their religion with ease is being steadily chipped away, while Israel's right to exist is challenged on every spurious grounds imaginable.

Behind the polished mask of political discourse is the ugly menace of unbridled bigotry and hatred. This evil dressed up as good is so utterly convincing that millions of good people have been persuaded to believe in it. It is specifically for them that the pillar of salt reminder is so important. Never before has the world been so blind to evil and so opposed to what is really moral. The world needs to see Lot's wife and come face-to-face with the futility of Sodom's aspirations. Ultimately, as we know, good always prevails over evil. The question is only – who will be in Sodom when it is destroyed?

CHAYEI SARAH

WHY THE DEVIL WEARS PRADA

first published November 21st, 2019

Most Hollywood movies are not particularly memorable, even the good ones, and it is rare for a feature film to make the kind of impact on popular culture that will outlast its run in the theaters and the next round of award ceremonies. But one movie that has made a lasting impression and continues to be considered one of the most iconic films of the last twenty years is the 2006 comedy-drama, *The Devil Wears Prada*, starring Meryl Streep and Anne Hathaway, which, according to reports this week, is about to be turned into a musical. Hathaway plays Andy Sachs, an aspiring young journalist who sidesteps her contempt for the fashion industry to get a job as assistant to Miranda Priestly, editor-in-chief of a major fashion magazine, played by Streep. The film focuses on the gulf that separates these two women, and particularly their very different attitudes towards the world of fashion.

The most memorable moment follows Sachs' involuntary disparaging chuckle as Priestly struggles to choose between two seemingly identical belts for a photoshoot – because they are "so different." In the short exchange that follows it becomes clear that Sachs cannot see the point in trying to detect the apparently meaningless differences between items of clothing or accessories, and why these things matter so much to those immersed in fashion.

Priestly gazes at Sachs contemptuously, noting her bright blue sweater, prompting her to launch into a scathing soliloquay.

"OK, I see, you think this has nothing to do with you. You go to your closet and you select that lumpy, loose sweater, for instance, because you're trying to tell the world that you take yourself too seriously to care about what you put on your back. But what you don't know is that that sweater is not just blue. It's not turquoise. It's not lapis. It's actually cerulean."

"And you're also blithely unaware of the fact that in 2002, Oscar de la Renta did a collection of cerulean gowns, and then I think it was Yves Saint Laurent who showed cerulean military jackets, and then cerulean quickly shot up in the collections of eight different designers. And then it filtered down through department stores, and then trickled on down into some tragic Casual Corner where you no doubt fished it out of some clearance bin."

"However, that blue represents millions of dollars and countless jobs, and it's sort of comical how you think you made a choice that exempts you from the fashion industry when, in fact, you're wearing a sweater that was selected for you by the people in this room from a pile of stuff."

The idea behind this startling put-down – which has incidentally been hotly disputed by fashion industry insiders – is that there is a trickle-down effect in the clothing world that ordinary non-fashion obsessed individuals are utterly unaware of. But their ignorance does not change the fact that what appears on fashion runways, however ridiculous these displays may appear to the uninitiated, influences what ordinary people wear down the line. Ultimately, we are all affected by things that go on far away from us, in arenas that are seemingly totally disconnected from our day-to-day lives.

Priestly's monologue came to mind as I delved into a fascinating piece in *Kedushat Levi*, the seminal Hasidic work authored by Rabbi Levi Yitzchok of Berditchev (1740-1809). The *Kedushat Levi* offers a fascinating explanation of the Torah's cryptic introduction to Rebecca in Parshat Chayei Sarah. When we first encounter Rebecca, she is presented to us as follows (Gen. 24:15): וְהִנֵּה רִבְקָה יֹצֵאת אֲשֶׁר יֻלְּדָה לִבְתוּאֵל בֶּן מִלְכָּה אֵשֶׁת נָחוֹר אֲחִי אַבְרָהָם – "And behold Rebecca emerged, who was born to Bethuel, son of Milcah, wife of Nahor, Abraham's brother." Rather than telling us that Rebecca was Bethuel's daughter, the Torah describes her as having been "born to Bethuel," deliberately detaching her from her biological father, while the remainder of the verse expressly connects her to Abraham.

For the *Kedushat Levi* the explanation is simple. Everything boils down to cause and effect, even when we don't relate an effect to the cause. Rebecca was chosen by Eliezer to marry Isaac based on her superlative kindness towards him, an unknown stranger in need of assistance. But where did Rebecca's kindness come from? Her father was so nondescript that he barely registers in the narrative at all, while her brother Laban was evidently an unpleasant and unscrupulous villain. Rebecca certainly did not learn how to be kind from them.

But just as when we fish out a cerulean sweater from some clearance bin, we are blithely unaware of the remote fashion industry world that resulted in that particular sweater being in that particular bin, the same is true in the spiritual realm. When someone does a mitzva, it has trickle-down energy that affects people and places well beyond that person's immediate surroundings. The mitzva brings a spiritual vibe into the world-at-large, and the knock-on effect results in numerous *mitzvot* by others, even people who have nothing to do with the person who did the mitzva.

Moreover, if the source of the mitzvah is the equivalent of a top-rated fashion designer, namely an exemplar of that particular mitzvah, the effect of his mitzvah is magnified exponentially. For example, as a result of one extraordinary person's life-changing charity and generosity in New York, someone else will help a friend with carpool or collect their friend's dry-cleaning in Los Angeles, and another person will volunteer to visit the sick in a Jerusalem hospital. The world will have become a different place, with *chessed* energy abundant and dynamic.

The Midrash says that as a result of Abraham's extraordinary kindness, human kindness changed forever. Which means that although Rebecca may have been Bethuel's biological daughter, her amazing kindness marked her out as Abraham's spiritual heir, and therefore she was a perfect wife for Isaac. This crucial detail of who Rebecca was is underscored by the Torah's introduction of her as having been born to Bethuel, but actually being more closely related to Abraham, whose kindness emanated through her in everything that she did.

FOR THE SUCCESS OF MERGERS AND ACQUISITIONS

first published November 9th, 2017

One of the riskiest areas of endeavor in the business world is known as "mergers and acquisitions." A merger joins two separate entities into one entity, while an acquisition is when one, usually larger entity acquires ownership of another entity's shares and assets. For someone unfamiliar with the technicalities, both of these processes amount to the same thing — a consolidation of assets and liabilities under the umbrella of one entity. The idea behind M&A, as it is known, is strategic growth. Every business enterprise has a glass ceiling beyond which it cannot grow, unless it can create a strategic union with competitors, or take them over, thereby neutralizing competition and dominating the marketplace. Another reason for M&A is diversification, allowing companies to move out of their own narrow field of operations into different market sectors.

But while all of this makes perfect sense, in reality a huge number of M&A deals either fall apart at the last minute, or fail spectacularly once they go through, despite the hundreds of people who have researched every detail of both entities, and experts on both sides who have negotiated skillfully over many months or even years to secure the best deal for all the stakeholders.

For example, in 2013 the software giant Microsoft began to feel left out of the smartphone revolution, having fallen behind Apple and Android in the platform wars, so they decided to acquire the cellphone division of the European communication conglomerate Nokia, which had great branding and a good reputation, but had steadily lost ground to competitors. In less than a year Microsoft had bought Nokia for well over $7 billion. Nevertheless, and in spite of the incredible synergies, the acquisition turned out to be an utter disaster for Microsoft, and instead of increasing Microsoft's share of the US smartphone market, in the three years since the acquisition their market share has fallen from 3.8 percent to 1.7 percent.

In 2007, Thomas Straub of the University of Geneva, published a book titled *Reasons for Frequent Failure in Mergers and Acquisitions*. The foreword, by economics professor J. Carlos Jarillo, did not pull any punches in identifying the dissonance between expectation and reality in M&A deals:

> *"Perhaps the most remarkable aspect of the [M&A] phenomenon is its very high failure rate. Study upon study... show value destruction in about two-thirds of the operations... [from] AOL/TimeWarner to Daimler/Chrysler, literally dozens of billions of euros are routinely destroyed. Why is such an apparently dangerous exercise pursued with ever-greater intensity, and why, being so crucially important for their companies, do managers fail almost systematically? Evidently, given the sums in play, one feels like asking everybody to stop until these questions are answered."*

I have not read the book cover to cover, so I cannot profess to know how Straub addresses these questions. However, I would speculate that his suggested solutions are rather less practical than he might have hoped, as they do not seem to have made the slightest difference to the overall success rate of M&A in the ten years since the book was published.

My own proposition, while it might not be of any value in terms of economic theory, addresses the rather more fundamental question of how complex arrangements and situations can ever evolve into something that works, rather than the other way around. After all, with so many moving parts, even if everything makes sense "on paper," it seems inevitable that any attempt to get everything to work in tandem will fail.

The answer can be found in the story of the quest to find Isaac a wife. Right at the end of the lengthy narrative describing the dramatic events leading up to his marriage to Rebecca, we encounter Isaac for the very first time (Gen. 24:63): וַיֵּצֵא יִצְחָק לָשׂוּחַ בַּשָּׂדֶה – "Isaac went out to meditate in the field." Many of the commentaries suggest that Isaac went to the field to ask for God's help in finding the right wife. At that very moment, he looked up, and there was Rebecca making her way towards him on a camel. The implication of this proximity, say the commentaries, is that God answers prayers even as they are being uttered.

But while the idea that prayers are answered instantaneously is wonderful, it hardly seems accurate to suggest a straightforward connection between Isaac's prayer and Rebecca's appearance. The long narrative preceding that moment makes it abundantly clear that Abraham dispatched Eliezer long before Isaac's prayer, without Isaac's involvement; that Eliezer had made extraordinary efforts to fulfill his mission; and that he had succeeded in returning to Canaan with Rebecca. Surely everything that happened prior to Isaac's prayer had already guaranteed Rebecca's arrival to be his wife?

In order to resolve this glaring contradiction, we are compelled to completely reappraise any preconceptions we may have about causality. It would appear that everything that had happened which led up to Isaac meeting Rebecca, beginning with Abraham's instructions to Eliezer, was God setting the scene in order to be ready to respond to Isaac's prayer. Although it was one of the most important M&A events in history, even if it looked good on paper, it would need Isaac's prayer to make it happen and turn this spiritual M&A it into an enduring success.

In every aspect of our lives, there are so many things that need to be aligned in order for them to succeed, and all of those things will have been in play long before we were even aware of them, or of their crucial role. What the story of Isaac and Rebecca teaches us is that the difference between success and failure has nothing to do with statistics, data, market forces, the right personalities, or anything else. All it really takes is a sincere prayer.

TURNING SLOGANS INTO SOMETHING REAL

first published November 24th, 2016

I recently did some research on the history of U.S. Presidential campaign slogans. You won't be surprised to learn that there is a website dedicated to this exact subject, along with numerous other online resources offering insights into the historical circumstances and politics that fed into each particular slogan.

Some of them are very obscure. In 1844, James K. Polk (1795-1849) ran under the slogan "54-40 or fight," apparently referencing a longstanding dispute with Great Britain over a piece of territory in Oregon. If the point of a slogan is to confound, this one was certainly a winner, although it was not just Polk's slogan that baffled people – apparently Polk was such an unknown quantity, he confounded voters even without a catchy slogan, leading his opponent, Henry Clay (1777-1852), to run under the catchphrase "Who is James K. Polk?"

In 1884, Grover Cleveland (1837-1908) ran with this unlikely tag: "Blaine, Blaine, James G. Blaine, The Continental Liar from the State of Maine." I guess it worked, because James Blaine (1830-1897) lost the election. His own slogan – "Ma, Ma, Where's my Pa, Gone to the White House, Ha, Ha, Ha" – was a reference to Cleveland's alleged fathering of illegitimate children. How either of these two slogans projected any useful information about the candidates' policies is a moot point.

In the end, it's always only about winning. Ask Abraham ("Vote Yourself a Farm") Lincoln, or Dwight ("I Like Ike") Eisenhower. But is it really only about winning? In 1916, Woodrow Wilson (1856-1924) ran for his second term under the slogan "He kept us out of war," namely the First World War, at that time raging in Europe and the Middle East. Then, within four months of beginning his second term, Wilson announced that American neutrality was no longer tenable. He spent the rest of his presidency vigorously advocating ever-more convoluted strategies to resolve the shifting sands of conflict among the industrialized nations of the world, damaging his health and his standing, both of them irreparably, a fate he might well have avoided had he not been so stubborn about American neutrality.

Republican president Herbert Hoover's fate was even more tragic. Having promised his voters he would put "a chicken in every pot and a car in every garage," his presidency was hit by the stock market crash of 1929, which in turn precipitated the Great Depression and twenty years of Democrat presidents.

In case you're wondering, my interest in slogans and promises was ignited by the dawning realization that many of Donald Trump's election promises were nothing more than dramatic hyperbole designed to get our attention, rather than policy commitments backed by well-considered strategies to see them implemented. And yet, while I understand the desire to scrutinize the president-elect, and hold him accountable, I think that doing so actually misses the point.

The description in Parshat Chayei Sarah of Abraham's purchase of the "Cave of Machpela" as the burial site for his wife Sarah seems overly long and detailed. Abraham clearly wants to buy this piece of real estate, and is willing to pay any price for it, which is odd, as everyone he engages with makes it abundantly clear he can bury Sarah there at no cost, and he would not be compelled to buy the land. Abraham's single-minded persistence prevails, and he ultimately takes legal possession of the land before burying his wife. But why was Abraham so determined to buy this land, and why was he willing to pay any price for it? The Midrash reveals that Adam and Eve were buried there, but although this may explain why Abraham was so fixated with the location, it does not explain why he had to buy it.

The relevant passage is immediately followed by another one describing the search for a suitable wife for Abraham's son, Isaac. Abraham is assertive, even anxious, demanding that his servant does exactly as he is told, namely find a wife for Isaac who is not a Canaanite girl, from the country of Abraham's origin. What was the sudden panic? God had promised Abraham on numerous occasions that his family would develop into a populous nation. What suddenly prompted Abraham to get into gear and ensure that it happened now, without delay, and in this particular way?

Sarah's death came as a terrible shock to Abraham. Although he had lived in Canaan for over sixty years, and had heard God promise him the most wonderful things, it suddenly dawned on him that he was in exactly the same position now that he had been in when he first arrived – no land of his own, and no great nation — just one unmarried son. Abraham's life had always been so intertwined with Divine involvement that he thought God's promises would simply materialize without any intervention. It took Sarah's death for him to see things differently. He realized that knowing something will happen in the future is not meaningful if we have no role in making it happen. God may have made promises, but those promises amounted to nothing if Abraham didn't act.

God had promised Abraham the land, but Abraham would have to buy the first field. God promised Abraham a great nation, but Abraham would have to ensure his son was married, and to a woman who was a suitable wife. God's promises are a vision of possibilities, possibilities that we must turn into reality by taking the necessary steps to ensure they happen.

Rather than looking to presidents and politicians to turn slogans into a better future, we must be the force for change so that a better future becomes the reality we all desire and require for our children and grandchildren. The president-elect and his opponent may have painted a picture of some version of a future we all yearn for, or not, but it is up to each of us to make the first move in the direction of those promises we would like to see happen so that we can make them happen. That is the only way a slogan will ever turn into something real.

TOLDOT

BE HONEST WITH YOURSELF

first published November 28th, 2019

In October 1897, Sigmund Freud (1856-1939) wrote to his close friend and confidant, the idiosyncratic German-Jewish otolaryngologist Wilhelm Fliess (1858-1928), inter-alia telling him that "being entirely honest with oneself is a good exercise." This piece of advice, among many others Freud gave Fliess before falling out with him in 1904, might have been lost to posterity had those Freud trusted followed his strict instructions to destroy all their correspondence. Luckily, Freud's copies of these important letters were saved by his acolyte Princess Marie Bonaparte (1882-1962), who was herself a psychologist, as well as being a great-grandniece of Emperor Napoleon I of France (1769-1821).

The importance of the Freud-Fliess correspondence cannot be overstated; the letters chart the development of psychoanalysis in its earliest stages, ideas later expanded upon and formalized by Freud. But the most important detail of Freud's vision of psychoanalysis and its goals is the quote mentioned earlier about self-honesty being the ultimate aspiration and guarantor of positive mental health. Peeling away every level of detail about one's life only has true value if it leads to a point when one can be "entirely honest with oneself." In other words – not just honest, but "entirely honest."

One of the greatest and most influential figures of modern Jewish history was a rabbinic educator called Rabbi Nota Hirsch Finkel, better known as the "Alter of Slabodka," or by his Hebrew name Rabbi Nosson Tzvi Finkel (1849-1927). Rav Finkel lived more-or-less contemporaneously with Sigmund Freud, although I doubt he was familiar with the founder of psychoanalysis. And yet, Rav Finkel's educational philosophy seems to have intuitively followed similar lines to Freud. He aimed to get to the essence of each of his students, so that they could maximize their strengths and work on their weaknesses. Basing himself on the *Mussar* ("Jewish ethics") ideals he had picked up and honed during his youthful studies at Kelm yeshiva, in the late 1800s Rav Finkel founded and quietly led a yeshiva in Slabodka, a nondescript suburb of Kovno, today Kaunas in Lithuania. His fame grew, and many of Slabodka's students went on to become significant religious leaders and educators in the Jewish world.

In 1924, Rav Finkel dramatically announced he was moving his yeshiva from Lithuania to Palestine, and later that year most of the faculty and student body moved to Hebron, where they remained until the horrific Arab massacre of Jews in Hebron in 1929, after which they relocated to Jerusalem, where his yeshiva remains to this day, thriving and successful. Slabodka and Hebron yeshiva graduates include some of the greatest orthodox rabbis of the twentieth century, such as Rabbis Aharon Kotler, Yitzchak Hutner, Yaakov Kamenetzky, and Eleazar Menachem Man Shach, along with countless other influencers and leaders – Ezriel Carlebach, founding editor of both *Yediot Aḥronot* and *Maariv* newspapers; Professor Saul Lieberman of Jewish Theological Seminary; and Chaim Herzog, sixth President of Israel.

As far as Rav Finkel was concerned, *Gadlut Ha-Adam* – "a person's greatness" – can only ever be achieved through self-awareness, which more often than not requires painful self-honesty.

Partial self-awareness is insufficient, as unless you have got to the bottom of who you are, you will never be the greatest version of yourself that you can be. And this ideal is beautifully illustrated by Rav Finkel's insight on Parshat Toldot.

It is immediately evident that Esau is the villain, although the narrative does not offer any hard facts as to why that should be the case. Yes, he was red and hairy at birth, and yes, he was an outdoors guy and a hunter. But why is that bad? Perhaps it is because being a "man of the field" is a rejection of spiritual pursuits. But, to be fair, there are plenty of farmers and hunters who are good people, faithful to God and responsible providers. What makes Esau so bad? Not everyone is cut out to be a spiritual trailblazer. Meanwhile, without much explanation, Jacob leverages Esau to part with his birthright for a mere bowl of lentil soup.

Unusually, Rav Finkel devotes a lot of attention to Esau's personality, analyzing his strengths and weaknesses so that we can better understand why the Torah regards him as such a villain. In discussing Esau, Rav Finkel poses a profound but important question: how did Jacob know Esau was willing to sell his birthright? Esau had returned home to find everyone mourning for Abraham, while Jacob was cooking lentil soup, a traditional mourning food. But Esau was hungry, and all he wanted to do was eat, prompting him to demand "give me that red stuff now." Rav Finkel notes that whenever anyone prioritizes something material without pausing to reflect, no amount of intervention will help, and it is this weakness that is Esau's hallmark.

Self-awareness is all about cultivating one's consciousness to pause before acting. But Esau was totally impulse-driven, a trait that undermined the responsibilities of his birthright. Remarkably, Esau was self-aware enough to realize that he lacked the discipline to be the person his role required of him, and this was how Jacob knew he could negotiate the sale. But here comes the kicker, a unique insight that only someone of Rav Finkel's profound understanding of human nature can ever reveal. Esau believed his birthright unworthiness was the result of him not being an elevated person – in itself, one might think, a great feat of self-honesty – but at the same time he was not aware that he was a bad person, nor did he recognize any real need for self-improvement.

Had Esau been honest with himself, he would have admitted that his "self-honesty" was not actually so honest after all, and in actual fact he had sold his birthright for instant gratification. Because, as it turns out, even when Esau was being honest, he was not being completely honest. The greatest test of self-awareness is not admitting your weaknesses, because even then you could be using contrived "self-awareness" as a cover to delay facing up to who you actually are. Or, as Freud wrote to Fliess in 1897, it is not being self-honest that is crucial, it is being "entirely" self-honest.

MAKERS OF HISTORY WHO ARE MADE BY HISTORY

first published November 9th, 2018

[This article coincided with the launch event of the author's debut book, *Mavericks, Mystics & False Messiahs.*]

Late last year, when I was putting the final touches to my first book, I decided to add quotes before each section, in an effort to capture the essence of what followed. For the book's introduction I chose two quotes. The first is from President Harry Truman (1884-1982), whose lifelong love of history originally stemmed from his having been excluded from sports activities as a child, due to his poor eyesight, which resulted in his obsession with reading, particularly history books.

The quote I chose – "There is nothing new in the world except the history you do not know" – uses a clever play on words to deliver a powerful message about the relationship of the present with the past. Truman's quote skillfully conveys the idea that concepts and events which appear novel and unusual in the present have generally played themselves out numerous times in the past, and the only reason they seem original is due to the ignorance of the observer.

The French have a saying for this: *plus ça change, plus c'est la même chose* – "the more it changes, the more it's just the same thing." Each successive generation wants to believe that they have an advantageous edge over previous generations. But those who know history see things quite differently. As the charming Yiddish comedian Shimon Dzigan (1905-1980) once quipped, "the only thing new in this morning's newspaper is the date."

My second introductory quote was from Martin Luther King Jr. (1929-1968): "We are not makers of history, we are made by history," he told his congregation in 1954 – a declaration that went on to become one of his best-known lines. This statement is usually understood to mean that humanity is subject to the forces of history whether we like it or not, and that the winds of change will sweep away those attempting to shape history to fit in with their warped worldview, although in reality King was reproaching his flock for not being more proactive in their battle for civil rights. Never allow yourself to become a victim of history, he was telling them – we are only "made" by history if we allow ourselves to believe that we are helpless to change its trajectory.

But actually, I prefer a third interpretation – one that is neither the way this quote is generally understood, nor the way MLK actually meant it. Rather, we are only makers of history as a result of being made by history – in other words, we are neither original, nor predetermined. Those who attempt to forge an original path, ignoring the direction of history which led them to the present, will surely be frustrated in their efforts, which will be inevitably short-lived and abortive. And those who refuse to be proactive in the present in the mistaken assumption that no effort will alter their predestined path, will have abandoned their responsibility and missed their own unique opportunity to contribute to history.

At the beginning of Parshat Toldot, we are introduced to the sad predicament of Isaac and Rebecca, who remained childless after several years of marriage. The bereft couple pray fervently for a reversal of fortune (Gen. 25:21): ... וַיֶּעְתַּר יִצְחָק לַה' לְנֹכַח אִשְׁתּוֹ וַיֵּעָתֶר לוֹ ה' וַתַּהַר רִבְקָה אִשְׁתּוֹ – "Isaac pleaded with God on behalf of his wife... and God responded to his plea, and his wife Rebecca conceived." In the previous verse, before informing us of Isaac's prayer, the Torah had reminded us that Rebecca was the daughter of Bethuel and the sister of Laban – seemingly superfluous information as we are already fully aware of her family background.

According to the medieval commentator Rashi, the Torah only mentions Rebecca's iniquitous father and brother in order to praise Rebecca, who was brought up in their home and was nonetheless a righteous woman. And yet, just one verse later we are informed that it was Isaac's prayer that was answered by God, not Rebecca's, and the very same Rashi informs us that this was due to her poor lineage as compared to Isaac's illustrious parentage.

Rabbi Moshe Teitelbaum of Ujhely (1759-1841), author of the influential Hasidic work *Yismaḥ Moshe*, has a radical interpretation of the words *l'nokhaḥ ishto* in the verse, which he suggests means "on the basis of his wife's merits." Isaac had always seen himself as living in the shadow of his father. He believed himself to have been made by history, as referenced in the verse at the beginning of Toldot (Gen. 25:19): "These are the generations of Isaac son of Abraham; Abraham begot Isaac." Meanwhile Rebecca was a maker of history; she had forged a new path for herself, different from that of her family, Bethuel and Laban.

Isaac was certain that Rebecca had a distinct advantage over him, as she had overcome the potentially crippling weakness in her background to become who she was. He therefore prayed to God *l'nokhaḥ ishto* – on the basis of her merits, and to the exclusion of his own, which he reckoned were utterly inadequate by comparison. But God's response is very revealing. Rather than responding to Isaac as the son of Abraham, *vaye'ater lo* – he responded to Isaac as himself. With this powerful statement God acknowledged Isaac's own originality even as he closely emulated his father.

The Torah's lesson is that Isaac was a maker of history who had been made by history. Rather than merely acting out an empty echo of his father's life, he had been able to forge his own path despite the weight of history, no less of a feat than that of his wife. And particularly when it pertained to prayers for children, God wished to convey the importance of family precedent, as well as the importance of forging one's own independent path in the shadow of that very same family precedent, keeping the traditional path fresh and dynamic, neither abandoning it nor submitting to it.

And although that may not have been what Martin Luther King Jr. actually meant in 1954, it certainly makes much more sense.

YOU CAN BE AS GOOD AS TIGER WOODS

first published December 1st, 2016

I have always been fascinated by the golf handicap concept. To those of you who regularly roam the fairways the handicap is something you are all familiar with. It allows novices to get into the game on an equal footing with more experienced golfers, by establishing a numerical measurement that calculates the ability or limitations of anyone who picks up a golf club. Better golfers with a low handicap might find themselves losing a game to a beginner with a higher handicap, but it is all in the spirit of gentlemanly sportsmanship.

Of course, the handicap system is never used in professional golf, otherwise I would have won the U.S. Open against Tiger Woods. And although that last statement is made tongue-in-cheek, it brings to mind an important point regarding modern education, and a particular educational technique that has become increasingly popular over the past fifteen years, called "Differentiated Instruction" (D.I.). Also known as "Differentiated Learning," this technique requires teachers to provide different students in the same classroom with avenues to learning tailored to their individual skills or weaknesses.

Taking into account diverse learning needs, an educator using this rubric personalizes classroom instruction for individuals within the group, setting different tasks and goals. Each student's results and grades reflect their own ability and effort rather than a standardized curriculum, enabling every child to be successful. Using this method, an 'A' grade for one student in a particular project or subject might be a 'C' grade for another, and vice-versa. It is the golf-handicap model, and everyone participates in the game on "equal" terms.

The logic behind D.I. also sounds remarkably similar to an idea expressed by Rabbi Samson Raphael Hirsch (1808-1888) in his commentary on Parshat Toldot. No two brothers were ever more dissimilar than Jacob and Esau, the twins born to Isaac and Rebecca at the beginning of Toldot (Gen. 25:27): וַיְהִי עֵשָׂו אִישׁ יֹדֵעַ צַיִד אִישׁ שָׂדֶה וְיַעֲקֹב אִישׁ תָּם יֹשֵׁב אֹהָלִים – "Esau grew up to be a hunter, a man of the field, while Jacob was a scholarly man, a tent dweller." Although they were treated alike and given identical educations, Jacob developed into the perfect child, while Esau went in a wayward direction, eventually becoming a completely depraved degenerate. One might think, says Rabbi Hirsch, that Esau had no reason to rebel. After all, his parents had handled him in exactly the same way as they had his twin brother. So why did he act up?

Rabbi Hirsch suggests that it was precisely the evenhandedness that caused the problem. Esau had a very different temperament to his brother. He was not studious, or eager to be educated. He was an outdoor, sporty type. But if only he had been offered the opportunity to shine in areas where he could excel, perhaps he would not have ended up the black sheep of his family. This proposition is thought-provoking, and very much in tune with the theory behind D.I. Nevertheless, and without wishing to sound disrespectful or dismissive, I must vehemently disagree with Rabbi Hirsch.

Rabbi Hirsch's suggestion lays the blame for Esau's adult wickedness squarely at Isaac and Rebecca's door, as if they were ultimately responsible for their son's later debauchery. This is entirely unfair. While no parent is perfect, and this even includes our biblical patriarchs and matriarchs, ultimate responsibility for an adult's actions must always lie with that adult, whose challenge it is to overcome impediments to his or her success, whether these impediments are environmental, familial, or personality based.

Lowering standards might be a gracious way to be as inclusive as possible in a game of amateur golf, but just as in professional golf no handicap concessions are made for the players, in real life there are no shortcuts when one wishes to achieve excellence. There comes a point when pretending everyone is equal is not a secret weapon to achieve world peace but has instead become a tyranny of mediocrity.

Interestingly, in the past couple of years a range of professional educators has begun to question the efficacy of Differentiated Instruction. One highly respected educational expert, Mike Schmoker, has described D.I. as a method that was conceived based "largely on enthusiasm and a certain superficial logic," but instead of having improved overall education, it has, in his words, "corrupted both curriculum and effective instruction." In the final analysis, he says, unless you aim high, the common denominator sinks ever lower as the teacher struggles to be all things to all students.

But perhaps Rabbi Hirsch's point is slightly different. Not every child can meet the highest expectations of his parents and of society, but this doesn't mean they cannot be encouraged to excel to the maximum of their own ability. Perhaps Esau need not have developed into the antihero he became, if only his parents had not insisted that he be just like Jacob. If this were the attitude of teachers, parents, and society, we might yet succeed in limiting the number of adult miscreants from those among us who will always struggle to match up to any standard of excellence.

Nonetheless, this approach can never be allowed to develop into an abandonment of all expectations. Surely one can let someone know that they are wrong or heading in the wrong direction without it being the cause of their lifelong downfall and failure. After all, no golfer with a hefty handicap who is told that they are not quite as good as Tiger Woods is going to give up golf for the rest of their lives.

ATHEISM IS NOT A MARK OF INTELLIGENCE

first published November 16th, 2017

[**On November 5th, 2017, Devin Patrick Kelley fatally shot 26 people and wounded 20 others during a mass shooting at the First Baptist Church in Sutherland Springs, Texas.**]

Recently, atheism has featured prominently in the news, and for all the wrong reasons. It turns out that Devin Patrick Kelley, the deranged gunman who killed 26 people and injured 20 more in the horrific Texas church shooting on November 5th, was a crazy outcast who prominently proclaimed his atheism to anyone who was willing to listen. Remarkably, local police felt compelled to issue a statement rejecting claims that the massacre had been inspired by Kelley's hatred of religion and its practitioners.

The denial came in the wake of mounting accusations that online atheist communities to which Kelley had been subscribed, had actively fostered an atmosphere of hatred against Christians, and were therefore responsible for the violent rampage. I must admit I was entirely unaware of this phenomenon, operating under an abiding misapprehension that online atheists are all a bunch of left-leaning pseudo-intellectuals promoting twenty-first century humanist claptrap to an audience of agitated metro-liberals. All it took was a couple of hours of research and I stand humbled and corrected. Allow me give you some examples.

Last month in Milwaukee, at a conference intriguingly titled "Mythcon 2017," a celebrity YouTuber atheist and alt-right sympathizer, Carl "Sargon of Akkad" Benjamin, jousted onstage with Thomas Smith, a rather more "traditional" atheist, even if the word traditional seems out of place as an adjective for atheists. The acrimonious debate eventually ended when Smith abruptly stormed off, after accusing his atheist interlocutor of being a misogynist racist. Yes, that's right – a humanist misogynist racist. Go figure!

And here is another example. In a stunning display of malevolence, online atheist bloggers targeted the churchgoers who were massacred by Kelley, condemning them as fools worthy of slaughter for having believed in a God that let them die. Meanwhile, the highbrow "Global Atheist Convention", an annual gathering due to take place in Melbourne, Australia, was called off, despite the promised appearance of the world's most famous literary atheist, Sir Salman Rushdie, after it became clear that ticket sales and sponsorships were never going to be enough to cover the costs.

It seems that while atheism may be an increasing phenomenon across the world, rather than attracting the cream of intelligentsia as its foot soldiers, the most vocal atheists are increasingly found among the belligerent fringes, with prominent academic celebrity atheists now reduced to acting as fig leaves for vile nihilism and ugly anarchic rhetoric. Not that we should be in any way surprised. After all, the twentieth century's most violent mass-murderers were all atheists: Adolf Hitler, Josef Stalin, Mao Zedong and Pol Pot.

Nevertheless, we have become so used to the narrative that extremist violence is always perpetrated in the name of religion, that we have almost forgotten that it is not belief in God that generates violence, but rather it is a denial of God. Those who trust in God, and appreciate His extraordinary patience with sin and benevolence towards sinners, do not feel the need to resort to violence as a means to any end. The wanton murder of those with whom one disagrees is the ultimate symbol of human weakness and insecurity. As I have written elsewhere, militant Islam, as promoted by groups such as Al Qaeda and ISIS, is just another branch of Godless atheism.

I was reminded of the correlation between the excesses of human violence and nihilistic atheism by a Midrash in Parshat Toldot about the story of Esau relinquishing his firstborn status to his brother Jacob. Immediately after their births, the Torah identifies Esau as a hunter-warrior, while Jacob is referred to as a tent dweller, underlining the contrast between the God-denying thug and the gentle God-believer.

But it is only in the first narrative involving the twin brothers that the Midrash picks up on this theme: the story begins with Esau storming in as Jacob prepares a lentil soup. Overcome with hunger, Esau demands soup from his brother, who proceeds to sell it to him in exchange for Esau's status as the firstborn son. According to the Midrash, lentil soup was a preparation associated with mourning, and this whole incident occurred on the day Abraham died. Esau saw the soup being made, and inquired who had died. When he heard that his grandfather Abraham had passed away, instead of mourning him respectfully, he exploited the information as an excuse to dismiss the existence of God. "If there were a God," Esau exclaimed, "he would never have allowed a righteous man like Abraham to die. There is no justice, and therefore there is no God." Declaring Abraham's death as an injustice is a feeble rationale for atheism, but seemingly this was all Esau needed.

The subtle message inferred by this Midrash is that rather than being the domain of intellectual giants and great philosophers, atheism is the domain of superficial fools who use artificial rationalizations to promote human supremacy. Abraham's death at the age of 175 was hardly an injustice or a tragedy, but it allowed Esau to free himself from the responsibilities that accompany faith in God and an acknowledgement of His existence.

Religious folk are often intimidated by the arguments mounted by acclaimed intellectuals against God and the Bible. But over the years I have discovered that atheism is no less a belief system than its religious counterpart, requiring similar if not greater leaps of faith for it to make any sense. Rather than being the exclusive territory of great minds, those who cling to godless views are usually abandoning reason rather than embracing it, in a vain attempt to justify human weakness and humanity's overpowering tendency not to bow to the wishes of a higher power. Which only goes to prove that atheism is not a mark of intelligence.

VAYEITZEI

THE MOST DANGEROUS ANTISEMITE OF ALL

first published December 5th, 2019

[This article was written just before the UK parliamentary elections of December 2019, in which the leading candidates for prime minister were Boris Johnson for the Conservatives, and Jeremy Corbyn for Labour]

By this time next week, Jeremy Corbyn could be the newly elected prime minister of the United Kingdom. The gap in the polls between him and his primary opponent, Boris Johnson, is closing. Even if Johnson's Conservative party gets more votes than Corbyn's Labour, the election could still result in a "hung parliament," which means no party has managed to achieve a majority, a situation which could also hand Corbyn the country's leadership – if he is able to cobble together a coalition with smaller parties to form a majority government.

Ordinarily, British elections barely register in news terms for those outside the UK, and unless one has a personal interest in the outcome, it hovers indiscernibly in the background of the 24-hour news-cycle. But this election is different. The Brexit debacle that has frozen British politics for the past three-and-a-half years is finally coming to a head, and the outcome of this election will have real and potentially damaging repercussions for a range of vested interests well-beyond the UK, and stakeholders across the globe, not just in Europe, are anxiously awaiting the result so that they can realistically plan for their future dealings with Britain.

For Jews in the UK and around the world, however, this election has very little to do with Brexit, and everything to do with the possibility that Jeremy Corbyn might become prime minister of a significant Western country like the UK. Because Jeremy Corbyn is an antisemite. It's as simple as that. Despite his vehement denials of any prejudice against Jews, or indeed anyone, and despite his protestations that the Labour Party he leads is devoted to fighting racism and prejudice in all its forms, Jeremy Corbyn clearly despises Jews (except, of course, those Jews who say they will vote for him, although, truthfully, he probably despises them too).

In a dossier published this week, the Jewish Labour Movement (JLM), a veteran socialist affiliate of the UK Labour Party, stunningly revealed that Corbyn "has repeatedly associated with, sympathized with, and engaged in antisemitism." Accusing the Labour Party of a "hostile response to antisemitism," and of "defending perpetrators," the dossier provides evidence that there has been a "cover-up" regarding antisemitism in the Labour Party – a cover-up that emanates directly from the leader's office.

An anonymous former member of Corbyn's inner team told JLM that when anyone demanded for former London mayor Ken Livingstone to be excluded from Labour for his antisemitic comments, they were accused of a being part of a "Jewish conspiracy" and of being engaged in a "political smear campaign."

Seamus Milne, Corbyn's head of strategy, when he heard that a Labour member had been suspended from Labour for virulent antisemitism, asked to have the suspension overturned on the grounds that she was "on friendly terms" with Corbyn. And a former compliance officer also told JLM that cases of "harrowing antisemitic abuse" were "routinely ignored" by Corbyn's office.

What strikes me most about Corbyn and the accusations of antisemitism is his insistent denials, as if we are all too stupid to interpret the evidence. In a 2009 speech in London, Corbyn described terrorist organizations Hamas and Hezbollah as his "friends," and although he later claimed to regret his statement, he has been openly friendly with Islamic extremists throughout his decades-long political life. His assertions that one has to engage with those one disagrees with in order to facilitate solutions ring very hollow; I am not aware that he has ever met with Binyamin Netanyahu, nor even representatives of Israel's Labor party or mainstream peace camp activists, at any stage of his political life. He has certainly not gone on the record to call them his friends.

In 2012, Corbyn attended a conference in Qatar which included two Palestinian militants recently released by Israel in exchange for a captured soldier: Abdul Aziz Umar, convicted in Israel for his role in a 2003 suicide bombing in Jerusalem in which seven people were killed, and Husam Badran, a former head of Hamas' military operations who planned suicide bombings which killed more than 100 people. Corbyn found their contributions at the conference "fascinating and electrifying."

The most insidious threats always come from people who deny that they pose any threat. If someone tells you how honest and straightforward they are, think twice before you invest any money with them. If someone tells you how easygoing they are, be aware that they are probably very sensitive, and just watch your p's and q's.

The effort to lull people into a false sense of security is as old as history itself, and the archetype villain masquerading as an upstanding person is none other than Laban, uncle and father-in-law of Jacob, whose duplicity is recorded in Parshat Vayeitzei. After Jacob completes seven years of working for Laban in return for his daughter Rachel's hand in marriage, in an act of extraordinary deceit Laban decides to give Jacob his other daughter Leah instead. But when he is confronted by Jacob, instead of admitting he has done something wrong, he simply dismisses the accusation as unfounded – "this is the way we do things here, the older daughter marries before the younger one," he tells Jacob, implying that Jacob had completely misread the situation. Rather than acknowledging his misdeed and apologizing, Laban pretends that his contemptable behavior had been misunderstood, and protests his innocence.

At Seder night on Passover we recall Laban's attempt to destroy the Jewish nation, which seems rather strange if one considers that the purpose of the night is to record the thwarted genocidal intentions of Pharaoh and Egypt many hundreds of years later. One explanation is that on a night devoted to Jewish survival, we should not just be focusing on obvious enemies, like Pharaoh, but also on deceptive enemies, like Laban, who act against us while insisting they are our friends, with only our best interests at heart.

Jeremy Corbyn, should he ever become prime minister, will undoubtedly continue to maintain that he loves Jews, and is doing everything in his power to prevent anything bad from happening to the Jewish community. But like Laban before him, he is not to be trusted. Let us just pray that he never gets into Downing Street.

ASSESSING SOMEONE'S IMPACT

first published November 25th, 2017

Last Sunday evening I received a phone call from a friend to ask whether I could conduct the funeral of a distant relative the following day. There would be very few mourners present at the funeral, he said, as the deceased woman had reached a ripe old age and never had any children. She was an only child, her husband predeceased her by ten years, and the closest relative was her husband's nephew, who was making all the arrangements for the funeral.

I checked and saw that I was free to preside at the funeral on Monday afternoon, but I needed to deliver a eulogy, so I asked my friend if he had information he could share about the woman who had passed away. As it turned out, he knew very little about her. Her sister-in-law had been his wife's grandfather's cousin – hardly very close in family terms. But my friend and his wife had treated her like family, as she was all on her own. Particularly after her husband died, they visited her regularly together with their children.

I decided to call the late woman's nephew, but discovered that he also knew surprisingly little about his aunt. He knew that she was born in London in 1917 and had turned 100-years-old in the summer. Other than that, all he could tell me was that she had moved to New York in the 1950s, where she met and married his father's brother, a Belgian Holocaust survivor called Hyman Skulsky. They moved to Los Angeles in the early 1960s, and Hyman and his brother Sam opened a lighting store in Pacific Palisades.

There was scant material for a eulogy, so I told the nephew I would try to research the family online using various resources that have been helpful in similar situations in the past. However, despite hours of research late into the night, I drew a complete blank. Perhaps we had her unmarried surname wrong, or perhaps she was known by a different first name when she was young. Or perhaps she was not even born in London, and came there with her parents as a young child from somewhere in Europe. Or possibly, it was all of the above. In any event, whatever the reason for the paucity of information, I resolved to weave together everything I had into a respectful eulogy, and also to ask her nephew to share whatever he knew, along with some personal reminisces.

I arrived at Eden Memorial Park Cemetery in Mission Hills a few minutes late, after struggling through worse-than-usual Los Angeles freeway traffic. Eden is famous for its many showbiz burials, including Groucho Marx, Lenny Bruce, and the ill-fated Catya, daughter of Vidal Sassoon. There were around twenty people in the funeral chapel, and we waited for a few more minutes as a few other latecomers joined us. A very sad looking elderly Israeli man asked if he could chant a chapter of psalms during the funeral service, and I immediately agreed. My friend and his wife were there, along with the nephew and his wife, and the rest of the small group looked to me like a typical range of Jewish Angelenos. I began with introductory verses, gave a brief eulogy, and then invited the nephew to say a few words. The

Israeli man rendered Psalm 23, I sang *Eishet Ḥayil,* and we were ready for the burial.

The burial site was close to the chapel, and the coffin was soon lowered into the grave, after which we covered it with earth. In the absence of any mourners, I was about to recite the special kaddish prayer designated for funeral services, when suddenly a woman caught my attention. "Rabbi, there are a number of us here who knew her," she said, "and we visited her regularly. With your permission, as there is not going to be a week of shiva mourning, we would like to say a few words here at her graveside." I looked across at the nephew, and he shrugged his shoulders. "If it's ok with you, rabbi, it's ok with me." I looked back at the woman. "Sure," I said to her, "go right ahead."

What happened over the next half hour was a powerful and moving experience that I will carry with me for the rest of my life. With the grave still fresh and not totally filled, and the California sun slowly setting on the western horizon, a dozen-or-so friends poured out their hearts, amidst emotional tears and bursts of laughter, as they recalled their personal interactions over the years with their dear beloved friend, the late Meta Koppelman-Skulsky.

Meta, it would appear, was quite a character. Decidedly British, with her fondness for Earl Grey tea served in china cups on saucers, she was well read, highly intelligent, full of cheeky humor, and in her later years – this, the cause of all the mirth – profoundly deaf. Meta seemed to have brought the best out in her friends, with many of them saying that their visits to her tiny house on Fiske Street did much more for them than they were doing for her. The common theme was how much this diminutive childless centenarian would be missed by her Pacific Palisades *ḥevre,* who all wept openly as I recited the final kaddish before we left the cemetery.

Rashi on the first verse of Parshat Vayeitzei (Gen. 28:10) notes that the Torah superfluously mentions Jacob's departure from Beersheba in order to stress that "the departure of a righteous person from their city makes an impression – as long as a righteous person is in their city, they are its glory, its splendor, and its beauty; but when they leave it, its glory, its splendor, and its beauty is also departed."

After such a memorable funeral it dawned on me that there is no scale attached to this rule, and Rashi could just as easily have been referring to Meta Skulsky as he was to the patriarch Jacob. The effect of any departure on those who are affected is the same, measured directly against the positive impact that person had on those with whom they interacted on a regular basis. It is a lesson I can never forget.

A PREREQUISITE TO SURVIVAL

first published November 19th, 2015

[On November 13th, 2015, a series of coordinated Islamist terrorist attacks took place in Paris, France, and the city's northern suburb, Saint-Denis. In three separate attacks, the terrorists killed 130 people, and another 416 people were injured.]

R eligious faith, and how the adherents of any faith practice their religion, is a complex subject. Which makes it almost impossible to say anything definitive about any religion. This week, for example, we heard a lot about the innate violence of Islam in the wake of the horrific events in Paris last weekend. The images of the dead and wounded, alongside photos of the perpetrators who all fit the bill as stereotypical Jihadists, reinforce the clumsy view that every Muslim is a violent killer, or at least a would-be violent killer. I say clumsy, because how does one then explain the selfless behavior of someone like Lassana Bathily, a devout Muslim employee of the Jewish supermarket in Paris attacked by a gunman last January? At great risk to himself, he hid twenty Jews in a cold storage facility, saving their lives. Surely, as a faithful Muslim, he should have facilitated the execution of these Jews? But apparently his version of Islam did not drive him to do that.

At the same time, whenever we hear America's President Obama or Prime Minister Cameron of the UK describing Islam as a "religion of peace" – as we did this week – we cringe. How can anyone refer to a religion that was the driving force motivating the group of young men who planned and executed the terrorist outrage in Paris as a "religion of peace"? So which is it? Is Islam a religion of non-violence, epitomized by Lassan Bathily, and millions of other Muslims, who seem to have no interest in violent Jihad? Or is it a religion of violence and mayhem, whose ultimate expression can be found in the murderers who behead innocents, or stab random Jews in Israel and ram them with their cars, or shoot revelers at a rock concert and in restaurants in Paris?

In his book *Not in God's Name*, former British Chief Rabbi Lord Jonathan Sacks carefully charts the origins of religious conflicts, and identifies Jihadism as something he refers to as "altruistic evil." Jihadists are convinced, he says, that they have no choice but to do what they do, for the greater good of their group, and the world. This strange worldview results from over simplistic interpretations of religious texts that seem to demand violent domination, although they can be also understood to mean something less destructive.

There has always been a tendency within faith groups for extremists to get fed up with compromises, and to campaign for the religion to go "back to basics," stripping away mitigating interpretations that soften some of the sharper statements or ideas found in their holy scriptures.

Second Temple era Sadducees believed in the supremacy of the literal text of the Torah, and thought that "an eye for an eye" (Ex.

21:24) meant exactly what it said, rejecting the Pharisaic interpretation that understands this verse to mean monetary compensation. The Catholic church's infamous Inquisition demanded that all Christians comply with a monolithic understanding of Christianity or face public execution for heresy.

But ultimately these movements did not and cannot endure, however much damage and pain they cause, because they defy the ultimate human instinct: survival. A religion can be extremely demanding and detailed and remain successful. Rabbi Sacks argues that a demanding religion can succeed in keeping people as part of a group more successfully than any other system. But what is very clear is that once adherence to a dogma threatens the very survival of those who believe in it, that dogma has failed and will ultimately disappear. The simplicity of a "black-and-white" system may seem attractive in theory, but in practice it cannot endure. As our Jewish tradition teaches us (Lev. 18:5): וָחַי בָּהֶם – "you shall live by them." God does not expect humanity to adhere to a faith which undermines human survival.

Our patriarch Jacob is a perfect demonstration of this dynamic at play. Initially identified as אִישׁ תָּם יֹשֵׁב אֹהָלִים – "a pure man, a tent dweller" (Gen. 25:27), he is suddenly forced to emerge from his bubble and confront the reality of an imperfect world. But Jacob seems ill-equipped for this challenge. The Hebrew word *tam* can also mean "simple," as we know from the Passover Haggadah, and for Jacob life had been very simple. He had spent it secluded at home, working on his relationship with God, and devoting himself to the facilitation of that goal without interference. But now, not only was he was compelled to run away from a fratricidal brother, but he had to find his wife in a foreign country, and then to form a productive relationship with a father-in-law who was a wily crook.

The conversation between God and Jacob as he left Canaan at the beginning of Parshat Vayeitzei revolves around this issue. Like the ladder of his vision, Jacob would have to keep his feet firmly on the ground if he was to achieve the ultimate relationship with God. God did not put him, or us, into an imperfect world so that we should reject it or try to destroy any part of it which doesn't chime with our version of perfection. On the contrary, God created a world with Esaus and Labans, challenges and disappointments, and even with crises of faith and identity. Jacob, who is the paradigm of spirituality, stands as a powerful lesson for us to see how someone can only fulfill their mission fully via engagement with the real world. In each and every story Jacob rises to incredible challenges and prevails, but at no time does he compromise his Godliness, nor does he shed blood, although he was prepared to do so if necessary.

I am not an expert on the Islamic faith or its adherents. Nevertheless, I would suggest that among the 1.57 billion Muslims in the world there are surely many who reject violence, and who seek to engage with the imperfect world as it is. I don't know who or where they are, or why their voices are not being heard, but it is nonetheless likely that they will outsurvive their Jihadist, fundamentalist coreligionists and become the future of Islam.

LUCID DREAMING, OR PROPHECY?

first published November 4th, 2014

I will assume you have never heard of Marie-Jean-Léon Lecoq, Baron d'Hervey de Juchereau, also known as The Marquis d'Hervey de Saint-Denys (1822-1892). Don't worry if you haven't – I had also never heard of him until earlier this week.

I won't bore you with the details of his full biography, except to tell you that he was a nineteenth-century French aristocrat who was an expert on China, with a particular interest in Chinese plant life and domestic animals, and in his most famous book he advocated numerous ways in which they might be introduced into the Western world.

Marie-Jean-Léon Lecoq's obsession with Chinese flaura and fauna is long forgotten. But he is still vividly recalled as the modern "father" of something known as "lucid dreaming." Although "lucid dreaming" sounds like a phrase out of a sci-fi movie, it is a real definition, coined by Lecoq in an anonymous 1867 pamphlet to describe something he had apparently been experiencing regularly since the age of thirteen. Lecoq claimed to have the rare ability of being absolutely aware of his dreams while they were happening, suggesting that he was as close to consciousness as it is possible to be while still remaining asleep.

In the pamphlet – which was titled *Les Reves et les Moyens de Les Diriger* – Lecoq maintained that people with the same ability as he possessed could actually manipulate the circumstances of their dream environment, and he recommended a variety of practical techniques. The eccentric Marquis was not just a theorist, and he went to great pains to put his methods into practice. In one experiment, for example, he threw himself off the top of the tallest building he could find – in his dream, of course – to see what would happen.

I will leave you to research, in your own time, the results of this particularly curious experiment, but suffice to say his unconventional theories and the associated experiments were treated by most scientists, then and for many years afterwards, as laughable pseudo-science. Until recently. Over the past couple of decades, with the increased ability to measure brainwaves more accurately and with greater understanding, the whole idea of "lucid dreaming" has been reborn. Neuroscientists have conducted numerous experiments with lucid dreamers, no less strange than those conducted by Lecoq, to understand the brain and the way it works while one is unconscious.

This week it emerged that a team in Bern University in Switzerland has conducted a number of experiments to measure the passage of time in a lucid dream, which, as it turns out, is up to 50% more drawn out than in real life.

Lucid dreaming was a phenomenon already understood by ancient Greek philosophers, such as Aristotle (384 B.C.E.-322 B.C.E.). The authors of the Babylonian Talmud were also acutely aware of lucid dreaming. A passage in the Talmud (Ber. 55b) discusses the difference between dreams that are vague while asleep and then instantly forgotten once one wakes up, and dreams which are vivid both when they occur, and later on when one is fully conscious once again.

Don Isaac Abarbanel (1437-1508), the fifteenth century Spanish rabbi and communal leader, comments that most dreams are simply a revelation of disorganized thoughts suppressed during waking hours, and then released during sleep. This is consistent with the modern understanding of dreams. Nevertheless, if it is true that lucid dreamers are able to manipulate the events they are dreaming about, this presents a thorny problem for Jewish theology. It is a central plank of our belief system that one form of prophecy occurs while the prophet is sleeping.

In fact, you don't even need to be a prophet. A person looking to understand his future through his dreams might seek guidance from a dream interpreter, as was the case with Joseph and his fellow prisoners, and later on with Pharaoh. But how would one know if a dream was a prophecy? Perhaps it is just a very realistic lucid dream?

It was this exact dilemma that bothered Jacob at the beginning of Parshat Vayeitzei. He understood with great clarity that manipulatable lucid dreams can seem like prophecy, and that a real prophecy could seem like nothing more than a lucid dream. So, when he awoke from his dream of the ladder leading to the heavens, with angels ascending and descending, followed, in his dream, by a communication with God, he exclaimed (Gen. 28:16): אָכֵן יֵשׁ ה' בַּמָּקוֹם הַזֶּה – "is it possible that God is in this place?"

Why would Jacob have been in any doubt? After going through the powerful experience of hearing directly from God Himself, as

He "stood over him," that he was being gifted the land of Canaan, that his descendants would be as plentiful as the "dust of the earth," and that the nations of the world would be blessed through him and his progeny – why would he have questioned the validity of such an experience?

It seems Jacob was puzzled by his initial lack of awareness – if this was such a holy place, why had he not sensed it earlier? Perhaps the "prophecy" was in fact nothing more than a lucid dream. Perhaps it was just a replay of his father's experience and his grandfather's experience with God, so well-known to him, which had resulted in his hopes and expectations traveling from his conscious mind into his unconscious mind to create this vivid revelation.

It was only once Jacob began to sense the extraordinary holiness of the place that he was able to accept the dream as a true prophecy, and not treat it as a mere neuropsychological phenomenon.

It was at this point that he declared, probably with some relief (Gen. 28:17): מַה נּוֹרָא הַמָּקוֹם הַזֶּה אֵין זֶה כִּי אִם בֵּית אֱלֹקִים וְזֶה שַׁעַר הַשָּׁמָיִם – "how awesome this place is, it must surely be the house of God and the gateway to Heaven."

VAYISHLACH

THE SECRET OF GREATNESS

first published December 10th, 2019

William Shakespeare's play *Twelfth Night* is probably his most enduring and popular comedy. At one point in the play, the unfortunate Malvolio discovers a letter he thinks has been written by Countess Olivia, with whom he is besotted. But the letter is a forgery, containing information that leads Malvolio to behave out of character, much to the amusement of those who forged it. But as with so many other Shakespearean peripherals, the fake letter contains a remarkable line which remains one of Shakespeare's best-known quotes: "Be not afraid of greatness. Some are born great, some achieve greatness, and others have greatness thrust upon them."

Those who achieve greatness often defy advance prediction. Such a man was the late Rabbi Eleazar Menachem Man Shach (1899-2001). A Lithuanian-born yeshiva-trained scholar lucky enough to emerge from Nazi-overrun Europe, in 1940 he settled in Palestine where he struggled to find income as a yeshiva teacher, despite his previous experience running a significant yeshiva in Europe. He was eventually hired to teach at Ponevezh, a remarkable institution created by the legendary Ponevezher

Rav, Rabbi Yosef Shlomo Kahaneman (1886-1969). Rabbi Shach proved very popular with students, although he was initially overshadowed by his colleague Rabbi Shmuel Rozovsky (1913-1979), a masterful pedagogue whose clarity and scholarship made him the undisputed superstar Talmud lecturer at the yeshiva.

In retrospect, Rabbi Shach was typical of many rabbis like him who had survived the Holocaust – qualified, competent, pious, a scholar, and deeply committed to the cause of reestablishing the world that had been destroyed. And just like most of these rabbinic colleagues, including those who had excelled in Europe, Rabbi Shach struggled to succeed in the postwar Jewish world, amid an atmosphere where old-world Judaism seemed very much in decline. Making a living was difficult, and incidental concerns, among them ideological leadership, were remote considerations, if they were considerations at all.

But in contrast to others, in the early-1970s, with the passing or decline of the older generation of rabbis who took on leadership roles after the Holocaust, Rabbi Shach emerged as the preeminent spokesperson for the non-Zionist Orthodox Jewish community who chose active if cautious cooperation with the State of Israel as its *modus operandi*. For over a quarter of a century he presided over this community, his pronouncements treated as holy law by hundreds of thousands of acolytes in Israel and across the world. Despite his humble origins, and despite the lack of exceptional credentials by any objective criteria, or at least any such credentials that would have made him preeminent earlier in his career, Rabbi Shach became one of the most outstanding leaders this community has ever had, unmatched by anyone since he faded into the background in the mid-1990s (he passed away in 2001 at the age of 102).

Obituaries published after he died gave the impression of an implacable, one-dimensional ideologue: "a zealot who repeatedly led his followers into ideological battles"; a "fiery leader" who was "uncompromising in his opposition to the liberal values of secular Israeli society." The truth, however, is far more nuanced, and it unlocks the secret of Rabbi Shach's incredible appeal as a leader who inspired such devoted and sustained admiration, even beyond the strictly-Orthodox community.

My late father took me to see Rabbi Shach several times when I studied in yeshiva in Israel during the late 1980s; I have a photo of one of those visits on display in my office. I was only in my teens, but even so was struck by Rabbi Shach's incredibly gentle nature and profound humility; he met us at the door as we arrived and escorted us back to the door when we left, despite being extremely elderly and having attendants to do it for him.

But what left the greatest impression was a speech Rabbi Shach gave on October 9, 1988, to thousands of people at the *Binyanei Ha'uma* conference center in Jerusalem. Elections for Israel's 12th Knesset were scheduled for November 1st, and Rabbi Shach requested a gathering of the faithful for him to share an important message in anticipation of the polls. His speech that day, if read as a dry text, appears harsh and unforgiving. Torah-true Jews needed to understand that their influence had to be asserted on Israeli society-at-large; ingrained secularism had turned Israel's youth into the antithesis of Jewish values; the very future of Judaism and the Jewish nation was in danger unless those who cared about Torah and traditional Jewish law seized the moment and turned things around. Rabbi Shach's biting criticism of modern Israel in that speech was merciless, contemptuous, and disdainful.

But the text of his speech belies the mode of its delivery. As Rabbi Shach began to describe the worst aspects of Israeli society's embrace of secular values he started to weep uncontrollably, his voice cracking with emotion. "My heart breaks within me," he cried, "to see how our nation's holiness is being consumed by evil." It was not about politics or censure; he was engaged in a battle to preserve the heritage of the Jewish people. Those who had abandoned tradition were not objects of hate, rather they were the misguided results of skewed priorities, souls ripe for reignition, if only his followers would take up the challenge and reignite them.

Remarkably, this powerful message is utterly consistent with Rabbi Shach's interpretation of a curious Midrash on Parshat Vayishlach. The Midrash attributes the tragedy of Jacob's daughter Dinah's kidnapping by Shechem to his not having given Dinah to Esau as a wife, instead hiding her in a box so that Esau wouldn't see her. Had Jacob allowed Esau to marry Dinah, suggests the Midrash, perhaps Esau would have repented from his sinful ways.

Many commentaries query this idea: does the Midrash seriously believe Jacob was wrong to protect his daughter from Esau? Rabbi Shach dismisses this notion. On the contrary, he says, Jacob did the right thing. Rather, the Midrash is taking Jacob to task for not being regretful that he had to hide his daughter. Just for a moment Jacob should have paused to consider his brother's inferior spiritual condition that forced him to hide her, and felt a moment of sadness.

We, who benefit from the incredible warmth and depth of Jewish tradition, should never forget that those who lack what we have are not "others," but "brothers," and their lack of Judaism must never be treated merely as an excuse to criticize. Instead, it should remind us that as members of our family, their reduced involvement in Jewish life is a terrible scar. And I believe that it was this visceral feeling of sorrow that elevated Rabbi Shach above his rabbinic peers, and the reason why greatness was thrust upon him.

THE POWER OF A NAME

first published November 21st, 2018

L ast Wednesday I crept quietly into a room at my daughter's apartment in New York, to catch my first glimpse of our first grandchild, a tiny beautiful baby girl, born to Shoshana and her husband Zion the Saturday before. A couple of days earlier Zion named the baby Miriam Emunah at his synagogue in Queens NY, after being called up to the Torah, as is our tradition.

Miriam was my mother's name, and the baby was named after her. My mother passed away quite suddenly in 2006 at the age of sixty-five. Born in Rotterdam in 1941, whilst Holland was occupied by the Nazis, she was adopted by a gentile couple who masqueraded her as their own baby. This incredibly generous act undoubtedly saved my mother's life. After the Allied victory against Germany in 1945, my mother was reunited with her parents, who had miraculously survived the war by hiding behind a closet at the home of a gentile friend. Only recently I discovered that my grandfather would occasionally sneak out of hiding to visit my mother. Although he did not reveal his identity to her, pretending to be a business associate of her foster father, he made sure to visit so that he could keep up with his baby daughter as she grew into a little girl.

It is a strange feeling to see baby Miri, as she will be called, and to know that she will bear my mother's name for the rest of her life. Jewish tradition places a lot of meaning in someone's name, and particularly if they are named after someone significant – whether it be a departed loved one or a great historical figure. Somehow their life is expected to echo the life of their namesake, or at the very least they are expected to emulate the qualities of the person they are named after. And very often, as time unfolds, one may observe the effect this has on people's lives – often positive, but occasionally negative, as they struggle to match up to the burden of expectation which accompanies their name.

The importance of a name is not an idea limited to Jewish tradition. Numerous studies have shown how much a name can impact a person's life. In 2011, the *Journal of Experimental Social Psychology* published a paper which included information from countless earlier papers proving that a person's name impacts on how they may be perceived even before people meet them. The authors also suggest that easily pronounced names "are judged more positively than difficult-to-pronounce names," which means, in practical terms, that you are more likely to get a job if your name has one or two syllables, rather than three or more.

Meanwhile, a 2009 study by a team from Shippensburg University in Pennsylvania shows that "unpopular names are positively correlated with juvenile delinquency." After producing irrefutable proof , the authors propose that "adolescents with unpopular names may be more prone to crime because they are treated differently by their peers, making it more difficult for them to form relationships, [and] juveniles with unpopular names may also act out because they... dislike their names."

The flip side of this phenomenon was presented in a 2013 German study which concluded, quite remarkably, that Germans with noble-sounding surnames, such as Kaiser ("emperor"), König ("king"), and Fürst ("prince"), are more likely to have senior roles at work than those with last names which indicate everyday occupations, such as Koch ("cook"), Bauer ("farmer"), and Becker ("baker"). This is despite the fact that the noble-sounding surname is not evidence of noble descent, or indeed any kind of superiority. Simply as a result of "associative cognition," the status linked to a name may spill over to its bearer and influence his or her occupational outcomes."

The subject of names comes up quite unexpectedly at the beginning of Parshat Vayishlach. On the night before Jacob's highly anticipated meeting with his brother Esau, he is suddenly set upon by a mysterious individual, who wrestles with him until dawn. Before departing, he asks Jacob to reveal his name, and upon hearing it promptly informs him that from now on he will be known as "Israel" – a Hebrew portmanteau which carries the message that Jacob had "wrestled with the Divine and with humans, and prevailed." In response, Jacob asks his enigmatic adversary – who the Midrash discloses was Esau's angel alter-ego – to reveal his name. But the angel replies (Gen. 39:29): לָמָּה זֶּה תִּשְׁאַל לִשְׁמִי – "why are you asking me for my name?" – and then abruptly departs the scene without answering the question. The commentaries all puzzle over his elusive response.

The legendary *Mussar* ("Jewish ethics") luminary, Rabbi Yehuda Leib Chasman (1869-1935), offers a powerful solution to the angel's evasion. By not answering Jacob's question, the angel actually answered it. A name defines a person's positive essence and potential. The angel who fought with Jacob embodied the opposite of everything positive; as Esau's protector he personified the idea of *yetzer hara* ("evil inclination"), which has no identity of its own. In spiritual terms *yetzer hara* is the epitome of nothing, a pyrotechnic display of smoke and mirrors. In the realm of God and truth *yetzer hara* does not actually exist, and therefore has no name. It is as a result of this that one may find it hard to identify the *yetzer hara*, and therefore avoid it. At the same time, it puts everything associated with *yetzer hara* into perspective – with no real substance, it is capricious, ephemeral, and ultimately utterly pointless.

When we carry the name of a beloved family member, or a revered biblical figure, or – as is often the case – both, we carry the potential for everything positive that characterized their lives into ours. My mother was a gentle, generous soul, who lived to do good and to share the goodness she had been given by God. Little Miri is lucky to bear her name, but more than that, she is lucky to be the vessel of that positive potential. That is the power of a name.

PRELUDE TO A BETTER FUTURE

first published December 16th, 2016

The destruction of the city of Aleppo in Syria and the wanton murder of its citizens has once again been dominating the news. This ancient metropolis, purportedly one of the oldest continuously inhabited places on Earth, has witnessed many wars, and been a part of many empires. For millennia Aleppo lay at the heart of the international "silk road," the famous trade route connecting China with the Mediterranean Sea.

After the completion of the Suez Canal in 1869, Aleppo's status declined, and except for a brief stint as the capital city of the State of Aleppo in the early 1920s, until recently it had receded completely from view, and particularly after the 1961 coup d'état that brought the Baathist regime to power in Syria. And so it would have remained had Aleppo not taken central stage in the vicious Syrian civil war that has raged over the past six years.

Beginning in 2012, the city began its descent into what can only be described as a living hell, occupied by Islamic extremist rebel forces opposed to President Bashar al-Assad, and subjected to a stranglehold siege and ruthless bombardment by the Syrian Army, assisted by their Russian and Iranian allies. The indiscriminate killing of civilians has led to over 30,000 deaths in four years, and this week it was reported that the Syrian Army, who claimed to have finally retaken Aleppo after offering rebel militants and their sympathizers safe passage out of the city, were shooting civilians in cold blood, including women and children, as they conducted mopping-up operations in neighborhoods now under their control.

The world-at-large has stayed silent as the Aleppo atrocities escalate. Despite widespread revulsion, the lack of affinity with either of the warring sides has left Western democracies in a dilemma that has become ever more frequent with localized wars in the early twenty-first century: who does one support to win, when one would prefer both sides to lose? There is no great ideal at stake, as there frequently was during the Cold War era, and with the shambolic strategic errors associated with the Iraq War still casting their toxic pall on international affairs, the idea that Western meddling will improve matters seems so remote and fanciful, that the world has opted to get on with its life as Aleppo burns and its civilians are slaughtered in the full "real-time" view of satellite feeds and social media posts.

Over the past couple of weeks there have at least been rhetorical attempts to address the Aleppo disaster. At a meeting of the U.N. Security Council this week — which, notably, failed to adopt any resolution to end the suffering of civilians in Aleppo — the U.S. Permanent Representative, Samantha Powers, delivered an impassioned statement, declaring that Aleppo would "join the ranks of those events in world history that define modern evil and stain our conscience decades later."

"Are you truly incapable of shame?" she asked the Syrian regime, together with its Russian and Iranian allies. "Is there literally nothing that can shame you? Is there no act of barbarism against civilians, no execution of a child that gets under your skin, that just creeps you out a little bit? Is there nothing you will not lie about or justify?"

Although these words strike an emotional chord for all champions of freedom and human rights, essentially it is all empty grandiloquence, as America's President Obama has deliberately avoided taking any kind of proactive role in the Syrian maelstrom. How can Americans point a finger at Syria or Russia when they have been absent for Syrians in Syria throughout the civil war? And not just for Syrians. The United States is the world's most powerful nation, a status that carries with it responsibility and duty, but over the past eight years it has all but disappeared from view, having taken a back seat approach to international affairs in a policy that has inevitably allowed violent turbulence to escalate and vicious despots to prosper.

I was struck by an interesting insight into Jacob's attitude towards his imminent confrontation with his twin brother Esau at the beginning of Parshat Vayishlach, that brings this folly into sharp focus. After more than thirty years away from Canaan, and from the brother who had vowed to kill him, Jacob had finally returned home with his large family and the great wealth he had amassed abroad, and was imminently going to face his nemesis, Esau. The Torah informs us that Jacob was very anxious about the meeting (Gen. 32:8): וַיִּירָא יַעֲקֹב מְאֹד וַיֵּצֶר לוֹ – "Jacob was extremely afraid and very distressed." The commentaries struggle with this statement. After all, God had promised him even before he left that he would be protected when he returned. So why was he overwhelmed with such fear?

The *Sefat Emet* offers a compelling answer in his remarkable commentary on the Torah. Rather than the fear and distress being an involuntary emotional reaction, he suggests that Jacob caused himself to be afraid, and consequently to be proactive in his defense. The greatest threat to peace and goodness is not war – it is complacency and hubris. Jacob could certainly have relied on God's personal assurance that he would be protected from any harm. But the stakes were too high. It was not just about his own personal safety. Jacob's confrontation with Esau amounted to nothing less than assuring the future of mankind. Brutality and evil would have to be subdued if the message of God was to prevail and thrive. Jacob urgently felt the need to actively defend his mission, so that monotheism would triumph over the dictatorship of malevolent God-denial represented by Esau. This assignment needed to fill him with trepidation.

It is the responsibility of ensuring the survival of freedom and a humane society that should be alarming the free world when it comes to places like Syria, Iran, Russia, and every country who perceive Western reticence to involve themselves in the protection of innocents as the proof that evil can prevail. And unless there is a drastic change of attitude, the future of mankind truly hangs in the balance.

VAYEISHEV

PUTTING IMPEACHMENT ON TRIAL

first published December 19th, 2019

I had not planned to write about the impeachment. Frankly, along with millions of others who live in the United States, and probably the rest of the world, I am sick and tired of the endless news coverage, and the never-ending sanctimonious drivel emanating from both the President's detractors and his supporters. Despite valiant attempts on both sides to convince people of one version of events to the exclusion of any other, everyone seems to have made up their minds a long time ago.

And yet, my Twitter feed continues to produce an avalanche of indignant partisan proclamations – wasted energy that achieves nothing more than increase rancor. Support for impeaching the President has actually diminished over the past few months, as reported in a startling article published by CNN earlier this week. In real terms, the nation is about equally divided between those who think the President should be impeached and those who don't, and the numbers have barely shifted since this whole saga began.

But in the end, I have decided to write about the impeachment, a decision I made after watching the debate in the House of

Representatives, and the unfolding situation since the articles of impeachment were voted through.

In 1972, the premier of China, Zhou Enlai (1898-1976), was asked what he thought about the impact of the French Revolution of 1789. He replied that he thought it was "too early to tell." As it turns out, or so the story goes, he believed he was being asked about the 1968 student protests in France, not the 1789 revolution – apparently the fault of an incompetent interpreter. Nevertheless, his reply to the question was not without merit. Democracy, as practiced by republics, remains relatively young in human history terms, and there are anomalies that have only become apparent many years after its advent.

One of these anomalies has thrust itself onto center stage over these past few weeks, and crystallized with the vote in the House of Representatives, and will most likely further display itself when the Senate votes on the articles of impeachment, whenever that happens. America's founding fathers were acutely conscious of the dangers of a monarchy, particularly as they had to contend with George III of Great Britain (1738-1820), who, despite having to govern via parliament, was for all intents and purposes an autocratic dictator. British government ministers bowed to his wishes, and short of a violent revolution of the sort that took place during the era of Charles I (1600-1649), who was executed by parliamentarians, there was no method of getting rid of him.

As a result, one of the key articles of the US Constitution enables the legislative branch to impeach a president for "high crimes and misdemeanors", in order to prevent the country from suffering the consequences of a monarchical president who abuses power.

In theory, it sounds great. The trouble is, American democracy is far too young, and consequently, the impeachment process has only been road-tested three times: in 1868, 1974 and 1998. On each of those occasions, it seems to have done its job, albeit for different reasons. For example, the impeachment of Andrew Johnson (1808-1875), although passed by the House, never made it through the Senate; despite an overwhelming Republican majority, enough Republican senators chose to vote against the impeachment to prevent a two-thirds majority in favor. And during the impeachment process aimed at unseating Richard Nixon (1913-1994), a number of significant Republican lawmakers broke ranks and refused to back him, resulting in his resignation before the House had voted. It would appear that the founding fathers banked on enough lawmakers setting aside their partisan views so that the right result would ensue.

This week, setting aside whether or not President Trump is guilty or innocent, the notion of such idealistic impartiality has been proved wrong. In other words, while the ability to impeach a president is a great idea, the process itself is deeply flawed. Besides for an inconsequential handful of Democrats who resisted the pressure to vote along party lines, Republicans have uniformly backed the President, and Democrats have more-or-less all favored impeachment.

Meanwhile, many senators have made clear that they are not impartial, and no amount of witnesses or evidence one way or another will sway them from their views. Clearly the impeachment process is not as robust as the founding fathers thought it would be. And everyone involved, left to right, top to bottom – including the media – are guilty of turning an enlightened ideal into an international joke.

There is an outstanding piece of commentary by Rabbi Naftali Tzvi Yehuda Berlin ("*Haamek Davar*"; 1816-1893) at the beginning of Parshat Vayeishev. After Joseph had his first dream, he sought out his brothers – who all despised him – to tell them about it. The Torah describes it as follows (Gen. 37:5): וַיַּחֲלֹם יוֹסֵף חֲלוֹם וַיַּגֵּד לְאֶחָיו וַיּוֹסִפוּ עוֹד שְׂנֹא אֹתוֹ – "Joseph had a dream that he told to his brothers; and they hated him even more." Interestingly, Joseph only began to tell them the details of the dream in the next verse. Why, then, did his brothers hate him more, even before they had heard what the dream was about?

The Talmud (Ber. 55b) teaches that one should only ever share a dream with a person one is close to. Joseph's brothers were so certain he was their sworn enemy, that as soon as he approached them with his dream, instead of seeing this as proof that he felt close to them, they suspected him of faking friendship, and of trying to lull them into a false sense of security while he undermined them behind their backs. Notably, there was no dissenting view among the brothers – they all immediately hated him more without pausing to reflect on whether or not their assessment of the situation was correct, ultimately leading them to justify Joseph's murder, without any consideration for the fact that they may have got themselves caught up in a false narrative.

In Jewish law, a unanimous guilty verdict in any capital case would result in a not-guilty verdict. Essentially, if nothing exculpatory can be found to say about the accused, something must be wrong with the judges. Any judicial process which is forced to rely on jurists who have made up their minds about the verdict before the process has even begun is a broken system – whether their view of the accused is guilty or innocent.

However positive the American democratic system has proved to be in just under 250 years, it is still "too early to tell" if it is strong enough to withstand the body blow of this flawed impeachment process. The lesson of Joseph's brothers is simple: if you refuse to be impartial or open to alternative viewpoints, you are treading on very dangerous ground.

FINDING GOD IN THE DARKEST HOUR

first published December 8th, 2017

My late grandfather, Rabbi Joseph H. Dunner (1913-2007), was a remarkable man. Born in Cologne, Germany, his family was devoutly Orthodox in an era when German Jewry had reached the zenith of assimilation. My grandfather aspired to continue in this path of devout Orthodoxy, and despite the enormous challenges he faced at a young age – his mother died when he was just five years old, and his father was then reduced to penury by Germany's interwar economic crisis – he never wavered from his faith-inspired goals.

In 1932, my grandfather enrolled at the prestigious Hildesheimer Rabbinical Seminary in Berlin, the only institution of its kind in Germany. The seminary trained young Orthodox men for the German rabbinate, under the guidance of first-class teachers and mentors, including the dean, Rabbi Yechiel Yaakov Weinberg (1884-1966), a Lithuanian-born Slabodka Yeshiva trained polymath, whose powerful personality and fiery genius left an indelible impression on his students as they prepared themselves for their rabbinical careers.

The ascendancy of the Nazis and Hitler's leadership of Germany, which commenced just a few months after my grandfather started at the seminary, did not deter him in any way, and he resolutely continued along his determined path. When

Berlin University informed him that the subject of his doctoral thesis was no longer acceptable under the law, as it focused on a Jewish theme, he refused to be disappointed, and persisted towards rabbinic ordination, which was conferred in 1936.

By that time German Jewry was reeling from the draconian antisemitic sanctions imposed on them by the Nazi authorities, but rather than seek a career outside the rabbinate, or attempting to emigrate, my grandfather accepted the position as rabbi of Konigsberg, once a thriving community at the heart of this East Prussian university town, but by then a shadow of its former self, struggling to deal with the ever-worsening situation.

On the fateful night of November 9th, 1938, during the countrywide pogrom that became known as *Kristallnacht* (Night of Broken Glass), my grandfather was dragged from his bed by Nazi thugs, as his apartment was trashed, and after being violently beaten, he was marched through the streets until he was eventually thrown into a holding cell at a nearby police station.

I once asked him to describe the experience to me. What was he thinking as he went through it? He had committed no crime, and yet his freedom was being taken away, and his life was in grave danger. He pondered over my questions for a moment, and then looked at me. "I felt very lucky," he said. My grandfather must have seen the surprise on my face, so he explained to me what he meant.

"You see, when they eventually put me in a cell, I knew it was going to be with somebody else. That person could have been anybody. For example, it might easily have been an antisemitic criminal who could have hurt me, or even killed me. But I was lucky. My cellmate turned out

to be my dear friend, Martin Miloslawer, the cantor from
the big synagogue. He knew all the prayers by heart, and
I knew mishnayot by heart, so we prayed together, and
we studied together – and I really felt very lucky."

This story encapsulates my grandfather's personality, and is redolent of a Midrash quoted by Rashi on a verse in Parshat Vayeishev (Gen. 37:25): וַיִּשְׂאוּ עֵינֵיהֶם וַיִּרְאוּ וְהִנֵּה אֹרְחַת יִשְׁמְעֵאלִים בָּאָה מִגִּלְעָד וּגְמַלֵּיהֶם נֹשְׂאִים נְכֹאת וּצְרִי וָלֹט – "[Joseph's brothers] looked up and saw a caravan of Ishmaelites coming from Gilead, and their camels were loaded with spices, balm, and myrrh."

Rashi points out that Ishmaelite merchants tended to trade fuel oil, not spices. How was it that the traders who bought Joseph from his brothers were carrying spices? According to the Midrash, this was not random. God was acutely aware of the unfolding drama between Joseph and his brothers, and although he was being sold into slavery, God did not want Joseph to suffer from the foul odor of fuel oil during his journey to Egypt, and therefore arranged for a caravan that was loaded with pleasantly scented spices.

But while this is a nice idea, and introduces the concept of Divine Providence into a story that is full of negative vibes, in reality, what difference does it make to a person who is being sold into slavery to be in a pleasant smelling wagon rather than a foul smelling wagon? How likely was it that Joseph, who had to deal with multiple traumas, would be consoled by the good fortune of being transported in a spice caravan?

It seems the Midrash is teaching us the exact point my grandfather was trying to stress in his recollections of Kristallnacht. If someone is able to see God's hand even as he is suffering, he will never feel abandoned. God remains with him even in the midst of his anguish; the evidence is right there in front of him. It is people who see God's providence at every turn who are able to hope that things will improve. If God has not given up on them, if He is still present in their lives, how could they ever give up on God?

When Joseph saw that his new Ishmaelite owners were transporting spices rather than oil, he realized that God was watching over him, notwithstanding the gravity of his situation. My grandfather, also named Joseph, had a similar moment when he was thrown into that Nazi jail together with his good friend, with whom he could pray and study Torah, and whose presence meant that his life was not in any imminent danger. And we, too, can look for that silver lining as we face the challenges of life, identifying God's presence even when things are tough, using His presence as proof that our dark tunnel has a shining light at the end of it.

SERVING GOD IN GOOD TIMES AND BAD

first published December 22nd, 2016

E arlier this week Jack Kagan passed away in London, at the age of 87. You've probably never heard his name. He was an unassuming man who lived most of his life in North London, although he was born and grew up in Novogrodek, a tiny town in Belarus. Before the Second World War, Novogrodek was known as Novardok, and was home to a thriving Jewish community as well as one of the most significant yeshivot in Eastern Europe. In September 1939, following the infamous Molotov-Ribbentrop Pact between Nazi Germany and the Soviet Union, Russian troops marched into Novardok, and deported thousands of the local residents to Siberia.

Jack and his family were spared Siberian exile, but their luck ran out when the Nazis invaded the Soviet Union in the early summer of 1941, and overran Novardok. The Kagan home was destroyed, and they were rounded up and herded into a ghetto along with the rest of the Jewish community. On July 26, 1941, the Nazi Jew-killing in Novardok began in earnest. Fifty-two Jews were gunned down in the town center while a Nazi orchestra played Strauss. A few months later 5,000 Jews were taken to pits just outside the town and shot dead. Jack was not killed in the massacre; instead he was thrown into a horrific local labor camp.

In 1943, after witnessing thousands of Jews dying or being murdered by the Nazi genocide machine, Jack and his friends mounted a daring escape via a tunnel they had been secretly digging for months, and then fled to the local forest where they joined the notorious Bielski partisans. Formed by the extraordinary Bielski brothers, the Bielski partisans successfully resisted the Nazis and survived the war, in the process saving over 1,200 men, women and children. Their story would later be made famous by the Hollywood movie *Defiance*, starring Daniel Craig.

After the war was over, Jack left his birthplace and eventually ended up in London, where he married and had three children, and where he remained for the rest of his life. He became a stalwart member of his local synagogue, and an active member of London's wider Jewish community. What was most incredible about this humble survivor, whose family was mercilessly slaughtered, and who endured suffering and hardship beyond our worst nightmares, was his simple faith and his unwavering dedication to Judaism and to his proud roots in Novardok.

In Parshat Vayeishev, we read about Jacob's family troubles, and the initial events that resulted, ultimately, in the Jewish nation's slavery in Egypt. Joseph and his brothers were unable to get along, leading to Joseph's kidnapping and sale into captivity. Reading the story of our nation's founding family in crisis is agonizing, and we desperately try to make sense of it, and to find merit in the actions of the various protagonists. The spotlight is mainly on Joseph. After arriving in Egypt, alone and totally remote from anything familiar, this former favorite son of a wealthy family is about as disadvantaged as a person can be, with no rights and no material security, and with absolutely no training to help him deal with such a crisis.

And yet, despite these handicaps, Joseph thrived, becoming the head of his master's household (Gen. 39:2): וַיְהִי ה' אֶת יוֹסֵף וַיְהִי אִישׁ מַצְלִיחַ וַיְהִי בְּבֵית אֲדֹנָיו הַמִּצְרִי – "God was with Joseph, and he was successful, and he was in the house of his master, the Egyptian." Puzzlingly, this verse duplicates the Hebrew word *vayehi* three times – the first time with reference to God, the second and third times referring to Joseph. Grammatically, the third *vayehi* could be folded into the second one, prompting the question: why the repetition? But actually, the message contained in this repetition is extremely powerful, identifying a crucial ingredient of faith. Some people only find God in challenging circumstances but abandon Him when things improve. Others relate to God when they are successful and their lives are easy, but find faith difficult when things turn tough.

Joseph's relationship with God was unaffected by life's events. When life was good he felt close to God, and when he was in testing circumstances, God also remained central in his life. His connection to God was constant, unaffected by what was going on around him. The wording of the verse now reads perfectly, and the repetition is explained. Joseph had God when he was successful, and equally so when he was the disadvantaged slave of his Egyptian master.

Jack Kagan, like so many other Holocaust survivors – a group that is rapidly and very sadly dwindling away – was not just an inspiration because of the horrific experiences he endured during the Shoah. He was inspiring for the fact that his faith never faltered, neither in good times, nor in bad.

This, too, is the message of the festival of Chanukah. The downtrodden Jews of Judea who were victorious against the unbeatable might of the Greek occupation immediately celebrated victory by finding a container of uncontaminated ritual oil, declaring their faith in God by lighting the Temple Menorah. Theirs' was a constant faith – like Joseph's, and like Jack Kagan's. It had not been extinguished by suffering under the Greeks, nor discarded following their successful military campaign against their antagonists.

And that is the way a Jew must be – always conscious of and engaged with God, and with the obligations that go with that consciousness, notwithstanding personal circumstances. Whether flying high or down in the dumps, the common denominator must always be to stay focused on the fact that our relationship with God is the primary reason for our existence.

THE MARK OF TRUE LEADERSHIP

first published December 10th, 2014

O n November 17, 1973, 400 Associated Press managing editors gathered in Orlando, Florida, to meet beleaguered President Richard Nixon (1913-1994) for a nationally televised press conference. The entire country was captivated by the dramatic events unfolding on an almost daily basis, in the saga that had become known as the "Watergate Crisis."

What began in the Summer of 1972 with the botched robbery of a political campaign office by bungling thieves, had resulted in the stunning arrest of some of the administration's loftiest officials, and there was widespread public dismay at the grubby self-interest of those charged with leading the nation. This press conference had been sought by Nixon, and was understood by everyone as being of critical importance. If Nixon was able to defend his record and articulate cogently why the public should give him their trust, everybody agreed that the crisis would fizzle out. If, on the other hand, he was unable to present himself as a credible leader, the road to his impeachment or losing the presidency before the end of his term was more-or-less guaranteed.

The press conference was intense. It went on for over an hour, with a barrage of question after question. The president was calm, coherent, and even humorous at times. Then, about halfway through, he was asked about possible irregularities in his personal finances, with the next questioner querying how, as chief executive of the administration, he could have allowed something like the Watergate affair to occur. After answering the questions separately, offering a fairly detailed defense of both his financial affairs and his record as president, Nixon offered a conflated answer to both questions that he felt would present, in a nutshell, why the focus on him was both unfounded and unfair.

> *"I [have] made my mistakes, but in all of my years of public life, I have never profited [...] from public service. I have earned every cent. And in all of my years of public life, I have never obstructed justice [...] people have got to know whether or not their President is a crook. Well, I am not a crook."*

Nixon's underlying thesis was simple. In the same way that he was fully transparent in his financial affairs, and it was clear that he done nothing illegal or even shifty in that sphere, his role in Watergate was equally pure, and his hands were completely clean. He was not, as he declared, a "crook." This statement became the most quoted phrase in all of the following day's news reports, and it was a statement that would haunt Nixon for the rest of his life.

The British journalist, David Frost (1939-2013), who famously interviewed Nixon two years after he left office, recognized that it was at this exact moment that Nixon's fate was sealed. The American people had wanted to see leadership. What they saw instead was a facile claim of innocence by association. At the end of three grueling days of interviews, Frost sought, and, incredibly, received, an acknowledgment by the ex-President, that his stubborn inability to admit fault and to shoulder responsibility in the Watergate affair had been an egregious crime against the citizens of the United States. In fact, many saw this weakness of character as worse than anything related to the original sin of Watergate, and even the subsequent cover up.

This insight into Nixon's downfall, in a reverse logic sort of way, helps us understand one of the most troubling chapters in all of Genesis – the story of Judah and Tamar. The inclusion of this episode in the Torah is usually understood in the context of showing the importance of owning up to wrongdoing. After being challenged by his erstwhile daughter-in-law, Tamar, in such a way that avoiding responsibility was an easy option, instead of obfuscating and mitigating his actions, Judah declared (Gen. 38:26): צָדְקָה מִמֶּנִּי – "she has right on her side." He admitted, publicly, that he was guilty of having prevented her from having children, as had been his duty.

But while it took great courage to admit fault, this still does not explain why we need to know that Judah was capable of such an admission. This only becomes clear much later on, when Jacob gathers his sons around his deathbed in Egypt. Reuben, Simeon and Levi, Jacob's three oldest sons, are passed over for the eternal leadership of the Jewish nation, in favor of Judah, not only as a result of their inherent faults, but also because Judah had the unique quality we all seek and hope for in our leaders – the courage to own up to mistakes.

In the episode with Tamar we see a powerful man with, it seems, everything to lose if he shows weakness. Nevertheless, he admits to having done something wrong – even though he could have quite easily covered it up. That is genuine greatness, and that is the mark of true leadership.

It was a family trait, and it continued through the generations, down to King David, and his son King Solomon. And ultimately it will be the reflected in the leadership of their descendent, the Messianic redeemer.

We mistakenly understand leadership as being purely about the ability to inspire, or delegate, or come up with powerful ideas and put them into action. But a real leader is not only capable of those things, but is also someone who is humble in the face of his or her own weaknesses.

MIKKETZ

ANCIENT EGYPT AND ANCIENT GREECE

first published December 14th, 2017

Although ancient Egypt and ancient Greece coexisted for over a millennium, they were different in almost every respect. Egyptian civilization emerged at the dawn of human history and continued until the first century BCE, while Greek civilization began in approximately 1100 BCE, and petered out in the second century BCE, when it was overtaken by Roman civilization.

The disparities between Egypt and Greece are usually assumed to be a factor of their different geographical locations. Mass travel and human migration were extremely limited in those days, and as a consequence cultural influences were contained. For example, the politics of ancient Egypt emphasized centralized authority, while the Greek political structure was far more diffuse, with power decentralized and distributed to local authorities. Artistically, too, the civilizations were very different. Egypt focused heavily on the creation of monumental structures, while the Greeks devoted themselves to less substantial art and focused instead on intricate literary works.

There were, of course, areas of commonality, but none so pronounced as in the area of religious belief. Although the range and structure of the two pantheons were very different, both systems shared a common theme that is both striking and revealing. In both cultures, either a deity was good, or it was evil. In Egypt, for example, the forces of darkness and destruction were represented by a god named *Apep* – the "Lord of Chaos" – who was the archenemy of the sun god *Ra*, considered the source of everything good in the world.

Ra was also known as "King of the Gods", although this appellation did not connote omnipotence; rather it suggested worthiness in the eyes of the faithful. If *Apep* gained the upper hand, *Ra* would be in decline, and Egyptians believed that each evening, as the sun set, *Apep* – who was lurking just below the horizon – would let off a mighty roar, as his might overcame the influence of his nemesis.

The Greek pantheon numbered a totally different set of gods, dominated by Zeus – god of the sky, law, order, and justice. But far from being omnipotent, Zeus was forced to deal with threats from other gods keen to steal his throne, not least of whom was his "wife," Hera, who together with Poseidon tried to stage a coup against Zeus, and almost succeeded. Another deity, Typhon, almost managed to kill Zeus, and the Iliad suggests that Zeus was extremely fearful of Nyx, the Greek goddess of the night. The similarities between this struggle for dominance between the distinct powers of good and evil, as seen in both Egypt and Greece, is conspicuous.

Contrast that with Judaism's understanding of an omnipotent God who presides over everything that happens, and who has no gaps in His powers, or weaknesses that might expose Him to the danger of defeat. I believe it is this contrast that explains a puzzle in the narrative describing Pharaoh's dreams. Although we would like to explain Joseph's ability to interpret dreams as a sign of his remarkable wisdom, the facts demand a more prosaic explanation. After all, correlating livestock and grain with the fortunes of Egypt's economy seems straightforward enough. Which forces the question – why were Pharaoh's advisors unable to interpret his dreams, and what did Joseph see that they failed to observe?

A number of commentaries suggest that the key lies in the fact that the dreams did not portray seven fat cows followed by seven skinny cows, instead they depicted seven skinny cows alongside the seven fat cows. This made no sense to Pharaoh's advisors, who believed that when good prevails, evil has no place. Had there been seven fat cows without the thin ones, the message would have been clear – Egypt would experience prosperity. Alternatively, had the dream only contained the emaciated cows, it would have been evident that a famine was on the way. What was confounding was the simultaneous appearance of fat cows together with the thin cows.

When Pharaoh called for Joseph to be brought from his prison cell, the verse says (Gen. 41:14): וַיְרִיצֻהוּ מִן הַבּוֹר – "and he was quickly brought from the dungeon." The primary kabbalistic text, the *Zohar*, suggests that the root of the Hebrew word *vayeritzuhu* is the Hebrew word *ratzon*, which means "will" or "desire." It was at the exact moment he was being freed from jail by royal command that Joseph suddenly realized that his own dreams all those years ago were never meant to unfold from one minute to the next. Each aspect of his tortuous path, and especially the challenges, had been part of God's will. The bad had combined with the good, so that in the end it was all good, and no separation existed between one and the other. Only a monotheist like Joseph could spot that nuance, and it was this exact nuance that helped him see past the image of fat cows and thin cows occupying the same scene, enabling him to interpret the dreams accurately and to Pharaoh's satisfaction.

Chanukah, which always coincides with the Torah portion of Mikeitz, epitomizes this very same message. We light menorah to commemorate the seemingly minor miracle of oil lasting longer than it should have, while many greater miracles have occurred in our history that have not generated annual festivals. More importantly, full military victory against the Greeks would elude the Maccabeans for many years after they had retaken the Temple. In which case, what exactly are we celebrating?

Chanukah teaches us that life is a patchwork of good and bad, and that bad is not actually always bad. Had the Greeks and their Jewish supporters not tried to Hellenize Jerusalem, Judaism might have declined into oblivion. And more importantly, our enemies' plans do not need to be completely thwarted for God's will to be realized, even if that means that a difficult journey lies ahead. What is imperative is for us to have an appreciation for the miracle of sustained light in an imperfect reality. That is truly a cause for celebration.

WHAT IT REALLY MEANS TO BE CHOSEN

first published December 10th, 2015

I t was a great privilege to attend the recent JNF annual breakfast at the Hyatt Regency Century Plaza as one of the 1,400 people there to support the State of Israel. JNF was founded in 1901 to buy land in Palestine from Ottoman landowners, and this fantastic organization has continued for over a century to be at the forefront of projects in the Land of Israel, for the benefit of the land and for the benefit of those living there.

The guest speaker was author and talk show host Dennis Prager. He always speaks well, articulating so clearly why Israel's critics are wrong, and how Israel is unfairly targeted by her enemies. As usual, his address was stimulating and informative, but something he said really stood out. During the course of his address he made the interesting point that "history has proven without question that the Jews are a chosen nation – how else is it possible to rationally understand the scope of Jews in world history?" So true, and yet so many Jews are embarrassed to call themselves "chosen" (unlike the Chinese, or the Japanese, who cheerfully declare their "chosen"-ness), while at the same time there are so many antisemites who profoundly hate the Jews precisely because they feel "chosen" (although those same people don't hate the Chinese or the Japanese for feeling that same way!).

The obsession with Jews that has morphed and regenerated over thousands of years is indeed a proof that we are "chosen." Is it not obvious that our being chosen is the only explanation for why Jews, a statistically insignificant group of diverse individuals who can barely agree on anything (you know the one – "two Jews, three opinions!"), are bunched together as the target of so much hatred and derision? Why is a Jew in Paris targeted for the supposed crimes of a Jew in Israel? Why are Israeli universities and their academic professionals banned, while Iranian, or North Korean, or Zimbabwean professors, or universities, are welcomed and feted by all? It only makes sense if the Jews are chosen. It is not ethnocentricity to say it – it is merely a statement of the facts.

As Prager was speaking, I thought to myself that perhaps those Jews who wish to deny their chosen status are related to Sholom Aleichem's fictional character, Tevye the Milkman, in the iconic movie, *Fiddler on the Roof.* Tired of the endless antisemitism and threat of pogroms in his little village of Anatevka, he laconically turns to God in the course of one of his monologues, and says: "once in a while, can't you choose someone else?"

I think, though, that the denial of this "chosen" status is a human-condition problem. We are searching for complex answers when simple ones make most sense. We come up with convoluted theories when the answer is staring at us right in the face. And I was particularly delighted to hear this idea expressed so beautifully regarding Chanukah. The festival of Chanukah has always puzzled me. It seems to be so schizophrenic. Are we celebrating the Hasmonean victory over the Greeks? Or are we celebrating the miracle of eight nights of Menorah lights that should have lasted only one night? Well, I guess it depends on who you ask, or where you look. To most people the Menorah symbolizes a spiritual affirmation of the military victory. But the truth is quite different.

The Chanukah battle was not between Greeks and Jews, as is often thought. It was between Jews who revered traditional Judaism, and Jews who wished to renounce their tradition in favor of Greek culture. The victory of Chanukah is a triumph of Judaism – as symbolized by the Menorah and by the miracle that occurred when the Temple was reconsecrated. Of course, it could never have happened without the military victory, but that was a means to an end, not the other way around. Which means that those who focus on the military victory have taken their eyes off the ball and have chosen to ignore the obvious.

Joseph and his brothers present us with a similar scenario. Many of the commentaries ask why Joseph went through the whole charade with his brothers, keeping one in jail as they brought back Benjamin, and then threatening to keep Benjamin and never set him free. The answer is obvious to us, but it clearly was not obvious to Joseph's brothers. Joseph realized that unless his brothers were able to recognize that their decision to sell him into slavery had been a dreadful mistake, the Jewish nation could not be born, as it needed to be, in unity and harmony. His intrigues and complex machinations were all executed only so that the brothers would themselves come to recognize the obvious – that Joseph had not deserved the fate they had foisted on him.

The process of catharsis begins in Parshat Mikketz (Gen. 42:21): וַיֹּאמְרוּ אִישׁ אֶל אָחִיו אֲבָל אֲשֵׁמִים אֲנַחְנוּ עַל אָחִינוּ אֲשֶׁר רָאִינוּ צָרַת נַפְשׁוֹ בְּהִתְחַנְנוֹ אֵלֵינוּ וְלֹא שָׁמָעְנוּ – "They said to each other: 'We must be guilty with regard to our brother, as we saw how deeply distressed he was when he begged us, and we did not listen; that is the reason we are going through such distress ourselves.'" With Judah's powerful soliloquy at the beginning of Parshat Vayigash, the process that began in Mikketz finally concluded, and Joseph revealed himself. The brothers' eyes had been opened and they were rehabilitated.

Let the festival of Chanukah along with the dramatic narrative of Joseph and his brothers act as a wakeup call to all those who refuse to acknowledge the obvious. There is no shame in being the Chosen People, nor is there anything wrong with defending Israel and denouncing its critics. We survived the Greek onslaught as the Chosen People, and we will continue to endure as long as we recognize that our Jewish faith and its continuity is nothing less than the will of God.

THE MIGHTY AT THE HANDS OF THE WEAK

first published December 17th, 2014

Another week, and more crazed, suicidal attacks by Islamic murderers, intent on killing innocent civilians. This week it was Sydney, Australia. And Peshawar, Pakistan. And Jos, Nigeria. Meanwhile, the London-based *International Centre for the Study of Radicalisation* last week issued a comprehensive report on all the deaths caused by Islamic murderers during the month of November. They tracked every bombing, shooting, beheading, and all other types of fatal attack by violent Islamists, for the thirty days of November, to offer a snapshot of jihadi violence.

Well, guess what. The number of people killed at the hands of these savages in November 2014 was 5,042. That's nearly twice as many people than were killed in the World Trade Center on 9/11. Oh, and on December 11, 2014, the day the report was released, a suicide bomber drove a car full of explosives into a group of pro-government Shiite fighters south of Tikrit, Iraq, killing nine people.

In 2009 there were apparently 1.57 billion Muslims in the world — give or take a few tens of millions. It is an overwhelming number, and even if a fraction of that number are the type of barbarians who happily murder for their faith, it still makes the threat from Fascism in the 1930's, and the threat of from

Communists during the Cold War, pale by comparison. Everyone has their own take on what do about this threat to civilized humanity. Some believe that moderate Muslims will eventually come to their senses and the problem will be dealt with internally. Then there are those who believe that the threat can be contained through a mixture of clever diplomacy and basic defensive measures.

Yet others believe that Muslims are in any event not a homogenous group, and that the fissures that exist between different Islamic denominations, nationalities, and even tribes, are so deep, that they will ultimately neutralize any real threat to Western civilization, however unsettling it is to regularly see people being beheaded or blown to smithereens. In the end, notwithstanding the existence of such brutality, Muslims do not pose a real existential threat to the rest of the world – or so the argument goes.

I wish I could be so sanguine. My own family experience of narrowly escaping certain death at the hands of the Nazis feeds into my heightened aversion for belittling danger, and dismissing threats from people who want to kill you or to destroy your way of life given half the chance.

Despite that, I remain entirely upbeat. While I believe that the world is going to go through various shades of hell as Islamic belligerence increases the pain and mayhem inflicted upon the West, I still firmly believe that the long-term picture is positive.

My confidence and optimism is based on an utter certainty that the eternity of the Jewish people is guaranteed, as is the survival of all those gentiles who carry and perpetuate the values of our ancient faith. And we need to look no further than the Torah portion of Mikketz for proof.

The verse tells us (Gen. 41:8): וַיְסַפֵּר פַּרְעֹה לָהֶם אֶת חֲלֹמוֹ וְאֵין פּוֹתֵר אוֹתָם לְפַרְעֹה – "Pharaoh described his dreams to [the wise men] and they were not able to interpret them."

The commentators all puzzle over the inability of these experts to come up with the correct interpretation. Clearly, they were people who had previously offered dream analyses to Pharaoh, and had been right, otherwise why would he turn to them now? In which case, why were they so mystified on this occasion? There are a variety of different answers, but the one that makes the most sense is that the two dream narratives were incompatible with the way things ought to be, and therefore were inexplicable to the soothsayers. Both dreams described large things being devoured by far smaller things, and yet those smaller things showed no material change. Thin cows eating fat cows – and remaining thin. Lean sheaves consuming fat sheaves – and remaining lean.

The Egyptian mystics, despite their expertise, were confounded by this defiance of the natural order, and it confused them so much that they could make no sense of what was being foretold.

Joseph, who was brought up in the house of the patriarch Jacob, was entirely comfortable with the supernatural, and so he declared (Gen. 41:25): אֵת אֲשֶׁר הָאֱלֹקִים עֹשֶׂה הִגִּיד לְפַרְעֹה – "that which God is doing is what is being told to Pharaoh." In other words, don't concern yourself with the natural order – if God wants it to happen, it will happen. The strong can collapse and be consumed without trace, even at the hands of the weak – who do not necessarily end up displaying any apparent sign of their victory.

This message is reinforced during the week of Chanukah, when we commemorate the victory of the Hasmonean rebels against the might of the Seleucid Greek army, led by Antiochus IV Epiphanes. During the prayer that we insert in our thrice-daily services we declare our gratitude to God: מָסַרְתָּ גִבּוֹרִים בְּיַד חַלָּשִׁים וְרַבִּים בְּיַד מְעַטִּים – "You delivered the mighty into the hands of the weak, and the many into the hands of the few."

Where is the might of the Greeks today? Gone. It has disappeared, existing only in history books and museums. And yet the Jewish nation, small and weak then as now, remains a force that endures, and all those who embrace the values contained in the Torah, and recognize the supremacy of morality over barbarism, and Godliness over mindless brutality, will similarly endure, while the threat from those who wish to dominate humanity with their morbid dogma of intolerance and violence will evaporate, to be the subject of future history books and academic deliberation. May that day come very soon.

VAYIGASH

ALWAYS LOOK ON THE BRIGHT SIDE OF LIFE

first published January 2nd, 2020

Ou've been asked the question before. Are you a glass-half-full kind of person, or is your glass always half-empty? You might think to yourself – who cares? After all, what difference does it make one way or the other? Well, in August 2019 a remarkable study revealed that if your proverbial glass is always half-full, you are much more likely to live to a ripe old age than those people who think their glass is half-empty. The statistics are astounding; optimistic women are 50 percent more likely to live until at least the age of 85, and optimistic males are 70 percent more likely to live that long. In other words, a pessimist's lifespan is profoundly affected – indeed, reduced – as a result of their negative disposition.

The lead researcher for the study was USC graduate Dr. Lewina Lee, Assistant Professor of Psychiatry at Boston University School of Medicine. She is clearly a glass-half-full type, because rather than seeing the results of the study as depressing for pessimists, she told reporters that the findings "raise an exciting possibility that we may be able to promote healthy and resilient aging by cultivating psychosocial assets such as optimism."

Lee and her team analyzed data from two other long-term research projects, one of them focused on a large number of female nurses and the other on a smaller group of men. The nurses were first evaluated for their optimism in 2004; at the time they had an average age of 70. The men were first assessed for optimism in 1986, when their average age was 62, and deaths were recorded until 2016. After splitting the more than 70,000 subjects into four roughly equal groups, based on how they scored for optimism, the research team then noted the lifespans of the most optimistic ones as compared to the lifespans of the least optimistic, while simultaneously accounting for other factors, such as age, race, education, and various physical and mental health conditions.

The study proved what has long been considered the case based on anecdotal evidence: positive people live longer and healthier lives. Yes, it's true – not thinking the worst of every situation, or imagining the worst outcome, can actually increase your lifespan considerably. The study's co-author, Laura Kubzansky, Professor of Social and Behavioral Sciences at the Harvard School of Public Health, says that the reason for this extraordinary phenomenon is really quite simple: "more optimistic people [are more] able to regulate emotions and behavior, as well as bounce back from stressors and difficulties more effectively."

Or, as the Israel-born Nobel Prize-winning economist, Daniel Kahneman (b.1934), put it so beautifully in his book *Thinking Fast and Slow*: "If you are genetically endowed with an optimistic bias, you hardly need to be told that you are a lucky person – you already feel fortunate." The corollary of optimism is that you eat better, you don't suffer the negative consequences of anxiety and depression, and you actually feel like you want to live longer because you enjoy your life, even when things are undeniably challenging. And it occurred to me that this entire concept can help us understand a puzzling Midrash about Jacob and how old he was when he died.

When Jacob had his audience with Pharaoh after arriving in Egypt, the ruler of Egypt was quite shocked by Jacob's very elderly and frail appearance and asked him how old he was (Gen. 47:8): וַיֹּאמֶר פַּרְעֹה אֶל יַעֲקֹב כַּמָּה יְמֵי שְׁנֵי חַיֶּיךָ – "Pharaoh said to Jacob, 'how many years are the days of your life?'" Jacob explained that the reason he looked so frail and old was because he had experienced a very hard life.

The Midrash comments that Jacob should have lived at least as long as his father, Isaac, who died at the age of 180. But Jacob died aged 147, a reduction of 33 years based on the number of words in this very exchange with Pharaoh as recorded in Parshat Vayigash. The medieval Tosafists explain that God reminded Jacob of all the times He had saved him from life-threatening and challenging experiences, with the implication that Jacob had nothing to complain about – after all Esau had not managed to kill him, Laban had not got the better of him, and in the end, Joseph had turned up alive-and-well as the viceroy of Egypt.

To be frank, this Midrash is absolutely bewildering. While it is true that God saved Jacob from Esau and Laban, and reunited him with Joseph, just because there was a happy ending did not diminish the trauma of the situation as it unfolded and before the happy ending had happened. The tension and anxiety take their toll, and one can hardly blame Jacob for mentioning it as an explanation for his very aged appearance.

But I think the Midrash is presenting us with the two approaches to life we mentioned earlier and highlighting the lifechanging consequences of each. Isaac could hardly be said to have had an easy life – pointedly, he was the subject of a harrowing near-death experience at the hands of his father at the *Akeida*. But it would appear he was a glass-half-full kind of person, and always saw the bright side of life, resulting in his remarkable longevity. Meanwhile, his son Jacob was a worrier, and always took the glass-half-empty approach. His conversation with Pharaoh in Vayigash simply highlights this attitude, and the Midrash uses it as an opportunity to explain that this was why his lifespan was shorter than Isaac's.

There is a quote often misattributed to Sir Winston Churchill (1875-1965), actually spoken by a long-forgotten British local politician, the mayor of Carlisle, Bertram Carr (1868-1927), better known for his family's eponymous biscuit company. In his 1919 keynote speech to a convention of social reformers, Carr addressed some of the great challenges they faced in achieving their utopian goals, telling delegates that they must: "view these [matters] in the spirit of the optimist to whom every difficulty is an opportunity, and not as the pessimist, to whom every opportunity presents some difficulty."

So true, and, as it turns out, your life may actually depend on it.

TRUE FORGIVENESS NEEDS CLOSURE

first published December 10th, 2018

Ⅰn 1976, the famous Holocaust survivor and Nazi-hunter Simon Wiesenthal (1908-2005) published a small book called *The Sunflower*. The book was inspired by a troubling and evocative memory that had plagued Wiesenthal ever since the Second World War. In 1943, while imprisoned at Janowska concentration camp on the outskirts of Lvov, Wiesenthal was suddenly spirited to the bedside of a dying 22-year-old SS soldier, Karl Seidl, who had told nurses to "bring him a Jew!" Wiesenthal found the dying soldier wrapped in bandages covering his entire face, with only holes for his mouth, nose and ears.

Seidl spoke to Wiesenthal at great length. He described his idyllic childhood as a Catholic altar boy from a loving non-Nazi home, and then spoke about his Nazi career, including his active involvement in the murder of hundreds of Jews whom he had burned alive and shot in cold blood. Now, as he lay dying, he was haunted by these heinous crimes, and felt compelled to offer a full confession to a Jew, and to obtain forgiveness from a Jew.

"I am left here with my guilt. In the last hours of my life you are here with me. I do not know who you are, I only know that you are a Jew and that is enough. I know that what I have told you is terrible. In the long nights while I have been waiting for death, time and time again

I have longed to talk about it to a Jew and beg forgiveness from him. Only I didn't know if there were any Jews left. I know that what I am asking is almost too much for you, but without your answer I cannot die in peace."

Wiesenthal sat and listened to Seidl, but said absolutely nothing in response and then left him. Later that night the SS murderer died. Years later Wiesenthal went to visit Seidl's mother, to find out whether the dying Nazi's description of his childhood had been accurate or overly idealized.

Seidl's mother turned out to be a fine, upstanding woman, and she told Wiesenthal her son had been a normal, caring, responsible young man who was absolutely incapable of cold-blooded murder. Once again Wiesenthal was silent, this time so as not to reveal what he had heard from her son about his evil violence against Jews in Poland.

But the experience haunted him. As the years went by, Wiesenthal began to wonder: had he done the right thing?

"Was my silence at the bedside of the dying Nazi right or wrong? This is a profound moral question that challenges the conscience of the reader of this episode, just as much as it once challenged my heart and mind."

In the first edition of *The Sunflower*, Wiesenthal reproduced the responses of ten people to whom he had posed the question. Ultimately this number increased to 53 men and women, whose responses appeared in subsequent editions. The reactions were from a wide range of people, including Christians and Jews, Buddhists and atheists; they came from the Dalai Lama and Deborah Lipstadt, from Cardinal Franz König of Austria and the

Jewish scholar Abraham Joshua Heschel, from a former West German justice minister and from a survivor of nineteen years in Chinese labor camps. And while the answers varied, many of those who responded felt – as Wiesenthal himself had felt – that they could not forgive someone for a crime that had not been perpetrated directly against them.

This week, as I reflected on one of the most enduring puzzles of Joseph's 22-years in Egypt away from his family, I was reminded of *The Sunflower*, and the answer I would have given Simon Wiesenthal had he asked me the question. Why did Joseph not just reveal himself to his brothers as soon as he saw them, and get it over with? And although the brothers were the guilty party in this entire saga, is it not true to say that Joseph also bore some responsibility for his father's misery? After all, are we to believe that he had never once had the opportunity to send a message home to his father, to let him know he was still alive? Certainly, as viceroy of Egypt, he could easily have been in touch. He may not to have been to blame for his father's despair, but he was certainly not blameless.

Maimonides ("*Rambam*"; 1138-1204) writes that atonement for sin requires more than just remorse (*Mishne Torah*, Laws of Repentance 2:4). Although being sorry for what you've done is certainly important as an initial step, true *teshuva* needs more than that – it requires a total character overhaul, so that one can say, "I am no longer the person who committed the sin; I am a totally different person." Maimonides even suggests (ad loc. 2:1) that the only way to know if one's atonement has been successful is to find oneself in similar circumstances to those of the original sin, and this time to desist from sinning.

Had Simon Wiesenthal asked me for my response, I would have said that while Karl Seidl was clearly sorry for what he had done, he was on his deathbed, and it seems unlikely he would have been so remorseful had he not been dying. In full health he might well have killed thousands more Jews. In which case forgiveness has no meaning. Just as Seidl's confession was the empty plea of a dying, scared man, Wiesenthal's forgiveness in that situation would have been hollow and superficial.

This might explain Joseph's decision to refrain from revealing himself to his brothers, and even from sending a message to his father at some point earlier on. Joseph knew his predicament was no accident, and when he saw his brothers, he realized that in order for the plan to unfold correctly, it had to all fall into place properly. He could have magnanimously forgiven his brothers immediately, and in that situation, needing him for food, and shocked at his rise to such a powerful position, they would have gratefully welcomed that forgiveness.

But Joseph also knew that this would not be enough. In order to draw a line under their monstrous behavior they needed to be confronted with their sin, and not repeat it. It was for this reason that Joseph orchestrated events so carefully, arranging for Benjamin to be suspected of thievery and taken away from his father. How would the brothers react? Would they repeat their sin? Although, this time the brothers acted differently. Judah stepped forward and said to Joseph, "Spare our brother, and send him back to his father; rather take me in his place." Only then was Joseph able to reveal his true identity, and only then could his brothers be properly forgiven.

Joseph instinctively understood that Jacob wanted what was best for his children, and would not want his sons to have unfinished, unfinishable business. If this meant not seeing or hearing from his beloved son until that outcome was possible, Joseph knew Jacob would not just accept it, but would be happy he had been part of a process that allowed his children to reclaim their self-esteem.

In the final analysis, forgiveness amounts to nothing if it is not accompanied by true closure.

IF ONLY THEY COULD TALK

first published December 21st, 2017

Animals communicating with each other and with humans have always been a feature of literary fiction, and over the last century this has spilled over into the world of movie entertainment. Science has long accepted that animals communicate, but until fairly recently animal interaction was thought to be rudimentary, and much of it was believed to be unpremeditated – meaning that when a monkey shrieks a warning about a predator, the shriek is an instinctive reaction to the predator, as is the response of the monkeys that hear it and run for cover.

The conclusion that animals and birds do not communicate intelligently is based on the view that animals do not have the brainpower to enable intelligent communication. Humans, on the other hand, do have the brainpower, and therefore do communicate intelligently, using sophisticated vocalizations of complex vocabularies that are the foundation of highly developed vernaculars.

But as attractive as this thesis may be, it is deeply flawed, and not simply in light of the study published last month, about which I will say more in a moment. Essentially, once we have established that animals and birds can communicate with each other, the level of their language sophistication becomes entirely irrelevant. As primitive as their interactions may be, the mere fact that they interact at all reduces the difference between human and animal language to a quantitative measure, as opposed to a qualitative one. Even among humans the level of communication sophistication differs enormously, and to draw any conclusion about animals or humans on the basis of their communication skills seems rather arbitrary if, in the end, they are capable of making themselves understood to the satisfaction of those around them.

In any event, the case for human communication superiority just got even weaker. A study published last month in *Science Advances*, authored by three eminent scientists spanning various disciplines, reveals that chimpanzees carefully tailor what they "say," depending on who they are "talking" to. Of course, we humans are very familiar with this concept. A professional talking to a layman will dumb down terminology so that the person he is talking to can understand what he is saying. When talking to a fellow professional, however, they won't hold back, as they know that the fellow professional will understand exactly what even the most obscure term means.

According to the study, chimpanzees vary their warning calls when spotting a venomous snake, if they know that other chimpanzees are already aware of the snake's presence. Rather than alerting their fellow chimpanzees to a new danger, they reiterate the snake warning less vigorously, either to note the snake's altered location, or to sustain awareness of the snake's presence as time progresses. These measured calls, as opposed to the rather more frantic initial reaction when the snake is first spotted, dismisses the notion that animal communication is instinctive rather than premeditated.

Judaism divides creation into four different categories: inanimate, plant life, animal life, and humanity. Interestingly, the Hebrew word used to describe humanity for this breakdown is *medaber*, which translates as "speaker." The implication seems to be that human beings are more elevated than animal life because we can communicate with each other via the medium of speech. But if animals can also speak to each other, even if their language skills are not a match for ours, how does it make sense for communication to be used as the defining characteristic of our superiority?

There is a puzzling line in the story of Joseph's final confrontation with his estranged brothers, in the immediate aftermath of his revelation as the long-lost brother they had sold into slavery. As if trying to convince them that he was who claimed to be, and that he meant them no harm, Joseph declares (Gen. 45:12): וְהִנֵּה עֵינֵיכֶם רֹאוֹת וְעֵינֵי אָחִי בִנְיָמִין כִּי פִי הַמְדַבֵּר אֲלֵיכֶם – "you can see for yourselves, and my brother Benjamin can see, that it is I who is speaking to you." According to Rashi, until this conversation occurred Joseph had only spoken to his brothers via an interpreter. Now, after revealing himself as their brother, he spoke to them in their native Hebrew, and, says Rashi, he wished to use his familiarity with their mother tongue as proof of his identity.

But was this really the most convincing proof Joseph could come up with? After all, perhaps he had met the "real" Joseph and learned Hebrew from him? The answer lies in the correct Hebrew term for the Hebrew language: *Lashon Hakodesh*, which means "sacred tongue." In other words, it is not the fact that we can communicate with each other that makes us superior; it is the fact that we can elevate our speech and sanctify it.

Joseph knew that his brothers' grudge against him was in part based on the stories he had relayed to his father about them, which they believed had painted them in a bad light (Gen. 37:2). With this gossip he had defiled his power of speech, and could not be considered a true *medaber*. But after 22-years of soul-searching and devoted character development, Joseph was no longer the careless, loose-tongued teenager his brothers had so reviled. He was now someone whose power of communication via speech had been finely honed, connecting him to the Divine in every aspect of its use. "Don't picture me as you knew me then, all those years ago," he was telling his brothers – "see me as I am now, the way I speak to you now, that is who I really am."

It is not our knowledge of Hebrew that turns us into anything special, nor is it our ability to communicate, nor, even, is it the volume and complexity of the words we use when we interact. Animals can also communicate with each other, and we are no different to them in that respect.

The only thing that separates us from all other communicators is if our interactions elevate us, and also elevates the world around us.

VAYECHI

MEMORIES OF MORDECHAI "PUPIK" ARNON

first published January 9th, 2020

I was 8 years old when I met him for the first time; truthfully, he was the first real "showbiz" star I ever encountered. In his heyday, Mordechai "Pupik" Arnon – who died last week aged 78 after a difficult battle with cancer – was one of Israel's most beloved stars. His moment in the spotlight was during the 1960s and 1970s, when Israel was experiencing its major post-independence explosion of art, film, music, and literature.

Pupik is Yiddish for navel, a nickname Arnon picked up because of his diminutive size, but although he was physically tiny, he was always the biggest personality in the room. He was a singer and an actor, but more than anything else Pupik was absolutely hilarious, a first-class comedian in whose mouth every story was funny, and every punchline was perfect. His close friends included Chaim Topol, with whom he costarred in the 1964 Israeli movie *Sallah Shabbati*, a whimsical social satire about Jewish immigrants directed by Ephraim Kishon and produced by Menachem Golan – all of them at the very beginning of careers that would propel them to international fame and celebrity.

During the Yom Kippur War of 1973, Pupik performed for Israel's beleaguered troops alongside the legendary Canadian singer Leonard Cohen (1934-2016) – the soldiers had never heard of Cohen and were apparently far more eager to watch Pupik perform. He was truly a rising star, with a bright future ahead of him. Hollywood and Broadway beckoned, nevertheless Pupik chose a different path, one that meant he would completely disappear from the public eye, despite his extraordinary talent and prodigious energy.

Pupik grew up completely secular and in his younger years had no social contact with religious Jews whatsoever. Then, in 1975, at the height of his success, he suddenly began to feel that his life was devoid of meaning – or as he put it: "I needed to find out why I existed." In desperation, he struck up a conversation with a group of religious Jews in Jerusalem, mainly to prove to himself that religion had nothing to offer that would enhance his life. In an interview with *Maariv*, he later said:

> *"I asked them many difficult questions, but they asked me even more difficult questions – questions that I could not answer. It was then that I realized I needed to examine my life more deeply. I tried many philosophies and ideas to answer my questions but realized that if I did not also examine Judaism seriously, I might end up living a lie."*

Within a few months Pupik dropped out of sight and went to study at Ohr Someach yeshiva in Jerusalem. When he reemerged, he was a fully committed orthodox Jew, a commitment he fervently maintained for the remainder of his life. Such was the impact of his startling metamorphosis, that several of his high-profile friends followed in his footsteps and also became religious – most notably the renowned actor and director Uri Zohar, and the celebrated artist Ika Israeli.

Having rejected his showbiz career, Pupik moved from Tel Aviv to the religious Shaarei Ḥesed neighborhood in Jerusalem, where he became a familiar fixture at the GR"A Synagogue. He devoted the rest of his life to raising an orthodox family, and to creating religious education programs for secular Israelis, often involving clever movie shorts and various other unusual gimmicks.

My family got to know Pupik after he quite randomly knocked at the door of my parents' home during Shavuot in 1978. I don't recall the reason he suddenly turned up out of the blue; all I can remember is that he had us all in stitches with his spontaneous sketches and riotous routines.

Thereafter he came every year, often together with Ika Israeli, occasionally with Uri Zohar – and I can even recall a fundraising event at my parents' home with Chaim Topol. The money Pupik raised all went to fund his groundbreaking educational projects.

Even as a fundraiser Pupik was original and creative. On one occasion a philanthropist was playing hard-to-get and not returning Pupik's calls, so he went to a passport photo booth and took dozens of photos of himself making different faces, stuck them to sheets of paper and faxed them to the philanthropist with a note saying "I am trying to reach you – these photos are just in case you've forgotten what I look like." It was so unique – classic Pupik.

Parshat Vayechi records the death of Jacob, or at least so it seems. At first we are told that he is old and sick; Jacob then tells Joseph he is going to die; soon afterward Jacob gathers his sons together for a final deathbed meeting and he blesses them; and finally Joseph and his brothers "saw that their father had died" and take him to be buried in Hebron, the last person to be interred in the "Cave of Maḥpelah."

But there is a problem with that narrative – the Torah never actually informs us that Jacob has died, instead telling us (Gen. 49:33): וַיֶּאֱסֹף רַגְלָיו אֶל הַמִּטָּה וַיִּגְוַע וַיֵּאָסֶף אֶל עַמָּיו – "he drew his feet into the bed, he expired, and he was gathered to his people." There is no direct mention of his death using the standard Hebrew word *vayamat*, and it is this anomaly that prompts the Midrash to propose the rather startling concept: "our forefather Jacob did not die." What makes this statement even more curious is that we later read of Jacob being buried.

Jacob is seen as the founding father of the Jewish nation. His alternative name, Israel, would later become synonymous with the nation that emerged from his descendants. Although his father Isaac and grandfather Abraham had a part in the foundation of Jewish nationhood, they also fathered other nations through their other children. But while these nations may have existed for centuries, their collective rejection of God rendered them lifeless even as they thrived, and part of Abraham and Isaac died with them. Jacob's descendants, on the other hand, by being the standard-bearers of God's mission and of God-belief in a world that rejects God, ensured that Jacob remained alive even though he was physically gone.

My friend Pupik made a remarkable life choice at the pinnacle of his career. Fame and fortune are ephemeral, he decided, a flash-in-the-pan that will not ensure eternal life. And so he abandoned his certain path to a life of stardom, and instead chose to be like Jacob – a choice to live on even after he had died, through a legacy of commitment to Judaism and a Jewish future that will long outlive his tiny physical presence on this earth.

AN EDUCATION IN JEWISH EDUCATION

first published December 20th, 2018

You have probably heard about the controversy over general studies at Orthodox Jewish day schools that recently erupted in New York. Actually, this story has been brewing for several years. In July 2015, fifty-two former yeshiva students, themselves parents of yeshiva students or former teachers at yeshivas, signed a letter that was sent to seven district superintendents in Queens and Brooklyn, and also to the New York City Schools Chancellor Carmen Farina.

The letter expressed "deep concern" about "the poor quality and scant amount of secular education" at the 39 schools in New York to which the signatories were affiliated. The central allegation was that these yeshivas failed to meet New York state laws that require all nonpublic schools to provide a "substantially equivalent" education to public schools.

As a result of the letter, New York mayor Bill de Blasio launched an investigation into a range of yeshivas in New York's five boroughs – institutions that serve some 57,000 students. But the investigation went nowhere, with activists alleging that New York politicians are far too cautious when dealing with the strictly Orthodox Jewish community, which comprises a crucial voting bloc. With the city inquiry stalling, the state stepped in. One month ago, on November 20, Mary Ellen Elia, who is New York

State's Education Commissioner, released updated rules which mandate how nonpublic schools will be regulated going forward, specifying what students in those schools must learn on a daily basis, and stipulating consequences for any school that is found to be in non-compliance.

The reaction was swift and fierce. "SHOCK: New NYS Guidelines Require Yeshiva Elementary Schools to Teach AT LEAST 6 HOURS A DAY of Secular Studies" screamed a headline on the popular ultra-Orthodox website *Yeshiva World* the following day. A week later the Satmar Rebbe of Kiryas Yoel "declared war" on the New York State Education Department in a "fiery speech." And since that time, two senior rabbinic leaders, Rabbi Elya Brudny of Mir yeshiva, and Rabbi Yisroel Reisman of Torah Vodaas, both located in Brooklyn, authored a joint op-ed in the Wall Street Journal, in which they noted:

> *"There will always be schools that need to improve and students who can be better served. But underperforming schools are the outliers, and they don't define the yeshiva system. Parents who want to send their children to a school offering a course list devised by the state enroll their children in the local public school. But parents who choose religious education want their children to have a specific moral, ethical and religious framework for life."*

It is noteworthy that both of the schools headed by these rabbis offer general studies that fully comply with state requirements. At issue is the state's objective to ensure that private schools provide an education that is "substantially equivalent" to that offered in public schools.

Even secular experts have warned that the revised rules may be a step too far, with Neal McCluskey of the Cato Institute writing in *Forbes* that "private schools must never be required to provide instruction "substantially equivalent" to state institutions," although he added that this should never lead to authorities giving "absolute deference to parents – [for] if a child is kept from attaining the basic skills necessary for self-government, that, too, is a denial of liberty."

At the beginning of Parshat Vayechi, Jacob informs Joseph that in future people would bless their children by referencing his two sons, Ephraim and Manasseh (Gen. 48:20): וַיְבָרֲכֵם בַּיּוֹם הַהוּא לֵאמוֹר בְּךָ יְבָרֵךְ יִשְׂרָאֵל לֵאמֹר יְשִׂמְךָ אֱלֹקִים כְּאֶפְרַיִם וְכִמְנַשֶּׁה – [Jacob] blessed them on that day, saying, "With you, Israel will bless, saying, 'May God make you like Ephraim and like Manasseh.'"

The ancient Aramaic explanatory translation, *Targum Yonatan*, adds two words which indicate that this blessing should be given at a Brit Milah, the ritual circumcision of an 8-day-old baby.

Rabbi Abraham Shmuel Binyamin Sofer ("*Ketav Sofer*"; 1815-1871) questions the specificity of this requirement. Why is this blessing particularly relevant to a tiny baby? His answer is based on a Midrash that suggests Ephraim and Manasseh excelled in different areas. Manasseh was a master of worldly matters; he spoke various languages and assisted his father in running the affairs of Egypt. Meanwhile, Ephraim was very spiritual, and spent all of his time studying with his grandfather Jacob.

At the very earliest moment of a child's life a choice must be made to go one way or another, says the *Ketav Sofer*, and therefore focusing on Jacob's formula at the Brit Milah is the greatest blessing of all. He goes on to suggest that parents should focus more on the Ephraim than the Manasseh in their children, citing the fact that Jacob switched the names around, putting the younger son Ephraim first.

But the *Ketav Sofer* was writing in the nineteenth century, when Orthodox Judaism was under phenomenal pressure to modernize and to dilute its ideals, both externally and from within the community. Consequently, it is perfectly understandable that he felt a need to stress Ephraim over Manasseh. The situation is markedly different in the United States in the year 2018. And in any event, besides for the fact that Orthodox Jewry is fully protected by the First Amendment to the U.S. Constitution, the *Ketav Sofer*'s reading of the verse is simply not true to the literal text of Jacob's declaration. Jacob did not suggest for the blessing to be "may God make you like Ephraim **or** like Manasseh," rather he formulated the blessing as "like Ephraim **and** like Manasseh."

Our children, from the youngest age, have to be given a dual-track education that both ensures their spiritual elevation and their ability to cope adequately, or better, in the world in which they live. And although we must always give primacy to Torah and the tenets of our faith, if we deny them their basic rights as citizens of the world, not only are we shortchanging them, we are also defying the very blessing first uttered by our patriarch Jacob, which forms a central part of our ancient tradition.

THE BENEFITS OF PILING ON THE PRESSURE

first published December 28th, 2017

O ver the past couple of decades, a new area of psychological research has emerged that has changed the way psychologists understand a very familiar aspect of human behavior. "Procrastination psychology," as it is called, is the study of why it is that people put things off when they have to do them, rather than getting them done immediately.

This cutting-edge branch of behavioral study has many applications, and it has quickly found its way into numerous other disciplines. Most of us see procrastination as just another form of laziness, or alternatively a consequence of poor time management skills, but psychological researchers have demonstrated that when someone chronically procrastinates, it is not about putting stuff off until tomorrow, or next week. It turns out that this ubiquitous human condition is actually a complex failure of self-regulation. Those who habitually procrastinate choose to delay important tasks, despite knowing that they will certainly suffer as a result of that delay. Although it may be true that laziness and poor time-management can make the problem worse, it is an inability to manage emotions that seems to be at the root of this all-too-common human failing.

One expert who has pioneered modern research on procrastination, Professor Joseph Ferrari of DePaul University in

Chicago, has shown through his research that at least twenty out of every hundred people are chronic procrastinators. According to him, chronic procrastination has nothing whatsoever to do with time-management. Moreover, he says that telling a chronic procrastinator to "just do it!" would be like telling a clinically depressed person to "cheer up!"

The arguments put forward by chronic procrastinators are that they work best under pressure, and rushing to do a task can itself produce poor results, so surely it is better to wait. But psychologists dismiss these excuses as self-serving rationalizations, and even see them as insidious, as they correlate positive traits – such as careful reflection and prioritizing – with the destructive habit of putting things off and then doing them poorly in the last minute.

Numerous studies now show that chronic procrastinators do worse than those who have a healthy, more proactive approach to their "to-do list," and in the final analysis the fleeting benefits of procrastination pale into insignificance when measured against the downside.

Remarkably, the more important the task, the greater is the propensity for procrastination. In one particularly revealing study, college students were told that they would be expected to do a math puzzle at the end of their class. Some of them were told that the task was an important test of their cognitive abilities; others, that it was just to have some fun.

Before doing the puzzle, the students were given a few minutes break, during which they could either prepare to do the puzzle by looking at some other examples, or just mess around on computer games. Incredibly, the chronic procrastinators only avoided doing anything that might have helped them prepare for the puzzle if they thought it was going to be a cognitive evaluation. If they were told it was for fun, their behavior during the break was identical to the non-procrastinators, and they happily worked on the examples. The researchers concluded that procrastination is a self-defeating behavioral problem, and chronic procrastinators seem compelled to undermine their own best efforts. Ironically, all of this research proves that the very opposite is true when it comes to non-procrastinators. Those who self-regulate best clearly understand the value of pressure as a motivator to get things done. They also understand that the more pressure you pile on, the greater the result.

I found this point beautifully demonstrated in Parshat Vayechi, in the story of Jacob insisting that Joseph takes an oath to bury him in Canaan instead of Egypt. All the commentators are puzzled by Jacob's insistence on an oath. Did Jacob think that his devoted son Joseph would not bury him in Canaan unless he took the oath? Naḥmanides ("*Ramban*; 1194-1270) answers that Jacob was concerned Pharaoh might not let Joseph fulfill his deathbed request unless it was reinforced by the oath, and he adds that Jacob believed the power of an oath would also be a great motivator for Joseph. This is not to suggest that Joseph would not have done his best had he simply agreed to fulfill the request, but it is a fact that if someone is a non-procrastinator, their "best" gets better if the level of pressure increases.

If someone says they are giving a task their 100%, this is only in the context of the situation they are in at the time. But if you put that same person in a more pressurized situation, somehow they will discover an extra few percentage points to add to their previous 100%. When failure is not an option, we discover untapped resources, and can achieve more, and do better.

The Midrash says that had Reuben known the Torah would record that he had saved his brother Joseph from death, he would have run home to his father with Joseph on his shoulders; and had Aaron known the Torah would record that he went out to greet Moses without being jealous of the fact that his younger brother had been appointed leader, and not him, he would have turned the encounter into ancient Egypt's version of a tickertape parade. At first glance it appears the Midrash is suggesting that Reuben and Aaron were motivated by the glory of a Torah citation. But that is absolutely not what the Midrash means. Rather, it is telling us that had these two biblical heroes known the Torah would record their incredible ability to rise above a challenging situation, they would have pushed themselves even harder, and found inner resources to do what they themselves were unaware they were capable of.

And it was for exactly this reason that Jacob added an extra layer of urgency and pressure to Joseph's mission, by asking him to take an oath, in the knowledge that this would ensure his prodigal son would excel beyond his ordinary measure of capability.

SHEMOT

SHEMOT

A BIT OF ENTHUSIASM CAN GO A LONG WAY

first published January 16th, 2020

One of the most remarkable of all Roman Emperors was the philosopher-king Marcus Aurelius (121-180 C.E.). His full name was Marcus Aurelius Antoninus Augustus, which led the nineteenth-century Talmud scholar and polymath Rabbi Shlomo Yehuda Leib Rapoport (1786-1867) to identify Marcus Aurelius as the Roman leader "Antoninus", whose close friendship with the editor of the Mishnah, Rabbi Yehuda Hanassi, is cited in various fascinating episodes and encounters recorded across the Talmud.

Marcus Aurelius is principally remembered for his refreshingly candid philosophical composition, known to us as *Meditations*, a compilation of personal recollections written to help him with his own moral improvement, and based on his deep commitment to Stoicism. The Stoics based their lives on the worldview propagated by a school of philosophy founded by the Greek philosopher Zeno of Citium (c.334-262 B.C.) in the early third century BCE. Their belief system supposed that humans have no control over – and therefore cannot rely on – external events, and thus only ever have ourselves and our response to events as the route to happiness and contentment. Most famously, true stoics teach themselves to become immune to misfortune, and to submit themselves to life's most challenging moments without complaint.

The late Professor Moshe Aberbach (1924-2007) and his son Professor David Aberbach (b.1953), in their jointly-authored essay on the close ties between Judaism and Stoicism, *Hebrew and Stoicism*, correctly point out that there are many parallels between our Jewish faith and the Stoic belief system, "because Stoicism deals with moral questions which are central to Judaism and is, therefore, closer to Judaism than any other philosophy in the ancient world," to which they add that "many fundamental teachings of Stoicism appear in some form in the Bible."

In 1910, after the unexpected death of Rabbi Eliezer Gordon of Telz (1841-1910) during a fundraising trip to London, he was succeeded as head of Telz Yeshiva by his son-in-law, Rabbi Yosef Yehuda Leib Bloch (1860-1929). An original thinker and gifted teacher, Rabbi Bloch founded a new branch of Mussar ("Jewish ethics") that he named *Shiurei Da'at*, presented as lectures to the students which were later published in four volumes. In Parshat Shemot he offers an observation that seems very much aligned with the idea of Stoicism being an elevated objective of Judaism.

The Midrash tells us that Moses admitted to a transgression with the word *az* when he protested to God (Ex. 5:23): וּמֵאָז בָּאתִי אֶל פַּרְעֹה לְדַבֵּר בִּשְׁמֶךָ הֵרַע לָעָם הַזֶּה – "ever since I came to Pharaoh to speak in Your name, he has dealt worse with this people." The Midrash adds that Moses later corrected his sin by using the exact same word – *az* – when he led an enthusiastic song of praise to God after the nation was saved at the Red Sea – *az yashir Moshe*.

In an attempt to explain this peculiar Midrash, Rabbi Bloch quotes a different Midrash which teaches us that despite the numerous miracles God performed before Exodus, no one had ever sung a song of praise until the splitting of the Red Sea. Not Abraham, not Isaac, not Jacob, nor any of Jacob's children – all of whom experienced miraculous and wondrous events during the course of their lives. However, says Rabbi Bloch, rather than this being the result of some failing on their part, it was actually a demonstration of their immutable faith. True faith in God means that you accept whatever comes your way as the will of God, whether it be bad or good. Why complain, or indeed sing a song of praise, when you believe that whatever happens has a purpose, whether or not you understand that purpose?

But Moses refused to accept the suffering of his brethren with equanimity. He probed and questioned God, because he could not see how God's glory was served by increasing the nation's pain and prolonging their servitude. And it was precisely as a result of his capacity to be stimulated by their distress that he also had the ability to be moved and therefore rejoice in song when he witnessed their miraculous salvation at the Red Sea. These were two sides of the same coin, which, to be sure, was a distinctly unstoical coin. Rabbi Bloch stunningly suggests that religious Stoicism is preferable to the Moses approach, a view he supports by citing a passage from the Talmud (Ber. 3b).

The passage paints a vivid picture of King David being woken in the middle of the night by the wind whistling through the strings of a lyre suspended above his bed. Unlike the song of Moses, which was prompted by a change from the *az* of slavery to the *az* of redemption, King David's lyre played music even as he slept, a constant song of faith that had nothing to do with prevailing conditions. It is for this reason that King David became the foundational figure for Messianic redemption.

But while this thesis is both neat and inspirational, it fails to take into consideration that Moses is held to have been the greatest leader the Jewish nation ever had – the man who led us out of slavery and into the metaphorical arms of God at Mount Sinai, where we received the Torah.

And, of course, it didn't end at Sinai. Moses went on to lead the nation for 40 years, through good times and bad, ensuring the survival of this fractious and often rebellious group, and ultimately delivering them to their destiny at the border of the Promised Land. Notably, Maimonides ("*Rambam*"; 1138-1204) includes belief in the prophecy of Moses as one of his thirteen articles of faith, but makes no mention whatsoever of Stoicism as a measure of faith.

Not allowing bumps in the road to affect one's equilibrium may be a demonstration of faith, but such placidity in the face of adversity may also mean reduced passion at moments of great triumph, as was the case for the great men and women of faith who preceded Moses, none of whom ever composed spontaneous songs of praise despite experiencing great miracles. Ultimately, human nature is human nature, and we are not robots on autopilot. And while Stoicism may sound wonderful, it fails to take into account our human need to react to events as they happen, and the importance of ensuring that all of our positive enthusiasm is directed towards faith in God, so that our relationship with him is not simply a monotonous flatline of acceptance and acquiescence.

Or, to quote the early twentieth century Supreme Court Justice Oliver Wendell Holmes (1841-1935), "it's faith in something, and enthusiasm for something, that makes a life worth looking at."

BACKS TO THE WALL

first published December 24th, 2018

As the row over President Trump's proposed border wall gathers pace, with thousands of Central Americans camped in Tijuana on the Mexican-American border, and the president holed up in the White House over the holidays in the midst of a government shutdown, the media has gone into an absolute frenzy.

From the moment Trump declared his candidacy in June 2015, he made building a wall spanning the entire southern border of the United States a central promise of his presidential campaign. At the end of his candidacy announcement speech, he pledged to "build a great, great wall on our southern border," adding that he would get Mexico pay for it. On January 17, 2017, immediately after becoming president, Trump signed Executive Order 13767, "to secure the southern border of the United States through the immediate construction of a physical wall on the southern border."

It goes without saying that Mexico has never had any intention of paying for a $22 billion border wall, and neither has Congress. Which has meant that the border wall has so far remained nothing more than a meaningless electioneering mantra. But with problems mounting for the beleaguered President, and his support base refusing to accept any capitulation on this issue,

Trump is digging in his heels, refusing to approve the government budget until it includes a $5.7 billion spending bill to fund the wall.

The face-off has resulted in a partial government shutdown, affecting hundreds of thousands of workers across nine federal agencies, and although a range of compromises have been discussed, so far they have all been summarily rejected by the President. And as we head towards a Democratic majority in the House of Representatives, it would appear that hopes for a "great, great wall on our southern border" are fading fast.

What strikes me most about this entire issue is that the conversation is all about the wall, and on the rights and wrongs of building a border-spanning barrier between the United States and Mexico. The benefits or otherwise of immigrants coming to the United States – a subject that is in desperate need of an honest national debate – has receded into the background, or disappeared completely, as politicians and pundits clamber over themselves to vilify the President's intransigence, or alternatively to hail his heroic stand.

What have we become if we allow ourselves to forget that this controversy is not simply about a wall? It is actually about people. And I am not just referring to the illegal immigrants already here, nor to those making the effort to get into the country. It is not solely about them, because ultimately it is also about us. All of us are affected by this issue. Not merely in terms of the economic benefits of dynamic legal immigration weighed up against the negative impact of unfettered illegal immigration – truthfully, that is something all of us non-economists will probably never properly understand. No. What I am referring to is how this issue affects us in terms of who we have become as people when immigration has evolved into nothing more than a political football, a talking point, an ideological badge.

The Book of Shemot opens with a fly-on-the-wall report of a conversation between Pharaoh and his courtiers regarding the dangers of the growing Israelite community in Egypt. Concerned by the ludicrous suggestion that the Israelites were a fifth column who would align themselves with Egypt's enemies in the event of a regional war and pose a security danger to Egypt, Pharaoh and his advisors proposed a draconian course of action to ensure that this outcome would never materialize. When reading Haggada at the Passover seder, we recall this moment by introducing it with a verse from the book of Devarim (Deut. 26:6) – Moses tells the nation: וַיָּרֵעוּ אֹתָנוּ הַמִּצְרִים – "the Egyptians dealt with us in a malevolent manner."

I have always found it puzzling that Pharaoh's closed-door strategizing is presented to us as his most malicious act against the Israelite minority in Egypt. After all, he went on to enslave them and wantonly mistreat them, and he also perpetrated mass genocide against their male babies. Surely this was far worse? In any event, why would we fault Pharaoh for being concerned about his nation's security?

The real issue with Pharaoh's solution was not the solution, rather it was his misidentification of the problem. There was never a threat from the Israelites living in Egypt, as they were never going to undermine his kingdom. But once Pharaoh and those around him had decided that the threat did exist, this "threat" became the source of everything that unfolded subsequently. Had the Israelites truly been enemies of Egypt, the campaign to neutralize them might have been justified. But they were not enemies, and therefore mislabeling them as such was Pharaoh's greatest act of malice.

Ironically, the Achilles heel of any public policy is very often the problem it is trying to solve. Once the problem is identified, any discussion will revolve around the relative merits of possible solutions. But what if the problem being addressed is not really the problem, or not quite the problem you think it is? It follows that any debate over potential solutions is by definition misguided. After all, even when one is certain about a problem, finding the right solution can be a challenge.

The debate over the proposed border wall and how it should be paid for concerns a controversial solution to the wrong problem. The United States is a country noted for its economic opportunities, understandably attractive to economic migrants. A recent Pew Study reported that more than ten million illegal immigrants are already resident in the United States, with almost eight million of them in the workforce, and that two thirds of them have lived here for more than ten years.

It is not the immigrants who are the problem, rather it is the lack of a workable and coherent immigration policy. The time has come for politicians to stop fuming over a wall that is nothing more than a distraction, and which will never solve the real problem, and instead they should start looking for solutions that will.

HUMAN WISDOM VS. DIVINE WISDOM

first published January 4th, 2018

Moses Maimonides ("*Rambam*"; 1138-1204) is surely one of the most fascinating Jewish personalities of the past thousand years. The remarkable output of this polymath almost defies explanation. There seems to be no subject he had not mastered, albeit limited by the scientific and historic knowledge of his day.

But even more impressive than his breadth and depth of knowledge was his ability to assimilate it all, so that every aspect of what he knew existed in the kind of harmony that can only be the result of an elevated ability to cross-reference information across disciplines and subject matter. So much so, that any inconsistencies in Maimonides' output are often at the center of discussions and deliberations in traditional Jewish studies, with the automatic assumption that any seeming contradiction is only there to reveal a deeper meaning or some important principle in relation to the matter at hand.

One of Maimonides' most important works was his *Dalālat al-Ḥā'irīn*, better known to us as *Moreh Nevukhim* ("Guide for the Perplexed"). Written in Judeo-Arabic in the year 1190 as a three-part letter to one of his students, it was translated into Hebrew in 1204, and has since become recognized as one of the most important works of Jewish philosophy ever written.

The main purpose of *Moreh Nevukhim* was for Maimonides to offer rational explanations for aspects of the Hebrew Scriptures and subsequent literature that grated against the thinking of his day. In Maimonides' view, any kind of anthropomorphism—associating God with a physical form, or any human emotion or characteristic—was tantamount to heresy. Although Maimonides borrowed heavily from Aristotelian philosophy, *Moreh Nevukhim* really fits into the genre of "apologetics" – defending traditional Judaism against objections. Maimonides claimed that God can never be defined by what He is, only by what He is not. Among other things, God is not corporeal, He does not occupy any physical space, and He is not subject to generation or decay.

Maimonides' understanding of God is consequently usually referred to as "negative theology," also known as "classical theism." But the idea that any positive definition of God's attributes marks the beginning of a slippery slope into heresy was firmly rejected by his literary nemesis, Rabbi Abraham ben David of Posquières ("*Rabad*"; 1125-1198), who thundered against Maimonides in a published riposte: "Why should anyone who understands God anthropomorphically be called a heretic? How many people better and greater than he [Maimonides] have held such opinions?"

Rabad's dismissal of Maimonides' extreme form of theism is usually understood to be a defense of Talmudic and Geonic sages who appeared to accept some form of Divine corporeality. Even among Rabad's contemporaries there were those who were quite comfortable with anthropomorphism. One example was the controversial Bohemian Tosafist, Rabbi Moses ben Chasdai Taku (1250-1290), who suggested in his writings that God intermittently adopted a defined form and moved around, if a given situation demanded it. Meanwhile, Rabbi Isaiah of Trani (1180-1250), a highly regarded Italian Talmudist, personally rejected any view that embraced anthropomorphism, but like Rabad did not consider those who held such views to be heretics.

Rabbi Moses Sofer of Pressburg (*"Chatam Sofer"*; 1762-1839), revered leader of Austro-Hungarian Jewry in the early nineteenth century, offers a different and somewhat counterintuitive view of Rabad's rebuttal of Maimonides, based on the exchange between Moses and God at the Burning Bush. In his view, any conception of God, even if it is entirely abstract and philosophical, is nonetheless limiting, and therefore no improvement on anthropomorphism. Rabad's comment that "better and greater people than Maimonides have held such opinions" was not a reference to those who were comfortable with anthropomorphism, says Rabbi Sofer, but rather to philosophers and thinkers who had come up with ideas about God that were limited to the parameters of human intellect. Any limited concept of God is no less of a theological problem than thinking that God has a physical body.

At the Burning Bush, Moses asked God to tell him what to say when the Israelites in Egypt asked him for the name of God. Surrounded by pagan deities, and drowning in a polytheistic culture that worshipped physical forms, the Israelites would inevitably want to know who and what God was. God answers in two distinct sentences. At first, He told Moses (Ex. 3:14): אֶהְיֶה אֲשֶׁר אֶהְיֶה – "I shall be what I shall be." Confusingly, God then instructs Moses to inform the Israelites that he had been sent by the God of their forefathers, Abraham, Isaac and Jacob. So which of them was He – was He the "I shall be" God, or was He God of the patriarchs?

Rabbi Sofer's suggestion is that the initial statement implies that the concept of who or what God is will be different for every person – "I shall be what I shall be." But even with the greatest level of understanding of God, and at whatever level, no person will ever surpass the understanding of God experienced by the patriarchs, whose profound relationship with God was at the highest possible level — and yet God said (Ex. 6:3): "and my name, God, was not known to them." Those who trail in their shadow need only to be satisfied to know that God exists, and that they are worshipping the God of Abraham, Isaac and Jacob. Any other theological concept of God, whether it involves primitive anthropomorphism or complex philosophy, is always a self-imposed limitation that results from weakness of the human mind.

At his trial for heresy, the Greek philosopher Socrates (c.470 – 399 B.C.E.) was asked how it was possible that he, who claimed to be the wisest person in Athens, was ignorant of the knowledge he sought. Socrates answered that he was the wisest person in Athens because he alone recognized that human wisdom is of little or no value when compared to Divine wisdom. And although I doubt Rabbi Sofer based his novel approach on this quote from Socrates, he would seem to be saying exactly the same thing.

THE DANGER FROM CONSPIRACIES

first published January 7th, 2021

The violent invasion of Congress by a mob of pro-Trump supporters has sent a paroxysm of fear across the United States, and the world. A bastion of democracy has been violated in a way that is horribly reminiscent of the Storming of the Bastille in Paris, France, on 14 July 1789. But there is a stark difference. In 1789, the protestors represented a popular movement trying to upend the autocratic rule of the French monarchy. They had right on their side, however misguided their violent actions. In contrast, the scenes out of Washington DC in 2021 reveal the efforts by retrograde anarchists and purveyors of chaos who are determined to undermine the rule of law and the stability of the world's greatest democracy. And in the wake of those alarming scenes at the Capitol, Senator Lindsay Graham – previously a devoted supporter of Donald Trump – declared at a press conference, "these people aren't patriots, they are domestic terrorists."

But even as the handwringing escalates, and condemnations gather pace, the most shocking aspect of this entire episode has been the loss of lives for the sake of a misguided cause. Five people died as a result of the invasion of Congress. One of them was Ashli Babbitt of San Diego, shot and killed in the halls of the U.S. Capitol by law-enforcement officers trying to repel the mob she was a part of, as they attempted to overrun the Senate.

Babbitt, a decorated Air Force veteran, was apparently an enthusiastic Trump supporter, but truthfully, what really matters is that she was an ardent believer in, and promoter of, the insidious QAnon conspiracy theory movement. According to Babbitt – and a significant number of fellow-traveling Americans – president-elect Joe Biden didn't win the 2020 presidential election, a startling notion that they base on countless conspiracy narratives which actively promote the idea that the election was stolen.

Simply put, Ashli Babbitt's death is the direct result of unsupported, inaccurate stories of wholesale electoral fraud across multiple states which, it is claimed, resulted in a "stolen election." This was the reason she flew from California to Washington DC. This was the reason she was willing to cheer Donald Trump as he peddled his election-fraud narrative at a rally. This was the reason she joined a bunch of reckless villains as they attempted to occupy the Houses of Congress. And this was the reason she was shot and killed by U.S. Capitol security personnel, whose job it is to protect the Capitol building and its inhabitants from exactly this kind of incursion. Yes, Ashli Babbitt died as a sacrifice to the incendiary lies promoted by QAnon and numerous other peddlers of false information – including Donald Trump – regarding every aspect of political and civic life in the United States. What an absolute disgrace.

According to a 2014 article in the *American Journal of Political Science*, about half of all Americans believe in at least one disproven conspiracy theory. The most dangerous propagator of conspiracies is the anonymous blogger QAnon, whose favorite conspiracy theory is that President Trump has been waging a secret war against a pedophilic ring of "deep state" elites linked to the Democratic Party. But there are numerous conspiracy theories out there, urban myths that are bled into the mainstream by a range of characters ranging from anonymous bloggers to mainstream media personalities: the COVID-19 pandemic is a hoax; the COVID-19 vaccine is injected with a microchip to keep track of those who are vaccinated; the world is controlled by an elitist group of individuals called "Illuminati"; and many, many others.

After the First World War, prominent German influencers and retired military leaders came up with a crazy theory they called *Dolchstoßlegende* ("stab-in-the-back myth"), an emotionally charged claim that Germany had not actually lost the war on the battlefield, but rather it had been betrayed by civilians – particularly Jewish financiers and anti-monarchists – who faked the military loss so that they could overthrow the Hohenzollern monarchy and destroy German power. No amount of proofs to the contrary made the slightest bit of difference to those who bought into this nonsensical narrative; instead the conspiracy was further stoked and promoted by political opportunists, particularly the Nazis, which directly resulted in the catastrophic rise to power of Adolf Hitler's Third Reich, a disaster for all of humanity.

The eminent French sociologist Émile Durkheim (1858-1917) was the first person to come up with the idea that a "social fact" is not necessarily true, but rather it is what society believes to be true. Even if evidence demonstrates this "fact" to be untrue, it makes no difference. Scientific fact and sociological fact do not necessarily intersect; if a broad group of people believes something to be true, then it is true for them, and even if it is not true, they will still behave as if it is. That is why a society may respond to the believed existence of something non-existent by mobilizing counter-measures to counteract it. They are fighting a shadow, a hallucination, but to them the fight is real.

At the beginning of Parshat Shemot, Pharaoh addressed a rally of his people so that he could reveal a grave danger that he believed was threatening Egypt – the Jews. No doubt his adoring fans all screamed their approval as he told them (Ex. 1:9): הִנֵּה עַם בְּנֵי יִשְׂרָאֵל רַב וְעָצוּם מִמֶּנּוּ – "Behold, the Israelite people are much too numerous and are stronger than us." And I am certain that Pharaoh rallied them all to his shameful cause by building on this unfounded myth of there being a Jewish threat to Egypt; the route from his incendiary rhetoric to violence, enslavement and genocide was short and sharp. Once the social fact was established, all bets were off, and despite the reality – namely, that the Jews were peaceful, and that great harm would come to Egypt if they persecuted the Jews – Pharaoh and his supporters were hellbent on going down the path they had chosen, a path that ultimately led to a devastating result for Egypt in general, and for Pharaoh in particular.

The U.S. political establishment has always been a beacon of civility and democracy – and particularly notable in its ability to execute a peaceful transition of power from one party to another. The embrace of damaging conspiracy theories by leading politicians and their followers has been an aberration, but it is an aberration that has resulted in one of the most devastating blows to American democracy in the history of the United States. It is now imperative for leaders and citizens of all political persuasions to take a deep breath, and to publicly repudiate every narrative that endangers the future of democracy and freedom. Any other route has the specter of Pharaoh's ill-fated campaign against the

Jews at the dawn of history hovering over it. We must stop this abomination in its tracks right now. The stakes are simply too high.

VA'ERA

first published January 22nd, 2020

O ne of the most idiosyncratic philosophers and cultural commentators of the postwar period was a Frenchman called Jean Baudrillard (1929-2007), renowned for his prolific academic studies focusing on modern media, contemporary culture, and the rapid growth of technological communication. I absolutely love his aphorisms. For example, he said, "we live in a world where there is more and more information, and less and less meaning." And here's another one: "Philosophy leads to death, but sociology leads to suicide." Although, to be sure, my favorite Baudrillard line is this caustic classic: "Americans may have no identity, but they do have wonderful teeth."

There was a poignant side to Baudrillard – despite his irreverent mockery of human nature and his boundless contempt for the mindlessness of modernity – which is best expressed in this quote: "Smile and others will smile back." Baudrillard understood very well that every human being desires positive contact with others, and that once an emotional bond has been initiated and established there is no limit; positive energy that is generated by positive energy is exponential in its growth and astonishing in its reach.

Truthfully, we don't need science to prove it. Common sense recognizes that whatever mood we are in impacts the people around us, and that their mood affects us. Have you ever felt irritable, and then you realize that the person you are with is miserable and depressed and that their mood is getting you down? Or that when you are with people who are irrepressibly cheerful, it puts you in a good mood even if you were previously having a bad day? We are constantly influenced by what goes on around us, which is why it is so important to surround ourselves with people who put us in good spirits.

But the effect does not stop there, by any means. Families and workplaces can be affected by the disposition of just one of their number. So too, communities, neighborhoods, cities, and even countries. Like a contagious infection, the knock-on effect can multiply exponentially and result in unpredictable and unexpected consequences.

In December 1972, at the 139th meeting of the *American Association for the Advancement of Science* in Washington DC, the intrepid mathematician and meteorologist Edward Lorenz (1917-2008) posed his later-to-become most famous question: "Does the flap of a butterfly's wings in Brazil set off a tornado in Texas?" The aptly named "chaos theory" has adopted this idea, now widely referred to as "the butterfly effect" which is defined as "the sensitive dependence on initial conditions in which a small change in one state of a deterministic nonlinear system can result in large differences in a later state."

Lorenz introduced us all to the shocking notion that the formation or path of a tornado can be influenced by imperceptible stimuli, such as the metaphorical flapping of a butterfly's wings, weeks before the tornado is even detected. But Lorenz's butterfly effect idea is not limited to weathercasting, and applies to every province of life, including the impact individuals and small groups can have on the world well beyond their immediate sphere of activity, in situations where cause and effect cannot be easily determined, or, indeed, determined at all.

In Parshat Va'era, after Moses has failed to convince the Israelites that God will set them free, God asks him to speak with Pharaoh to convince the despot to redeem the enslaved nation.

But a crestfallen Moses remonstrates with God (Ex. 6:12): הֵן בְּנֵי יִשְׂרָאֵל לֹא שָׁמְעוּ אֵלַי וְאֵיךְ יִשְׁמָעֵנִי פַרְעֹה – "The Israelites would not listen to me, surely Pharaoh will not listen either." According to Rashi (ad loc.) this is one of ten instances in the Torah where the *a fortiori* logical device is used. Referred to in Hebrew as *kal vaḥomer*, the *a fortiori* rule is a form of logical reasoning in which a fact is inferred to be even more certain than another; this is one of the devices later used frequently by the Talmud to formulate Jewish law.

The problem with Rashi's assertion is that the Torah says quite explicitly (Ex. 6:9) that the reason the Israelites would not listen to Moses was because "their spirit was crushed by cruel bondage." Under the devastating burden of their slavery, they simply could not believe in the vision of freedom proposed by Moses in God's name. But Pharaoh was not a slave, he was a privileged king – why, therefore, would he not have accepted that freedom awaited Moses' enslaved brethren? There appears to be no basis for a *kal vahomer* to be used here, as Pharaoh's reaction cannot be inferred from the earlier reaction of the Israelites.

But according to the *Sfat Emet*, the answer is simple. The nations of the world are only able to appreciate and attach themselves to God if God's chosen nation finds itself in an elevated spiritual state. When Jews are strong in their faith, Gentile nations will see the Divine light with greater clarity, and their own faith will be enhanced. However, if Jews are remote from God, everyone, even those who have nothing whatsoever to do with Jews, will struggle to connect with God. We can call it the "Jewish butterfly effect."

On that basis, Moses' *kal vahomer* argument was actually a perfectly formed logical device. If the Israelites were not able to believe in God's promise of redemption, how could God expect him to convince Pharaoh that God would redeem His nation? The Israelites may have lived in their own neighborhoods and communities, but every Egyptian, including Pharaoh, was affected by their disheartened state, and by the fact that they had given up on God.

This is an incredibly powerful idea, although it is one that burdens us with great spiritual responsibility. By flapping our spiritual butterfly wings in our own seemingly limited vicinity we can literally unleash a tornado of faith and spirituality across the world. All we need to do is smile with the joy of God in our lives, and before long the whole world will smile back.

GIVE ME YAVNEH AND ITS SCHOLARS

first published January 3rd, 2019

S ome weeks ago, I hosted the journalist Melanie Phillips for dinner at my home in Beverly Hills. Although Melanie and I are both from London and had met briefly in the past, over the years we have never really had a proper opportunity to exchange views and compare notes. Our few hours together over dinner flew by in a whirlwind of discussion on a variety of topics, ranging from the Iraq War to Brexit, and of course the existential issues facing Jews and Judaism in the twenty-first century.

Melanie started out life on the left-wing side of politics, but over the years morphed into a conservative thinker and writer, seeing herself – in Irving Kristol's words – as "a liberal mugged by reality." In Jewish terms, both she and her husband and fellow-journalist Joshua Rozenberg were undereducated, but that changed dramatically when their daughter went to Israel in 2000 for her gap year. Melanie's previously detached position vis-à-vis Judaism and Israel evolved considerably into proactive advocacy and support, as she began to detect the latent and occasionally open hostility towards Israel among generally benign opinion formers in the UK, and particularly as she realized that they automatically bunched her together with all the vocal Israel supporters they so reviled simply because she was Jewish.

In December 2001, shortly after 9-11, Melanie was hissed and booed during a live TV show after suggesting that Israel had every right to tackle terrorists in its own back yard if the world cheerfully allowed Americans to root out terrorists halfway across the world from their country, in Afghanistan. She later wrote about this formative experience.

> *"For myself and countless British Jews watching the show, this [primal, negative reaction] was a defining moment. In that instant, I realized this was not some rogue set of attitudes. British Jews had been living in a fool's paradise during the half-century since the discovery of the Nazi extermination camps had sent Jew-hatred underground... Mainstream opinion had become infected by an animus against Israel that was simply impervious to reason..."*

Following our meeting in November, Melanie wrote an article in London's *Jewish Chronicle* provocatively titled *Tikkun Olam, the supposedly Jewish social justice, is a fraud*. Challenged during her visit to the States by anxious American-Jewish parents concerned by the drift away from strong Israel support among the emerging generation, Melanie told them bluntly that "young American Jews are turning against Israel principally because they are disconnecting from Judaism." In her article, Melanie assertively blames the parents, who generally belong to the progressive Jewish denominations that promote Tikkun Olam, namely "the idea that liberal universalist values are authentic Jewish values." But Tikkun Olam is nothing of the sort, Melanie insists; in fact, she claims that it is "inimical to Judaism."

One orthodox rabbi she spoke to seemed less alarmed by the prospect of this demographic timebomb. "Just give me Yavneh," he said, a reference to the year 70 C.E., when Rabbi Yoḥanan ben Zakkai negotiated a reprieve for the yeshiva town of Yavneh with the Roman general who was about to sack Jerusalem. Yavneh went on to become the cradle of Jewish life after the Temple's destruction, ensuring the survival of Judaism and the nation. Melanie went on to write about what the rabbi she met actually had in in mind:

> *"What the rabbi in America meant, was that he had given up on the wider American Jewish community. No longer would he even attempt to persuade them they were on the path of communal self-destruction. They would never listen or change. Within a fairly short time, given the accelerating rate of intermarriage and assimilation, that part of the community would have effectively disintegrated. But spiritually, ethically, Jewishly, it was already lost. In dramatic contrast, the much smaller Orthodox community was growing by leaps and bounds. So all efforts... needed to go into supporting and financing that Orthodox world, because that's where the Jewish diaspora future lay."*

Citing the town of Lakewood as an example, the rabbi suggested that if someone wanted to make a good investment in the future of Jewish life in America, they should look no further than this nondescript suburban township in southern New Jersey. The eponymous yeshiva founded there in 1943 with 13 students, now has 1,000 new students enrolling each year, sparking a glorious Jewish revival. The diverse and culturally rich Jewish community that has grown around this institution is nothing short of astounding – almost 500 synagogues; 35,000 kids in Jewish day schools; and 85,000 Jews who are committed unabashedly to the Jewish people and to the survival of Israel. Compare this incredible community success with the declining Reform and Conservative communities in the United States, and you begin to understand the point. If there is quality Judaism, quantity will follow. The reverse, sadly, is almost never true.

The Talmud (Sanhedrin 111a) links two verses at the beginning of Parshat Va'era, suggesting that just as Joshua and Caleb were the only two out of the 600,000 Israelites who left Egypt to make it to the Promised Land, only two out of every 600,000 Israelites who were slaves in Egypt actually left Egypt, while the remaining 599,998 died during the plague of darkness. Clearly this exaggerated fraction makes no sense whatsoever, as Rabbi Meir Simcha HaCohen of Dvinsk (1843-1926) points out in his commentary on the Torah, *Meshekh Hokhma*. It would therefore seem that what the Talmud is trying to say is quantity should never be the priority when quality might be at stake. Every one of the many miracles performed for the Israelites in Egypt and later on in the wilderness were worth it, even if just two out of 600,000 people achieved the spiritual expectations God had for them.

Based on this Talmudic lesson, we should not despair when we see that the masses remain oblivious to what God wants from them. We should offer everyone a warm and welcoming home, so that those who have drifted away can easily experience the Judaism they outright reject as outmoded and outdated. But the majority of our resources must be devoted to "Yavneh and its scholars" – ensuring the survival of the Jewish people via the few who will become the many of the future, rather than to the many who will dwindle into the few, and then disappear. As the Talmud makes clear, using the glorious story of our nation's founding in the Book of Exodus as proof – it is always going to be the few committed individuals in whose merit the nation will be protected, and ultimately redeemed.

CAN A SECRET BE A NON-SECRET?

first published January 11th, 2018

The infamous bon-viveur, Anthony Haden-Guest (b.1937), is purported to have once told a friend, "of course I can keep secrets; it's the people I tell them to that can't keep them."

Haden-Guest was certainly aware of the inherent contradiction in this remark, no doubt the source of much merriment when he said it. As we all know, a secret is something you tell no-one, and once you share it, the secret is no more. Consequently, it is impossible for something to be a secret and not a secret at the same time. Or is it?

It would seem pretty obvious that if something is true it cannot simultaneously not be true. And yet, Greek philosophers saw fit to delineate this idea in the first two fundamental rules of classical logic, which Aristotle (384–322 B.C.E.) referred to as the axioms of human thought. The first is the law of non-contradiction, which states that for all propositions (p), it is impossible for both "p" and "not-p" to be true. Just as an example, this means that if something is wet, it cannot also be dry.

The second is the law of the excluded middle, in which either "p" or "not-p" must be true, and no third truth is possible. Using the same wet/dry example, if something is either wet or dry, it cannot be defined in any other way.

As with all definitive laws, experts seem to most enjoy trying to disprove them. One of the earliest Greek philosophers was a misanthropic savant called Heraclitus (c.535 – c.475 B.C.E.), often remembered for having tried to cure himself from acute edema by burying himself in cow manure. Heraclitus apparently rejected the law of non-contradiction, with the observation that "the road that goes up and the road that goes down are one and the same." Plato (c.428–c.348 B.C.E.) would later qualify this rejection as counterintuitive, with his own observation that to the person using the road at any given moment, either it is going up, or it is going down—but it cannot be doing both.

Contemporary philosophers and logicians have invented a term for the antithesis of non-contradiction: "dialetheism" (dialetheia is a portmanteau word combining the Greek *di*, or two, with *aletheia*, which means truth). In the world of dialetheism, self-contradictory propositions can be both true and false, and are referred to as "true contradictions." This idea has most famously been used by the modern philosophy guru, Graham Priest (b.1948), to resolve the ancient "liar's paradox," the problem of assessing liars who state that they are lying. Are they lying, in which case they are telling the truth, or are they telling the truth, in which case they are lying? Dialetheism resolves this paradox by asserting that in that particular situation, the law of non-contradiction does not apply—a liar remains a liar, while the statement that they are lying is also true.

In her 2016 book, *A Theology of Nonsense*, British theologian Josephine Gabelman notes that although this idea undermines the inflexible logical underpinning of atheism, "dialetheism is seldom included in modern theological discourse." Her observation is correct, and theologians are clearly slow off the mark.

A perfect opportunity for the use of dialetheism can be found at the beginning of Parshat Va'era, when God responded to Moses after Pharaoh intensified the workload for the Hebrew slaves as a direct result of Moses' intercession on their behalf. Moses was very despondent, in the belief that he was to blame. Moreover, the new draconian impositions on the slaves made no sense at all if he had been sent by God as the redeemer. After all, if it was time for redemption, why were things getting worse? And if the time for redemption had not yet arrived, why had he been asked to lead it?

God enigmatically informs Moses that He revealed himself to the patriarchs as *El Shadai*, rather than as the God of the tetragrammaton, the four-letter name which represents the most elevated version of divine presence. What was God talking about? And how does His statement explain the situation?

Rabbi Naftali Tzvi Yehudah Berlin of Volozhin ("*Haamek Davar*"; 1816-1893) explains that the *El Shadai* name of God is always used in situations that reflect the ultimate purpose of creation, which is to reveal God's glory for all to see. If God does anything to increase or enhance our awareness of His existence and greatness, the name that best embodies such a moment is *El Shadai*. Meanwhile, the tetragrammaton projects the concept of God's immanence, and His utter control of every aspect of creation at any given moment, even though His presence in the physical universe is completely hidden.

The significant problem posed by these two different names of God is that they represent a profound theological contradiction. If God's glory-revealing interaction with the world is the ultimate purpose of creation, why is God invisible? And if God's most elevated form is utterly invisible, how do public displays of His presence reveal His glory? But this paradox is only a problem if the law of non-contradiction applies to God, and it was exactly this that confounded the patriarchs. And now, in Egypt, this same paradox had caused Moses to doubt his role.

God therefore told him that although the patriarchs may have found the contradiction challenging, they accepted it for what it was. They understood how it could be explained using dialetheism, which allows for self-contradictory propositions to work in circumstances where no other choice makes sense. For God, both the importance of revelation and hiddenness can be true at the same time. He can be behind the increased oppression of the slaves, which seems to epitomize His concealment, while simultaneously that same situation can form an intrinsic part of the revelation of God's glory. In reality, it is entirely possible for something to be a secret and not a secret at the same time.

Now, I wonder what Anthony Haden-Guest would make of that!

BO

TURNING PHYSICAL REDEMPTION
INTO SPIRITUAL REDEMPTION

first published January 10th, 2019

In the final lecture of my most recent Jewish History series, I recalled the extraordinary life of Rabbi Avraham Yitzchak Hacohen Kook (1865-1935), known to all simply as "Rav Kook," a man who was undoubtedly one of the most remarkable rabbinic leaders of the past two centuries. A visionary with the disposition of a saint, Rav Kook developed a unique religious foundation for the emerging reality of a Jewish sovereign state in the Land of Israel, and although he died in 1935 – 13 years before the establishment of Israel – his far-reaching theological concepts continue to inspire new generations, helping them appreciate Zionism and the miracle of Israel, which he firmly identified as the launchpad for Messianic redemption.

Rav Kook is best remembered for establishing a Chief Rabbinate for Eretz Yisrael in 1921, and for his highly original works, particularly *Orot*, published in 1920, amid furious opposition from the more conservative elements of the Orthodox community. Less well known is his attempt to create an umbrella organization for Torah-observant Jewry incorporating both pro-

and anti-Zionist factions, to operate in parallel with the secular-Jewish controlled Zionist movement, as a vehicle to promote the religious significance of Jewish hegemony in the Promised Land.

The organization, called *Degel Yerushalayim*, was launched in 1918, but never really got off the ground. Rav Kook dispatched his son, Rabbi Tzvi Yehuda Kook (1891-1982), to visit Jewish leaders across Europe to galvanize their support, but the reaction was lackluster, exposing the sedentary nature of traditional Jewish leadership, which feared the outcome for Jewish life of any major shift in focus, and which was united in its unwillingness to embrace a proactive redemption narrative.

In his excellent article on *Degel Yerushalayim*, Yosef Avneri describes Rav Kook's attempts to reassure the Zionist leadership – including the religious Zionist movement Mizrachi – that he was not trying to undermine their political efforts, by telling them that he was merely going to augment their efforts by giving political Zionism a religious parallel. Nevertheless, says Avneri, it was clear that "the very establishment of *Degel Yerushalayim* signified disappointment, if not despair, at the Zionist movement ever serving as the instrument through which the traditional national vision would be implemented."

Sadly, *Degel Yerushalayim* found itself caught between Mizrachi Zionists who were unwilling to risk losing their influence, limited though it was, within the mainstream Zionist movement, and the conservative rabbinic establishment, which saw any innovation as risky, and which particularly concerned that involvement with this new idea might unintentionally lead people to believe that it supported Zionism. The organization had isolated chapters in various cities, and sputtered along for a few years before falling apart altogether. But with the benefit of hindsight, we can see how prophetic the concept was. Once the political goals of Zionism were achieved, only religious commitment, powered by deep faith in the role a Jewish state plays in our historical aspirations as a people, would keep the passion burning.

According to the medieval commentator Rashi (Ex. 12:6), God ordered the Jewish people in Egypt to take the Passover lamb into their homes four days before it needed to be killed so that they would have a mitzvah to merit the reward of redemption. The time to fulfill Abraham's covenant had arrived, and the nation needed to do something to earn the pledge. But Rashi's suggestion is quite puzzling. If redemption had been promised to Abraham for his descendants, whether or not they deserved it, surely that redemption was inevitable? And if redemption was inevitable, why was the additional requirement of taking the lamb into their homes necessary to accrue extra credit?

Rabbi Shmuel Bornsztain of Sochaczew (1855-1926), in his commentary *Shem MiShmuel*, notes that there are two aspects to exile: the physical exile in a foreign land, living under oppressive conditions; and the spiritual exile, namely the loss of our ability to perform God's commandments properly, resulting in a diminished spiritual existence. Abraham was told that his children would have to endure a physical exile, but it was the conflict between Joseph and his brothers that resulted in a spiritual decline, and this exile also required a redemption.

There is no doubt that God would have fulfilled his promise to Abraham of redemption from Egypt for his descendants no matter what, but what would that redemption have been worth if all it amounted to was a redemption from the physical restrictions of slavery in Egypt? God was determined that His people also be redeemed from spiritual bondage, and that could only happen if they heeded His commandments, and became conscious of their spiritual role in God's world. By taking the lamb into their homes, they demonstrated a commitment to God and to their heritage as Abraham's spiritual heirs, especially as the Passover lamb would be shared by many, and be eaten together at a meal that would celebrate Jewish spiritual identity and their commitment to God's mission.

For Rav Kook, the idea of a Jewish state was not just to provide a solution to the "Jewish Problem" as it was to so many others, Jews and gentiles, for whom the "problem" of a Jewish minority in the diaspora needed to be resolved by the creation of its own homeland, giving an identity to a stateless people who had struggled to survive endless persecutions and prejudice.

Although Rav Kook knew this was important – even crucial – it was equally if not more important that this be coupled with a spiritual revolution, a renewed commitment to Jewish faith that would enable physical redemption to result in a Messianic era, as promised by the prophets of our bible, and by every traditional text of Judaism.

Our job as Jews today is no longer to ensure the goals of the original Zionist project – after 70 years of Israel the challenge of meeting those goals are thankfully behind us. Rather, our goals today must be to revive the ideals of *Degel Yerushalayim*, and to ensure that our physical redemption is coupled with a spiritual redemption, achieved through an ever-greater commitment to

Torah and *mitzvot* in every aspect of our lives, so that we merit to greet the Messiah.

THE SECRET OF JEWISH ENDURANCE

first published January 19th, 2018

The recent arrest of David and Louise Turpin in Perris, California, was immediately followed by details of their wretched saga, undoubtedly one of the most disturbing news stories in quite some time. The authorities described the alleged abuse carried out by the Turpins against their thirteen children over a period of several years — abuse that defies rational explanation and societal norms. The emaciated, undernourished children were apparently held captive in shackles at their home, punished with beatings, and prevented from engaging with the outside world.

Remarkably, the 17-year-old who alerted authorities to the abuse had been planning to escape with her siblings for over two years, before finally plucking up the courage to bolt. To get out, she jumped through a window together with one of her siblings — but even at that stage, her sibling was too frightened to go through with the plan, and returned home.

Although news reports of murder and violence are ubiquitous — often featuring family members as perpetrators and victims – we are not generally used to seeing the family structure itself used as the weapon to destroy lives. This is undoubtedly the most disturbing aspect of the Turpin story – the normal family structure was used to terrorize their children. Parental authority, group dynamics, and reward and punishment were all exploited to create an environment of fear and dependency that prevented the children from developing into healthy members of society.

In 2002, a study that compared 50 years of research papers looking into the routines and rituals of family life concluded that it was the fundamental aspects of inter-generational dynamics that were "important to the health and well-being of today's families trying to meet the busy demands of juggling work and home." It added that "family routines and rituals are powerful organizers of family life that offer stability during times of stress and transition."

Bedtime stories, silly names for each other, inside jokes, daily or weekly meals together — all of these things make the mundane aspects of life special, and make the special things more memorable. And later in life, when the earlier generation has gone, we pass down these treasured habits and routines to our own children and grandchildren, developing a home that bonds disparate family members together even when they are far apart.

We also rely on these memories and dynamics as an invaluable resource in times of crisis.

The first directive given to the Israelites as a nation was the instruction by God to acquire a lamb for the night of redemption from Egypt (Ex. 12:21): מִשְׁכוּ וּקְחוּ לָכֶם צֹאן לְמִשְׁפְּחֹתֵיכֶם וְשַׁחֲטוּ הַפָּסַח – "take for yourselves a sheep for your families, and slaughter the Passover offering." The reference to "your families" seems somewhat superfluous in the context of this commandment. Nevertheless, it represents possibly the greatest miracle of all — greater than all the wondrous plagues and the splitting of the Red

Sea combined — namely, the creation of a nation that has endured for thousands of years.

A people that had been downtrodden and enslaved for generations — totally dehumanized and humiliated — were brought together and elevated to the heights of chosen nationhood, and this was all done via the medium of family togetherness. The Passover offering was not an individual responsibility; rather it was a family ritual, bringing each family unit together for a joint project that would be unique and special for them as a group, setting the tone for the future, and establishing the family at the heart of Jewish life for all time.

Throughout our turbulent history, and to this day, Passover is celebrated together as a family — with every family coming together annually, each with its own traditions and customs to commemorate the origins of our identity. A 2013 Pew Study reported that 70% of American Jews participated in a seder, compared with just 53% who observe Yom Kippur. That number includes 40% of unaffiliated Jews, for whom the seder is probably the only Jewish ritual that they observe each year.

While the dreadful Turpin story represents the aberration of a family unit gone horribly wrong, we are all far too familiar with the fragmentation of our society over the past few decades. Family units are no longer valued as a priority, and the breakdown of family life is common. Western civilization celebrates individuality and independence, but these values often come at the expense of family unity and cohesiveness, with families torn apart as the individuals within them pursue their own aspirations. And while Judaism is not opposed to individuality per-se, the importance of family, and the nurturing a solid sense of family identity, must always be at the forefront of who we are.

This idea stretches beyond the family, and into community as well. Each community is a large extended family, united by its shared experiences and unique makeup, strengthened by its bonds, and representing a unit that is ultimately greater than the sum of its parts. The miracle of Jewish endurance has been the success of family and community, resources that not only ensure our ability to function in regular life, but also guarantee our resilience in crisis. This critical factor has seen our people outsurvive numerous civilizations and empires, starting 3,330 years ago — when we departed Egypt, and left Egyptian civilization trailing in our wake.

THE DESTRUCTIVE STRENGTH OF PHARAOH'S ADDICTION

first published February 2nd, 2017

 One of modern psychology's most researched topics is the phenomenon of addiction. We know more about addiction today than at any point in human history. Notwithstanding this, most people still assume addicts are deliberately amoral individuals, and that all it would require to halt their addiction would be inner strength and willpower.

The literature and numerous studies reveal quite a different story. Addiction is an extremely complex disease, and getting out of addiction requires much more than acknowledging the problem and having the desire to be rid of it, however genuine that desire may be. Without getting into a discussion about chemical dependence that often results from addiction – the most obvious example being the regular use of hard drugs, such as heroin – it is clear that the trigger that leads to dependence has nothing to do with the chemical, and everything to do with a desire or need to engage in self-destructive behavior. People who compulsively use drugs, or smoke, or abuse alcohol, nearly always start doing so long before they have any kind of physical addiction. This explains how it is that people frequently switch addictions from one drug to another, or even from drugs to a non-drug form of addictive behavior.

Beginning in the early 1960s, one of the most effective and widely used forms of addiction treatment, in terms of halting an addiction in its tracks and beginning the addict on a road of rehabilitation and recovery, has been a method known as direct intervention. This involves close family and friends, accompanied by a mental health professional, staging an ambush style meeting with the addict during which each of them explains how they have been harmed by his or her addiction, and then appealing to the addict to seek treatment using the leverage of consequences if treatment is not sought.

The brilliant insight of those who came up with this idea is that a well-planned and properly executed intervention preempts the inevitable "rock bottom" consequences of long-term addiction by precipitating the consequences artificially before they actually occur. A compulsive gambler, or alcoholic, or drug addict, may ultimately lose their family, or their status, or their material possessions, and could even lose their lives, as a direct consequence of being enslaved by their addiction. The intervention dramatically dangles these dire consequences in front of the addict, while offering him or her the chance to prevent them from gaining traction if they seek help. What happens as a result of the intervention is that the part of the addict that wants to beat the addiction joins forces with the external pressure, and those combined strengths have the power to gain victory over the dominant addiction force that has hitherto ruled the addict's life.

Another form of intervention is known as "forcible intervention." This last-resort type of intervention involves implementing drastic consequences on the addict, such as the loss of his or her civil liberties. Such an intervention will only ever be used in a situation where the addict is a danger to himself or those around him.

Over the past couple of weeks, as I have been studying the strange story of Pharaoh's refusal to allow the Jews out of Egypt, I was struck by the thought that the addict/intervention paradigm fits very neatly into this narrative, and in the process it can help us explain a number of puzzling aspects that have vexed commentators for millennia.

Hundreds of years earlier, God had told Abraham that his descendants would one day experience bondage in a foreign country, before being miraculously redeemed, after which they would return triumphantly to the Promised Land. But at no point in His covenant with Abraham did God suggest that external actors would be involved in the story. Strangely enough, though, the Exodus story seems to be far more about Pharaoh than it does about the Jews, who seem quite marginal to the narrative as Moses and Pharaoh spar, while Egypt sinks ever deeper into an abyss of supernatural chaos. Even more troubling than this is the "hardening" of Pharaoh's heart by God, as explicitly stated in the narrative (Ex. 14:8): וַיְחַזֵּק ה' אֶת לֵב פַּרְעֹה – "and God hardened Pharaoh's heart." Why would God do this, and how could a man – and his country – be punished, if God induced all of his actions?

Ultimately, the Exodus story is a narrative that runs parallel to the account of the Plagues and Pharaoh's stubbornness. The Exodus story recalls the events surrounding Jewish slavery followed by their redemption, as promised to Abraham; the account of the Plagues and Pharaoh's stubbornness has a different purpose – it describes the insidiousness of evil, which ultimately destroys those in its thrall, along with all those to whom they are connected.

Pharaoh is the epitome of an addict – compulsively and uncontrollably doing the same things again and again, long after it has become evident that he is battling against forces that far outstrip his ability to counter them. Moses begins the process of weaning him off his addiction with a well-constructed direct intervention involving consequences, but Pharaoh refuses to play ball. So the intervention process escalates into a full-on forcible intervention, where a nightmare range of consequences rain down on Pharaoh and Egypt, with the aim of compelling him to give up his addiction to God-denial.

Then, in the final chapter, Pharaoh receives a gift every addict truly craves – the ability to withstand any attempt to separate him from his addiction of choice. Every person has their breaking point, but even as they fold, they wish they didn't have to. Pharaoh's strength was really his greatest weakness, a destructive force that would have consequences on his country long after the Jews had gone.

And all of this happened so that the Jews would observe it before they received the Torah, to teach them that the power of God's will transcends any human desire to overcome it. Although we may be living some 3,300 years later, Pharaoh-type addicts still abound, and you can be sure that nothing has changed. This lesson is as relevant today as it was when the Jews left Egypt.

BESHALACH

THE MYSTERY OF THE FIRST SHABBAT

first published January 17th, 2019

Sometime in the eighteenth century, a group of Russian-Orthodox Christians revolted against the strict hierarchical religious environment of the Russian-Orthodox church and embraced Judaism – or at least that is what they thought they were doing. This group soon became known as *Subbotniki* – "Sabbath observers" – as a result of their decision to adopt Saturday as a holy day instead of Sunday, and to observe Shabbat as a day of rest.

The lack of any ethnic Jewish origins of this unusual religious sect has fascinated scholars, ever since they were discovered and studied by anthropologists and historians during the nineteenth century. The sect – also known as *Shaposhniki* ("hat wearers") – first appeared prior to the Russian Empire's annexation of the areas in Poland later referred to as "the Pale of Settlement," which was home to a significant Jewish population. Before that time Jews were not permitted to live in Imperial Russia, and although Subbotniks were eager to claim Jewish descent, it would appear that their Jewish-inspired belief system was entirely self-generated, evident from the absence of any Hebrew in their liturgy, and also from the nonexistence, at least initially, of any laws or customs originating in the Talmud.

Unsurprisingly, the Subbotniks were viciously persecuted, despised both by the state and by the devoutly Christian population, and by the end of the 1830s most of them had been exiled from European Russia to Siberia or the Caucasus. Additionally, Subbotnik children were forcibly taken from their parents and given to Christian families for adoption. In the late 1800s, a large contingent of Subbotniks who had formally converted to Judaism joined the first wave of Aliyah to Eretz Yisrael to escape the endless hostility, and a number of Israel's most prominent public figures were descended from these Subbotnik immigrants, including Ariel Sharon (1928-2014), whose mother Vera Schneirov-Scheinermann (1900-1988) was of Subbotnik descent; and former IDF Chief of Staff and government minister Raful Eitan (1929-2004).

Today there are approximately 20,000 Subbotniks scattered across the former Soviet Union, mainly in tiny communities that are either shrinking rapidly or disappearing at a rapid rate. Some efforts have been made to bring them to Israel, but this is complicated by the lack of certainty as to their Jewish identity and their consequent exclusion from the Law of Return.

Earlier this week, I found myself thinking about this obscure quasi-Jewish sect while trying to figure out a puzzling Talmudic reference to Shabbat observance. The Talmud (Sab. 118b) quotes the great Babylonian sage Rav: "Had the Jewish people properly observed the first Shabbat ... no nation would have ever ruled over them."

Rav goes on to cite a source text from Beshalach to prove the nation had flunked their very first Shabbat-observance test (Ex. 16:27): וַיְהִי בַּיּוֹם הַשְּׁבִיעִי יָצְאוּ מִן הָעָם לִלְקֹט וְלֹא מָצָאוּ – "and it was on the seventh day, some of nation went out to gather [manna] but they did not find it." Having been given specific instructions regarding restrictions on Shabbat, there were still those who disregarded Moses and went to look for manna. Tosafot (Sab. 87b) is mystified by Rav's assertion that the first Shabbat had been defiled. A few verses earlier the narrative describes an incident at Marah (Ex. 15:25), when the nation was given "a statute, a law, and there He tested them."

According to the Talmud (San. 56b), at Marah, Moses told the nation about Shabbat and stressed its centrality to the Jewish faith. There is no indication whatsoever that the nation desecrated this Shabbat, which was their actual first, a fact that rather undermines Rav's assertion about the long-term negative effect of the nation's failure to observe their first Shabbat. Rabbi Judah Loew of Prague ("*Maharal*"; c.1526-1609), suggests an intriguing solution to this obvious contradiction. The Shabbat defined by Moses at Marah involved positive precepts, but no restrictions. Only later on, when the rules regarding manna were handed down – rules which included restrictions concerning the collection of manna on Shabbat – did the observance of this holy day of rest take on real meaning. And it was these flouted restrictions that Rav proclaimed had resulted in Jewish suffering at the hands of gentile nations.

The Maharal's explanation is profound. Nothing worthwhile can ever be defined purely by what it is; what it is only ever has meaning when contrasted with what it is not. Shabbat is a day devoted to God because it is a day when we desist from our mundane daily tasks. Without these associated restrictions, all the actions of Shabbat lack true meaningfulness and depth.

Rabbi Hershel Shachter (b.1941), Rosh Yeshiva of Yeshiva University, takes this idea even further. By definition, the concept of sanctity necessitates prohibitions. For example, a *kohen* is considered sanctified as a result of the restrictions imposed on him regarding who he cannot marry, and the fact that he is restricted from any contact with the dead. The Land of Israel is considered sanctified as a consequence of the many restrictions placed upon any produce that grows there. Similarly, Shabbat is holy because of the many activities which are prohibited on that day. Our challenge is to take this time sanctified by restrictions and turn it into a meaningful holy day via the medium of mandated and permitted actions.

Although the Subbotniks denied the divinity of Jesus, and rejected the notion of a Second Coming, interestingly, it was not their heresy that defined them for the Russian authorities, but their observance of Shabbat. Indeed, it was this aspect of their religious sectarianism that gave them their name – not the fact that they gathered in their houses of worship on Saturdays and prayed. After all, in this respect they were no different to Christians who went to church on Sundays. Rather it was because they refused to work on Saturdays, and took upon themselves, to the best of their knowledge, all the restrictions of Shabbat observance.

The Zionist thinker and essayist, Ahad Ha'am (1856-1927), famously quipped: "More than Jews have kept Shabbat, Shabbat has kept the Jews" – an astounding observation from someone who had himself abandoned Shabbat observance in favor of cultural Judaism. But notwithstanding his own drift away from adherence to Shabbat restrictions, on this point he hit the nail squarely on its head.

THE CURSE OF ATTENTION SEEKING

first published January 25th, 2018

Palestinian leader Mahmoud Abbas recently called together a meeting of the PLO's Central Council, and delivered a speech marked more by its rancor than by its accuracy. For well over two hours Abbas ranted against a whole range of characters, both historical and contemporary, whom he blamed for the dire situation of his people.

According to Abbas, all the problems began with Oliver Cromwell (1599-1658), who "staged a coup against [King Charles I of Great Britain] and became the head of a republic... 300 years prior to the Balfour Declaration." It was Cromwell who "came up with the idea of transferring the Jews from Europe to the Middle East... because they wanted this region to become an outpost to protect the interests and the convoys coming from Europe to the East." According to this twisted narrative, Jews were the expedient pawns of colonialist expansion.

Next up on the blame list was Napoleon Bonaparte (1769-1821), who, in Abbas's alternate universe, had declared that "a Jewish state must be established in Palestine." He was only thwarted in this aspiration when he "failed at the walls of Acre," a victory Abbas claimed for the Palestinians, even though no such national entity appeared until the second half of the twentieth century. This fantasy thesis, popular among anti-Zionist pseudo-historians, is based on a French newspaper article of May 1799, which reported that Napoleon had invited "all the Jews of Asia and Africa to gather under his flag in order to re-establish the ancient Jerusalem." Most respectable historians dismiss this as a wartime rumor, and even those who take the report seriously consider it a tactical gesture by Napoleon, who hoped such a declaration would help tip the battle of Acre in his favor. In short, no serious academic believes Napoleon was a proto-Zionist.

The rest of the names on the Abbas hit list were equally bizarre: Warder Cresson (1798-1860), the first United States consul in Jerusalem, later a convert to Judaism and founder of an agricultural settlement in Palestine, but by no means a political operator; Colonel Charles Henry Churchill (1807-1869), a nineteenth-century British diplomat in Damascus (who Abbas erroneously identified as Sir Winston Churchill's grandfather); Sir Henry Campbell-Bannerman (1836-1908), a British prime minister who is spuriously purported to have authored the "Campbell-Bannerman document" in 1907, proposing the creation of a buffer state in the Middle East to serve European interests by preventing Muslim nations from gaining an upper hand in world affairs.

The list of supposed crimes and criminals went on and on. David Ben Gurion forced Jews to move to Israel after its creation (as if you can force Jews to do anything); American air carrier TWA transferred 50,000 Jews to Israel from Yemen as part of a US conspiracy against the Palestinians; anyone who refers to Palestinians as terrorists is guilty of willful misrepresentation; Palestinians have never rejected negotiations. Abbas's rambling speech presented an alternative reality that is utterly deranged, and its author is clearly unhinged.

Meanwhile, this week, former US Secretary of State John Kerry sent Abbas a message to "hold on and be strong" in his resistance to President Trump, proof that even senior diplomats fail to understand the level of cognitive dissonance prevalent in the Palestinian narrative. "Maybe it is time for the Palestinians to define their peace principles and present a positive plan," Kerry suggested. Really? On what planet? No Palestinian who believes in a Zionist conspiracy dating back over 350 years is ever going to "define peace principles," nor will a Palestinian fantasist such as Abbas ever come up with any kind of peace plan. But, I hear you say, surely the Palestinians want to end their miserable existence as the perpetual victims of the modern era?

Actually, it would appear that this is exactly what they do not want, a fact that dawned on me as I studied a Midrash that addresses an anomaly at the beginning of Parshat Beshalach. The portion begins (Ex. 13:17): וַיְהִי בְּשַׁלַּח פַּרְעֹה אֶת הָעָם – "and it came to pass when Pharaoh sent away the nation." The Talmud (Meg. 10b) has a principle that whenever the Hebrew word *vayehi* is used in scripture, it indicates the beginning of a sad story. And yet, surely a chapter that ends with the destruction of the entire Egyptian army is happy, not sad? In which case, why does this chapter begin with an opening word that has negative connotations?

The Midrash explains that the opener reflects Pharaoh's perception of events, and offers an analogy to explain. Someone kidnaps the son of a mighty king. The king sends him letters and messages to release his son, but the kidnapper takes no notice. Eventually, the king comes to the kidnapper's hideout and rescues his son. Afterwards, the kidnapper complains that while he had held the prince captive, he had been the recipient of daily communications from the king. With the prince gone, the king was ignoring him. The analogy is simple. With the Jews gone from Egypt suddenly Pharaoh was no longer the center of attention, and he was upset. For months he had interacted constantly with God, via Moses and the ten plagues. Now God was ignoring him.

This Midrash is extremely peculiar, appearing to suggest that Pharaoh enjoyed being God's victim, craving the negative repercussions of God's daily attention. How does this make any sense? But in truth, it shows a remarkable understanding of a well-known psychosis associated with a range of personality disorders and with Munchausen's syndrome, in which attention-seeking is achieved by chronic victimism. Pharaoh realized that after the Exodus God was no longer interested in him and his nation. He therefore manufactured a situation that would demand God's attention, even if it meant utter devastation and disaster.

Abbas is a modern-day Pharaoh, craving the world's attention. But rightly or wrongly, the world has passed him and his people by. He therefore wishes to perpetuate a narrative of wanton victimhood stretching back centuries, and involving multiple international actors, so that the Palestinians continue to attract the attention of world players. Defining peace principles and coming up with a definitive peace plan would end the attention forever. This seems to be something the Palestinian leadership cannot and will never accept, and unless the younger generation take over soon, this is a broken record we will continue to hear for years to come.

IT'S O.K. TO CRY

first published February 6th, 2020

O
ne of the hardest aspects of being a pulpit rabbi is bereavement. As a rabbi, you grow close to the members of your shul, becoming intimately involved in their lives over many years, as they traverse the challenges we all face during the course of our limited time on this earth. My relationships with shul members cannot be classified as clinical or professional, rather they are special and meaningful.

Members of my communities past and present – people who I have seen regularly at synagogue and social events over the years, often for many years – have become lifelong personal friends. We laugh together, we celebrate together, we pray together, we study together, we know each other's children, and we know about everything that is going on in each other's lives. And then one day, out of the blue, I will get a call or there will be a knock at the door – "I'm so sorry rabbi, I have some terrible news…", so-and-so has been diagnosed with cancer, or they've had a heart attack, or a stroke. Or even worse, they have died suddenly and unexpectedly. Such devastating news always hits me hard. Someone so close to me dying is literally like losing a member of my own family.

Often, over the last few weeks or months of their lives, I will spend quite a bit of time with my shul member friends – chatting, laughing, bolstering their spirits, and almost always being inspired by their bravery and faith. After any bereavement, the family left behind are devastated by the loss of their loved one, even if the loss was totally expected. Judaism has a sensitive and well-thought-out bereavement process, honed to perfection over millennia, and based on scripture and Talmud. But although slotting into the groove of Jewish rituals for mourning can be comforting, truthfully every person grieves in their own way, and sometimes the details and expectations that go with Jewish rituals can be overwhelming, and can even get in the way of personalizing one's feelings at such a vulnerable moment.

Modern psychology has conducted deep research into the grief one experiences after the loss of someone close, and psychologists and therapists acknowledge that the death of a loved one is one of the greatest sorrows that can occur in a person's life. And yet, despite what we know based on countless scientific studies – namely, that mourners can have uncontrolled crying spells, difficulty sleeping, reduced appetite, lack of work productivity, and even intense feelings of anger or guilt, only one state in the United States – Oregon – requires employers to offer bereavement leave.

Meanwhile, Judaism is way ahead and insists on bereavement leave, having done so for thousands of years, thereby allowing mourners to recuperate and get themselves together during a full week of Shiva, during which they remain at home and receive condolence visitors.

Recently, a mourner at my synagogue told me she had found herself weeping after the loss of her mother and questioned me about it: "Why am I crying," she said, "after all, I knew my mother was dying – and frankly, after years of illness and disability, she's in a much better place now, with no more pain or suffering. Why am I crying?"

To be candid, I admit to having asked myself the exact same question after the loss of my own parents – it felt embarrassing, and almost demeaning, to be so emotional about something that is just a normal part of the cycle of life. Surely we know from the moment someone is born that they are going to die, so why are we so shocked and upset when it happens? Our emotional reaction seems exaggerated and entirely out of proportion.

The medieval commentators are similarly puzzled by Moses' inexplicably hysterical reaction in Parshat Beshalach when he spots the Egyptian army chasing after the Israelites following their Exodus from Egypt. Moses knew exactly how things were going to unfold, as he had been explicitly told by God that the Egyptians would chase after them, and would then be crushed (Ex. 14:4): וְחִזַּקְתִּי אֶת לֵב פַּרְעֹה וְרָדַף אַחֲרֵיהֶם וְאִכָּבְדָה בְּפַרְעֹה וּבְכָל חֵילוֹ – "I will stiffen Pharaoh's heart and he will pursue them, that I may gain glory through Pharaoh and his entire army." Why, then, did Moses get so upset when the Egyptian army appeared on the horizon?

The Midrash identifies the three advisors whom Pharaoh consulted regarding the fate of the Israelites as Balaam, Job, and Jethro. Balaam advised Pharaoh to wipe out the Israelites, and was consequently killed just before the nation entered the Promised Land. Jethro implored Pharaoh to behave decently towards the Israelites, and not to enslave or murder them, and as a result became a wanted man. Forced to flee, he ended up in Midian, and later merited Moses as his son-in-law.

Job remained silent, and the Midrash informs us that for this silence he was punished with all the dreadful suffering recorded in the Book of Job.

On the face of it, this Midrash is extremely disturbing. What did Job do so wrong that resulted in such misery and torment? Is it not possible that he was waiting for the right moment to intercede on the Israelites' behalf, thinking to himself that it was best to wait until his intervention would have the greatest effect?

Rabbi Yitzchak Zev Soloveitchik of Brisk (1886-1959) explains that such rationalizing is just an excuse. Whenever you're in pain, you don't sit around and strategize, you scream and cry. Job had been informed of the clear and present danger to the Israelites, but his actions indicated he felt no pain. For this reason he was punished with pain and suffering. According to the *Sefat Emet*, this same idea can be applied to Moses' reaction on the shores of the Red Sea. Even though he had been informed the Egyptians would chase after the Israelites, and that God would make an example of them, when confronted with the reality of the situation his human emotions kicked in – the pain was real, and he cried and prayed for their salvation.

This visceral reaction is also the reaction of any mourner who loses a loved one, even though they were fully aware of what was going to happen long before it happened. God has hardwired us to get emotional following the loss of a mother or father, or any other close relative or friend. Indeed, says the *Sefat Emet*, it is this instinctive emotion that makes us righteous and virtuous, not the false dignity of a stiff upper lip.

YITRO

EYE OF THE BEHOLDER

first published January 31st, 2019

I have just returned from Israel, where I spent an exhilarating week with my family. During our short visit we visited many places and met a range of wonderful people. I never fail to be amazed at the vitality of this extraordinary country; how is it possible that such a physically small space can be home to so many different types of people and experiences? Although, for those of us who see the modern State of Israel as a prelude to the Messianic era, the fact that all these disparate parts can hold together to make a functional whole, and that it all somehow works, is just further proof that something higher is at play – a force that defies our comprehension, and that is greater than any and all attempts to define it or undermine it.

Our last stop on the way to the airport just before leaving was a visit to the Israel Children's Museum in Holon, where we took part in a tour called "Dialogue in the Dark." Billed as a "fascinating social, moral and emotional journey," it was a formative experience for all us, instructive in ways we never imagined it would be. For about an hour we were led through a series of rooms in complete darkness by a guide named Sabir, who helped us navigate a variety of different settings from everyday life, including a supermarket and a public street. We stumbled around trying to get our bearings in surroundings that would have been very familiar had we been able to see. Initially our boys were boisterous and energetic, but as the hour unfolded, the sobering reality of sightlessness calmed them down. Finally, before exiting the darkness, we sat together with Sabir and shared our reactions with her, and with each other.

Never again would we take sight for granted; we now had some understanding of what it means to be blind or visually impaired; how sad it must be for those who cannot appreciate the kaleidoscope of colors and contrasts the world around us has to offer. These were just some of the thoughtful reactions of our sons Eli, 19, Meir, 16, and Uri, 12, who for the first time in their lives were compelled to consider the world from the perspective of someone with a debilitating handicap. And these messages were hammered home when we finally saw Sabir for the first time, as we emerged, squinting, into the light. For as we discovered, Sabir is severely visually impaired.

We continued discussing our experience among ourselves as we drove to the airport. One of the things we had done in the museum was try and identify different everyday objects and fixtures just by touching them. We had found a car and a mailbox in the street, and fruits and vegetables in the supermarket, but we had not been able to see them. What colors were they? We simply could not say. We realized that seeing something takes our consciousness of it to a whole new level. Sabir had also told us how it was impossible to describe a color or distance to someone born blind, as neither of these can ever be adequately explained to someone who has never physically seen them.

In Parshat Yitro, the Torah describes the Sinai revelation experience using the curious expression (Ex. 20:15): רֹאִים אֶת הַקּוֹלֹת – the Jewish nation "saw the almighty sounds." Rashi explains this to mean that "they saw that which should be heard, something impossible... on any other occasion." This phenomenon was a miracle unique to Sinai. But why was it not enough to hear the sound of God's voice? Why did it need to be seen?

Rabbi Chaim of Volozhin (1749-1821) was once extolling the virtues of his son Rabbi Isaac (1780-1849) to his students, suggesting he would have been considered a great Torah scholar even in the era of Talmudic sages. His audience was shocked by this hyperbole, particularly because they knew Rabbi Chaim was not prone to empty praise. If this was how he described his son, they asked, how would he portray his revered teacher, Rabbi Elijah, the Gaon of Vilna (1720-1797), whom he considered the epitome of rabbinic scholarship?

Rabbi Chaim dismissed his students' astonishment, and suggested that the difference between Rabbi Isaac and the Vilna Gaon was simple. If one was to ask someone to verbalize in reverse order any text or number sequence with which they are very familiar, they would certainly be able to do it, but only once they had first been through the text in their minds in the correct order.

Rabbi Isaac had the ability to do this with the entire text of Torah and Talmud, said his father, but the Gaon of Vilna's ability transcended this superlative gift; he could cite the previous word without having to run through the text from the beginning.

When someone is asked to recite a familiar text by-heart in reverse order, they rely on something called auditory memory, which means they must first go through the text in their minds in the correct order. But if they have the text open in front of them, all they need to do is look at it and read it backwards, hardly a significant feat. For the Vilna Gaon, said Rabbi Chaim of Volozhin, every word of the Torah was virtually visible before of him at all times. It was this that put him head-and-shoulders above Rabbi Isaac.

The revelation at Mount Sinai was not an auditory memory experience; every aspect of it was a vision, seen by those who were present. Even God's voice was experienced as if it was seen and not just heard. Parshat Mishpatim, which is the next portion in the Torah after Yitro, begins with the laws of *Eved Ivri* – an indentured Jewish servant. If, after six years, he wishes to remain a servant, the Torah instructs for him to be brought to the rabbinical court where his ear is pierced. Rashi explains that the ear is singled out, as it is "the ear which heard at Sinai that the Children of Israel are My servants and not servants to a servant."

By choosing to remain indentured, the servant has demonstrated that for him the Torah is merely an auditory memory, not a vivid vision seen in all its glorious color and texture. And just as colors and distance cannot be explained to those who were born blind, the dynamism of a Torah life can never be truly appreciated by those who have never seen its beauty.

THE DANGERS OF EXAGGERATED CAUTION

first published October 4th, 2018

I don't expect that you have heard of Dr. Ian Walker, a professor at Bath University in England.

Usually described by the media as a "traffic psychologist," his official title is "senior lecturer in the Department of Psychology with research interests in environmental behaviors and traffic safety." Just to be clear, Dr. Walker studies how people behave when they are driving cars, with a focus on safety issues.

Walker emerged into the limelight in 2006 with a shocking find. After years of research, he discovered that when people driving cars drive past cyclists, if the cyclist is wearing a helmet they will pass them at a closer distance than they would a cyclist with no helmet. As astonishing as it may sound, subconsciously drivers make a judgement call about cyclists without a helmet, believing them to be more vulnerable to permanent damage in the event of an accident. Consequently, they are extra careful when driving alongside them, opting to give them more room. Ironically, this means that wearing a helmet may actually be more dangerous for cyclists. While a helmet offers only limited protection if there is a collision, passing drivers will probably be less cautious if the cyclist is wearing one.

The most recent figures available for bicycle accidents in the United States involving cars or trucks resulting in a fatality is for the year 2015: 818 cyclists were killed on American roads that year, averaging more than 2 per day. And yet, despite the existence of Walker's research, the detailed 2015 report includes no information on how many of the fatalities were wearing helmets at the time of their collision, and it ends with the following warning: "All bicyclists should wear properly fitted bicycle helmets every time they ride. A helmet is the single most effective way to prevent head injury resulting from a bicycle crash."

But surely the NHTSA should be warning cyclists that wearing a helmet may lead to a greater risk of collisions, and that those wearing a helmet should act with greater caution while riding? Not least because Walker also reports that cyclists who wear a helmet often engage in risky behavior while on the road. For example, in an experiment where participants were told they were testing eye tracking while they played a computer game, half the participants were given a hat to hold their eye tracking equipment and the other half were given a bicycle helmet. Those wearing the helmet played the game in a far riskier fashion than those who were not wearing one.

The conclusion: wearing a helmet gives people a false sense of invincibility and empowers them to take risks that they would not ordinarily take, even though the helmet has no logical way of protecting them from those risks.

Make no mistake, I am not suggesting that cyclists no longer wear helmets, but it is certainly worth noting that Dr. Walker's research highlights an important aspect of decision making when it comes to added protection for cyclists. And as it turns out, sometimes adding too much protection can be counterproductive.

Quite astoundingly, Rashi highlights exactly this point regarding a detail of the biblical story of Eve eating from the Tree of Knowledge. Eve initially rejected the serpent's invitation to eat from the tree, citing God's prohibition (Gen. 3:3): וּמִפְּרִי הָעֵץ אֲשֶׁר בְּתוֹךְ הַגָּן אָמַר אֱלֹקִים לֹא תֹאכְלוּ מִמֶּנּוּ וְלֹא תִגְּעוּ בּוֹ פֶּן תְּמֻתוּן – "God said, 'don't eat from the tree in the middle of the garden, and don't touch it, lest you die.'" But the serpent summarily dismissed Eve's caution, assuring her that she was "not going to die!"

Rashi explains that his confidence was boosted by Eve's exaggerated vigilance. The Talmud explains that God had not forbidden her from touching the tree; He had only said that she and Adam should not eat from it. The Midrash, quoted by Rashi on the Talmud, has the serpent pushing Eve into the tree to demonstrate that nothing would happen to her, thereby lulling her into believing that eating from it would similarly lack any consequences.

In his commentary on this passage, Rabbi Moses Sofer of Pressburg ("Chatam Sofer"; 1762-1839) poses the following problem. How is it that Eve's extra boundary was any different from the countless boundaries set by the Talmud to stop us violating Torah prohibitions? His answer is as simple as it is astute. Exaggerated boundaries end up encouraging violations rather than preventing them.

The Talmud has a maxim, gezeira ligzeira lo gazrinan – "one must not add a restriction to a restriction." Had Eve's restriction been limited to not touching the fruit of the Tree of Knowledge to make it less likely that she would eat it, this would have been a limitation that made sense. But not touching the entire tree was a restriction too far, and opened the way for the serpent to take advantage of her.

And this same idea of not creating a double restriction appears in Parshat Yitro, in the section that precedes God's revelation to the nascent Jewish nation at Mount Sinai (Ex. 19:23). Rashi's grandson, Rabbi Samuel ben Meir ("*Rashbam*"; c.1085– c.1158), explains the verses at the end of Exodus 19 as a dialogue between God and Moses regarding the setting of proper boundaries. Moses had proposed that staying away from the mountain was not enough, suggesting that God also wanted the nation not to gaze at it from afar. But God overruled this proposal, responding that one level of restriction was more than sufficient. Extra boundaries can actually create more problems than they resolve

This easily overlooked aspect of the story of Adam and Eve, and similarly regarding Mount Sinai, is a cautionary warning from the dawn of human history. It acts as a reminder that self-congratulation as a result of exaggerated caution can easily result in complacency, and complacency inevitably leads to self-endangering hubris. The gravest danger is always the threat that hovers over those who feel they are well protected, while people who recognize their own vulnerability are far less likely to fall victim to a looming hazard.

LIKE ONE MAN, WITH ONE HEART

first published June 9th, 2016

One of my favorite Midrashic narratives describes God's attempt to find a nation willing to accept His Torah (*Sifrei Devarim* 343). The narrative depicts the nascent Jewish nation's willingness to embrace the Torah, and juxtaposes their enthusiasm with the reaction of various other nations who refused the Torah as it included elements they deemed intolerable.

God approaches the descendants of Ishmael and asks them if they want the Torah. "What does it contain?" they inquire. "Do not steal," God replies. "In that case, it is not for us." The descendants of Esau similarly reject the Torah, because it prohibits murder, while the descendants of Ammon and Moab, nations whose origins are rooted in an incestuous liaison between Lot and his two daughters, rebuff the Torah because it forbids incest. The narrative concludes with God offering the Torah to the Jews, who make no inquiries as to its content, declaring in unison נַעֲשֶׂה וְנִשְׁמַע – "we will do whatever it says, and we will listen to whatever it tells us."

The account is obviously fanciful and clearly the interactions between God and these nations never actually took place in the way the Midrash describes them. Instead, the idea behind this Midrashic narrative is message orientated, and the message appears to be the Jewish nation's unconditional willingness to abide by the Torah, as opposed to the other nations cited in the passage.

But the problem with this being the only takeaway is that it fails to acknowledge the unfairness of God's exchanges with those other nations. After all, if God's first and only demand of these other nations was that they renounce their favorite sin, surely He was setting them up to say no? Why didn't He tell them that the Torah contains celebratory days of rest and family time called Shabbat and *chagim*? Why didn't he inform them about the laws concerning sacrifices, or honoring one's parents? Perhaps these would have been mitzvot they could have embraced immediately, and then, in the fullness of time, their observance of less objectionable parts of the Torah might lead them to abandon their cherished sin.

It is also worth reflecting on the fact that God confronted each nation with their Achilles heel, driving them into an Orwellian "Room 101" even before they had even had the chance to see what else the Torah had to offer. Would the Jews have fared any better in the same situation?

It is all very well to say that we declared our allegiance to the Torah without demanding to know its content, but over the weeks and months and years that followed we failed God and His Torah on countless occasions. I hesitate to say this, but perhaps those other nations should even be commended for having been more honest in their response. By rejecting the Torah, they had demonstrated a greater self-awareness than we did.

To answer this pointed question, the late *rosh yeshiva* of Kerem BeYavneh, Rabbi Chaim Yaakov Goldvicht (1924-1994), offered a compelling suggestion: the response of the Jews to God's inquiry demonstrated they had conquered their greatest weakness of all – an almost instinctive lack of unity and mutual respect. When they declared in unison "we will do, we will hear," they showed their ability to rise above the sum of their parts by putting aside their differences, becoming one nation in the service of God. This idea is also hinted at elsewhere in the story of Mount Sinai: in anticipation of the Sinai revelation the Torah first says of the Jews that "they came to Sinai, they camped in the desert" – all in the plural. But once the Jews arrived at Mount Sinai, they are referred to in the singular. With reference to this anomaly, Rashi quotes a Midrash stating that at Mount Sinai the nation was "like one man, with one heart."

Although Rabbi Goldvicht's thesis is persuasive, it still leaves an open question. If the nations of Ishmael, Esau, Ammon and Moab each collectively rejected the Torah, surely their unity for this purpose is equally laudable? But the answer to this question lies in the difference between unity based on selfishness and unity based on empathy for others.

One of the definitive characteristics of sociopaths and psychopaths is their lack of empathy. They have little or no ability to understand and share the feelings of others, which results in behavior that is risky or harmful to others, as they are not inhibited by guilt, fear, anxiety, self-doubt, or remorse. The unity of the nations that rejected the Torah was based purely on selfishness and self-interest – each nation was a collection of psychopaths and sociopaths acting not as a singular unit, but as a unit of multiple individuals motivated by common interest.

But ultimately there is no such thing as common interest for a psychopath, only mass individual self-interest. God needed to know if these nations could let go of the parts of their national culture that would eventually lead to a complete breakdown of their societies. But the answer was an unequivocal "no!" — and He knew then that these nations were all doomed to oblivion.

The Jewish nation was different. Uppermost in each of their minds was a desire to help others and to be there for each other, even if this meant their individual lives would suffer. If God assured them that the Torah was good for the nation as a whole, even if as individuals they might struggle with all of its many rules, even if they were unable to match up to its requirements, they instinctively knew what they had to do. Of course they failed to live up to this ideal from time to time, and even frequently to start with, but overall, and over millennia, our success as a nation has stemmed from this one overriding trait – the individual desire of each and every one of us to concern ourselves for the welfare of others at our own cost, so that our nation as a whole can thrive and prosper, and be true to our original declaration of נַעֲשֶׂה וְנִשְׁמָע — "we will do, we will hear."

MISHPATIM

CHARITY SHOULD BE ABOUT CHARITY

first published February 24th, 2017

I f you live in the United States, you may be aware that the century-old unlimited charitable tax deduction on individual tax returns is in danger of being scrapped. Or maybe you are not aware of this proposal, so let me tell you about it. Legislation currently being considered for fast-tracking through Congress could reduce the number of people who can claim the deduction to just one in twenty taxpayers. The Urban-Brookings Tax Policy Center in Washington DC has published a detailed analysis of President Trump's proposed tax plans, and suggests that the cap on charitable deductions would devastate charitable receipts if it were ever passed into law.

The financial incentive offered by the charitable deduction tax break is a powerful motivator in charitable giving, and is often a clincher when making a decision about donating to a charitable cause. To be clear, the proposed change is far from a done deal, and will have to be properly vetted by experts as well be passed by Congress before it hits anyone in their pocketbook.

Although this issue is not yet in the spotlight, it is worth noting that the "charities economy" generates abundant jobs across the country, and a dip in charitable giving could have serious repercussions elsewhere that will need to be factored in before action is taken. And, it goes without saying that every charity has a champion in Washington DC, and every lawmaker is connected to multiple charities, large and small, who will make every effort via heavy lobbying to protect themselves from the inevitable repercussions of the proposed changes.

Parshat Mishpatim contains the first references in the Torah to charity-related legislation. One of them discusses extending loans to the needy (Ex. 22:24): אִם כֶּסֶף תַּלְוֶה אֶת עַמִּי אֶת הֶעָנִי עִמָּךְ...לֹא תְשִׂימוּן עָלָיו נֶשֶׁךְ – "if you lend money to my nation, the poor man among you...do not charge him interest." This statement seems to indicate that lending money to a needy individual is a voluntary act, and not obligated by the Torah – "if" you lend money to the poor man, as opposed to "you must" lend money to the poor man – the choice seems to be up to the lender.

But the Talmudic sage Rabbi Yishmael rejected this interpretation and insisted that this instance is an exception to the normal use of the Hebrew word *im*, which usually means "if." Here, he says, it means "when" – putting more pressure on the charitable lender to do his duty. Although, even if Rabbi Yishmael is correct, it is still puzzling that the Torah would use such an ambiguous word. Besides, the second phrase in this statement – "the poor man among you" – also seems superfluous. Isn't it self-evident that the prohibition against charging interest is to prevent the exploitation of those in need?

The eighteenth-century rabbinic luminary, Rabbi Chaim ibn Attar ("*Ohr Hachaim*"; 1696-1743) offers an intriguing suggestion to explain this puzzle, which cuts to the core of the

Jewish theological understanding of charity. For many people life is extremely challenging, he says, not least because they struggle to earn enough money to pay for their own needs and the needs of their loved ones. And yet, although the yoke of this challenge may be a heavy burden, it can be understood in the context of God wanting each person to seek out a relationship with Him through prayer and devotion, as part of their personal journey through life. God gives us challenges so that we will connect with him on a daily basis to ask for help.

But while this explains the need for financial hardship, where does this paradigm leave us when it comes to financial success? How is it that there are those whose financial accomplishments preclude any such need for God? And if the answer is that God rewards those who have merited his blessing, hence the existence of wealth, this only prompts the question as to why God would reward anyone with more than they need?

Rabbi Chaim ibn Attar proposes that this phenomenon is an equally important part of God's overarching plan. There are those in the plan who must struggle for their livelihood. And then there are those to whom He gives more than they need, so that those in need will have someone to go to who can help them plug the gaps in their finances. It would seem that God wants the needy to ask for money from a real, live person from whom the answer could just as easily be "no" as it could be "yes." Meanwhile, the role of the givers in this equation is to understand that any extra money they have is given to them in trust by God, so that when solicited by those in need they can act as God's agents to deliver the money where it is required.

As it turns out, the interaction between asker and giver is an interface with God for both parties. Once one is aware of this incredible fact, a mundane fundraising meeting about charity can suddenly turn into an extraordinary spiritual event. It also explains the meaning of the ambiguous word and the superfluous phrase in Parshat Mishpatim. If someone knocks on your door and asks for help, you can be sure it is because you are in a more privileged position than they are: "if my nation comes to you for a loan" – "if" you happen to get that knock on your door, be cognizant of the fact that "the poor is with you," in other words, that the money which belongs to the poor is "with you," and it is now your duty to act out your role in God's plan.

All kinds of extraneous distractions are factored into charitable giving, not least of which is the lure of a tax deduction. Notwithstanding the outcome of the proposed tax changes – and it is extremely unlikely that the proposals will be passed into law – perhaps the proposals are nonetheless a good thing, prompting us to recall the true objectives of charity.

THERE IS NO SOCIAL JUSTICE WITHOUT GOD

first published February 4th, 2016

I have just read a report about the Pro-Life Congress that took place last week in Santa Ana, California. Before I delve into what caught my eye about the report, let me say that Orthodox Judaism does not fit into any of the "camps" when it comes to the abortion debate, as halakha neither bans abortion completely, nor does it allow arbitrary abortion as a method of birth control.

The eighteenth-century rabbinic heavyweight, Rabbi Yaakov Emden (1697-1776), even went on the record to say that abortion is permitted (see: *She'ilat Yaavetz*, Vol. 1, #43), and as part of his ruling on abortion stated as follows: "Not only in an instance where there is a need to save the mother's life, but even if it is only to save her from the harassment and great pain that her fetus is causing" — which according to many modern interpretations would include extreme psychological or emotional distress.

Rabbi Emden also permitted the abortion of a child conceived by adultery to prevent the birth of what is known in Jewish legal terminology as a *mamzer*, a genetically transmitting stigmatizing halakhic impediment that lasts forever. And although Rabbi Emden's leniencies are undoubtedly at the extreme end of the spectrum of rabbinic opinion, even those who disagree with him do not suggest or even hint that his rulings are beyond the pale of normative halakha.

But let's get back to last week's conference in Santa Ana. The keynote speaker was Catholic Archbishop José Horacio Gómez of Los Angeles (b.1951), and what he said was profound. To be clear, it was not the detail of his address that I found significant, but rather a fundamentally important general point.

> *"Abortion and euthanasia raise basic questions of human rights and social justice in our society – questions of what kind of society we are and what kind of people we want to be. Never before has there been so much talk about human freedom and dignity and self-realization, and yet we find ourselves more and more indifferent to the cruelty and injustice that we see all around us."*

The Archbishop did not limit himself to abortion and euthanasia. He also mentioned racial discrimination, unemployment, homelessness, and environmental pollution, as examples of how a society that claims to care about human rights does not, in reality, care at all. And he ended his address by saying this: "If we really believed that God is our Father and that every person is a child of God made in his image – the world could be changed overnight." The essence of his message is extremely powerful, and – as you will see in a moment – it is embedded in Jewish tradition as far back as the revelation at Mount Sinai over three thousand years ago.

We are all familiar with the concept of humanism, an ideal that governs much of the social policy prevalent in modern-day Western society. Humanists define their beliefs as an outlook that attaches superior importance to the human rather than to Divine, or supernatural, matters. In other words, a humanist believes that if we focus on God it will simply distract us from creating a caring society where there is justice for all, and due consideration for the needs of others. After all, they argue, if it is only God's word that counts, how would it be possible to put the needs of humanity before the needs of God? Humanism posits that only by taking God out of the equation can one truly focus on improving society, and ensuring no one falls through the cracks.

But the Archbishop articulated something that we all know to be true – namely, if you take God out of the equation not only will it not help society, society will ultimately disintegrate completely. Hundreds of years after atheism entered into the mainstream there is, if anything, more suffering, not less, and no amount of grandstanding can hide the fact that while a religious system demands true concern for those around us and the world we live in, humanism often results in moral relativism and a self-indulgent "morality" that discriminates against more people than it defends.

Which is why Parshat Mishpatim, a portion that discusses seemingly mundane civil law – such as the laws pertaining to respect for one's fellow man, respect for parents, financial crime, capital crime, and other comparable human concerns – begins with words: וְאֵלֶּה הַמִּשְׁפָּטִים אֲשֶׁר תָּשִׂים לִפְנֵיהֶם — "**and** these are the laws you should place before them." The connecting Hebrew letter *vav* at the beginning of the sentence joins up the previous narrative describing the Sinai Revelation to the laws governing civil society. This conveys the message that a moral, caring society is a prerequisite for any relationship with God. Without one you will never have the other.

I would add that the word אֵלֶּה – "these" – stresses the fact that it is only civil laws mandated by the Torah that lay the groundwork for the relationship. Rabbi Israel Meir Kagan (1838-1933), the venerated Chofetz Chaim of Radun, was once at the mikva on Friday afternoon and saw a man come out of the mikva pool and use someone else's towel without permission to dry himself. The rabbi immediately challenged him: "How can you possibly believe you are cleansed from sin if you have just dried yourself with a stolen towel?"

Modern society is ostensibly focused on social justice and the rights of the individual, but in the headlong rush to form such a society without the guidance of a Divine map, they have lost their moral compass and created a morality that is both hollow and corrupt. I don't often find myself looking to an Archbishop for inspiration, but we would all do well to heed Archbishop Gomez's message. God has created a world where we must care for others, just as He cares for us. Or as the Archbishop put it so well: "God is our Father and he sees only His children – and when one of God's children is suffering or in danger, He calls the rest of us to love and compassion."

TERUMAH

LOVE LANGUAGE OF VERY FEW WORDS

first published February 28th, 2019

I n October 2010, the *Journal of Personality and Social Psychology* published a fascinating article about the remarkable linguistic synergy that exists between couples who are in a long-term relationship. Authored by two academics from the University of Texas at Austin, Molly Ireland and James Pennebaker, the article proposed that people who fall in love and remain in love will mimic and repeat the words and phrases each of them uses, and will end up sounding very much like each other. But if the relationship breaks down, the common language breaks down with it, and the couple's speaking and writing styles will drift apart.

The genesis of the article arose out of a study in which the authors looked at the language used by 2,000 college students responding to class assignments. Evidence showed that when an essay question was written using "a dry, confusing tone, students responded with dry, confusing answers," but if the assignment question used informal language, students responded using colloquial expressions and slang words. Spurred on by this discovery, the researchers began to look at historical figures to see what "Language Style Matching" (LSM) could reveal about the relationships between famous personalities.

For example, pioneer psychologists Sigmund Freud (1856-1939) and Carl Jung (1875-1961) corresponded frequently for over seven years. With the help of "style-matching statistics," the researchers charted the two men's stormy relationship from initial joint admiration to later mutual contempt, by focusing on pronouns, prepositions and other words that don't have much meaning outside the context of the sentence.

But all of this research paled into insignificance when the research team began to look at the poetry of the celebrated Victorian poet couple, Elizabeth Barrett (1806-1861) and Robert Browning (1812-1889), and their twentieth-century counterparts, Ted Hughes (1930-1998) and Sylvia Plath (1932-1963). Researchers discovered that similarities in the language used by the famous couples became more intense as their relationships intensified. In the case of Hughes and Plath, whose relationship was far more volatile than Barrett and Browning, and eventually ended in Plath's tragic suicide, the commonalities dramatically reached a zenith and then foundered as their marriage disintegrated.

In an interview about their findings, Pennebaker and Ireland explained that talking alike is so instinctive that it is almost imperceptible. When two people start a conversation, they usually begin talking alike within a matter of seconds, and because style matching is automatic it serves as an unobtrusive window into people's close relationships with others. Indeed, LSM is considered a major factor in assessing the success or breakdown of a relationship, and analyzing LSM is now used as a matter of course by marriage therapists when couples come for help, as a barometer to gage the state of a relationship.

A 1993 study also found that couples in happier marriages often use a private dialect that only they understand, peppering their everyday conversations with nicknames, codewords, and in-jokes. In fact, when people are very close, they may not need to say anything at all—a look, a nod, or just a twinkle in their eye, will be enough to tell their spouse everything they are trying to convey. Meanwhile, the more distant people are from each other, the harder it will be for them to communicate and to relate to each other through words, or indeed by any other means.

This insight into the nature of communication helps to explain a problem that has bothered countless Torah commentators. The laborious details of the Mishkan's construction take up no less than four Torah portions – Terumah, Tetzaveh, Vayakhel and Pekudei – amounting to hundreds of verses. And yet, axiomatic to our faith is the idea that the Torah is a concentrated source book, concisely written for the Oral Torah to elaborate upon. Why does this paradigm change so dramatically when the Torah addresses the construction of the Mishkan, a temporary Temple sanctuary, the details of which were to become irrelevant as soon as the permanent Temple was erected in Jerusalem?

One famous suggestion is that this anomaly demonstrates God's devoted love for the Jewish people. Although the nation had sinned against God in the episode of the Golden Calf, God granted them this special gift of a Mishkan to show His enduring affection for His chosen people. When it comes to love, no amount of words is ever truly adequate, and in describing the construction of this love-shrine, the inflated number of words are a reflection of God's superlative love for the Jewish nation.

But while this idea is heartwarming and wonderful, surely it would be more appropriate for God's love to be reflected in the form of a hyperbolic poem, not in the mundane, tedious details of a construction project? Perhaps for this reason, Rabbi Menachem Mendel Morgenstern of Kotzk (1787-1859) takes a rather more prosaic approach. When the Jewish nation is close to God, the LSM-rating is fantastic. So much so, that the Talmudic sage, Rabbi Akiba, used the individual decorative crowns on each Hebrew letter of the Torah to derive important messages from God.

The Talmud (Ned. 22b) declares that had the Jewish nation not sinned, they would only have required the Pentateuch and the Book of Joshua. The addition of so many other works in the Hebrew Scriptures was a reflection of how their relationship with God had been affected and diminished. The more distant one is from another party, the more words it takes to convey even the simplest ideas. The sin of the Golden Calf profoundly distanced the nation from God, and it is exactly this idea that is reflected in the verbose portions dealing with the construction project whose primary aim was fixing that broken relationship, enabling God to reside in our midst.

Those who struggle with prayer, or who find it difficult to relate to, or conform with, the requirements of the Jewish faith, should consider the possibility that their God-relationship LSM-rating is far lower than it should be. Having come to that realization, they should carefully consider how the relationship can be fixed, so that even the crowns on each letter cascade them with information.

CHARITY IS IN YOUR HEART, NOT YOUR WALLET

first published February 7th, 2019

S ome years ago, I came across an article that began with the rather startling statement: "If you raise money for charity, you're probably oppressing someone." The article turned out to be a tongue-in-cheek tirade against charitable campaigns and campaigners, written in the style of socialist ideologues who believe charity is a deliberately misleading public-relations ambassador for capitalism, enabling the very system that results in the poverty and the needy causes it purports to prevent.

At the time, I researched this subverted logic phenomenon further, and found myself in a labyrinthine maze of articles and studies on – believe it or not – the "evils of charity." I recently went back to research the same topic, and was confronted by a similar more recent range of indignant condemnations of charity. "Poverty is inevitable in capitalist systems due to the necessity of its exploitative nature to force the masses to consume and produce," declared one blogger, adding that "the true horrors of [charities] lies within their own profitability from this suffering." And do not imagine for a moment that this radical corner of the internet is sparsely populated; the aforementioned blog boasts more than 172,000 followers.

This ideological antipathy towards human altruism dates back to the nineteenth century, even before socialism and communism had gained a foothold in the administration of countries. In 1891, Oscar Wilde (1854-1900) wrote a lengthy, whimsical article titled *The Soul of Man under Socialism*. "The chief advantage that would result from the establishment of Socialism," he began, "is undoubtedly the fact that Socialism would relieve us from that sordid necessity of living for others." Society needed to be recreated, he continued, so that poverty would be impossible, and charity unnecessary. The only thing getting in the way of this utopian enterprise was misplaced philanthropy.

> *"Just as the worst slave-owners were those who were kind to their slaves, and so prevented the horror of the system being realized by those who suffered from it, and understood by those who contemplated it, so... the people who do most harm [in our society] are the people who try to do most good."*

Wilde's article is replete with equally ridiculous assertions, although it presciently notes the danger of socialism and communism developing into their own version of tyranny, an outcome he clearly – and quite foolishly – felt was preventable. But the most notable aspect of Wilde's thesis, and of the many other articles which advocate the same theories, is that there is an inherent evil in the fact that there are have's and have-not's, and that the job of society is to eliminate this distinction.

It is not surprising, then, that die-hard socialists and communists are uncharitable. Claudia Jacobs, a philanthropy expert, wrote about her experiences on a visit to Cuba. During the visit she inquired about individual and institutional philanthropy in Cuba by Cubans, and was consistently met "by puzzled looks... the concept seemed alien." Meanwhile, the number one charitable country in the world in 2018, as calculated by the Charities Aid Foundation in its annual World Giving Index, was Indonesia, hardly a bastion of capitalism, and certainly not a stronghold of socialism or communism. Two things stand out about Indonesia: the large percentage of people living below the poverty line, and the simple religious faith of many of its citizens.

This latter fact has a simple explanation: people of faith are more likely to give money than those who don't believe in God – a phenomenon I have previously addressed, and which is evident in a recent study published in Israel about Haredi charitable giving. Moreover, rather than poverty being a barrier to charitable giving, the poor are often more likely to give charity if they can, and to aspire to charitable giving if they do not have the funds at present.

Virtually every commentary on the second verse of Terumah asks the same question. God instructs Moses to embark on the first major charitable fundraising campaign in Jewish history (Ex. 25:2): דַּבֵּר אֶל בְּנֵי יִשְׂרָאֵל וְיִקְחוּ לִי תְּרוּמָה מֵאֵת כָּל אִישׁ אֲשֶׁר יִדְּבֶנּוּ לִבּוֹ תִּקְחוּ אֶת תְּרוּמָתִי – "Tell the Israelites to take gifts for Me; from every person whose heart so moves him you shall take my gift." Surely, the commentaries all ask, Moses should have been instructing the nation to give the gifts, not to take them?

The nineteenth-century rabbinic giant, Rabbi Moses Sofer of Pressburg ("*Chatam Sofer*"; 1762-1839), suggests a number of answers, mainly focused on the theme of God's ownership of everything, including those things we consider ours. But there is one idea tucked away at the end of his answers that is both compelling and inspiring. At the dawn of Jewish history, these recently redeemed slaves were being asked to part with their most precious commodities – gold, silver, bronze, jewels, fine cloth – to build an edifice they could easily have argued they neither needed nor wanted. And what about those among them who did not own any of the items on the campaign wish list? What would they give, or were they off the hook?

The powerful lesson of this verse, says Rabbi Sofer, is that for someone who is charitable, giving is in their nature, whether they have the resources or not. A "person whose heart so moves him" is not looking for excuses not to give; indeed, he or she will experience distress if they are unable to give. During the collection for the sanctuary no one had the precious stones required for the High Priest's breastplate, and this greatly distressed the leaders of each tribe, who were eager to donate them. So God included the jewels in their manna one morning, enabling them to give what they so wanted to give. If their heart desires it, God was telling Moses, I will afford them the opportunity to fulfil their heart's desire – they will take it from me, for me. God will always be there to help those who wish to help others.

Hardline socialist ideologues who argue that the capitalist system is purely selfish and greedy miss the point completely, while – and this is the greatest irony of all – simultaneously advocating for a system that ultimately legitimizes mean-spiritedness. There will always be those people who have more than others, but charity is in a person's heart, not in his wallet; and if it is in their heart, the resources will follow.

WHERE IS THE ARK OF THE COVENANT?

first published February 15th, 2018

Last month, if you were visiting Addis Ababa in Ethiopia, you would have witnessed an astonishing sight. Every January, the Ethiopian Orthodox Tewahedo Church celebrates a festival called *Timkat,* during which their senior priests parade through the streets of Ethiopia's capital carrying a replica of the Ark of the Covenant, as onlookers drop to their knees in reverence.

Astoundingly, this obscure branch of Christianity has approximately 50 million adherents, most of whom live in Ethiopia. And aside for this sect's curious affinity to the Hebrew Scriptures and Jewish practices—evident in their observance of some form of kosher laws, separation of the sexes in their churches, and the treatment of Saturday as Sabbath rather than Sunday—they also make the extraordinary claim that the Ark of the Covenant, Judaism's most revered object, is in their possession, and has been for almost 3,000 years.

The current location of the Ark, first described in Parshat Terumah (Ex. 25:11-23), has long been a subject of fascination for religious believers and archeological adventurers, most famously portrayed in the 1981 movie *Raiders of the Lost Ark,* in which the intrepid archeology professor, Indiana Jones, competes against

Nazis and supernatural forces in a swashbuckling escapade to find this ancient treasure.

Jewish tradition on this topic is ambiguous. Tosefta, a Talmudic work compiled in the second century C.E., offers two accounts of the Ark's fate. In the first, King Josiah of the Kingdom of Judah secreted the Ark away, along with several other sacred relics, in order to prevent their theft by Babylonian invaders, who would doubtless have taken them back to Babylon after destroying Jerusalem's First Temple. The second account suggests that this feared outcome is exactly what happened—the Ark was removed to Babylon, never to return. Meanwhile, the second Book of Maccabees contains another version of the story; in this account, the prophet Jeremiah concealed the Ark on Mount Nebo, vowing that the location would remain a secret "until God finally gathers his people together and shows them mercy." (2 Macc. 2:7)

It is certainly the case that the Ark was missing from the Second Temple, and there is no record of anyone being aware of its location in contemporaneous documents or traditions. Although, rather predictably, none of this has prevented countless dubious claims of the Ark's discovery over the years. The most recent claim came in 1982, when Ron Wyatt (1933-1999), an eccentric amateur archaeologist and Seventh Day Adventist, proudly proclaimed to have found the Ark buried in a cave under the remains of the Old City in Jerusalem. Intriguingly, he was the only one to see it, and claimed to have revisited it several times.

But the assertions of the Ethiopian Church far outstrip Wyatt's tantalizing story. These faithful Christians believe the Ark of the Covenant was taken from Jerusalem 3000 years ago, to a place called Aksum, in northern Ethiopia, where it has remained ever since, housed in a small unassuming church, and zealously guarded by the monks of Saint Mary of Zion. The story has its origins in an ancient text called *Kebra Nagast*, which begins with the story of the Queen of Sheba, who traveled from Ethiopia to Jerusalem to benefit from King Solomon's wisdom, and gave birth to his son on the way home. This son, named Menelik, later visited his father, and returned with a group of Israelite princes who had stolen the Ark without Menelik's knowledge, and taken it with them to Ethiopia. When Menelik discovered the theft, he decided to keep the Ark rather than return it—hence its presence in Aksum.

No one besides for a designated guardian is ever allowed to see this Ark. In 2007, reporter Paul Raffaele of the *Smithsonian Magazine* spent considerable time in Ethiopia in an attempt to gain access to the vault where the purported Ark is kept. But after countless adventures, he was thwarted at the eleventh hour by the impassive guardian, and found himself unable to "judge whether the Ark of the Covenant truly rested inside this nondescript chapel," or not. Determined not to be disappointed by his failure, he decided "that simply being in the presence of this eternal mystery was a fitting ending to my quest." Meanwhile, presumably the obsession with keeping the "Ark" from prying eyes has less to do with religious dogma, and far more to do with this relic's dubious provenance, and the fear that scientific testing will show that whatever it is, it certainly cannot be the Ark of the Covenant.

Jewish tradition has never obsessed about religious relics, and has no particular interest in the Ark's location, only in its symbolism. Various commentaries find it significant that the

Ark's measurements include half cubits, unlike all the other Temple vessels, whose measurements were rounded off to whole numbers. Rabbi Jacob ben Asher ("*Ba'al ha-Turim*"; 1269-1343) proposes that this anomaly is a reference to the Ark's contents—the sacred Tablets of Sinai and a Torah scroll, symbolic of a Torah scholar—and conveys the idea that a Torah scholar must always remain humble and see himself as only halfway there on the journey to his full potential.

Another lesson is learned from the poles used to transport the Ark. The Torah instructs for these poles never to be removed from the rings that held them in place (Ex. 25:15). Even though the other Temple vessels had rings and poles to transport them, this prohibition against pole removal only applied to the Ark. The commentaries explain that the poles for the other vessels were there purely for transportation purposes, while the poles of the Ark represent those who value and support Torah. It is imperative for Torah scholars supported by others to remember that they must never discard those who support them. These supporters are and will always remain a critical component of Torah preservation for the Jewish nation. Not only must they never be removed from the Ark, but they remain alongside it in the most sacred space of the Temple—the Holy of Holies—a fitting tribute to their commitment towards our sacred tradition.

TETZAVEH

THERE'S MORE THAN ONE MR PRESIDENT

first published February 14th, 2019

On December 5, 2018, four former US presidents and their wives attended the funeral of George H.W. Bush in Washington DC – Jimmy and Rosalynn Carter, Bill and Hillary Clinton, Bush's son George W. Bush and his wife Laura, and Barack and Michelle Obama. As it happens, the attendance of so many former presidents at the elder Bush's funeral was not a record breaker. The first time four ex-presidents were together in one geographic location was in November 1991, at the inauguration of the Ronald Reagan Presidential Library, and there have been a number of similar occasions since.

Even the phenomenon of five living ex-presidents from January 2017 until Bush sr.'s passing was not a first; in 1861, after the inauguration of President Abraham Lincoln (1809-1865), there were five living ex-presidents: Martin Van Buren (1782-1862), John Tyler (1790-1862), Millard Fillmore (1800-1874), Franklin Pierce (1804-1869) and James Buchanan (1791-1868) — although it is unlikely these five were ever together in one place, particularly after Tyler was elected to the Confederate House of Representatives. The more recent five ex-presidents actually did meet and spend an evening together, at the *Deep From the Heart* hurricane relief concert in Texas, in October 2017.

The United States has an interesting etiquette when it comes to former presidents—despite it attracting the attention of protocol critics. For the remainder of their lives after they leave office former presidents are always referred to as "Mr. President" or "President", followed by their name, rather than as "Former President". Which makes Jimmy Carter – who served as president for just one term but is the longest-serving ex-president in US history – the only president of the United States to be referred to as Mr. President for well over forty years.

I have always wondered how the emcee at an event attended by multiple former presidents begins his formal introduction. Is it "Good evening, Mr. President, Mr. President, Mr. President," etc.? Surely that must get rather confusing. Even referring to them all as "President" followed by their names would be quite disconcerting, particularly for the sitting president, whose stature and self-esteem would surely be diminished in such unusual circumstances.

In Parshat Tetzaveh the Torah introduces us to the concept of a Jewish High Priest, the person appointed to preside of the most elevated ritual affairs of Judaism in its most sanctified location – the Temple. The Talmud (Meg. 9b) records a debate between Rabbi Meir and Rabbi Yose regarding the status of a former high priest, understood to mean someone who has served as interim high priest until the official high priest becomes available to take up his post once again.

Rabbi Meir argues that the former high priest still retains the status of a high priest in a number of significant ways, and should therefore resume regular temple duties after stepping down, but still wear the vestments of the high priest.

Rabbi Yose disagrees. In his opinion the former high priest is in a kind of professional limbo. Wearing the vestments of a high priest while doing the duties of the temple is out of the question, as doing so could upset the incumbent. But at the same time the ex-high priest cannot possibly carry out temple duties in the vestments of an ordinary priest, as this would violate the Talmudic principle of מַעֲלִין בַּקּוֹדֶשׁ וְאֵין מוֹרִידִין – "one may elevate a level of sanctity, but one must never reduce it." In other words, once a high priest, always a high priest.

The medieval rabbinic Talmud annotators, Tosafot, are puzzled by the use of this principle, and pose the following question: if it makes sense for the former high priest to be treated like a high priest, and the only reason not to do so is to avoid hurting the feelings of his replacement, why does Rabbi Yose invoke the principle of not lowering levels of sanctity to explain why a former high priest cannot revert to his status as an ordinary priest? Clearly, once a high priest, always a high priest, notwithstanding any issues there may be with donning the associated uniform?

Tosafot offer an intriguing answer. Just like public officials in the modern world, a high priest can be impeached by order of the king or by a vote of the priestly caucus. Appointment to the high priesthood is a privilege, not a guaranteed lifetime position. Consequently, were it not for the concept of not reducing levels of sanctity, the presumption would be that an impeached high priest goes back to being an ordinary priest, and in that role wears the vestments of an ordinary priest. It is only because we cannot reduce sanctity once it has been elevated, that even someone whose unsuitability to the high priesthood resulted in his impeachment can never be treated as ordinary again.

Whatever the personal qualities or failings of a high priest may be, or a president for that matter, to be treated as commonplace after having held such an elevated position would be an affront to the position they once held. It is the duty of society to sustain the eminence of a leadership position, a worthy goal that was as evident to the sages of the Talmud as it is now.

Another uniquely American tradition is for former presidents to leave a handwritten note to their successor, and to leave it on the Oval Office desk for them to open and read on their first day as president. Partisanship and personal rivalries are set aside, with the departing president offering words of encouragement and support to their replacement. The most poignant such letter in recent memory was certainly the one from George W. Bush to Barack Obama:

> *"Very few have had the honor of knowing the responsibility you now feel. Very few know the excitement of the moment and the challenges you will face. There will be trying moments. The critics will rage. Your "friends" will disappoint you. But, you will have an Almighty God to comfort you, a family who loves you, and a country that is pulling for you, including me. No matter what comes, you will be inspired by the character and compassion of the people you now lead. God bless you."*

Worthy and inspiring words, particularly in these very troubled times.

DESIGNER UNIFORMS IMPART THE WRONG MESSAGE

first published February 28th, 2018

P arents of children attending the prestigious Taimei Elementary School in Tokyo were recently shocked to discover that buying a new school uniform for their children will set them back a staggering 80,000 yen (approximately $700). Although the school is state-funded, it is located in the luxury shopping district of Ginza – home to Tokyo's equivalent of Rodeo Drive – and enrolment is extremely competitive. Apparently, the school's administration took this coveted exclusivity to a whole new level by commissioning designer label Georgio Armani to design their new uniform— resulting in the hefty price tag.

Unveiled just a couple of weeks ago, the uniform includes a chic hat and a cute looking bag. But no one from the school's administration seems to have allowed for the fact that as wearing the uniform is mandatory, each child must own at least two full sets, if not more, and depending on how many school-age kids a family has, this can turn into a major financial burden. Irritated parents launched a campaign against the innovation, and last week the furor was raised at a session of the Japanese parliament, forcing government ministers to apologize.

The whole sorry saga began back in November, when headmaster Toshitsugu Wada informed parents of the uniform change in April, which is the start of the Japanese school year. But none of the parents expected a designer collection, and certainly not a uniform designed by Giorgio Armani—whose Japanese head office is conveniently located just two hundred yards from the school. "I was surprised such luxury brand-designed uniforms were picked for a public elementary school," one unnamed mother told *HuffPost Japan*, adding that she was "worried the wrong notion, that something expensive is good and something cheap is bad, could be imprinted on children."

A noble ideal, which captures one of the essential values represented by sartorial uniformity, a practice that has all but disappeared in American schools. Although, maybe that is about to change. Starting next school year, all public-school students in South Carolina will be required to wear school uniform, if a bill currently being tabled is voted into law.

There is endless data to demonstrate that buying stuff for kids ahead of a school year costs parents many hundreds of dollars, and often thousands. In the case of teenagers, much of this money is spent on new clothes. Step in South Carolina state lawmaker Cezar McKnight, who is proposing that all students attending state schools wear the same outfit, and that the uniform in question be limited in cost. The bill also proposes that students from low income families be provided with five sets of uniforms free-of-charge. "If they all wear uniforms, the children who can't afford the really nice clothes won't have to be ashamed of what they're wearing," one mother said.

The preamble to the bill details the phenomenal peer pressure that sees parents laying out small fortunes on designer clothes for their kids to wear at school. Although, despite this reality, not everyone agrees with McKnight's bill. "If I'm going to spend money, I'm going to go out and buy what my kids want," another mother told a local newspaper. "Kids should have the freedom to wear whatever they want to school." An enterprising student has even launched a petition to stop the bill, which, if it is passed, will result in mandatory statewide school uniform as early as this coming August.

Neither required clothing nor uniform appearance is a hallmark of Judaism. I recall hearing from former British chief rabbi, Rabbi Lord Jonathan Sacks, that he once attended a United Nations religious leadership conference at the invitation of the World Council of Religious Leaders. It was at this meeting that he discovered that Judaism is unique in not having a formal dress code for its religious leaders. At the closing session, every faith leader was asked to attend in their official vestments for the purposes of a group photo. It suddenly dawned on Rabbi Sacks that he didn't have anything in particular to wear, and in the photo he appears alongside dozens of other clergy, almost all of them in flowing robes and garments of every color imaginable, while he is dressed in a plain suit and tie—almost the only one without some external vestige of his faith role.

It is a remarkable observation, and what would appear to be obvious exceptions are in fact further proof of the fact. For example, the elaborate costume worn by contemporary Sephardic chief rabbis of Israel is a throwback to the mandated uniform worn by Jewish religious leaders of the Ottoman Empire, while the striking garb worn by Hasidic leaders (and their followers) can be traced back to the clothes worn by eighteenth century Ukrainian and Polish noblemen.

There is, however, one exception, even if it has no contemporary application — the clothing prescribed for priests while they performed the duties of the Temple, described in detail in Parshat Tetzaveh (Ex. 28:2): וְעָשִׂיתָ בִגְדֵי קֹדֶשׁ לְאַהֲרֹן אָחִיךָ לְכָבוֹד וּלְתִפְאָרֶת – "you shall make sacred garments for Aaron your brother, for honor and for glory."

The eighteenth-century commentator, Rabbi Chaim ibn Attar ("*Ohr Hachaim*"; 1696-1743) notes that these clothes, however intricate and beautiful they may have been, were not important in-and-of-themselves, evident from the fact that Moses was not required to wear them during the first week after the Temple was ready, before Aaron and his family took over. Rather they represented an ideal, with the four "white" garments signifying the unutterable four-letter name of God, and the four "gold" garments signifying the less elevated four-letter name of God whose pronunciation is permitted.

Priests were expected to serve the people, and to help atone for their sins, both sins of faith, as represented by God's elevated name, and sins of human weakness, characterized by God's other name. The garments acted as a reminder of this dual expectation, a clear demonstration that drawing some kind of uplifting inspiration from what you are wearing is the true purpose of any uniform, something it is safe to say could never be achieved by wearing an outfit designed by Giorgio Armani.

ATHEISM IS NOT PROGRESSIVE

first published February 18th, 2016

For many years I have instinctively believed that atheism thrived in the ancient world. I have relied on this hypothesis when teaching about aspects of Judaism in its earliest days and throughout its formative stages, as recorded in Jewish scripture and the Talmud. Although, until recently I was on thin ground. People could have taken issue with me and argued that the Jewish rituals we are familiar with from scripture were formulated as a direct response to pagan rituals that were the mainstay of religious life at the time Judaism emerged. The Temple, sacrifices, priests, and the complex societal rules – all of these things were the ubiquitous furniture of everyday polytheistic culture, and Judaism needed to embrace them if it was to successfully compete with everything else religious that was out there.

But despite this being a compelling analysis, I have never been entirely comfortable with it – even though it underpins much of Maimonides' exposition of biblical Judaism as found in his seminal apologetic work, *Moreh Nevukhim* ("Guide for the Perplexed"). My discomfort is rooted in a belief that Judaism is more than a two-dimensional religion set up to deter wavering monotheists from getting sucked into polytheism. Furthermore, the analysis also disingenuously infers that atheism might be a more progressive form of belief system than monotheism. After all, if it came later, this might lead one to think that the rejection of polytheism through the adoption of monotheism is best understood as a convenient segue into atheism.

Thankfully, I was recently vindicated, with the publication of an incredible new book titled *Battling the Gods: Atheism in the Ancient World* (Vintage Press, 2016), by Tim Whitmarsh (b.1969), Professor of Greek and Classics at Cambridge University. Whitmarsh has researched the topic in great detail, and concluded that the ancient world was brimming with skeptics and atheists. The most famous of these was the Greek philosopher Socrates, executed in 399 B.C. for the crime of heresy, or more precisely "impiety" for "not believing in the gods of the state." Until Whitmarsh's book was published, I imagined Socrates to be a one-off contrarian who paid for his cynicism with his life. But actually, he was one of many.

So why has history ignored ancient atheism and atheists? Whitmarsh posits that as it is always the victors who record history, with the Christian domination of the Western world in the early Common Era, atheism was essentially snuffed out for centuries and driven deep undercover. Whitmarsh also proposes that atheism is as old as Judaism, suggesting that at the same time as our ancestors were rejecting pagan gods in favor of the "Creator God of Israel," Xenophanes of Colophon was cheerfully satirizing all god-belief in his witty poetry, although he was principally concerned with primitive anthropomorphism and the idea that any deity would have an interest in human affairs.

Whitmarsh's thesis is compelling for the reasons I have already mentioned, and also because it confirms that human nature never changes, and must be the same now as it was when the Torah was given. Numerous rabbinic works discuss the tension between God-belief and God-rejection, and none of them present this tension as a binary system that confines any rejection of God to polytheism. On the contrary, heresy is complex, and it encapsulates any number of theologies and ideologies, including, among others, both polytheism and atheism.

It is certainly true that if you look at the Torah it seems dominated by rituals and practices that appear to echo the religious rituals of polytheism and pagan worship. And yet, if you look carefully, you will find that time and again the Torah references belief in God in such a way that it cannot have been addressing pagans, all of whom, by definition, believed in the concept of a deity. And while everything about the creation of the Temple sanctuary and the priestly vestments seem to directly relate to pagan worship, even in its construction process we see statements that clearly refer to the allure of atheism.

It is in this light that we can best understand a curious set of statements in Parshat Tetzaveh. After instructing Moses about the various sacrifices that he and Aaron would need to offer as part of the consecration of the priests, God describes how His presence will become evident once that process is complete, promising as follows (Ex. 29:45): וְשָׁכַנְתִּי בְּתוֹךְ בְּנֵי יִשְׂרָאֵל וְהָיִיתִי לָהֶם לֵאלֹקִים וְיָדְעוּ כִּי אֲנִי ה' אֱלֹקֵיהֶם – "I will dwell among the Children of Israel, and be their God, and they will know that I am God, their God."

The statement "they will know" seems out of place. If God was going to dwell among the Jews, clearly they would "know" that He was there. And that is exactly the point. Perhaps they would not "know." For those of them who had pagan tendencies, a Temple and associated rituals would be enough to assure them of God's presence. But for the atheists and skeptics among them, no amount of pomp and ceremony would suffice. God therefore reassured Moses that the Tabernacle would not just serve to satisfy those who were drawn to polytheism, but it would also convince doubters, who would, through its existence, "know" that He was God, the only God, and their God.

This and other similar statements prove to us that atheism is not as progressive as its promoters would have us believe. If anything, it is regressive. It is as ancient as human civilization. The revolutionary system of belief is the one that proposes one omnipotent God who created the entire universe and all intelligent life.

In the final analysis, both polytheism and atheism amount to one identical idea – the rejection of God. That both polytheism and atheism existed in ancient times simply confirms what I have always suspected – that the revelation at Mount Sinai was truly a revelation, as well as a revolution, enabling humanity to interface with God, and, with the help of the Torah, reject any system that militated against His existence.

KI TISSA

BEAUTY IS IN THE EYE OF THE BEHOLDER

first published February 21st, 2019

A few weeks ago, at the Western Wall in Jerusalem, our youngest son Uri put his *tefillin* on for the first time. In May he will turn thirteen, the age of adulthood for Jewish boys. In anticipation of that milestone moment – when he will become obligated to observe all those mitzvot that until now have merely been educational experiences – Uri prepared himself for the mitzva of *tefillin*, which he will don every day for the rest of his life. What more appropriate place to initiate him into this primary religious obligation than at the most sacred site of Jewish tradition – the location of our Temple in Jerusalem.

But why are *tefillin* considered so important? The odd-looking black boxes with attached leather straps are undoubtedly the most enigmatic religious accessories of Judaism—not only because they are purely ritual, but also because they occupy such an elevated place in our tradition and heritage. The mitzva of *tefillin* is the first practical mitzva mentioned in the *Shema* prayer that we recite each morning and evening, when we declare our faith in God, and promise to love Him in every possible way. That the first method of demonstrating this love is expressed through wearing *tefillin* conveys just how central this mitzva is to our faith.

And not a month goes past without an inspiring *tefillin* story. Just last week, the *Jewish Journal* in Los Angeles reported the miraculous reunion of a 91-year-old Polish Holocaust survivor, Al Kleiner, with his Holocaust-victim brother's *tefillin*, brought by his cousin from Poland to Israel after the Holocaust, where they remained forgotten until last year. Out of the blue, Al's cousin's daughter discovered the little red velvet bag with embroidered initials and immediately realized whose they were. She sent them to Al's family in Los Angeles, and, amid great emotion, he put them on for the first time since having been in hiding from the Nazis in 1943-4.

Some years ago, I was in Northbrooke, Illinois, for the High Holydays, and the synagogue president told us how he had recently sent his late Holocaust-survivor father's *tefillin* to New York to have the parchments checked. These were *tefillin* that had remained hidden with his father throughout his time in concentration camp, which he had diligently put on each day, from his thirteenth birthday until his passing. The *sofer* ("ritual scribe") called a few days later, his voice trembling.

> *"These are the most perfect tefillin parchments I have ever looked over during my entire career as a sofer – and for them to be decades old, and to have gone through the hell of Auschwitz – your father's father, who purchased these tefillin, must have been an extraordinary man, because I can assure you these tefillin did not come cheap."*

The late Lubavitcher Rebbe, Rabbi Menachem Mendel Schneerson (1902-1994), famously launched a "Tefillin Campaign" in the weeks leading up to the Six-Day War, to ensure that as many post-barmitzva Jewish boys and men as possible put on *tefillin* each day. This remarkable campaign has since resulted in millions of Jews putting on *tefillin* in thousands of locations all over the world, often after being stopped in the street, or in some other public place, by intrepid young Lubavitch yeshiva students.

During the early stages of the computer revolution, Rabbi Schneerson was once asked where computers could be found in the Torah. He replied simply, *"tefillin"* – and went on to explain that the essence of computers was efficient thinking and enhanced connectivity, and *tefillin* are the same, enabling us to think more spiritually, and connecting our heart, our hands and our brain at the start of each day so that they unite with each other with the sole purpose of serving God.

In the Torah portion of Ki Tissa, Moses is granted a glimpse of God's "back" after being told he would not be able to see God's "face" (Ex. 33:23). Rashi, quoting the Talmud, explains that Moses was shown the knot of God's *tefillin*, that for us is located at the nape of the neck when the head *tefillin* are worn. This mystical allusion is understood to mean that only part of the link between man and God was revealed to Moses, while everything else remained concealed.

According to another Midrash, a more complete vision was granted to the second century sage, Rabbi Akiba, and his contemporaries. Using a source text in Job (28:10), the Midrash underscores Rabbi Akiba's supremacy: וְכָל יְקָר רָאֲתָה עֵינוֹ – "all of your glory my eyes have seen," and tells us that "this [verse] refers to Rabbi Akiba and his friends—things which were not revealed to Moses were revealed to them." Commenting on the use of the word *yekar* ("glory") in Megillat Esther, the Talmud (Meg. 16b) informs us that this word refers to *tefillin*.

How are we to understand that Moses only saw the back of God's *tefillin*, while Rabbi Akiba was able to see God's *tefillin* in all its glory? Embedded in Judaism is the idea that Moses was the greatest prophet who has ever lived, and Rabbi Akiba, notwithstanding the fact that he was one of the greatest of all the Talmudic rabbis, was not even a prophet.

The innovative nineteenth-century Hasidic master, Rabbi Mordechai Yosef Leiner of Izbitza (1801-1854), suggests an astonishing distinction between Moses and Rabbi Akiba. Moses transmitted the foundational text of the Torah, and therefore had to convey the bad along with the good, specifically punishments for transgressing the word of God, acknowledging the possibility of human failing, and a rift between man and God. Meanwhile, the Talmud (Makk. 7a) records a statement of Rabbi Akiba and his friend Rabbi Tarfon, who said that "had we been members of the Sanhedrin, no person would have ever been executed." As far as they were concerned, no Jew could ever be so distant from God that they would potentially be liable for capital punishment. And, according to Rabbi Akiba, "Love your neighbor as yourself" (Lev. 19:18) is the most important principle of the Torah (JT Ned. 30b).

If we understand that *tefillin* represents the potential perfection in every Jew and our duty to love every Jew notwithstanding any disconnection with Judaism, Rabbi Akiba's view of God's Tefillin was complete, unmarred by any doubt or cynicism, while Moses' view was somewhat less favorable. During the month of Adar, and specifically on the festival of Purim, we are expected to see everyone as if they are resplendent in *tefillin*,

Judaism's representation of God's essence in all of us. It is our faith's version of seeing the glass half-full, as opposed to seeing it as half empty.

PROXIMITY TO THE RIGHTEOUS

first published March 1st, 2018

E very March, thousands of Jews from all over the world travel to the sleepy town of Lezajsk (Lizhensk), in Poland. The travelers are all pilgrim visitors to the tomb of the eighteenth-century founder of Polish Hasidism, Rabbi Elimelech Weisblum (1717-1787), whose *yahrzeit* (date-of-death anniversary) is on 21st Adar, exactly one week after the festival of Purim.

The Hasidic branch of Judaism, founded by Rabbi Israel Baal Shem Tov of Medzhybizh (1698-1760), originated and flourished in Western Ukraine, particularly after it was popularized by Rabbi Israel's devoted disciple, Rabbi Dov Baer of Mezhirichi (d.1772). In general, mainstream Jewish leadership rejected the mystical doctrines of Hasidism as too radical, and even as heresy. But the Jewish grassroots largely embraced the warm spirituality of Hasidic theology, which offered a counterpoint to the rigid academic traditions and intellectual snobbery that had dominated European Jewish community life for centuries.

Poland was at the center of this traditional approach to Judaism, and Rabbi Elimelech was a pioneer, bringing the vitality of Hasidic passion for the seemingly mundane aspects of Judaism into the heartlands of Polish Jewry, which resulted in Poland becoming the focal point of the Hasidic revolution in Jewish life that continues to reverberate today. Visitors to Lezajsk deposit paper notes inscribed with their names at Rabbi Elimelech's gravesite, and also pray in proximity to his last resting place, hoping that infusing his inspiration into their prayers will see their innermost aspirations crystallized.

Appropriately, Rabbi Elimelech emphasized the importance of a *tzaddik* ("righteous one") as an essential component of an enduring Judaism. A *tzaddik* can best be defined as an elevated soul who helps ordinary Jews connect to the Divine by acting as a kind of mediator, offering access to God in the spiritual sphere, and also in all other aspects of one's daily life. This refreshing idea was just one of many ideas set out by the "*Tzaddik* of Lizhensk" in his seminal work, *Noam Elimelech* ("Graciousness of Elimelech"), first published in 1788 by his son Rabbi Eliezer Lipman Weisblum (1742-1806), and republished dozens of times since.

Rabbi Elimelech used his fascinating *tzaddik* doctrine to illuminate a particularly troubling anomaly in what is certainly the best-known challenge to the concept of a personal God, namely the apparently unfair suffering of the righteous, and the abundant success of sinners, in spite of their sinful lives. The Talmud (Ber. 7a) informs us that Moses made three requests of God, one of which was for God to explain how He manages the world, a request that was granted, at least according to the majority opinion quoted in the Talmud. This is evident from the statement in Parshat Ki Tissa (Ex. 33:19): וְחַנֹּתִי אֶת אֲשֶׁר אָחֹן וְרִחַמְתִּי אֶת אֲשֶׁר אֲרַחֵם – "I will have mercy on whom I will have mercy, and I will have compassion on whom I will have compassion."

According to the majority opinion, this verse means that the righteous who have it good are perfect in their righteousness, while the righteous who suffer are not entirely perfect. Meanwhile, a sinner who suffers is utterly wicked and therefore deserves to suffer, while a sinner who has it good is clearly not entirely bad, and is thus rewarded for the good he has done. Puzzlingly, the Talmudic sage Rabbi Meir appears to disagree with this majority opinion, and rejects the idea that God responded to Moses' request. In his minority opinion, this verse means that God will reward even those who do not deserve to be rewarded.

Step in Rabbi Elimelech of Lizhensk, who explains that the disagreement between Rabbi Meir's minority view and the majority view has nothing whatsoever to do with the obvious meaning of the verse. Evidently, if someone righteous suffers, even when such suffering appears unfair; or if the wicked prosper, even if the prosperity seems undeserved; there is a reason that broadly accords with the majority view explanation found in the Talmudic discussion. Rather, he suggests, Rabbi Meir is addressing the anomaly of those who are truly undeserving, but nonetheless seem to have blessed lives. This unwarranted blessing is only made possible through their proximity to a true *tzaddik*, who is a beneficiary of abundant blessings, not all of which are for that *tzaddik*'s personal benefit.

Righteous individuals who personify God's presence through their conduct and example are conduits of blessings to the world around them, and those blessings permeate every aspect of their lives. Included in this are the lives of those who are associated with them, even if they are not fully worthy themselves. By finding a spiritual mentor who inspires and advances their connection to

God, they become the beneficiaries of blessings beyond their own merits.

The flip side of this coin is equally true. Those who distance themselves from the righteous, or worse still, denigrate and humiliate them, are not only missing out on blessings-by-association, but are also exposing themselves to the dangers of their own iniquities, most pointedly by disparaging those whose behavior embody righteousness and godliness. Perhaps in their own self-contained lives they are paragons of perfection, but this is only one part of the equation. The other side of the equation is going to reflect their relationship with a spiritual guide, a relationship that can determine blessings or the contrary in a way that will often seem counter-intuitive if this is not taken into account.

It is precisely this idea that inspires thousands of people to visit Rabbi Elimelech's tomb more than 230 years after his passing. Paying tribute to a true *tzaddik* is not something that comes to an end when that *tzaddik* is no longer alive. The blessings such a *tzaddik* has accumulated continue to be available to those who recognize his greatness, and who understand that true righteousness is a rare and valuable commodity, to be cherished by those who on their own might sink and flounder.

THERE IS NO APARTHEID IN ISRAEL

first published February 25th, 2016

Many of us were extremely disturbed to see a full-page advertisement that appeared in this Wednesday's edition of the *Los Angeles Times*. Sponsored by an organization calling itself *Jewish Voice for Peace* (JVP), and by the *U.S. Campaign to End the Israeli Occupation*, the $10,000 advert – ostensibly aimed at Oscar nominees who have been offered an all-expenses paid VIP trip to Israel – refers to Israel as an "apartheid state." This same ad had previously been rejected by *Variety*, who explained to JVP that the "topic is too sensitive," although this neither-here-nor-there excuse falls far short of the explanation *Variety* should have given JVP when they vetoed the ad.

To call Israel an apartheid state is not just a lie, it is brazen antisemitism. The clear aim of this provocative statement is to identify all Israelis and Jews who associate themselves with Israel as racists who deliberately segregate Palestinian Arabs and treat them as non-citizens, or worse, simply because they are Arabs.

That this is a total lie is self-evident to any unbiased person who has ever visited Israel. Benjamin Pogrund, a South African Jewish journalist now living in Israel, who actively battled apartheid from the 1960s onwards, has written frequently on this subject, and he is hardly an apologist for Israel. On the contrary, he feels very strongly that a solution must be found for the plight of Palestinians, and yet, although he is sympathetic to the cause of Palestinian statehood, he rejects any comparison between apartheid South Africa and contemporary Israel. In an article published last year, Pogrund wrote:

> *"I have now lived in Israel for 17 years, doing what I can to promote dialogue across lines of division. To an extent that I believe is rare, I straddle both societies. I know Israel today – and I knew apartheid up close. And put simply, there is no comparison between Israel and apartheid.'*

He goes on to explain why this is so, and criticizes "well intentioned" people who fall for this comparison, and allow themselves to get sucked into a propaganda campaign run by activists who have only one intention:

> *"[They] want Israel declared an apartheid state so it becomes a pariah, open to the world's severest sanctions. Many want not just an end to the occupation, but an end to Israel itself."*

Most strikingly, the late Nelson Mandela (1918-2013), unquestionably the person most identified with anti-apartheid activism, not only visited Israel, but heaped praise on its achievements – despite, as he mentioned when he was there, Israel's earlier association with South Africa's apartheid government. How do JVP "apartheid state" activists explain the fact that at no time during his visit, nor at any time before or after, did Mandela ever suggest or even hint that Israel was an apartheid state? Of course he didn't, because it isn't. He knew that, as does anyone else who has any knowledge of what it meant to be black in South Africa during the apartheid era.

And that is exactly the point. JVP activists are not interested in the accuracy of any historical analogy, only in the propaganda value of using such an incendiary word. By referring to Israel as an "apartheid state" they are setting the stage, they believe, for the complete collapse of Israel's governmental infrastructure and the legitimacy of its constitution, similar to the collapse of South Africa in the early 1990s, which was precipitated by the concerted delegitimization campaign of anti-apartheid activism.

There is a very powerful message here, and it is a message that can be similarly drawn from the episode of the Golden Calf in Parshat Ki Tissa. A careful reading of the narrative, as explained by various commentaries, reveals that the Golden Calf began as an innocent attempt to find a non-deity replacement for Moses, who had disappeared and was feared dead. One thing led to another, and the Golden Calf was the unfortunate result.

Even this, while misguided, would not have amounted to idol worship had it not been for an insidious campaign mounted by the *Eirev Rav* ("mixed multitude") element within the Jewish population – Egyptians who had insinuated themselves among the Jews during the Exodus. Once the Golden Calf was formed, the commentaries inform us that it was the *Eirev Rav* who announced (Ex. 32:4): אֵלֶּה אֱלֹהֶיךָ יִשְׂרָאֵל אֲשֶׁר הֶעֱלוּךָ מֵאֶרֶץ מִצְרָיִם – "This is your god, Israel, who brought you out of Egypt." How could any Jew who had been present at the Mount Sinai revelation ever have fallen for such a lie? Clearly this physical effigy was not the God who had presided over the Exodus. And yet there were

Jews who fell for it, mesmerized by the deceptive allure of the *Eirev Rav*.

That is the danger inherent in any kind of Golden Calf, however innocent or "well intentioned." The Jews had every reason to be concerned by Moses' absence, and to request new leadership. Without Moses, they lacked the guidance he offered. He was their link to God, and to God's plan for their future. But in their haste to replace Moses they ended up with something so destructive that it almost finished off the Jewish nation before it had even begun.

It is entirely legitimate for us to be concerned for the wellbeing of all those who fall under Israel's jurisdiction, Jew and non-Jew alike. Even Israel's fiercest advocates and defenders know that the situation as it stands is not perfect, and we watch as Israel struggles with this issue on an ongoing basis. But in the headlong rush to improve matters there are many Jews, both in Israel and beyond, who have allowed themselves to fall under the spell of the *Eirev Rav*, whose only objective is to dismantle the Jewish State and destroy all the good that it represents. Our duty, therefore, is to fight the "apartheid state" label with every fiber of our being. Nothing less than Israel's survival depends on it.

VAYAKHEIL/PEKUDEI

AN UNFINISHED WORK OF ART

first published March 7th, 2019

On April 12, 1945, the Russian-born American artist, Elizabeth Shoumatoff (1888-1980), began work on a portrait painting at a sleepy private vacation retreat in Warm Springs, Georgia, known as the "Little White House". It was noon, and her subject was Franklin Delano Roosevelt (1888-1945), recently elected to his fourth term as President of the United States. An hour later, over lunch, the President complained of a severe headache, and soon slumped over, unconscious. The attending physician confirmed the President had suffered a cerebral hemorrhage, and by 3:35pm President Roosevelt was dead.

Understandably, Shoumatoff's portrait was never completed. It remained a partial depiction, becoming known as the "Unfinished Portrait," and today it hangs on the wall at the Little White House, now a President Roosevelt memorial museum. Curiously, it joins numerous other unfinished works of art, music and literature – a genre considered by scholars to be an intriguing but important, if somewhat marginal element of the creative world. Perhaps the most famous example of this phenomenon is Franz Schubert's "Unfinished Symphony", while the most jarring is undoubtedly the bizarre portrait by Benjamin West of the delegates at the Treaty of Paris in 1783, which, as a result of the British delegates refusing to pose with their American counterparts, is a painting with half the canvas totally bare.

Interest in unfinished works of art has gained quite a bit of traction over the past few years, and was the subject of a major exhibition at the Met Breuer in New York, in 2016. The exhibition included over 190 artworks, many of them left incomplete by their makers for reasons unrelated to the art itself, but in that state offering insights into the creative process, along with other aspects of the artist.

Also featured as part of the exhibition were works considered *non finito*—intentionally unfinished. This branch of art actually dates back to the Renaissance period—it was originally pioneered by Donatello (1386-1466), and particularly typical of Michelangelo (1475-1564) in his later years. But while Renaissance-era *non finito* art – usually sculpture – was deliberately left incomplete by the artists to convey the Platonic philosophical point that no art can ever truly resemble its perfect heavenly equivalent, in the modern period this genre has taken on a whole new meaning, with the artists conveying a sense of temporariness, or even decay.

One such piece presented at the exhibition – *Lick and Lather* by Janine Antoni – is a series of self-portrait busts, half of which are made of chocolate and the other half from soap, "fragile materials that tend to age quickly." After completing the busts using a rough mold, Antoni "unfinished" them by licking the ones that were made of chocolate and using the soap ones when she washed, "stopping once she had arrived at her distinctive physiognomy."

As with much of this kind of modern art, I am not quite sure what to make of it, but I am definitely quite taken with the idea behind *non finito*. Kelly Baum, one of the curators of the Met exhibition, suggested that "an unfinished picture is almost like an X-ray, [allowing] you to see beyond the surface of the painting to what lies behind ... [it] demands your creative and imaginative investment in a picture, because you have ... to fill in the blanks."

It is exactly this that makes unfinished art so compelling, and it is also this that offers a wonderful insight into the temporary nature of the Mishkan, and particularly to explain a strange contradiction in the Torah regarding the final sum collected by Moses in his fundraising campaign for the Mishkan building project, described as both "enough" and "too much" (Ex. 36:7). Rabbi Chaim ibn Attar ("*Ohr Hachaim*"; 1697-1743) asked the obvious question: surely if what was collected is described as being just enough, what could there have been that was extra?

The Midrash teaches us that the Mishkan needs to be seen as a microcosm of the world, and the process of constructing the Mishkan is actually compared to the creation of the world by God. The Mishna in Avot (5:6) declares that *mazikim* ("destructive spirits") were created at dusk on the Friday of creation week. By the time God created these spirits, it was Shabbat, and it was too late to create bodies for them, so they were left as creatures without bodies. The idea that God ran out of time as Shabbat approached is patently ridiculous, a fact noted by Rabbi Judah Loew of Prague ("*Maharal*"; 1520-1609), who proposes that the statement in Avot is only there to teach us that the world is incomplete – not because God was unable to complete it, but because God wanted it that way.

Just like the modern version of *non finito* art, our world is deliberately unfinished to convey an important point, and the negative connotation of *mazikim*, along with the fact that it is they who are only half-created, is just a way of delivering this message – that our world is missing something, and that incompleteness is not a good thing. We must constantly be aware that our world – as beautiful as it may be as a piece of art, and even if we feel utterly filled with faith in God – is missing some element, however tiny, that we just cannot quite get to no matter how hard we try.

The Mishkan reflected this reality – it was beautiful and had everything it needed, but it was still temporary and incomplete. Even though the nation brought everything that the Mishkan needed, and completed the construction of every element, there was still more that it could contain. What they brought was enough, and at the same time it was too much.

Our lives are also like the Mishkan: *non finito* – fully rounded and complete, but nonetheless always remaining a work in progress. This powerful message resonates down the millennia, as relevant today as it was when the Mishkan was first erected.

THE SEVEN-DAY WEEK PHENOMENON

first published March 8th, 2018

Without any doubt, the most durable phenomenon in history is the seven-day week. Its origin continues to baffle anthropologists and scholars of ancient history, and numerous theories have been suggested to explain how ancient civilizations settled on seven days as the length of the unit of time known as a week.

One popular theory, first proposed by the controversial German historian, Friedrich Delitzsch (1850-1922), suggests that seven relates to the 28-day cycle of the moon, which neatly divides into four units of seven, with the quarterly division prompted by the beginning of each of the four significant moon shapes in every monthly cycle (initial crescent, waxing half-moon, full moon, waning half-moon). The problem with this theory – besides for the fact that a moon cycle is longer than 28 days – is that there is zero evidence of any ancient culture correlating the beginning of each month with the beginning of a new week.

The fact is that the number seven does not appear to correspond to any naturally occurring phenomenon, whereas days, lunar months and solar years do. Five-day weeks, six-day weeks, eight-day weeks, or even ten-day weeks, would make more sense than a seven-day week. Interestingly, all of these other permutations have been tried, and all of them have failed.

The early Romans instituted an eight-day week, which included one full day at the end of the week designated just for shopping. There is plenty of evidence that the seven-day week came first, though, and it is notable that the shopping day immediately followed a seven-day period.

In any event, Roman attempts to dislodge the seven-day system was far from the only one. Following the French Revolution of 1789, the radical social atheist, Sylvain Maréchal (1750-1803), promoted what became known as the Republican Calendar, in an attempt to eradicate religious and monarchical influences from French society, and in order to fully decimalize France.

Although Maréchal's system maintained the existing twelve-month cycle, albeit with modified names for the months, each month was divided into three equal weeks of ten days. Adopted by France in 1793, the Republican Calendar lasted for just twelve years before it was abolished by Napoleon. The ten-day week was the first element to be abandoned – it was never popular with the working classes, who were unhappy having to wait extra days for their day off.

But the most aggressive attempt to uproot the seven-day week was initiated by the despotic leader of the Soviet Union, Joseph Stalin (1878-1953), who imposed five-day and six-day workweeks for the Soviet workforce, with the inclusion of a day of rest. This system, which lasted from 1929 until 1940, was strictly imposed across the Soviet Union, and was principally motivated by Stalin's fervent desire to eliminate religion, and any opportunity to practice religion, within soviet society.

Much has been written about the seven-day week phenomenon, usually in an attempt to dismiss its religious significance. And yet this curious way of marking time has persisted throughout history, despite its indisputable origin in the Hebrew Scriptures, which underline the seven-day week with a day of rest we refer to as *Shabbat* ("the Sabbath"). First noted in Genesis 1, it was reaffirmed in the Decalogue (Ex. 20:8-11), and its governing laws were closely associated with the construction of the Tabernacle in the wilderness. Historically, even those who accepted the phenomenon of a seven-day week, and who never gave it a second thought, nonetheless aggressively assaulted the relationship between Shabbat and Saturday. The early church designated Sunday as the "Lord's Day", replacing Saturday with Sunday as the Sabbath.

Although Christian scholars have suggested a range of reasons as to why Sunday became the new Sabbath, the change from Saturday to Sunday undermines the original source for a seven-day week, which prompts the question – why is the seven-day week still so important to Christians? Meanwhile, Islam abolished the Saturday Sabbath, and replaced it with a day of prayer on Friday, which presents a similar dilemma. After all, the seven-day week only makes sense if you accept the biblical insistence that Saturday is Shabbat.

The Talmud (Shab. 118) extols the virtues of those who treat Shabbat with proper reverence, promising countless benefits to anyone who embraces the opportunities presented by such a unique day – which, if properly observed, fuses lofty spiritual opportunities with a range of material pleasures. But among the many statements made by the Talmud in this vein, there is one that is particularly confounding: אִלְמָלֵי מְשַׁמְּרִין יִשְׂרָאֵל שְׁתֵּי שַׁבָּתוֹת

כְּהִלְכָתָן מִיַד נִגְאָלִים – "If only Israel would observe two Sabbaths according to the law, they would be redeemed immediately."

Although the idea seems wonderful, the commentaries all ask the same question – why two Sabbaths? Why is one not sufficient? Rabbi Elijah ben Solomon Zalman (1720-1797), the celebrated "Gaon of Vilna," offers a compelling explanation that underlines the centrality of a seven-day week in our religious faith and adds further proof of its spiritual significance.

Shabbat follows a six-day workweek as the seventh day, exclusively serving that seven-day period as its day of rest. If everyone were to observe just one Shabbat, the preceding period would far exceed six days, and the day of rest they observed would not be sufficient to serve that extended period. But if everyone observed a second Shabbat, it could perform its function as the closing day of the preceding six-day period, with the seven-day week sandwiched between the Shabbat before it began, and the Shabbat at its conclusion.

Consequently, it makes perfect sense that the prohibitions of Shabbat relate to the activities required to build the Tabernacle. Shabbat offers us access to God without the medium of a physical location; the day itself is a portal into the Divine. And although we may have lost our Temple, destroyed and obliterated by enemies of God, no amount of effort to destroy our other Temple – Shabbat – has ever succeeded, nor will any such effort ever succeed.

DOES SIRI HAVE THE ANSWER?

first published March 23rd, 2017

Anyone who uses an iPhone or a MacBook is familiar with the silvery voice of "Siri", an electronic personal assistant that (who?) responds to questions for information. You can ask Siri anything and "she" will either give you a one-sentence answer in a monotonic woman's voice, or pull up the most relevant answer from the internet and send it to your screen.

Siri's creators realized early on that users related much more closely with the disembodied voice coming out of their device than they did with words on a screen, and were asking her questions she was not equipped to answer. This ultimately led them to develop a parallel response framework that is not purely informational, but is instead geared towards the more informal or even personal, and occasionally humorous, questions that users ask Siri. For example, if you pose the following question to Siri: "How much wood would a woodchuck chuck if a woodchuck could chuck wood?" – she will respond:

> *"A so-called 'woodchuck' (correctly speaking, a groundhog) would chuck — that is, throw — as much as the woodchuck in question was physically able to chuck (ibid.) if woodchucks in general had the capability (and, presumably, the motivation) to chuck wood."*

Alternatively, the answer might be: "As environmentally responsible creatures, I suspect woodchucks would encourage the recycling of wood over simply chucking it."

The relationship that users have developed with Siri is so humanized that they are not just asking her frivolous questions about woodchucks, but also more fundamental questions, such as "what is the meaning of life?" Siri's writers put a lot of thought into scripting various responses to this particular question, ranging from the rather cheesy philosopher-related pun "I Kant answer that. Ha-ha!" to the more evasive, "that's easy... it's a philosophical question concerning the purpose and significance of life or existence in general," and "all evidence to date suggests it's chocolate."

But for all the cleverness that these answers demonstrate, this question and many other questions are misdirected if aimed at electronic repositories of knowledge. The ubiquity of electronic information — a revolution that has mushroomed exponentially over just a couple of decades — has had some quite extraordinary consequences, one of them being the use of devices rather than humans such as parents or teachers to get information.

An astonishing study carried out by UK's Birmingham University in 2012 discovered that more than half of children aged 5-15 used Google as their first point of call when seeking information for research purposes. And if, by some chance, Google is not able to provide a satisfactory answer, 20 percent go to Wikipedia as their next stop, while just 3 percent of them – that is just 3 out of 100 children! – ask their teacher or parent for assistance.

Shockingly, the study confirms that parents have shifted from top spot to second place. The study showed that 26 percent of children turn to digital devices for an answer before asking a parent, while 34 percent of children don't think their parents are capable of helping them with their homework at all. After all, why bother asking Mum or Dad if Siri knows it all better? And – she has a better sense of humor!

Judaism is entirely geared away from this emerging model of solitary study that relies almost exclusively on non-human informational resources. Jewish tradition is heavily based on mentoring and role-modeling, not just on information and knowledge. It is a message that emanates loud and clear from Parshat Vayakhel, which begins with Moses congregating the entire nation together at God's request, to teach them the laws of Sabbath observance.

The Midrash observes that there is no portion in the Torah that begins with the words "Moses congregated the people" besides for this one. This unique opening indicates that God particularly wants important information, such as the complex laws of Sabbath, to be imparted only when there are groups of people together, and one should certainly not study alone using inanimate learning tools as the means by which to gain knowledge. The Talmud uses this as the source for the custom that in the lead-up to any festival, and particularly Passover, one should arrange public lectures during which subject matter pertaining to the festival will be taught and studied, evidently in as interactive a way as possible.

The whole concept of learning, and certainly Torah learning, is not just about obtaining and absorbing factual information.

There is something much more valuable than facts, namely the interaction that goes on between people discoursing and reviewing those facts.

Neither Google nor Siri will ever be able to help children or adults understand the importance or otherwise of information. If, however, you ask your parent, or rabbi, or doctor, or teacher, for information – their facial expression and method of delivering their response may teach you as much or more about what they are saying as the facts themselves. Excising this crucial element of learning from the equation is not just a mistake, but potentially dangerous.

I am certainly no Luddite – after all, I am partial to both Google and Siri, and use them frequently. But it is clear to me that information is always one-dimensional if it doesn't involve interaction with others, and I am acutely aware of how much both my knowledge and my quest for knowledge is the direct result of my parents, my teachers, my study partners, and of all of my real, live intellectual interlocutors.

The most venerated Jewish learning of all is Jewish mysticism, referred to as Kabbalah, which conveys the crucial message that one cannot truly understand the esoteric subject matter unless it is "received" from someone who in turn received it similarly from their teacher. Siri may be great, but she will never be able to teach us as much as we can learn from each other.

THE POWER OF HUMILITY

first published March 10th, 2016

Data is the mortal enemy of assumption. We often assume we know things, or we go along with accepted wisdom, but when we later examine the cold hard facts we will discover that reality is quite a different thing altogether. I had that feeling while reading through an article this week titled *The Power of Humility*, by Professor Amy Ou of the National University of Singapore Business School.

We all expect successful people in the corporate world to be arrogant and full of themselves. It is the inevitable cloud attached to the silver lining of great accomplishment. People who are hardwired to push their weight around and who constantly wear their success on their sleeve are the ones who will be the most successful of all. We make a similar assumption about all successful leadership, not just about leadership in the business world. Self-promoters and those with the pushiest personalities are the ones who get things done, and who get them done best.

Professor Ou's article dispels this myth with irrefutable data. It turns out there is a "significant and positive relationship between a company's bottom-line performance and CEO humility."

CEOs and their top managers from 105 small-to-medium-sized American firms were interviewed, and evaluated with a focus on the following criteria: CEO personality, top management team dynamics, executive incentive structures, firm strategy, and performance. To be clear, 105 companies is a significant sample in research terms, and guess what – the researchers discovered that companies led by humble CEOs do significantly better in revenue terms.

The details are all there in the study. Humble CEOs are willing to admit their weaknesses, and therefore "appreciate the strengths and contributions of others." They will also be open to self-improvement, and get the fact that they don't need to dominate the limelight – which means they will be willing to embark on lucrative projects even if the projects won't result in self-glory. Additionally, they are less likely to demand excessively high salaries or suppress the pay of their management colleagues. And by behaving in this way, humble CEOs empower their management team, which leads to better performance and greater profits.

So why is it that we think the opposite to be true? Surely the most successful companies in the world are all run by self-obsessed egomaniacs? Actually, that's not the case at all. Professor Ou gives two examples of humble CEOs of major corporations, and there are plenty more. Most likely the reason we have got it wrong is because egomaniacs tend to be the ones who dominate headlines, and all they do is tell us how prosperous they are. More often than not, they are not half as effective as they make out, while their quieter, more humble counterparts are far more successful – whether in their business affairs or in their personal lives.

In Parshat Pekudei, after Moses completed each of the various tasks necessary for the construction of the Mishkan and the

tailoring of the priestly vestments, we are told (Ex. 39:43): וְהִנֵּה
עָשׂוּ אֹתָהּ כַּאֲשֶׁר צִוָּה ה' כֵּן עָשׂוּ – "[Moses] did just as God had
instructed him – that is what he did." The statement is puzzling,
and the repetition at the end is even more puzzling. What exactly
is the Torah trying to tell us? Would Moses have done anything
differently to the way God had instructed him? Of course not! So
why mention it at all? And even supposing it needs to be
mentioned, surely once would have sufficed?

It is an axiom of Jewish history that Moses was our greatest
leader. He brought a slave nation out of Egypt and single-
handedly turned that nation into God's Chosen People. This was
no easy task. Time and again Moses dealt with discontent,
disobedience, and even rebellion. And yet, not only was he
successful in using each challenge as an opportunity to improve
the durability of the nation in his charge, but he also acted as a
relentless advocate for them to God, making sure that none of the
bumps in the road would lead to an abandonment of the project.
One might have expected Moses to be an arrogant, egotistical
man. After all, he was even ready to remonstrate with God. On
that basis we can allow ourselves to admire him, but up close we
could easily imagine him to have been tiresome and
objectionable.

In fact, though, the opposite was true. It was Moses' humility
that underpinned his success, and which resulted in a nation that
has endured for thousands of years. It was Moses' humility that
allowed others to share the limelight – Aaron and his family as
priests, and Bezalel and his team as the artisans who built the
Mishkan. The net result was a broader group of talented people
all committed to the same goals as he was. And even when it came
to carrying out the tasks given to him by God, instead of saying

"Moses did this," or "Moses did that," Moses took himself out of the equation, making sure that what was recorded for posterity was only that he had acted purely as an instrument of God.

Ironically, without this humility, the Jewish Nation project might have ended before it began. There would never have been an Exodus. There would never have been the revelation at Mount Sinai. There would never have been a Mishkan. And the Jews would never made it to the Promised Land. Forty years later, in an ultimate act of self-sacrifice, Moses would hand over the reins of leadership to Joshua. For Moses the handover was a no-brainer. Despite his sadness at not being the one who led the Jews into Canaan, he knew it had never been about him; he had simply been the facilitator. So "he did just as God had instructed him." That is the true "Power of Humility."

VAYIKRA

VAYIKRA

THE HUMILITY OF ABRAHAM LINCOLN

first published March 15th, 2019

T he Book of Leviticus begins with the Hebrew word *vayikra* (ויקרא). Curiously, in a Torah scroll, the letter *aleph* at the end of the word is written smaller than the other letters. The medieval commentator, Rabbi Jacob ben Asher ("*Baal Haturim*"; c.1269-1343), explains the reason behind the mini-aleph. Although Moses was a great man, he was also extremely humble, an attribute that is best illustrated in the exchange between Moses and God regarding the word *vayikra*:

> *"Moses only wanted to write 'vayikar', without the aleph, which implies chance – as if God only appeared to him in a dream, just as he appeared to the gentile prophet Balaam. But God told him to write the word with an aleph, which implies that God appeared to him deliberately. Moses, in his humility, responded that he would only write it with an aleph if he could write the aleph smaller than all the other alephs in the Torah, and that is what he did."*

Although, quite frankly, this whole "Moses was very humble" idea seems rather ridiculous. True, we are told that there was no humbler man than Moses on the face of the earth (Num. 12:3), yet the image of him as exceedingly modest hardly matches up with what we know about him. Moses was raised in Pharaoh's palace by a royal princess – hardly humble beginnings. Then, in the first recorded story of his adult life, he stumbles on an Egyptian beating up a Jew — and immediately kills the Egyptian to save the Jew. And while what he did to save his fellow Jew was certainly brave and praiseworthy, it can hardly be considered humble; killing someone is not the kind of behavior we associate with a humble man.

Later on, God calls on Moses to save the Jews and redeem them from slavery. Moses' response? A flat-out 'no'. What kind of person refuses a direct request from God? Certainly not a humble one. Upon discovering that the Jews had created and worshipped a golden calf, Moses broke the Tablets given to him by God, and although we know God subsequently praised him for this impulsive act, surely it was incredibly arrogant for him to break them in the first place? After all, who was he? A mere human being. How was it possible for him to take God's gift and smash it? How could we ever consider this the act of a humble man?

In that same episode Moses remonstrates with God, telling Him to "erase me from your Torah" if God refused to forgive the golden calf sinners for their sin (Ex. 32:32). What was that about? Why would Moses imagine that God cared if he was in His Torah or not? Who did Moses think he was? Where is the humility? And this just precipitates the biggest question of all. Let's face it – who was the person who wrote the Torah down for posterity? Moses. And how many times is his name mentioned in the Torah? Not once, not 10 times, not 100 times – Moses' name is mentioned in the Torah no less than 616 times, multiple more times than anyone else's name. So forget the mini-aleph — if Moses was actually so humble, why does his name appear in the Torah so often?

Some weeks ago, I received a gift from my friend Ben Shapell — *Lincoln and the Jews*, a book co-authored by him together with another dear friend, Professor Jonathan D. Sarna. *Lincoln and the Jews* is a fascinating book, all about President Abraham Lincoln (1809-1865) – a man who shaped the destiny of the United States at a crossroads moment – and his relationship with the American Jewish community of his day. Interestingly, although Lincoln is consistently rated as the best president in US history, during his tenure at the helm of the executive branch, he was hated and reviled. And yet, even though his enemies found fault in almost everything he did for the country, they still admired him.

Edward Dicey (1832-1911) was a British journalist with a reputation as a fierce Lincoln critic. During his extended visit to the United States in 1862 he was introduced to Lincoln at a social event and later said: "In my life I have seen a good number of men distinguished by their talents or their station, but I never saw anyone, so apparently unconscious that this distinction conferred upon him any superiority, as Abraham Lincoln." But despite this widely held view, the fact that Lincoln was considered modest and unassuming is puzzling, and it has always amazed me. He may have been polite and deferential in social company, but he was also incredibly forthright and opinionated.

In 1863, the *New York Tribune* challenged Lincoln to come out in favor of the abolition of slavery, now that he was at war with the Southern states that supported slavery. Infuriated, Lincoln fired off a letter to the editor which was completely unequivocal:

"[My interest in pursuing this war is to] save the Union. I would save it the shortest way under the Constitution. The sooner the national authority can be restored; the nearer the Union will be "the Union as it was." If there be those who would not save the Union, unless they could at the same time save slavery, I do not agree with them. If there be those who would not save the Union unless they could at the same time destroy slavery, I do not agree with them. My paramount object in this struggle is to save the Union, and is not either to save or to destroy slavery."

The letter continued on — relentless, unyielding, and uncompromising. Of course he hated slavery, Lincoln said, but as President of the United States he was not going to be told by some newspaper editor what his priorities should be in running the country. And while he was undoubtedly right, his blunt stance and harsh rhetoric hardly seem humble.

One of the best-known stories regarding Lincoln's humility concerns his letter to General George Meade (1815-1872), a senior commander of the Union Army during a decisive period of the American Civil War. After the Union victory at the Battle of Gettysburg in June 1863, in which Meade played an important role, instead of pursuing and capturing General Robert E. Lee (1807-1870) and his Confederate army, thereby ending the war, Meade and his colleagues gave Lee and his men the chance to flee across the river, and the war dragged on for almost two more years. Lincoln was livid and vented to his White House staff— against Meade in particular. The news of Lincoln's irate response quickly reached Meade and he immediately threatened to resign, defensively dismissing Lincoln's aspersions regarding his competence.

Upon hearing of Meade's indignant response, Lincoln sat down and wrote him a harsh letter to explain his irritation at the general's inexplicable decision to allow Lee the opportunity to get away:

> *"My dear general, I do not believe you appreciate the magnitude of the misfortune involved in Lee's escape— He was within your easy grasp, and to have closed upon him would, in connection with our other late successes, have ended the war. As it is, the war will be prolonged indefinitely... Your golden opportunity is gone, and I am distressed immeasurably because of it."*

If Meade had thought about resigning before the letter, he would certainly have immediately resigned — and probably gone into exile — after he received it. But Meade never did receive it, because Lincoln never sent it. He waited until the following morning and then decided, on reflection, not to send the letter after all. Instead, he wrote on the letter: "to Gen. Meade, never sent, or signed." It then went into filing, and did not reappear for over a century.

Lincoln experts all cite this story, and marvel at Lincoln's humility, his self-control, and his fantastic character. But when I first heard about this letter, I could not help thinking to myself – humility? – if Lincoln was that humble, surely he would have taken the letter and ripped it to shreds. By preserving it in his files and noting that he had never sent it, wasn't he ensuring that posterity would know just how "humble" and "restrained" he was? Where is the humility in that?

But in reality, this query regarding Lincoln's behavior is based on a false understanding of humility. Because we all imagine humility to mean a complete lack of ego: "nothing is about me and my opinions are not that important." But this is not the definition of humility at all, it is a definition of low self-esteem. Ego is not evil. It is only when ego propels a person into narcissism and self-indulgence that it become evil and destructive. Self-confidence which leads someone to stand up for truth is a paramount trait of good leadership, and coexists beautifully with humility. When something is for the greater good, even the humblest person on earth can stand up for what they believe in. Humility only becomes evident and relevant when no purpose is served by projecting one's ego.

When it came to the duties of the presidency, Lincoln was fierce. But when he felt the need to vent his personal frustrations, and to settle a score with a recalcitrant general, Lincoln was humble – indeed, he was the humblest of men. But how would anyone learn that lesson if no one knew that Lincoln had written the letter and then decided not to send it? Lincoln wanted future generations to learn this important lesson in humility, and what better way to ensure they would than to file away the contentious letter he had never sent.

Moses was undoubtedly the humblest person who ever lived. But when it came to a situation involving the greater good, he allowed his ego, his self-confidence, his genuine superiority, to act and be heard. When approached by God to lead the Jews out of Egypt, Moses genuinely felt he was not the right person – surely there were others among the Israelite elders who were more up to the task? And so he spoke up, for the greater good. Later on, when he realized that the Jews had worshipped a golden calf – Moses genuinely felt that the Tablets were too precious for them, and so he smashed them, for the greater good. And he was absolutely right – as God confirmed.

In fact, each time Moses remonstrated, argued and pleaded with God, using his position and even his name as leverage – it was all for the greater good. But when it came to the word *vayikra*, Moses was convinced that no greater good would be served by anyone knowing that he had personally communicated with God. In his view using the word *vayikra* was nothing more than self-indulgent ego. That was why he asked God to take out the *aleph*.

Except that God refused, and insisted on leaving the *aleph* in, wanting a record to exist that would help us differentiate between using one's ego for the greater good and allowing ego to turn you into a narcissist. It was on this basis, and this basis alone, that Moses agreed to keep the *aleph* in *vayikra* — but only as long as he could shrink it, to add the lesson that humility must never be misunderstood as a lack of backbone. Instead, humility is defined by a complete disinterest in self-promotion or self-projection, unless a greater good is involved.

NOT THE END OF THE WORLD

first published March 16th, 2018

The Chinese philosopher Confucius (551–479 B.C.E.) is purported to have said, "If you make a mistake and do not correct it, this is called a mistake."

I am not sure if I find the fact that nothing much has changed in human nature over the past two and a half thousand years gratifying or depressing. Perhaps it's a mixture of both. The world that surrounds us is obsessed with perfection—an obsession that often results in wanton self-destruction. In the final analysis, there is no such thing as perfection, and while we may hold up an ideal that equates with perfection, we would be foolish to pretend there is any such thing.

Years ago, when I was the rabbi at The Saatchi Synagogue in London, we invited Nigella Lawson to speak for us at a Friday night dinner. Nigella is a well-known and much-loved TV chef in the UK, whose father Nigel Lawson was Chancellor of the Exchequer in Margaret Thatcher's government. That Friday night Nigella closed her talk with a story that I found both poignant and valuable. She told us that on one occasion she had prepared a cake for her TV show with the cameras rolling. After blending the various ingredients and pouring the mixture into a cake pan, she stuck the pan into the oven so that it could bake. When she took it out, despite having done everything by the book, the cake had developed a large deep crack straight down the middle.

The show's director pressed her to prepare another cake off camera. He told her that the crew would film the new and presumably unblemished cake being taken out of the oven, and the viewers would then see a perfect cake as it was meant to be. But Nigella rejected the director's suggestion, because she felt this was a wonderful opportunity to present the viewers with life as it really is. Even a cake prepared properly can, for no apparent reason, have an ugly crack going through it. That is real life, and real life isn't perfect. Mistakes happen, things go wrong, and embracing this reality is healthy and constructive.

The recent passing of Stephen Hawking (1942-2018), arguably the most famous scientist of the modern era, has caused quite a stir in the media. In 2013, during a lecture he gave at Cedars Sinai Hospital in Los Angeles, Hawking made a startling admission, informing the audience that his earlier-held belief that everything swallowed up by a black hole would be lost forever was wrong, and had probably been the biggest blunder of his scientific career. He now believed that there was something that could escape from black holes – radiation.

Hawking's astonishing confession was undoubtedly prompted by a very similar statement made by his illustrious scientific predecessor, Albert Einstein (1879-1955), who initially altered his general theory of relativity to take into account his belief that the Universe was static, and does not expand, by proposing something called the Cosmological Constant. When some years later, the Russian mathematician Alexander Friedmann (1888-1925) proposed an expanding universe model in what is now called the Big Bang theory, and Edwin Hubble (1889-1953) demonstrated Friedmann's theory as true with empirical evidence, Einstein lamented his Cosmological Constant theory, viewing it as his "greatest mistake".

One of the hardest sections of the Torah for us to relate to is the Book of Leviticus (Sefer Vayikra). Neither animal sacrifice nor meal-cake sacrifice has been practiced by Jews for almost two thousand years, and nonetheless, year after year, as the Torah cycle reaches Vayikra, we read the details of sacrificial activity by priests in a temple setting, and wonder to ourselves how any of this is relevant to us. Reform Judaism has long dispensed with references to sacrifices in prayer; it was one of the first ritual observances to be excised in their zeal to remodel Judaism in the nineteenth century. But Orthodox Jews continue to include sacrifices in their daily prayers, and the section of the prayer service known as *mussaf* on Shabbat and festivals is devoted to the extra sacrifices offered on these days when the Jerusalem Temple was active.

I will not presume to resolve this vexed issue in a brief article, but at the very least I will offer my understanding as to why practical responses to a variety of aspects in our lives, in the form of sacrifices, served an important purpose, and could help us draw powerful lessons for our own lives, even if these sacrifices are no longer brought. In Parshat Vayikra, the first portion of Sefer Vayikra, the Torah instructs us regarding a variety of sacrifices. One of them is the "sin-offering" (Lev. 4:27): וְאִם נֶפֶשׁ אַחַת תֶּחֱטָא בִשְׁגָגָה מֵעַם הָאָרֶץ – "if an individual from among the people shall sin unintentionally by transgressing one of the commandments of God," a sin-offering must be brought by the unintentional sinner.

Truthfully, the fact that one is required to bring an offering for an entirely inadvertent act is puzzling. What could possibly be the point? What's done is done, and let's just move on. But it would appear that the sin-sacrifice gives a practical application to an important value – the acknowledgement of one's mistakes, and the opportunity to learn from them. By offering up a sin-sacrifice we are reminded of our error in a formal setting, even if the error was entirely innocent. We can use the opportunity to acknowledge our human frailty, and embrace the chance to reflect on how we did things in such a way that allowed a mistake to happen, and in that way ensure that the mistake doesn't happen again.

The Talmud teaches us (Gittin 43b): "A person does not properly grasp a Torah principle unless he has erred in it." The pattern of human behavior always includes mistakes, and by bringing the sacrifice we are showing that our cakes can have a giant crack in them, without the whole world collapsing around us. And after all, if geniuses like Hawking or Einstein could admit to their mistakes, why can't we do it too? It's not the end of world.

NOT BOUND BY THE LAWS OF CONVENTION

first published March 18th, 2015

I am going to depart from my normal practice and start this article from the end. Rather than examine a contemporary topic and bring it around to the Torah portion, I will begin with a theme from the Torah portion and relate it to a current burning issue: Bibi Netanyahu's stunning victory in the Israeli elections. Let's begin with what is possibly the most famous debate between the two medieval rabbinic titans, Maimonides ("*Rambam*"; 1138-1204) and Naḥmanides ("*Ramban*"; 1194-1270).

Maimonides was the author of a major philosophical work called *Moreh Nevukhim* ("Guide for the Perplexed"), as well as *Mishneh Torah* ("Repetition of the Torah"), the first comprehensive organized code of Jewish law. He was also the foremost rabbinic rationalist of his day, always attempting to understand Jewish history and Judaism through the prism of rational ideas. Naḥmanides, although trained in medicine and philosophy, is best known as a staunch fundamentalist, who refused, for example, to explain away biblical miracles by finding logical explanations for them. Nor would he mitigate disturbing Jewish practices by offering reasoned justifications for their origins – both of which Maimonides did wholeheartedly in *Moreh Nevukhim*.

In Parshat Vayikra we find the perfect storm for these two conflicting worldviews when we are introduced to the concept of mandated animal sacrifice in the context of the wilderness sanctuary – the Mishkan. These laws later became the central feature in the Jerusalem Temples, only ceasing with the Roman destruction of Jerusalem in the year 70 C.E.

But before delving into the disagreement between Maimonides and Naḥmanides, it is worth noting that by the time they debated this topic, no Jew had sacrificed an animal for religious purposes for well over a thousand years. Maimonides was clearly conscious of the fact that the "progressive" religions of his age, Islam and Christianity, saw animal sacrifice as primitive. This contemporary reality no doubt resulted in the infiltration into the Jewish world of a revulsion for animal sacrifice, and Maimonides clearly felt compelled to defend animal sacrifice against Jews who questioned it. And little has changed since then. We, too, have ambivalent feelings toward animal sacrifice, as we puzzle over the purpose of offering up slaughtered animals to a non-anthropomorphic deity.

Maimonides writes that the Torah-mandated obligation to offer animal sacrifices to God was a consequence of the ubiquity of animal sacrifice in the dominant pagan culture at the time of the Exodus from Egypt and during the centuries that followed. God figured that it would be virtually impossible for those early Jews to abandon animal sacrifice, and that this problem would persist for as long as such practices continued to flourish. He therefore created a system in which all such worship was done only for His sake, and only according to His rules.

But Naḥmanides vehemently disagrees and sharply dismisses Maimonides' explanation, declaring it to be without any merit, and instead suggests that animal sacrifice to God preexisted any similar pagan worship, beginning with Abel and Noah, who both brought sacrifices in which God took great pleasure. Although Naḥmanides then offers his own rational explanation for animal sacrifice, although in the end he dismisses even this and concludes that the idea of animal sacrifice is independent of any explanation, conceived of by God as a way of connecting with His chosen people, whether we understand how that works or not. Our connection to God, says Naḥmanides, is about believing that He knows what is best for us, and that is why we do it. It is not about doing something because gentiles do it, or because the culture around us is so pervasive and overwhelming that trying to avoid doing it is pointless.

In truth, Naḥmanides' rejection of Maimonides by offering an alternative rationale would have been sufficient. It seems, however, that he was not satisfied with this alone. Evidently Naḥmanides felt compelled to dispel the notion that Judaism and Jewish values are a reaction to the world around us. What God wants from us, and who we are, is not contingent on the fads that come and go, nor on the realities that dominate one era but are historical footnotes in the next. Our mission and our passion for Judaism must be about what is right for us, beyond any time, and beyond any space.

Which brings me, finally, onto the subject of this week's Israeli elections, and Bibi Netanyahu's unexpected victory. My abiding impression of those who opposed Bibi during this election, whether it was those who protested over the way he initiated it, or whether it was the uproar over his supposed disrespect towards the White House by speaking in the US Congress, or whether it was the Israeli opposition parties' obsession with resuming "peace" talks with the Palestinians, was that it was all about what President Obama or the Europeans or what the UN think of the State of Israel.

What they all seem to be saying is that if the President of the United States is not happy about an Israeli Prime Minister speaking to Congress about Iran, then the Prime Minister must comply and cancel his planned appearance. Moreover, if the world continues to demand a two-state solution even though realities have shifted monumentally and overwhelmingly since the idea first crystallized on the White House lawn in 1993, Jews must obsequiously submit to this demand, notwithstanding the incredible risks. Such is life, they say, and shrug their shoulders. Our continued existence is contingent and conditional on the world around us, and to deny this is to deny reality.

But anyone who has seen what Naḥmanides says about sacrifice rejects this notion as theologically unsound heresy. Although Naḥmanides was always respectful of Maimonides, in this instance he rejected his thesis outright, calling it misguided and stupid. The existence of the Jewish people is not rational, and our continued existence cannot be based on what the world thinks of us or what they do as a result of what they think of us. And thankfully the Jewish citizens of Israel voted resoundingly for a destiny that defies the demands of the world, and that relies on God's promise that we will endure. God's relationship with us is not restricted to or confined by contemporary actualities, and yes, Bibi's victory means that we really are beyond time and space.

TZAV

HIGH OFFICE IS NOT ABOUT GLORY

first published March 24th, 2016

Thousands of words have been written about this year's AIPAC Policy Conference in publications across the world. It seems everyone has wanted to weigh in on this gathering of pro-Israel activists, as 18,000 Jews and gentiles who support Israel and are concerned for the strength of the US-Israel relationship gathered in Washington DC to reaffirm their commitment to this important cause. Although, of course, it wasn't just this that drew the intense interest in Policy Conference 2016. The real attraction at this year's Policy Conference was the appearance of the various candidate hopefuls for US president, and particularly the appearance of the real-estate mogul turned Republican firebrand, Donald J. Trump.

I sat in the vast Verizon Center among delegates from every state in the US and across the world, as the various candidates slugged it out, trying to outdo each other in their pro-Israel pledges and sentiment. Even if you were listening carefully it would have been difficult to choose between them based purely on what they said. If a strong US-Israel relationship is the key to your support of a candidate, then any one of them sounded fine. They are all suspicious of Iran, and concerned about increased violence in the Middle East, and committed to US military support for Israel, and critical of Palestinian terrorism and violence, and so on and so forth. And as expected, they all declared that the US-Israel relationship would be most safe in their hands, as opposed to any of the other candidates and the current administration.

Ultimately it is not the speeches that count. We need to know what these people are really thinking. Professional speechwriters prepared well-phrased speeches that were slickly delivered, but – for fear of sounding cynical – we have heard it all before. In this critical year, it is essential for us to know what is really going on in their minds, so that we don't allow our imagination to determine our opinions, and our actions. Over the past four years in particular, realities in the Middle East have shifted dramatically, and the person who occupies the White House for the next four years, or possibly eight, will need to have an unshakeable love of and commitment to Israel, so that Israel's many enemies will not be able to exploit trending animosity in situations where US support will be vital.

We learn this exact lesson as we read Megillat Esther on Purim. We see a king getting rid of his wife, a beautiful woman whose family origins had been the force that propelled him to the throne, on the spurious basis that her refusal to appear at his drunken party would foment rebellion against him across the Persian Empire. It turned out that his commitment to her was fickle, discarded easily when it was expedient. That same ruler, King Aḥashverosh, was also apparently willing to participate in genocide against the Jews, and then, later on, he changed his mind. On every occasion that he needed to make a major decision it was expedience which underpinned the decision, not conviction. His love for Vashti was dispatched in favor of showcasing his authority. Similarly, his commitment to his closest advisor, Haman, whose power was second only to his own, was ultimately cast aside on a whim.

King Aḥashverosh was not a man of principle; he was a fair-weather friend whose warm words of amity were, as Hollywood mogul Sam Goldwyn (1879-1974) once said, not worth the paper they were written on. The Jews of the Persian Empire were not safe even after the Purim story was over, and after King Aḥashverosh's death, the Jewish diaspora lobbied his successor to permit the exiled community to return to their homeland, Israel, and rebuild the Temple in Jerusalem.

In Parshat Tzav we encounter the duties of the High Priest in the Temple. The same man whose elevated position demanded that he preside over the Yom Kippur service was also expected to clean up the ashes from the altar (Lev. 6:3): וְהֵרִים אֶת הַדֶּשֶׁן אֲשֶׁר תֹּאכַל הָאֵשׁ אֶת הָעֹלָה עַל הַמִּזְבֵּחַ וְשָׂמוֹ אֵצֶל הַמִּזְבֵּחַ – "he should pick up the ashes where the fire has consumed the burnt-offering on the altar, and put them next to the altar." The commentaries all puzzle over this instruction for the High Priest to carry out such a lowly task. Couldn't one of the ordinary priests have done it?

The powerful answer to this puzzling question is that the embers on the altar embodied the continuity of Jewish life. Each and every day the Menorah in the sanctuary was lit using fire taken from the altar, and it was also used to burn the sacrifices of the day. If that fire was ever extinguished all the sacred functions of the Temple would cease, and the High Priesthood would have been a redundant job. The message of *terumat hadeshen* – the disposal of the ashes so that the altar fire wouldn't die out – was to stress the importance of continuity and consistency, and even the holder of the most elevated position in Judaism must be cognizant of the fact that no task is too insignificant when continuity and consistency is at stake. That was why the High Priest himself would carry out this lowly task. His office was not about glory; it was about the service of God, and representing the will of God as spiritual leader of the people.

With this in mind as I reflect on my three days in Washington DC, having witnessed candidates and political leaders revel in the glory and hype of their role in US politics, I must admit that none of the pomp and ceremony around them particularly impressed me. Ultimately what we need to be looking for is devoted attention to the small details of the US-Israel relationship, as well as a genuine commitment to consistent support for Israel that will transcend electoral needs and political pressures. It is these qualities that are the mark of true leadership and true friendship.

ONLY THE FINEST AND THE BEST WILL DO

first published March 26th, 2015

T he truth is, it was probably inevitable. Two nice Jewish boys who ended up as partners in an internationally acclaimed food brand were bound to decide that they needed to produce a "Kosher for Passover" product before they retired. I refer, of course, to Ben Cohen and Jerry Greenfield, the Brooklyn-born founders of the world's quirkiest ice-cream brand, *Ben & Jerry's*, who recently launched a *charoset*-flavored ice-cream just in time for Pesach.

Although, it isn't so surprising if you consider the frankly staggering Passover product sales statistics. According to Lubicom, the leading marketing consultant for the kosher food industry, the Passover product business is worth a cool $2.5 billion in North America alone, of which $86 million is generated by the sale of matza. Which could mean that Ben and Jerry had nothing to do with the blatant exploitation of Pesach by their eponymous brand. After all, Unilever obtained a majority stake in their business in 2010, and since then the company has relentlessly pursued every possible avenue to capitalize on the frozen dessert company's idiosyncratic image – and *charoset*-flavored ice-cream certainly fits with the business model. Perhaps, if this new flavor is successful, next year we will see a full range of Seder-night themed flavors, such as *karpas*, *afikoman*, and sickly-sweet wine – the sky is literally the limit!

The whole Passover product phenomenon is actually getting a bit much. Recently I went shopping for Pesach supplies, and I felt besieged by the proliferation of Passover product manufacturers, all of whom seemed to be greedily tempting me with countless familiar looking products, each one of them exponentially more expensive than their non-Passover counterparts. Every year I am asked by concerned community members how it is possible that rabbis "allow" such exploitation, as if we rabbis are somehow responsible for manufacturers who respond to the insatiable public demand for Passover products that are identical in every respect – including packaging – to their non-Passover versions.

Can I share a secret with you? I have discovered that there is a very simple way to avoid overspending on Passover supplies – simply don't buy "Crispy-O's Passover Cereal" (pseudo-Cheerios, made out of potatoes), or the appropriately named "Dayenu" company's pre-packaged "Passover Pizza" (pseudo pizza-base, made out of potatoes), or indeed any other such faux products. Instead, just buy an ample supply of raw potatoes before Pesach, and then cook and eat them over the festival in the way that potatoes ought to be eaten. In the meantime, once the festival is over, you can buy and eat as many chametz Cheerios and as much proper pizza as you want.

Although, when it comes to Seder night and the obligatory foods of the Seder, Jewish law is very explicit. You need to buy the best, even if it is more expensive. For example, don't drink grape juice for the Four Cups if you are healthy and able to drink proper wine – even if the wine is more expensive. And if you have a choice between "*kiddush* wine" and a decent table wine, you should certainly use the decent table wine, even if it will set you back more money. The same rule applies to matza. Although all

Passover matza is non-chametz, on Seder night we must use only the highest quality matza, called *shmura* matza – made from wheat which remained under constant supervision from the moment it was harvested. And don't be surprised if *shmura* matza is more expensive; just remember that we are expected to use only the best for Seder night.

In order to understand the reason for this *halakha*, let me share a relevant idea about Parshat Tzav. It begins with a commandment about the mandatory daily animal sacrifice known as *Korban Tamid* (Lev. 6:2): צַו אֶת אַהֲרֹן וְאֶת בָּנָיו לֵאמֹר זֹאת תּוֹרַת הָעֹלָה – "**command** Aaron and his sons and tell them that these are the laws of the *olah* offering." There is a marked difference between this sacrifice and all the others that stands out and demands an explanation. As opposed to all the other sacrifices, for which Aaron and his sons were merely instructed, for this sacrifice Moshe was asked to "command" (*tzav*) the priests, implying that without this "command" the priests would not have done what they needed to do. Which then prompts the question: what made the *Korban Tamid* a sacrifice the priests would treat improperly?

Rashi explains that the priests needed to be compelled to perform their *Korban Tamid* duties properly, as it was paid for by public funds, which might have led the priests in charge to be frugal. This prudence would inevitably lead to low-quality animals being used for the daily sacrifice, and for this reason the priests needed to be given strict instructions to buy the best, and only the best. But if anything, Rashi's rationale seems somewhat counter-intuitive. After all, if it wasn't the priests' money that was being used, and the *Korban Tamid* was being paid for from public funds collected specifically for this purpose, why would the priests be frugal? Surely they would want to perform this mitzvah in the best possible way?

The answer lies in the dual nature of most *mitzvot*, a duality that is less apparent in the *Korban Tamid*. All *mitzvot* which involve physical objects have both a material and a spiritual component. The material component centers around some physical sensation which benefits the person doing it – for example, in the case of an animal sacrifice, a part of it was eaten. Meanwhile, the spiritual component of a mitzva is the intent, and for a sacrifice there was also a part of it that was offered up to God.

But the *Korban Tamid* was different. Unlike most other sacrifices it was completely incinerated on the altar. As a result of this, according to Rashi, the priests might have felt that the material element of the sacrifice was less important, as the focus was entirely on the spiritual – and if it was all going to God, what difference would it make if the animal was cheaper and didn't have as much meat on it? All that really mattered was the intent.

This is why the Torah uses the word *tzav* – "command." God wanted to make absolutely clear that even when a physical object is used purely for spiritual purposes, it must still be of the highest quality. God placed us in a physical world and gave us an appreciation of quality and beauty so that we can discern the best and serve Him better by using it. For this reason, when it comes to Pesach, even though we might think "it's only matza, so who cares?" or "sweet *kiddush* wine will do" – we need to remember the word *tzav* and realize that in the service of God, only the finest and the best will do.

FAITH IS CONTINGENT ON DOUBT

first published March 12th, 2014

The most intriguing aspect of the Purim story, and the principle feature that differentiates it from other Bible narratives, is its total lack of, or seeming lack of, Divine involvement. The events leading up to the salvation we celebrate on Purim seem, on the face of it, totally random – a somewhat lucky series of coincidences that resulted in the happy ending with which we are all so familiar. Ascribing some kind of supernatural causative force to explain these coincidences seems altogether rather contrived.

In fact, agnostics seize on instances such as the events of Megillat Esther to prove to themselves that those who have faith in God often saddle ordinary events with supernatural meaning, simply to create a raison d'etre for their religious beliefs, and with the story of Purim, at least superficially, this accusation seems to have some foundation.

The real question about Purim is why we insist on celebrating it to the degree that we do. While it is certainly the case that the Jews of ancient Persia experienced a fantastic reversal of fortune, ultimately it was the involvement of some well-placed people of influence and the success of a well-planned and well-prepared military campaign that really did it for the Jews. Why should any of this have any kind of religious significance, to the extent that it was turned into a religious holiday?

If anything, Purim should be considered a national holiday, a celebration of the Jewish nation's incredible resilience in times of crisis, a day that highlights how resilience and unity can make the difference between national destruction or national survival.

In Parshat Tzav we are given a positive commandment by God regarding the fire on the sacrificial altar (Lev. 6:6): אֵשׁ תָּמִיד תּוּקַד עַל הַמִּזְבֵּחַ – "a constant flame should burn on the Temple altar." This instruction is puzzling, as we are explicitly informed that a fire would descend from above to consume every sacrifice brought on the altar. Why bother with a "constant flame" if there is no practical need for it?

For an answer to this question we must turn to the *Sefer HaChinuch*, which informs us that every one of God's miracles is obscured by a certain degree of *teva* – a Hebrew word that we translate as "nature." In other words, there is some rational explanation as to how the miracle occurred, even though it is considered a miracle. Even when the Red Sea split and allowed the Israelites to flee the oncoming military might of the Egyptian army, the splitting sea was facilitated by a strong easterly wind – offering enough of a rational explanation for a doubter to argue that it was a natural phenomenon.

Similarly, with regard to the altar, we are commanded to ignite our own flame in order to camouflage the incredible miracle of fire descending from the heavens. And there is a distinct reason for this – a reason that cuts to the very core of faith, and to the essence of creation and even the meaning of life. The more obvious God is, the less value there is in believing in Him. If someone observes what they perceive to be an open miracle, and that catapults them into believing in God, the resultant faith conviction is just too easy. But if logic militates against belief, and one nevertheless chooses to see God's hand – that is a belief with real value.

God knows He's God, but we were created with the ability not to believe in Him, and with the ability to rationalize and deny. If, in spite of our instinctive agnosticism we still see God and recognize His hand in seemingly ordinary events, we are fulfilling the very purpose of our creation. And there is no festival more perfect than Purim that can enable us to celebrate this important aspect of faith. If we can see God in a story devoid of prophecy and supernatural miracles – that is a real demonstration of our faith, and a true cause for celebration.

SHEMINI

THE WORK OF YOUR HANDS

first published March 28th, 2019

Did the Democratic party's 2020 presidential candidates deliberately shun AIPAC's 2019 Policy Conference in Washington DC? It was a question I heard time and again at the Walter E. Washington Convention Center as the conference got underway this past Sunday. As far as Vice President Pence was concerned, there was no doubt. "As I stand before you," he declared during his address, "eight Democrat candidates for president are actually boycotting this very conference." Some in the audience of 18,000 booed and hissed, while the *Washington Post* took the vice president to task, questioning the veracity of his statement.

But while the semantics of the word "boycott" might vex journalists and pundits, the facts speak for themselves. Eight candidates publicly confirmed in advance that they were not going to attend, citing a range of reasons – including "scheduling conflicts" and meetings with AIPAC delegates on Capitol Hill – although one of them, Bernie Sanders, let it be known that his absence was a deliberate rebuke, resulting from his concern "about the platform AIPAC is providing for leaders who have expressed bigotry and oppose a two-state solution." Meanwhile, another four of the candidates didn't issue announcements; they just didn't show up.

The fact that these absences come in the wake of Congresswoman Ilhan Omar's belligerent tweet presenting support for Israel as "allegiance to a foreign country" speaks volumes. Moreover, there is a misconception on the left that antisemitism is a right-wing problem. On Tuesday Omar's (Jewish) communications director Jeremy Slevin tweeted angrily in response to the recurrent assertions at AIPAC that his boss was an antisemite. "Antisemitism is a right-wing force," he thundered, repeating the phrase another seven times in the same tweet. But he could not be more wrong.

The difference between right-wing antisemitism and left-wing antisemitism is very simple. On the far right they readily acknowledge their hatred of Jews, but on the left they deny that any such hatred exists. Unsurprisingly, there are no Jews on the far-right – there are, however, plenty of Jews on the progressive left, many of whom have eagerly embraced the insidious liberal progressive narratives that vilify Israel and its supporters, and they are simultaneously in complete denial about the lion's den they have made their home. No amount of logic will sway them, and their uncritical support actively enables trope-peddling hypocrites like Omar.

And to those who say there is nothing to worry about, on the basis that fringe opinions on the left pose no danger to the US-Israel relationship or Jewish Americans, just ask the Jewish community in the UK what they think of that. For decades Ken Livingstone and Jeremy Corbyn were dismissed as fringe politicians, referred to in the media as representatives of the "loony left". And then one of them became Mayor of London, and the other became leader of the Labour Party. Now, as the UK flounders in the midst of a mounting constitutional crisis, the chances of Jeremy Corbyn becoming prime minister seem quite real. And if he does, he will have been elected by an electorate who were bamboozled into believing he is not an antisemite, because "antisemitism is a right-wing force." In the meantime, hostility towards Jews and Israel is on the rise in the UK, all under the guise of legitimate criticism of Israel.

The Democrats who avoided AIPAC may not see themselves as antisemites, but by pandering to the zeitgeist – even as they deny that the zeitgeist is antisemitic – they have become unwitting partners in a trajectory towards a dark future. Whether it was a deliberate boycott or not won't make an iota of difference when that future arrives.

Meanwhile, I was delighted to note the increased attendance of overtly Orthodox Jews at AIPAC, including a noticeable number of black hats and yarmulkes. This marks a real change from years gone by, when kippot-wearing delegates were few and far between. In the past, whenever I challenged my Orthodox friends for not attending the conference, they made excuses – America's support for Israel is clearly God's doing, they said, so why waste time and money going to Washington?

Such quasi-religious justifications are nothing but a lame excuse. Actively supporting pro-Israel efforts at AIPAC and elsewhere is crucial – particularly if you are a fully observant Jew. In Shemini (Lev. 9), the Torah describes the various rituals that took place during the Mishkan consecration. Towards the end, Aaron raised his hands towards the people and blessed them. The

Midrash informs us that Aaron intoned the three verses of priestly benediction, although the actual words were only recorded in Parshat Nasso (Num. 6:24-27). A few moments later Moses joined Aaron in the tent of meeting, and when they emerged, they blessed the nation again; it was at this point that the glory of God entered the sanctuary.

How was the second blessing different to the first? Rashi cites a Midrash that has Moses and Aaron blessing the nation as follows: "May it be God's will that the Divine Presence rest upon the work of your hands," to which the nation responded: "May God's favor be upon us; let the work of our hands prosper and succeed." These same words were later recorded for posterity by King David (Ps. 90:17), and we continue to recite them each week at the conclusion of Shabbat, asking God for the work of our hands to be blessed during the week ahead. Although Aaron's initial blessing was important, it was all about God's blessings, as if the recipients were inanimate objects. But the second blessing changed that completely and took the task of any fulfilment of God's blessings to the people.

In order for God's blessing to work, it needs to rest upon the work of our hands. Yes, God is the source of all prosperity, but if we do not initiate, the prosperity blessing has nowhere to land.

That the most powerful nation on earth, the United States, has Israel's back at every turn is unquestionably God's blessing – but this blessing needs to rest upon the work of our hands, whether at AIPAC, on campuses, in the workplace, or in any other forum. And never has this fact been more important than it is today.

KOSHER PORK AND THE MESSIAH'S ARRIVAL

first published April 12th, 2018

The latest *kashrut* scandal to hit the news is not what you might expect. A couple of weeks ago, in an interview for Israel's widest read daily newspaper, *Yediot Aḥronot*, Rabbi Yuval Cherlow of Petach Tikva suggested that lab-grown pork, when it becomes available, will be kosher for consumption — and will even be permitted together with dairy products.

Science has been toying with the idea of producing meat and egg products out of laboratories for years. A controversial Silicon Valley company called Hampton Creek began working on an eggless mayonnaise in 2011. The company has now been renamed JUST—after the entire board of directors quit last year—and has had a lot of success growing meat from cells, after incubating them with heat and feeding them nutrients. The results are not just edible, but actually taste remarkably like the real thing.

JUST's CEO is Josh Tetrick (b.1980), a social entrepreneur whose devoted goal it is to create environmentally friendly meat and egg products. In a February interview for *Wired*, Tetrick claimed his company has finally made the faux-meat production process cost-effective enough to take to market, and by the end of 2018, an as yet undisclosed lab-grown meat product will start retailing in the United States, the first time such a product will have been made available in stores. And that's probably not a bad thing. Thanks to an insatiable and ever-growing demand for meat, and the modern world's streamlined industrialization of livestock farming, we eat far more meat today than at any point in human history.

Not that lab-grown meat will stop us eating animals—but it could help to drastically reduce the number. In the United States alone, a staggering 26 billion pounds of beef is eaten annually. And if you consider the fact that just one cow consumes as much as 11,000 gallons of water each year, and that livestock may be producing as much as 15 percent of the world's greenhouse gas emissions, any alternative that reduces this environmental footprint must surely be warmly embraced.

Tetrick's claim that his company's meat will be available to the public in stores later this year at affordable prices is nothing short of extraordinary. Just five years ago, in the full glare of the international media, Professor Mark Post (b.1957) of Maastricht University unveiled and then fried a "cultured beef" burger in London's Riverside Studios, at an event that was more like a freak TV chef show than a science-oriented press conference.

According to Professor Post, the unremarkable looking patty—predictably nicknamed "frankenburger" by the media—cost him and his team more than $330,000 to produce. The question posed to Rabbi Cherlow by *Yediot Aḥronot* was whether this kind of "meat" would have "meat" status according to Jewish ritual law, or if it would be considered "parev", which is how neutral food is referred to in rabbinic literature.

Rabbi Cherlow's response was that if the process of production results in a food completely losing its flavor and becoming inedible, which is certainly the case with lab-grown meat that is grown from cells, then it loses its original status, and there is no halachic prohibition against eating the meat product that emerges out of a lab-process together with milk, and one would even be permitted to eat the product if the foundation cells originated in pig meat, despite the fact that pork is strictly prohibited by Jewish law.

Rabbi Cherlow acknowledged that his opinion would be disputed by rabbinic colleagues who are more conservative in their approach than he is, although it seems he already has allies in the campaign for orthodox Jews to embrace scientifically produced meat. In 2013, Rabbi Menachem Genack of the Orthodox Union's kosher division, announced that the lab-grown patty unveiled by Professor Post could certainly be consumed together with dairy products. The only addition Rabbi Cherlow has made to Rabbi Genack's ruling is to include lab-grown pork on the list of permitted "meats," albeit this is extremely significant, given the visceral Jewish aversion to pig meat, an aversion that has its origins in Parshat Shemini.

I found Rabbi Cherlow's opinion particularly intriguing in light of a puzzling and somewhat obscure rabbinic prognostication regarding the kosher status of pork in the Messianic age.

Although we have no record of it in our Talmud and Midrash texts, a number of medieval rabbinic commentaries on the verse that proscribes pig meat for Torah-observant Jews (Lev. 11:7), quote a Midrashic source as saying: לָמָה נִקְרָא שְׁמוֹ חֲזִיר שֶׁעָתִיד לַחֲזוֹר לִהְיוֹת מוּתָּר – "Why is [the pig] called *chazir*? Because it is destined to be returned [*lachazor*] to permitted status."

Most rabbis have dismissed this prediction as an example of fanciful Midrashic hyperbole, just a small part of the wide and eclectic range of apocalyptic traditions regarding the Messianic age.

Even those rabbis, such as the early nineteenth-century conservative opponent of Reform Judaism, Rabbi Moses Sofer of Pressburg ("*Chatam Sofer*"; 1762-1839), who accept that pork will be permitted for consumption after the Messiah arrives, suggest that this will only happen because at that stage pigs will evolve into ruminant animals, like cows and sheep, thus removing the impediment for their permissibility.

The bottom line is that in the past there was no way any rabbi could ever have contemplated Jews eating pig meat, as that would have meant abandoning an explicit directive of the Torah – and even the Messiah would not have the mandate to legislate such a break with tradition. But perhaps Rabbi Cherlow has hit upon something we had all missed, and frankly, he might have missed it himself. What if it was possible to eat pork and bacon that does not come from a pig? Perhaps this ancient Midrashic prediction never meant actual pigs becoming kosher, but was telling us that when it becomes possible for Jews to eat pig meat – as it soon will, when lab-grown pork hits the market – it will be time for us to look out for the Messiah's imminent arrival.

ON THE DEATH OF AN ANTISEMITE

first published April 16th, 2015

Earlier this week, the German novelist and political activist, Günter Grass, died in Lübeck at the age of 87. I highly doubt that you have ever waded through his dense prose; he was certainly not a writer for the mass market. Nevertheless, his turgid verbiage and rather pompous air, along with storylines that dissonantly combined moralizing angst and amoral characters, clearly did not deter the decision makers at the Swedish Academy. In 1999 they awarded him the coveted Nobel Prize for Literature, and in their award announcement the judges fawningly praised him as someone "whose frolicsome black fables portray the forgotten face of history."

During the decades after the Second World War, Grass was a vocal spokesman for the cause of German atonement and contrition, pushing hard for social democracy, and advocating relentlessly for universal non-violence. Despite his socialist leanings, he was an outspoken opponent of aggressive left-wing radicalism, and he also opposed the reunification of Germany in 1989 and 1990, asserting that a reconfigured Germany would inevitably reassert itself as a dominant and aggressive nation within the international community.

Grass's own personal history was that of a child born into Nazism, and forced to grow up alongside the belligerent racism of his childhood milieu. He publicly acknowledged his membership of the notorious Hitler Youth, but everyone understood that no child growing up in those years could avoid it. There was never any mention of him having been a willing Nazi who deliberately took part in the German war effort, or worse.

Then, in 2006, we were hit with a shocking revelation. Apparently, in 1945, as Nazi Germany was crumbling in defeat, Grass served as a combat soldier, not in the regular army, but in the infamous Waffen SS. What was particularly stunning about this revelation was that at no time throughout his years of moralizing, and public efforts to help his country deal with its ignominious past, did he ever admit to or face up to his own shameful past. Thoroughly discredited, Grass descended into crude antisemitism and bitter anti-Zionism. In 2012, in a poem entitled "What Must Be Said," he ludicrously compared Israel to Nazi Germany, with the protagonist of the poem depicted as an Iranian survivor of an imaginary Israeli nuclear attack on Iran.

There is no surprise in any of this. Günter Grass joins a long and terrible list of so-called peace-loving moralists and self-declared friends of the Jewish community, who later turn out to be the greatest antagonists of the Jews. Grass had made such an effort to repel Germany's Nazi past, and to somehow make-up for it, that it seemed inconceivable that he was what he actually turned out to be. Sometimes it is this kind of enemy that is the scariest of them all – the friend who is actually your enemy. And it is this exact idea that prompted our Talmudic sages to single out one non-kosher animal as particularly reprehensible.

In Parshat Shemini we are given, for the first time, a definitive list of kosher and non-kosher animals and birds. Mammals, we are informed, are kosher if they are cloven hooved and ruminators. As an example of a mammal that does not possess both of these features, the Torah identifies the pig. The pig is not a kosher animal, and its meat cannot be eaten, despite the fact that it has cloven hooves, and can be easily domesticated for meat consumption purposes – simply because it does not ruminate. The absence of this crucial feature means its meat is forbidden.

What is interesting about the pig is that while other non-kosher mammals are not considered "bad," Jewish ritual law is particularly stringent when it comes to pigs, prohibiting not just the consumption of bacon and pork, but also the ownership of a pig farm, for example. The Talmud even suggests that one should avoid saying the Hebrew word for pig. So why are the rules regarding pigs so draconian?

The Midrash, in a passage discussing Rome and its behavior as a ruling power, explains the hostile Jewish attitude towards pigs, and therefore towards the Romans, as follows (see *Yalkut Tehillim*, 247:830): הַחֲזִיר הַזֶּה כְּשֶׁהוּא שׁוֹכֵב הוּא פּוֹשֵׁט טְלָפָיו לוֹמַר שֶׁאֲנִי טָהוֹר כַּךְ אֵלּוּ חוֹמְסִים וְגוֹזְלִים וּמַרְאִים עַצְמָם כְּשֵׁרִים – "When the pig lies down it stretches out its legs, as if to say: 'I am pure.' Similarly, these [descendants of Esav] plunder and steal, and portray themselves as honest." Rather than lie down on its legs and hooves while sleeping, as do the majority of mammals, the pig sleeps on its side, leaving its cloven hooves conspicuously visible. The Midrash is suggesting that this instinctive behavior is a deliberate fraud, hardwired into the pigs' DNA. By sleeping that way, the pig is attempting to mislead us into believing it is actually a kosher animal, when in truth it is not.

In an era when our greatest allies regularly declare their devotion to Israel, and to the survival of the Jewish nation, while vocally condemning those who speak ill of the Jews and of Israel, it might be wise to analyze which of these "friends" could actually be using their cloven hooves to distract us from seeing who they really are. The Günter Grass example should heighten our awareness, and should ensure that we constantly remain on our guard.

TAZRIA/METZORA

WHAT A BOLLYWOOD MOVIE CAN TEACH US

first published April 4th, 2019

Y ou will be excused for not having heard about the latest Bollywood movie sensation, a film called *Mard Ko Dard Nahi Hota*, which translates as "The Man Who Feels No Pain." The movie charts the story of a young boy, Surya, born with a rare medical condition that means he feels no pain. Beatings don't hurt him, and neither do broken bones or burns. The movie is partly a martial arts extravaganza, showcasing the latest in slow-motion action sequences, and partly a *Marvel Comics* style superhero movie, featuring an indestructible hero with a heart, who is pitted against an evil villain. The movie is already a runaway success – the YouTube trailer, uploaded in early March, has been viewed almost 9 million times.

The movie's central premise so intrigued me that I decided to investigate. Was Surya's condition merely science-fiction, a fantasy created to make the movie more exciting? Or was it actually a documented medical anomaly, used here by the moviemakers as a means to entertain? I soon discovered that CIP, or "congenital insensitivity to pain," is a real, if extremely rare, condition. Also known as congenital analgesia, there are less than 300 reported cases in the entire world. Most curiously, there is one village in Sweden, a tiny place called Vittangi, which just happens to be home to 40 CIP sufferers, and it is believed that the condition originated there.

But while Bollywood filmmakers may have framed CIP as a superpower, in reality the inability to feel pain is not a desirable condition. Feeling pain is crucial, as pain is used by the human body to identify problems so that they can be dealt with quickly and effectively. According to experts, "lack of pain awareness often leads to an accumulation of wounds, bruises, broken bones, and other health issues that may go undetected [and] these repeated injuries often lead to a reduced life expectancy."

In a 2017 interview with BBC Future, Stefan Betz, a 21-year-old German CIP sufferer, described how he can place his hand in boiling water and not feel any pain, and is even able to have an operation without anesthetic. Despite this, he thinks of his condition as more of a curse than a blessing. "People assume that feeling no pain is this incredible thing and it almost makes you superhuman," Betz said, "[but] for people with CIP it's the exact opposite. We would love to know what pain means and what it feels like to be in pain. Without it, your life is full of challenges."

Interestingly, there is a connection between CIP and Parshat Tazria. The Midrash on Tazria (*Vayikra Rabba* 15:4) opens with a strange parable. Someone pays a visit to the king's palace and the first thing he notices is a dungeon filled with a range of torture equipment. He is immediately reduced to a state of absolute terror, but the king calms his visitor down, telling him that the dungeon and implements of torture are not meant for him, rather "they are meant for disobedient serfs, while your experience at the palace will be good food, good wine, and a great time."

The Midrash explains that the parable is a metaphor of the Jewish nation and God. When the Jewish nation heard about the dreadful affliction known as *tsara'at*, they were understandably alarmed and petrified. God immediately reassured them that *tsara'at* was not meant for them; instead it was meant for the wicked gentile nations, while the Jewish nation's lot would be joy and bliss.

This Midrash is beyond puzzling. No gentile has ever been afflicted by *tsara'at*, as the entire purpose of this biblical malady is to keep the Jewish nation in check. What does the Midrash mean? It was only as a result of an explanation by the *Sefat Emet* commentary augmented by my new knowledge of CIP that I was able to make any sense of it. The *Sefat Emet* points out that it is the priest whose must declare when someone is fully cured of *tsara'at*, as a demonstration of the fact that in Judaism, priests are seen as paradigms of kindness. In which case, why must it be a priest – and no one else – who diagnoses the *tsara'at* in the first place? How is it kind to tell someone that they have a debilitating malady?

Perhaps the answer is simply that while good health is certainly good news, to know that you are not in good health is far better than not knowing, and can also be considered good news. Just ask a CIP sufferer like Stefan Betz what it means never to feel pain, and never getting the message when something is medically or physically wrong with you. Although pain may be uncomfortable, it is almost always a symptom of something more serious that needs to be addressed. Similarly, *tsara'at* is a symptom of something wrong that needs to be addressed; consequently, the priest who delivers that message is performing a great kindness by doing so.

The guy in the parable who visits the palace and spots the torture chamber is naturally fearful of gratuitous pain, as anyone would be, but the king reassures him that any pain for pain's sake is strictly reserved for the wicked among the nations; meanwhile, for him there will only be joy – namely, pain that will result in joy because it is a first step in the rehabilitation process which will see his relationship with God resurrected.

Particularly in an era when popping painkillers has become an ubiquitous addiction, and resulted in countless unnecessary fatal drug overdoses, we would do well to welcome wake-up calls when we get them, and to treat them as a blessing instead of a curse.

TRIBUTE TO A CONEY ISLAND SIDESHOW

first published April 27th, 2017

This past week, a remarkable breakthrough in the field of premature childbirth was announced.

An artificial womb – a plastic sac, filled with temperature controlled amniotic fluid to mimic the mother's womb – has apparently been successfully used in trials with premature sheep. The team behind the new technology believes these "wombs" could soon be used to transform the lives of newborn human babies.

The details of the project seem more like science fiction than real science. Lambs were "hatched" at the equivalent of 23-weeks in human pregnancy, and kept alive in artificial wombs until they were "born" at full term, delivered out of the artificial wombs into the real world. While floating inside the transparent sacs, the lamb fetuses developed normally, and if this technique could indeed be used for humans, it would radically improve the prospects for babies born so early in a pregnancy that they cannot breathe on their own, nor feed, or fight infection, without intensive and extremely invasive medical intervention, which scars the babies for life and can even cause severe intellectual disabilities or physical deformities.

Currently, what is known in medical terminology as the "limit of viability" — namely the earliest time during pregnancy that a newborn baby has at least a 50% chance of survival — is 24-weeks. But the risks of serious brain damage and other potential long-term handicaps at 24-weeks are extremely high, even if the babies survive. The new technology will not only bring the "limit of viability" to an earlier point, but will also reduce the long-term health complications so common in pre-term babies.

It is hard for us to comprehend that until just a century ago, the chances of survival for a baby born a few weeks early were almost zero. In the late 1870s, French obstetrician, Stephane Tarnier (1828-1897), invented an incubator for pre-term babies, inspired by chicken egg incubators he had seen at a farming exhibition. Suddenly, babies born too early began to survive into childhood, no different than their full-term counterparts.

In the United States the most outstanding premature baby pioneer was an enigmatic German-Jewish immigrant, Dr. Martin Couney (1869-1950), a man who may not even have been a medical doctor, but whose determination to ensure the survival of premature babies was streets ahead of mainstream medical practice. By the time he died in 1950, Couney had helped over 6,500 babies survive life-endangering premature birth during over fifty years of dedicated work in the field.

In the early days, when most ordinary parents were unable to pay for the cost of the intensive care required to help the babies survive, Couney funded his incubator ward by setting it up as a sideshow exhibition in Coney Island, New York, with visitors paying twenty-five cents to see the miniscule babies in their individual incubators. He was widely ridiculed, even criticized, for his efforts, and the New York Society for the Prevention of Cruelty to Children publicly accused him of exploiting the babies and endangering their lives by putting them on show. But history judges Couney differently, and today he and his fellow pioneers are revered for their efforts.

It is serendipitous that news of the artificial womb development was released in the week when we read Parshat Tazria, which records a mother's duty to separate herself from her husband and any holy object for a prescribed period after giving birth, and then to bring a penitential offering. Personally, I have always found these laws troubling. Surely giving birth should elevate one's level of sanctity, not reduce it? After all, why would childbirth render a mother ritually impure, forcing her to separate from her husband and God? And why is the period of ritual impurity twice as long after a girl is born than the time required for a boy?

I don't profess to fully understand the reasons behind our ancient laws of ritual purity and impurity, most of which do not apply nowadays as we do not have a Temple in Jerusalem.

What I do know with great certainty is that these laws have nothing whatsoever to do with cleanliness or hygiene, nor is a ritually unclean person considered a pariah, or sinful. Rather, they are expected to separate themselves and go through a process of ritual self-cleansing that is distinctive in each situation.

The most compelling explanation for ritual impurity is that a required period of separation, along with physical acts of self-cleansing, will undoubtedly involve much time for self-reflection and introspection, creating a closer bond with God once the process of purification is complete.

Similarly, the monthly separation required by Jewish law between husband and wife compels a regular reignition of the relationship with one's spouse, which, if managed properly, will refresh the mutual connection, creating a deeper bond with one's life-partner.

Perhaps the lengthy ritual impurity period after childbirth is a reflection of the great significance Judaism places in procreation. Although it is no longer the case, this week's news serves to remind us of the great risks associated with childbirth. With medical technology having profoundly reduced those risks, we have forgotten that until very recently many women were doomed never to have children, and many that did either died in childbirth or shortly afterwards, as did their newborn children.

We are all familiar with the Jewish idea that states: עוֹסֵק בְּמִצְוָה פָּטוּר מִן הַמִּצְוָה – "someone who is engaged in a mitzva is exempt from doing other mitzvot" (Sukka 25a). Could it be that God wishes for a mother who has just given birth to be devoid of any external obligations for an extended period? Is it the biblical version of mandated maternity leave? For forty days in the case of a boy, and for double that time with a girl, God expects nothing of the mother besides for the nurturing of herself and her newborn baby. Rather than wasting time on ritual duties, or on her marital relationship, she must devote every minute to herself and her new baby.

And yet, though there is nothing more holy than ensuring a newborn child and its mother are as healthy as possible, everyone has to go back to normal life eventually, and this is marked with a penitential sacrifice — not because childbirth has sullied the mother, but because rejoining society has as an inevitable consequence a reduction of the mother's attention to her newborn baby. And while the mother's attention to a baby boy is important, it is superseded by the mother's duties to a newborn girl, who will herself one day be the mother of newborn children.

THE PINOCCHIO NOSE PHENOMENON

first published April 23rd, 2015

News has been released that Disney is working on a live-action movie based on the nineteenth-century children's story, *The Adventures of Pinocchio*. This whimsical tale of the puppet that longed to be a boy has always fascinated me. The protagonist marionette comes to life shortly after he is formed by the gentle carpenter, Geppetto, and then traverses through a series of mishaps and adventures, full of pathos and tragedy, but also humor and charm. The original book, written by the Tuscan author Carlo Collodi (1826-1890) in 1881, is a timeless piece of literature, made exponentially more famous by Walt Disney's classic 1940 animated picture. Undoubtedly the live-action version will give the mischievous Pinocchio a whole new generation of fans, and further perpetuate his enduring popularity.

The most arresting and well-known aspect of Pinocchio's idiosyncratic features is unquestionably the growth of his nose every time he lies.

> *"Where are the gold pieces now?" the Fairy asked.*

> *"I lost them," answered Pinocchio, but he was lying – they were in his pocket. As he spoke, his nose, long though it was, became at least two inches longer.*

> *"And where did you lose them?" she inquired, innocently.*

"Er, in the wood nearby...." he responded, a little hesitantly. At this second lie, his nose grew a few more inches.

"Oh well, if you lost them in the wood," said the Fairy, "we can look for them and surely find them."

"Oh, yes, now I remember," Pinocchio blurted out, "I didn't lose them, I swallowed them when I drank the medicine!" At this third lie, his nose became so long that he couldn't even turn his head.

If he turned to the right, he knocked his nose against the bed or into the windowpanes; if he turned to the left, he struck the walls or the door; if he raised it a bit, he almost poked the Fairy's eyes out......!!

When I first saw the cartoon version of Pinocchio as a child I was very taken by the "your-nose-will-grow-if-you-lie" curse and actually imagined it to be true. There was this one man at the synagogue our family attended who had a really prominent nose, and I wondered to myself whether he had been a terrible fibber as a child, and never having made amends, found that his nose had stayed permanently elongated. Meanwhile, short-nosed people were, I assumed, all thoroughly honest.

A little simplistic, I know, but then again – wouldn't it be great if negative character traits could be identified via external physical signs in the people we come across in our daily lives? On the flip side, the danger of physical symptoms generated by uttering untruths would almost certainly ensure greater care in what we said. Just imagine what a difference the "your-nose-will-grow-if-you-lie" curse would make to an election campaign if every time a candidate lied we would see his or her nose grow a couple of inches. An amusing, if somewhat disturbing, thought.

All of this and more crosses my mind whenever I study the double Torah portion of Tazria/Metzora, which describes the various manifestations of a malady known as *tsara'at* in Biblical Hebrew, usually and incorrectly translated as "leprosy." The Torah gives us no indication as to why this disease affected people, although elsewhere we hear that Miriam, Moses' elder sister, was afflicted by *tsara'at* for speaking ill of Moses to her brother Aharon.

The medieval commentator Rashi explains that *tsara'at* results from having engaged in slander. He is quoting the first of seven opinions collated by the Talmudic sage Rabbi Yoḥanan in Tractate Arakhin (16a): "*tsara'at* can result from seven different causes: slander, murder, false oaths, immorality, arrogance, theft, or envy." The common denominator of these seven is that they are all behaviors which undermine the viability of a harmonious, God-fearing, and moral society.

Tsara'at publicly identifies its victims as corrupted individuals, and forces them to repent and rehabilitate themselves, while at the same time protecting society from their ill-effects.

So why does it no longer exist? Although codified as law by Maimonides ("*Rambam*"; 1138-1204), there is no incidence of this ailment in contemporary times, nor has there been for many hundreds or even thousands of years. The absence of *tsara'at* is mystifying. Surely there are plenty of people who would benefit from being afflicted by *tsara'at*, and wider society would certainly benefit in tandem.

Rabbinic commentaries have struggled with this question, particularly because the Torah goes into such vivid detail vis-à-vis identifying *tsara'at* and getting rid of it, as does the Talmud.

Some rabbis suggest that without the priestly expertise required to diagnose *tsara'at*, God removed it so as not to condemn sufferers to a lifetime of exclusion. Others suggest that it does still exist, but we are not qualified to recognize it. The nineteenth-century rabbinic luminary, Rabbi Akiva Eger (1761-1837), readily acknowledged that he was stumped by *tsara'at's* apparent extinction.

My own suggestion, based on an early rabbinic opinion that coincided its disappearance with the destruction of the Jerusalem Temple, is that if people genuinely aspire to spiritual greatness, they will welcome and embrace *tsara'at* as a tool for self-improvement, both individually and as a society. But with the degeneration and disintegration of such aspirations, crystallized by the destruction of the Temple, God decided to do away with it.

A society that is neither reflexively self-improving nor aspirational could not function smoothly and effectively if every individual who erred was afflicted by *tsara'at*. There would be a deluge of sufferers and its point would be lost. Just as Pinocchio's nose curse would be unworkable in real life, *tsara'at* today would be destructive instead of constructive. That this is the case is a poor reflection on us, perhaps, but in the meantime let us hope for a time when *tsara'at* will be welcomed by all as a guiding tool in our ongoing collective journey to elevated spiritual heights.

KEEPING UP WITH THE JONESES

first published April 11th, 2019

O n November 10, 1987, artist Arthur R. Momand died in New York at the age of 100 years old.

Although a short obituary appeared in the New York Times, his passing went largely unnoticed. Truthfully, this is hardly surprising, as even in his heyday he was hardly a household name – and his heyday ended almost 50 years before he died. Nevertheless, Momand ought to be celebrated for having made an indelible mark on both the English language and popular culture as the originator of the idiom "keeping up with the Joneses."

Fondly referred to as "Pop," Momand was a strip-comic artist originally hired by the *New York World* in 1905. A talented satirist, he succeeded in producing a number of popular strip-cartoons which were syndicated across the country. After his marriage in 1910, and flushed by his moderate success, Momand moved from New York City to Cedarhurst in Nassau County, where he soon found himself struggling to make ends meet as he attempted to stay materially on-par with his neighbors. As he later admitted, "we were living far beyond our means in our endeavor to keep up with the well-to-do class." By 1912 he had given up the fight and moved back to Manhattan, where he and his wife lived in a cheap rented apartment.

Momand was so affected by his encounter with the social-climbing fast-lane, it inspired him to launch a comic-strip to share his experiences. Originally conceived as "Keeping Up with the Smiths," the strip ended up being called "Keeping Up with the Joneses" and ran weekly from 1913 until 1938, charting the life of the fictional McGinis family. The comic's main focus was the family's endless efforts to "keep up" with the lifestyle of their neighbors, the never-seen but often-mentioned Jones family. The public loved it, and "keeping up with the Joneses" entered English vernacular, where it remained long after the cartoon was forgotten. The phrase is still used, describing those who compulsively engage in social competition.

The Hungarian game theory pioneer John Harsanyi (1920-2000), recipient of the 1994 Nobel Prize for Economics, posited that "apart from economic payoffs, social status seems to be the most important incentive and motivating force of social behavior." More notably, he added that "this concern for social status is perhaps more conspicuous in those societies, like the American, where the ruling ideology encourages a striving for upward social mobility, for movement to higher social status positions."

The sages of the Talmud were rather more direct, pithily observing (*Kohelet Rabba* 1:13) that "he who has one hundred will want two hundred, and he who has two hundred will want four hundred." The commentaries add that even when one hundred is enough, those who need to keep-up-with-the-Joneses will never be satisfied if others around them have two hundred.

Parshat Metzora records the purification process for a person afflicted by *tsara'at*, without which he or she cannot reenter society. *Tsara'at* was a disease afflicting those who engaged in *lashon hara* ("evil gossip") and it resulted in an enforced period of quarantine. After seven days of isolation, the priest would sacrifice a guilt-offering on the person's behalf and then wipe some of the blood on his or her right ear, thumb and big toe, as part of the rehabilitation process.

This unusual ritual has just one parallel in Jewish law—the inauguration of a new priest into active service. But why would a process marking the elevation of a priest, Judaism's most auspicious religious position, be echoed for an individual who has been ousted from society as a result of their antisocial behavior?

The Talmud (Sotah 9a) records the sin of the primordial serpent in the Garden of Eden, and reveals that God originally intended the serpent to be king of all beasts, portraying the snake as a creature that walked upright and communicated like a human being. But because the serpent "placed his eyes on that which was unfit for him, and desired that which was not given to him, what was in his possession was taken away from him."

The serpent is often used as a symbol of slanderous gossip; here it is told by God that it would never enjoy its food, an idea seen as a metaphor for the uselessness of slander as a tool for personal growth. According to the Talmud (Bava Batra 165a), only a minority of people stumble into a life of wanton immorality, although the same cannot be said about theft. However, no one – not one person – is immune to the temptation of *lashon hara*. This curious observation flies in the face of any rational understanding. Humans are primarily motivated by gratification, hence the fatal attraction of promiscuity and theft. But why would anyone be attracted to petty gossip if there is no material benefit?

It seems that our Talmudic sages understood human psychology only too well. Every person craves a sense of self-worth. Society actively promotes material competition as the medium by which we can attain our goals in life, and victory over others is seen as the way to measure our value. We are who we are only when we can be evaluated vis-à-vis our contemporaries – or so we are led to believe. But "keeping up with the Joneses" is a slippery slope. Instead of developing our inner potential we forge a path based on the success of others. Worst of all, we might resort to pushing others down so that we can rise above them. But rather than feeling accomplished, success in the rat race only results in us feeling vacant and needy – we may have one hundred, but we end up wanting double.

Our desire for self-worth results in *lashon hara*, in the mistaken belief that denigrating others will somehow elevate us. But *lashon hara* is a compulsion that drives us off our beaten track, diminishing our self-worth rather than building it up. The ordained priest of ancient Judaism was meant to embody the pinnacle of spiritual achievement, and the ordination ceremony confirmed that he was an outstanding individual. Using the very same ritual to initiate them as the one used for those emerging from *tsara'at* sends the message that there is no need for negativity to reach the pinnacle of who you can be. Rather than "keeping up with the Joneses," you could just be yourself.

ACHAREI MOT

ORTHODOX ANTIVAXXERS ARE BETRAYING GOD

first published May 1st, 2019

In February 1998, a group of medical professionals and scientists led by physician Andrew Wakefield published a research paper in the highly respected British medical journal *The Lancet*. The study focused on twelve children with developmental disorders that Wakefield and his colleagues had linked to the MMR vaccine. Most controversially, the study claimed that the MMR vaccine could result in autism.

Although Wakefield announced his findings at a press conference, initially the response was muted. But in 2001, after Wakefield began suggesting that the British government sponsored immunization program was unsafe, the anti-vaccination storm gathered strength. Hysterical parents shared anecdotal stories about their children, who they alleged had been adversely affected by the MMR vaccine, and a media firestorm erupted. Then, in 2004, an investigative journalist discovered that Wakefield's so-called study was heavily compromised; there were multiple undeclared conflicts of interest and Wakefield had manipulated evidence so that the study's "results" matched his thesis.

In 2010, after years of fierce debate, the study was finally retracted, and *The Lancet* admitted that its findings were "utterly false." Wakefield lost his medical license and was completely discredited. And yet, despite the fact that scientific consensus repudiates any link between the MMR vaccine and autism, and although the MMR vaccine's benefits clearly outweigh any risk, anti-vaccine campaigners continue to beat their drum. Particularly over the past few months this has become a serious issue among some strictly Orthodox communities in the United States, with a growing number of parents in these communities refusing to vaccinate their children claiming that it puts them at risk.

It was recently reported that there have been more than 700 recorded cases of measles this year in the United States – the highest number for decades, and more than 500 of those affected are people who have not been vaccinated. New York is the worst hit, and while it is not exclusively the Orthodox community who are at fault, New York city officials recently closed two Orthodox schools who refused to comply with an order to exclude unvaccinated children.

For clarity's sake, let me make my opinion on this issue very clear. Any parent who refuses to vaccinate their child is guilty of willful neglect and of endangering public health, and individuals and institutions who in any way enable those who refuse to vaccinate their children are guilty of gross negligence and a callous disregard for civic responsibility. Our duty as individuals extends beyond our own children and encompasses the community as a whole, and although I believe parents should be persuaded to comply with vaccination requirements, children whose parents categorically refuse to have them vaccinated should be forcibly vaccinated by public health officials without parental consent.

Part of the "antivaxxer" problem stems from a distrust of corporate medicine, but there is also this lingering notion that modern science has lumbered us with a greater susceptibility to disease by creating an infection-free bubble, which means we are all vulnerable to infection the moment we venture beyond it. Surely we would be safer if we were exposed to germs and built up natural immunity? Or so the argument goes. This theory has its roots in the notorious "hygiene hypothesis" first proposed by British epidemiologist David Strachan in 1989. Strachan suggested that the modern phenomenon of less infections in early childhood – the result of our obsession with hygiene – might explain the meteoric rise of allergic diseases such as asthma and hay fever over the past century.

It isn't a huge leap from there to imagine that "natural" measles is better than an injected manufactured vaccine version of the disease. But while there is an argument to say that cutting out bacteria completely might make us vulnerable, wanton exposure to bacteria is certainly far worse, and those who say the opposite are playing with people's lives.

Parshat Acharei Mot begins with a warning to the newly appointed High Priest, Aaron, informing him that he is forbidden to enter the inner sanctuary at will. To reinforce the message, the warning includes a mention of Aaron's two sons, Nadab and Abihu, who entered the inner sanctuary without permission and died. Rabbi Shmuel Bornsztain ("*Shem MiShmuel*"; 1855-1926) finds this idea puzzling. The Torah informs us that Nadab and Abihu died as a result of bringing improper incense. Talmudic and Midrashic sources offer a number of other explanations for their abrupt deaths – but none of them mention their uninvited presence in the inner sanctuary. In which case, how would their deaths serve as a warning to Aaron not to enter that hallowed spot?

To answer this question, we need a greater understanding of God's system of reward and punishment. Fault and virtue are not calculated based only on what a person does in isolation; rather it is calculated relative to who the person is and what that person is capable of. A mitzva performed by someone who lives a life largely without *mizvot* is valued in that context, while someone who grew up in a mitzva-observant family and community and then chooses to wantonly abandon his Judaism might be shown much less recognition for doing that very same mitzva. The more we include God in our lives, the greater the potential for God's displeasure when we fail – as opposed to someone who leads a life less connected to God.

Aaron's sons were guilty of a sin ordinary people would not have been punished for. Their elevated spiritual status meant increased scrutiny, and God punished them harshly exactly because they were so close to Him. To enter the inner sanctuary demands such a level of purity that even the slightest blemish results in a fierce negative reaction. That is why the inner sanctuary is reserved for the holiest day of the year, and only after rigorous preparation.

I don't need any scientist to tell me that a hygiene bubble might make me more vulnerable to germ exposure. And I get it – being vulnerable to infection is scary. But the advantages of our hyper-hygienic environment coupled with the astounding success of modern vaccines far outweigh the downside of any alternative, just as closeness to God is far better than never knowing God or not having God in one's life. If there is a risk attached to being close to God, it is entirely insignificant when measured against the benefit. And this message is one that religious Jews ought to understand better than anyone else.

HOW TO AGREE TO DISAGREE

first published April 26th, 2018

T he most significant political revolution of the modern era is the idea that dissent is not rebellion. The prevailing view for thousands of years was that a society cannot tolerate dissidents in its midst. The result was unbearable suffering for anyone suspected of deviating from the norm. Perceived as traitors and therefore a grave danger to society-at-large, dissidents were universally targeted, discriminated against, tortured and killed.

Jewish history is full of such persecutions, and we are all familiar with the attempts by ancient Persians, Greeks, Romans, Christians and Muslims to eliminate Jews and Judaism simply because Jews refused to accept the authority of a dominant power or creed. But we are not unique. The Romans were equally brutal with early Christians, who themselves turned out to be completely intolerant of any kind of dissent. Christian "heretics" were executed by Christians as a matter of course for centuries, the last one hanged by the Spanish Inquisition as late as 1826.

Meanwhile, Muslim dissenters continue to be murdered by their co-religionists to this day.

And people were not just killed for religious dissent. During the French Revolution's yearlong "reign of terror," more than

16,000 were guillotined – all of them for expressing viewpoints that clashed with the views of those in power.

Eventually France came to its senses, and with the execution of the killing frenzy's primary advocate Maximilien Robespierre in 1794, the idea that vocal opposition amounted to an existential threat was abandoned in favor of freedom of belief and expression, ideals that have become the hallmark of a free society. Three years earlier, the United States added the First Amendment to its constitution. This supplement to the country's foundation document was added to prevent Congress from ever getting in the way of individual freedoms, such as the freedom to practice a religion, the freedom to speak freely and publicly on any subject without fear of official sanction, and the freedom of the press, among others.

The effect of this revolutionary idea has been profound. We can all immediately recognize an oppressive regime when we see one, using the First Amendment as our yardstick. We have also come to accept that people are entitled to live in and benefit from a society, even if they profoundly disagree with some fundamental aspect of that society's ideals. Or, as one of the founders of Methodism, George Whitefield (1714-1770), put it, "we can agree to disagree," a phrase that entered popular culture after it was quoted as part of a generous-spirited eulogy delivered at his funeral by one of his staunchest opponents, John Wesley (1703-1791).

But are there limits to this axiom of modern values? The answer is a tentative 'yes', and there have been rare instances in which it became clear that First Amendment freedoms cannot be treated as a blank check, most famously in the 1919 United States

Supreme Court decision, "Schenck v. United States," when Judge Oliver Wendell Holmes, Jr. (1841-1935) established that the First Amendment did not protect speech that encouraged people to resist military service in a time of war, or as he famously put it, "the most stringent protection of free speech would not protect a man in falsely shouting fire in a theatre and causing a panic."

In my view there is an additional limitation that should be applied to freedom of speech, one that does not revolve around constitutional rights, but is nonetheless equally important. The modern State of Israel was founded on the same principles of democratic rights and individual freedoms as are found in the rest of the Western world. You only need to glance at the Israeli press, or familiarize yourself with Israel's national discourse, to see how this ideal has been embraced to its core. And yet there is something palpably uncomfortable about the freedom of expression in Israel that undermines the viability of that freedom, and even of the state itself. I am referring to the unbridled aggression and bristling discord that threatens to tear the country apart.

Parshat Kedoshim contains one of the most powerful expressions of human compassion ever composed (Lev. 19:18): וְאָהַבְתָּ לְרֵעֲךָ כָּמוֹךָ אֲנִי ה' – "you shall love your neighbor as yourself, I am God." The great Talmudic sage, Hillel, informed a prospective convert not to do to others that which he did not want done to him, telling him that this principle was all he needed to know, as it contained the entire Torah. A century later, Rabbi Akiba called the ideal of loving your neighbor as you do yourself the most important Torah principle of all. But what does it really mean? If someone is your friend, why would you need an instruction to love them? And if they are not your friend, why should you love them? Besides, how is it possible to love someone as much as you love yourself? What exactly does loving yourself actually mean?

There are several Hebrew words for "friend," but the one chosen for this directive – רֵעַ – is curious in that it contains the same letters as the Hebrew root word for "bad." Perhaps the Torah is telling us that although we may not be perfect, and our views or way of life may seem wrong to others, we nonetheless expect to be treated with respect, compassion, and even love, by those who are different or think differently to us.

For this reason, to the extent that any of us feels the need to express our disagreement with others, God directs us to be mindful of how we articulate those opinions by instructing us to reflect on how we would want those who disagree with us to articulate their disagreement.

We are entitled to our opinions, and to disagree with others. We are also entitled to express our opinions, even if they are a minority view. But confrontation and hostility must be completely out of bounds. Although we may agree to disagree, we must always remain agreeable.

THE SADDUCEES OF MODERN AMERICA

first published May 5th, 2016

S eymour Rosenbloom is a Conservative rabbi who gave 36 years of distinguished service as the spiritual leader of Congregation Adath Jeshurun in Elkins Park, Pennsylvania. Rosenbloom graduated from the Jewish Theological Seminary in 1972, and we must assume he studied under both Professors Saul Lieberman (1898-1983) and Professor Abraham Joshua Heschel (1907-1972). I mention their names only because I had wondered how they, in particular, might have reacted to the opening line of Rosenbloom's recent article, in which he declared that "the Conservative movement's leadership must drop its ban on Conservative rabbis officiating at interfaith weddings — before it's too late."

Apparently, the Conservative movement has forbidden any of its rabbis from officiating at interfaith marriages, and both bride and groom must be Jewish from birth or have converted to Judaism prior to the wedding. Most Reform rabbis have long abandoned this taboo, and Reform Judaism's Central Conference of American Rabbis has chosen to tolerate this aberration, with the official Reform website stating that "rabbis are given autonomy in such matters and each rabbi interprets Jewish tradition according to his or her own understanding." Rosenbloom argues that it is time for Conservative Judaism to move in the same direction, declaring that: "Reality has overtaken us. Sixty percent of Jews who wed, marry someone from another faith. The Conservative movement's prohibition is ineffective as policy if our goal is to reduce intermarriage."

He has a point. Marriages between Jews and non-Jews are on the rise, and refusing to embrace such unions has resulted in an alarming demographic decline. Rosenbloom's own community numbered 1,000 families when he began his tenure in 1978. He retired in 2014, by which time that number had shrunk to 650 families. Moreover, as he admits in the article, this subject is personal – last year his stepdaughter became engaged to a non-Jew and asked him to officiate.

"We talked about it. They wanted the ceremony to be as Jewish as possible… so I agreed. Looking back, I can't believe I even gave it a second thought."

There was another interesting article that appeared recently, also authored by a Conservative rabbi, Professor David Golinkin (b.1955). Framed as a ruling on Jewish ritual law, the article explains why the custom for Ashkenazi Jews to refrain from *kitniot* – rice and legumes – on Passover, can be discarded, as "it causes exorbitant price hikes… it emphasizes the insignificant and ignores the significant… it causes people to scoff at the commandments… [and] it causes unnecessary divisions between Ashkenazim and Sephardim." You might be thinking that Golinkin also has a point, and one that might be closer to your own heart than Rosenbloom's point.

Rabbi Samson Raphael Hirsch (1808-1888) was the rabbi of Frankfurt's breakaway Orthodox community, after it became evident that the umbrella Jewish community in that city was drifting ever further away from normative Judaism, causing fully observant Jews under its auspices to drift away with it. His commentary on the Torah, published in German between 1867 and 1878, is a tour-de-force. It contains numerous coded references to his struggles with the Reform, and there is one particularly relevant example in Parshat Acharei Mot.

Rabbi Hirsch notes an anomaly regarding the Sadducee view of the Temple incense offered up by the High Priest on Yom Kippur. The Sadducees were a sectarian group that emerged during the Second Temple period that discarded rabbinic law as practiced by their nemesis, the Pharisee sect. They became 'purists', only willing to follow laws exactly as they appeared in the text of the Torah and claiming that rabbinic law was a human creation with no basis in the will of God.

When it came to the Yom Kippur incense, however, they made an unusual exception.

The Torah states (Lev. 16:12): וְלָקַח מְלֹא הַמַּחְתָּה גַּחֲלֵי אֵשׁ מֵעַל הַמִּזְבֵּחַ... וּמְלֹא חָפְנָיו קְטֹרֶת סַמִּים... וְהֵבִיא מִבֵּית לַפָּרֹכֶת וְנָתַן אֶת הַקְּטֹרֶת עַל הָאֵשׁ – "He should take a full pan of fire coals from the altar, and a handful of incense, and bring them into the sanctuary, and then put the incense onto the fire."

The order is clear – outside the sanctuary the incense remained separate from the fire, and only once the High Priest was inside the sanctuary, he put the incense onto the fire. But the Sadducees insisted that the incense must be placed onto the coals before he entered the sanctuary, in defiance of the Torah's explicit instructions, and explained this inconsistency in their position by saying that it would be disrespectful to treat God differently than one treats a human being. Incense is always lit before someone enters a room, so that the excessive smoke the ignition creates will not be irritating. To do it any differently for God would be extremely rude, they said.

Rabbi Hirsch suggests that this idea is nothing less than a negation of the Torah. To suggest that one should change the incense production procedure on the basis of human concerns places man before God. On that basis, says Rabbi Hirsch, it is evident that rather than having disappeared, the Sadducees have endured, today embodied by people who reject the authority of rabbinic law, and who ridicule or discard any mitzvah or custom that makes no sense to them, or offends their morality or sensibilities. Rather than serve God, they seek God only on their own terms. If something makes no sense (to them), it must be abandoned as an outmoded useless relic.

Forbidden interfaith marriages and the prohibition of *kitniot* on Passover share, on the face of it, very little in common. But the reasons that underpin their rejection by those who oppose upholding these laws share a lot in common. It is all about doing away with something that is inconvenient. If we value our history, and the religious system that has been developed over millennia, we are best advised to cling to all aspects of it that have preserved us and delivered us as committed Jews into the present, in order for us to make it into the future.

KEDOSHIM

A TRUE FRIEND INDEED

first published May 9th, 2019

We all need friends. We all have friends. And we all have something to say about friendship.

But defining friendship is far more elusive than you might think. What exactly makes a friend? How does one know if one has experienced true friendship?

Socrates (c.470 – 399 B.C.E.) urged caution before committing to any friendship but encouraged steadfast loyalty once such a bond is formed: "Be slow to fall into friendship; but when you are in, continue firm and constant." Intriguingly, though, he does not tell us how to identify a friend. Abraham Lincoln (1809-1865) was similarly obscure when he quipped, "do I not destroy my enemies when I make them my friends?" The sentiment is wonderful, but surely one needs to know what friendship is in order to transform an enemy into a friend?

The pioneering gossip columnist Walter Winchell (1897-1972), who spent his career charting the lives of others in his widely syndicated column, defined a real friend as someone "who walks in when the rest of the world walks out." Tragically, despite leading a roller-coaster social life, Winchell seems to have experienced more of the latter than the former. During his final years the man who single-handedly invented the concept of modern celebrity was a barely remembered recluse; his funeral in 1972 was a lonely affair, attended by just one person – his adopted daughter Walda.

Thomas J. Watson (1874-1956), pioneering founder of IBM, understood friendship as a relationship which transforms you into a better version of yourself: "don't make friends who are comfortable to be with; make friends who will force you to lever yourself up." A noble ideal, but does it accurately define the friendships we all have with our friends? The noted humorist and writer Arnold Glasow (1905-1998) saw friendship rather differently than Watson. In his view, "a loyal friend laughs at your jokes when they're not so good and sympathizes with your problems when they're not so bad." Surely a more familiar model of friendship.

So which is it? Are our friends those people who challenge us to be our best, or are they more like a comfortable sweater, allowing us to feel okay just the way we are? The Torah weighs in on friendship in Parshat Kedoshim, with one of the most quoted biblical verses of all time (Lev. 19:18): וְאָהַבְתָּ לְרֵעֲךָ כָּמוֹךָ – "you shall love your fellow as yourself." This enigmatic directive has generated numerous interpretations. One of the earliest is in *Pirkei Avot* (2:10), which suggests that we give our friends the same level of respect we expect for ourselves. But a little later on (4:12), the mishna quotes Rabbi Eleazar ben Shamua as saying: "let the honor of your student be as dear to you as your own, and the honor of your friend as the respect for your teacher, and the respect for your teacher as the reverence of heaven." The clear implication of this statement is that we are to have more respect for a friend than we would ever demand for ourselves.

To dismiss this inconsistency as a difference of opinion is problematic; divergent opinions are more routinely quoted side-by-side in the Talmud, and here they are separated by two chapters.

More puzzlingly, Rabbi Eleazar ben Shamua's position seems to contradict the verse in Kedoshim, where the expectation is explicit – treat your friend as you would yourself, not as you would treat someone greater than yourself.

In *Moreh Nevukhim* ("Guide for the Perplexed), Maimonides ("*Rambam*"; 1138-1204) quotes the Greek philosopher Aristotle (385-322 B.C.E.), who noted that people have many different sorts of friends during the various stages of their lives. Most of these friends are people with whom one shares the simple experiences of life. Nevertheless, although we may enjoy their company, oftentimes we maintain a facade so that our vulnerabilities remain hidden. Maimonides refers to this kind of relationship as *ahavat hato'elet*, which loosely translates as "a relationship of convenience."

Finding a friend who we can trust with our innermost secrets and weaknesses is exceptionally rare, and almost all of our friendships are *ahavat hato'elet*. That is not to say these friendships are meaningless, or even superficial; rather they are more like the friendship described by Glasow, as opposed to the one defined by Watson. That is because a Watson-friendship can only happen when one is absolutely certain that this friend is both dedicated to your growth and motivated by your best interests. As it turns out, there is no inconsistency in *Pirkei Avot*, as each mishna identifies a different kind of relationship.

The majority of our friends – those who fall into the Glasow category – should be treated as we would wish to be treated by them. Most of our friends are in this group, even our lifelong friends. They are people whose company we enjoy and appreciate, but the friendship does not venture beyond that. The Torah directs us to love these friends as we do ourselves, thereby encouraging us to elevate the relationship beyond one of mere convenience and self-interest into one of meaningful affection.

Meanwhile, Rabbi Eleazar ben Shamua is referring to a different kind of friend – those rare friends whose friendship results in us reaching our true potential. This type of friend – the Watson friend – is not just a pal or buddy, rather they are more like a teacher who needs to be venerated and respected. Most importantly, this is the type of friend we must try to be for others, so that we are not merely the person who laughs at jokes and listens to complaints. Because ultimately, the secret of good friendship is to remove self-interest from the equation, and to put our friend's needs above our own.

Or, as the American writer Dale Carnegie (1888-1955) put it so well, "you can make more friends in two months by becoming interested in other people than you can in two years by trying to get other people interested in you."

THE TRUTH ABOUT TIKKUN OLAM

first published May 4th, 2017

There has always been an inclination among Jews to present contemporary political views as being in line with Judaism and the doctrines of the Jewish faith. Perhaps the most notorious example of this phenomenon was a sermon delivered by Rabbi Morris Jacob Raphall (1798-1868) to his congregation at New York's Bnai Jeshurun synagogue in December 1860. The sermon was a response to the last-minute attempt by outgoing President James Buchanan (1791-1868) to avoid the breakup of the union by calling for a national day of "Humiliation, Fasting and Prayer," and was provocatively titled "The Bible View on Slavery."

Rabbi Raphall proposed that the Torah and ancient Jewish law believed that "slaveholding [is] not only recognized and sanctioned as an integral part of the social structure…[but] the property in slaves [is] placed under the same protection as any other species of lawful property." Clearly, he was caught up in the fear of a nation descending into chaos while desperately trying to avoid civil war, leading him to present the case that slavery was not inherently evil, evidenced by the support for it in the Bible, thereby creating an opening for abolitionists to tolerate slavery in their midst which would, in turn, prevent the disintegration of the union. A neat thesis, perhaps, but even in 1860 this was regarded as a highly controversial view. And today? Today we look back at what Rabbi Raphall said aghast and wonder how he could have got it so wrong.

Actually, it makes perfect sense. Rabbi Raphall was not presenting his audience with pure theology, nor with halakhic discourse. What he was trying to do was fabricate an unassailable backdrop for a controversial political position within a vexed contemporary reality. After all, if abolitionists – many of whom were devoutly religious – revered and respected the Hebrew Scriptures, they would surely have to concede that those very same scriptures did not disparage slavery or slave-owners. It was a classic case of the tail wagging the dog.

The same is true of any political creed claiming its entire philosophy is based on the Torah. I have seen this all too often over the years – clever ideologues cherry picking laws and concepts from the Torah and Talmud and using them to demonstrate that their doctrine alone is the one that is founded in Judaism. Whether such claims come from the left or the right, they all have one thing in common — they never quite add up.

Let us take Tikkun Olam as an example of this phenomenon. The concept of Tikkun Olam has in recent years become a buzz phrase for American Jewish progressives. "Let us take care of the poor and downtrodden," proponents advocate, "whether they are in our back yard or anywhere around the world – that is what the Torah wants us to do." To proponents of Tikkun Olam, this Hebrew phrase has come to mean "Healing the World" – which, curiously, is not what it implies when it appears in Jewish legal texts, where it means ensuring that the execution of law does not result in a disintegration of society; nor does it mean that when it appears in Jewish mystical texts, where the word *tikkun* connotes a reconciliation between the spiritual and material worlds.

In any event, while "Healing the World" is undoubtedly a lofty aspiration, I find it hard to see any kind of meaningful differentiation between Tikkun Olam as an ideology, and contemporary liberal progressivism. Charity and kindness to others are certainly core Jewish values, but they are just one of many hundreds of *mitzvot* — and many of those others are far more unique, by which I mean more "Jewish." And before your hackles are raised in indignation, and before you rush for your Hebrew Scriptures to prove me wrong, let me share with you the central text of Tikkun Olam – literally the verse in the Torah that is the foundation of the entire Tikkun Olam movement – and show you how it has been misconstrued. The verse can be found in this week's Torah portion (Lev. 19:18): וְאָהַבְתָּ לְרֵעֲךָ כָּמוֹךָ – "you should love your neighbor as you do yourself."

The implication from this verse is clear. The Torah expects more than brotherly love and more than a sympathetic concern for others. It expects us to prioritize the needs of others no differently than we would our own needs. Moreover, in the Jerusalem Talmud the great Rabbi Akiba expands on this directive and tells us that it is כְּלָל גָּדוֹל בַּתּוֹרָה – a "great principle of Torah."

Surely Rabbi Akiba's statement indisputably proves that Tikkun Olam is of far greater significance than any other mitzva?

In reality, however, that is not what he is saying at all, and anyone who suggests otherwise is engaging in a fatuous Rabbi Raphall type justification. What Rabbi Akiba is trying to teach us is that we need to pay as much attention to the small principles of Torah as we do to the great ones, and the reason he refers to this directive as a "great principle of Torah" is because he is aiming his statement at precisely those people who believe that taking care of others and being a "good" person is more important than anything else.

The Western world has been engulfed by this notion of being a "good person," as though this is the only thing that matters. Ritual obligations, belief in God, concern for honoring the past or respecting your heritage, can all be discarded and dismissed without a second thought – as long as I'm a "good person." Rabbi Akiba – who had himself been very disparaging of rabbis and tradition in his youth – informs us that this view is utterly warped and misguided. Loving your neighbor is only ever a "great principle" if it exists *BaTorah* – in the context of an unshakeable commitment to every other Torah obligation.

MISPLACED PITY IS AN INSIDIOUS INJUSTICE

first published May 11th, 2016

Until last week, I thought that I had heard just about everything bad anyone had to say about Israel — and that no anti-Israel statement would ever shock me again. But it seems I underestimated the vile and insidious nature of those who criticize Israel. And I'm not talking about Hamas leaders, Iranian mullahs, or anonymous bloggers. I'm talking about respected Western politicians and opinion formers who are subject to the scrutiny of the free press, as well as disciplinary repercussions. Anyway, as it turns out, I was wrong — very wrong.

You may or may not have been following the escalating crisis engulfing the UK Labour Party, one of the two main parties in British politics. Over the past several months, a number of incidents have exposed a raw antisemitic element within Labour. The most recent incident started when one of Labour's lawmakers in the British parliament, Naz Shah, was revealed as having posted a message on her Facebook timeline in 2014, where she said that the Jews living in Israel should all be relocated to the United States. Desperate not to lose her job, she offered a fulsome apology in the House of Commons, but was nonetheless suspended from the party.

Amazingly, her suspension was greeted with disdain by many of her Labour friends, anti-Israel fellow travelers, some of whom spoke up in her defense. Her most vociferous defender was former Mayor of London and senior Labourite, Ken Livingstone, a left-wing firebrand notorious for his negative views on Israel. In a TV interview, he unsurprisingly dismissed Shah's noxious Facebook post as something she had written in the heat of the moment during the Gaza War.

He then went on to say something so jarring that I was completely stunned. Even now I cannot quite understand how he segued from defending Shah into what he said. Here it is, word for word:

"Let's remember when Hitler won his election in 1932, his policy then was that Jews should be moved to Israel. He was supporting Zionism — this before he went mad and ended up killing six million Jews."

Did you get that? According to Ken Livingstone, Adolf Hitler was actually a supporter of Zionism, and wanted Jews to move to Israel. Never mind that Hitler wasn't remotely interested in Zionism, only in ridding Germany of its Jews without caring where they went. And never mind that "Israel" didn't exist until 1948; in 1932 the territory where Israel is today was known as the British Mandate of Palestine. These inaccuracies are completely beside the point, because Livingstone wasn't trying to share historical facts. What he was doing was deliberately correlating Hitler with Zionism.

And lest you think that however tasteless this may be, at least his statement was not aimed against Jews, just remember that as far as Livingstone is concerned — and he is the unfiltered mouthpiece for millions like him — any Jew who supports Israel or lives in Israel, whether they be left or right, religious or secular, is a Zionist. Which makes almost every Jew a Nazi, in his warped understanding of the world. And as for the few Jews who do conscientiously object to Israel, they are the reprehensible fig leaves used by people like Livingstone so that they can claim not to be antisemitic.

In any event, as a result of his bizarre statement, Livingstone was suspended from the Labour Party, although rather than stop him in his tracks, it only seemed to spur him on. Earlier this week he gave an interview in which he declared that the creation of Israel was "a great catastrophe" and suggested that after the Second World War, displaced Jews should have been resettled in the UK and US. The creation of Israel was a great injustice, he said, imposed on the Arab communities of British-controlled Palestine by a world racked with guilt over the Holocaust, and, in essence, that the Jewish claim to Israel is nonexistent, making Israel's creation a travesty.

Putting aside the factual inaccuracies and the deliberate distortions contained in Livingstone's statements, what should we make of the claims that Israel's existence is a de facto injustice? Israel's existence has certainly resulted in realities that have negatively affected the life of Arabs who have roots in what was previously known as Palestine.

The answer is simple. Justice is an objective reality, not a subjective whim. In the Torah portion of Kedoshim, rabbinic judges are warned that when meting out justice (Lev. 19:15): לֹא תַעֲשׂוּ עָוֶל בַּמִּשְׁפָּט לֹא תִשָּׂא פְנֵי דָל וְלֹא תֶהְדַּר פְּנֵי גָדוֹל בְּצֶדֶק תִּשְׁפֹּט עֲמִיתֶךָ – "don't pervert justice; do not be partial to the poor or show favoritism to the great; judge your neighbor fairly." The Talmud expands on this theme, warning rabbinic judges not to allow their pity for an indigent litigant to influence their verdict if his opponent is wealthy. A judge should never rationalize that if the rich guy loses the case, it won't affect his overall prosperity, and therefore it doesn't really matter. Right is right, and wrong is wrong, and if what is right results in a devastating loss for the poorer litigant, so be it.

One of the greatest challenges to Jewish identity in modern times is the widespread conviction that Israel's existence is inherently iniquitous, and that the only solution is for Israel to make sweeping concessions to the Palestinians. This is not a view based on justice, but rather on misplaced pity. Just because the Palestinians may be destitute and desperate doesn't make them right, and just because Israel is a thriving country whose economic success and incredible achievements are the envy of all its neighbors doesn't mean the Jewish State needs to make concessions.

The idea that it has to be a two-state solution, or some other solution where Israel gives and the Palestinians take, is the greatest injustice of all. We must hold our heads up high and be strong in the face of such unfair demands and all of the contemptuous insults that accompany them.

EMOR

first published May 16th, 2019

This week, my good friend Yossi Fachler WhatsApped me from Poland. He is there on a trip with yeshiva high school students visiting a range of Jewish heritage sites, and his messages included photos of their visit to Izbica, a small nondescript town near Lublin. Today there are no Jews in Izbica; of the almost 3,000 Jews who lived there in 1939 just 14 survived the Holocaust, and they all relocated to Israel. But from the mid-nineteenth century until the Nazis overran Poland, Izbica was unique in that it was inhabited almost exclusively by Jews, with gentiles making up less than 10% of the town's population.

Izbica was also the birthplace of one of Hasidism's most unusual sects, and the seat of that sect's enigmatic founding leader, Rabbi Mordechai Yosef Leiner (1800-1854). Rabbi Leiner – known in the Hasidic world as "The Izhbitzer" – started out as a disciple of Rabbi Simcha Bunem of Przysucha (1765-1827). After the latter's death, Rabbi Leiner joined the circle of his fellow Przysucha devotee, Rabbi Menachem Mendel Morgenstern of Kotzk (1787-1859). But in 1839 the Izhbitzer had a dramatic falling-out with Rabbi Morgenstern and left him to form his own

Hasidic sect centered in Izbica, attracting thousands of followers from across Poland and beyond.

I was introduced to the teachings of the Izhbitzer in my late teens by the iconoclastic Jewish singer, Rabbi Shlomo Carlebach (1925-1994), who interspersed his concert performances with Hasidic stories and lessons. Rabbi Carlebach focused mostly on the works of Rabbi Nachman of Breslov (1772-1810), particularly those ideas that diverged from the very conservative outlook usually featured in normative rabbinic literature. But even Rabbi Nachman's most outlandish propositions paled in comparison to the ideas proposed by the Izhbitzer. The Torah's most prominent villains are presented as being righteous; stories you thought you understood are turned on their heads; and, most jarringly of all, everything that happens is the will of God, including sin. The Izhbitzer is so uncharacteristically counterintuitive for a traditional Orthodox rabbi, it is hardly surprising that for some years after his passing the publication of his works resulted in outrage and protest.

Today, all that that remains of the once vibrant Jewish community of Izbica is a cemetery. During the Holocaust years, the Izbica cemetery was heavily desecrated, and numerous headstones were looted for use by the Nazis to build a prison facility. After the Shoah, with no one to repair the damage, the cemetery remained in a terrible state for decades. Then, in 2006, the embassy of the Federal Republic of Germany in Poland joined forces with the Foundation for the Preservation of Jewish Heritage to undo the horrendous damage. The prison building was demolished, and the rescued headstones were affixed to the walls of the Izhbitzer's "Ohel" – the prayer chapel over his grave

– a reminder that this spiritual giant was still a shepherd to his devoted flock.

Inspired by the Izbica photos Yossi had sent me I decided to check out what original ideas the Izhbitzer had to say about Parshat Emor. I was not disappointed. The very first piece on Emor in his book *Mei HaShiloaḥ* directly challenges Maimonides' famous theological apologetics for the existence of evil. According to Maimonides ("*Rambam*"; 1138-1204), it is not God who is to blame for evil, rather it is the lack of God. In other words, what we refer to as evil is essentially the absence of God. When two countries go to war and people die, those deaths are not God's fault, they are man's fault. Natural disasters and devastating diseases are not directed by God, they are simply the unfortunate byproducts of a world which operates according to the laws of nature.

For example, the physical world requires gravity in order to function, but occasionally the same gravity that allows us to operate normally can result in death, as when someone falls to their death from a high place. So too with disease; our bodies function in a certain way so that we can lead our daily lives, but those same natural processes sometimes lead to misfunction and death. This, says Maimonides, is simply the price of living in a material world governed by nature.

But according to the Izhbitzer, this theology is outright heresy. Nothing that happens can be dismissed as the random byproduct of nature, or as the will of man without God.

The ultimate ambassadors of God's determinism are the priests, who preside over the religious and ritual duties of Judaism for the nation. For this reason, God instructs Moses (Lev. 21:1):

אֱמֹר אֶל הַכֹּהֲנִים בְּנֵי אַהֲרֹן וְאָמַרְתָּ אֲלֵהֶם לְנֶפֶשׁ לֹא יִטַּמָּא בְּעַמָּיו – "talk to the priests the sons of Aaron, and say to them: let none defile himself for a dead person among his people." Priests must epitomize the backbone of faith, namely that God is behind everything that happens, and nothing in life happens by chance occurrence. One must never blame the forces of nature, or human folly, or mere chance, for things that go wrong. Every detail of our lives is directed by God.

Nevertheless, the paradoxical danger of such a worldview is that it can lead to a decline of faith. After all, how can one have faith in a God who is responsible for incomprehensible evil?

For this reason, says the Izhbitzer, God warns the priests not to allow themselves to become defiled when those closest to them suffer or die. Don't allow your absolute faith in My providence result in questions about My actions, God says, as this will inevitably result in a loss of faith.

In a final twist, the Izhbitzer adds that the seminal kabbalistic work, the *Zohar*, interprets the word *Emor* to mean "a whisper." Even in the midst of the harshest "evil" God's faithful must always hear a whisper, reminding them that while the positive aspects of God's providence may not be evident, one can never lose faith. And as I looked at the photos of the cemetery in Izbica sent to me by Yossi Fachler, representing the devastation of a flourishing community obliterated by the Shoah, I strained to hear the faint whisper of the Izhbitzer in my ear: "Remain faithful. There is a God."

THE MARK OF LEADERSHIP IS OPTIMISM IN ADVERSITY

first published May 3rd, 2018

This week, we were offered two demonstrations of leadership in the face of adversity, and they could not have been more different. On Monday, Israel's Prime Minister, Benjamin Netanyahu, theatrically unveiled an astounding collection of secret files from Iran, obtained by Israel's espionage agency, Mossad. The cache reveals how Iran has consistently lied in claiming that it only ever sought nuclear power for peaceful purposes.

The 55,000 pages of secret information prove that Iran has engaged in a nuclear weapons program for over twenty years, despite its oft repeated denials. Netanyahu's argument was simple. Iran never had any intention of complying with the so-called "Iran Nuclear Deal" of 2015, and the mothballed archive proved the regime was ready to reactivate its nuclear weapons ambitions at the first opportunity.

It was a busy week for Netanyahu. On Sunday, a presumed Israeli airstrike bombed a complex near Hama, in Syria. The attack destroyed approximately 200 missiles and killed 16 people, at least 11 of them Iranians. Meanwhile, Israel's Knesset voted on a bill to empower a reduced "security cabinet" to declare war if necessary, and, in "extreme circumstances," on the orders of the

Prime Minister and Defense Minister alone. Even the *New York Times*, no fan of Netanyahu, grudgingly acknowledged the Israeli Prime Minister's remarkable ability to take control of the agenda in the midst of rapidly changing circumstances.

What is even more extraordinary is that all this is happening while Israel is threatened by Syria and Lebanon in the north, and incursions at the Gaza border in the south. In the meantime, Netanyahu and his wife are also being investigated for corruption in at least four separate investigations, all of which involve exhaustive police interviews and relentless coverage by Israel's vigorous media. Netanyahu's upbeat demeanor and can-do attitude in the midst of all this is an inspiring model of leadership in the face of adversity.

Meanwhile, in Ramallah, at the same time as Netanyahu was dazzling the world with his multimedia presentation, Palestinian Authority president Mahmoud Abbas addressed the 23rd session of the Palestinian National Council, in a speech that left his supporters in the Western world shocked and dismayed. The speech, which was an opportunity for Abbas to reenergize his leadership, turned into a three-hour long rambling farce that would have been pathetic and pitiful had it not been so vile.

This was the first PNC meeting for 22 years. The last meeting, in 1996, took place during the heady post-Oslo period that many believed would result in a Palestinian state alongside Israel before the millennium. The situation now is notably different. Gaza is controlled by Hamas, and despite feverish efforts to effect a reconciliation between Hamas and Abbas before this week's meeting, Hamas was notably absent, and Gaza remains out of bounds for the Palestinian Authority. International support for

Abbas and the Palestinians has waned considerably, most conspicuously in the Arab world.

At a meeting with Jewish leaders in New York last month, Saudi Arabia's powerhouse Crown Prince Mohamed bin Salman openly criticized Abbas for having consistently rejected opportunities for peace with Israel. According to unnamed sources who attended the meeting, the Crown Prince said it was "time the Palestinians accept [peace] offers and agree to come to the negotiating table — or they should shut up and stop complaining." In the same week, the Crown Prince told *Atlantic* he believed both "the Palestinians and the Israelis have the right to have their own land," the first time a Saudi leader has publicly acknowledged Israel's right to exist.

But instead of creating optimism for the Palestinian cause, Abbas launched into a tirade against Jews and Israel that included antisemitic tropes, long discarded to the margins of political discourse: the Jews brought the Holocaust upon themselves because they were usurers; there is no such thing as a "Jewish people"; there is no connection between Jews and the land of Israel; Israel was established as "a colonial project" to protect European interests in the Middle East, and so on. We've heard it all previously, but this time it reflected the ineffectiveness of the Abbas leadership like it never has before. Suddenly, "the king had no clothes".

The same *New York Times* that openly despises Netanyahu issued an editorial under the heading "Let Abbas's Vile Words Be His Last as Palestinian Leader." The editorial admitted that Abbas had lost "all credibility," and it was time for the Palestinians to find "a leader with energy, integrity and vision." Around the world, friends and critics concurred – this was the end of the road for Abbas. What a contrast. Two leaders under pressure – one projects hope and optimism, the other spouts bile and projects doom.

Parshat Emor opens with a verse instructing Moses to speak to the priests about their mourning practices (Lev. 21:1): אֱמֹר אֶל הַכֹּהֲנִים בְּנֵי אַהֲרֹן וְאָמַרְתָּ אֲלֵהֶם – "speak to the priests, the sons of Aaron, and say to them." Rashi picks up on the repetition of the Hebrew word *amar* (*emor* and *ve'amarta*) and explains it to mean that adults had to take responsibility for their children, in Hebrew: *l'hazhir gedolim al ha'ketanim* – "to caution adults with regard to the children." In other words, adults have a responsibility to ensure that their children comply with the Torah's requirements, and not just worry about themselves. The reason this concept crops up here is because priests serve a double function, as parents to their children, and as leaders of the nation. How they behave, particularly in times of stress such as when they are in mourning, would impact on how the entire nation behaved.

The Holocaust martyr Rabbi Aryeh Zvi Frumer (1884-1943) – known by all as the "Kozhiglover" – takes this concept even further. The Hebrew word *l'hazhir* is the verb form of the word *zohar*, which means shining. In order to be a good leader, one must inspire by being a shining example of positivity and optimism. Particularly in times of adversity, this is the mark of true leadership.

A THREAT TO THE SYSTEM

first published May 9th, 2017

For more than a thousand years after the Exodus from Egypt, the greatest threat to monotheism was polytheism, better known to us as idolatry. This form of religious faith focuses on something other than the Creator God of monotheism as an object of worship. In fact, idolatrous religions usually have multiple gods, and to this day polytheism thrives in certain countries, such as in India, where Hindus have a choice of no less than 33 million pagan gods to choose from.

The decline of polytheism in the Middle East and the Mediterranean Basin began in antiquity, during the period of the second Jerusalem Temple, approximately 2,500 years ago. Although it would take many centuries for idolatry to die out as a mainstream force — during which time its advocates oftentimes attempted to force their belief system onto those who had rejected it — among Jews there was no longer an enduring compulsion to worship multiple gods, an urge that had been overwhelming and ubiquitous during the First Temple period. The Talmud (Sanhedrin 64a) attributes this profound collective shift to the devoted prayers of a leadership group known as *Anshei Knesset Hagedolah* ("Men of the Great Assembly"), who painstakingly reinstated Judaism after the return of exiles from Babylonian exile.

If the devastating destruction of the First Temple had been the result of widespread idolatry, it followed that if all such heretical distractions were removed, the Second Temple would continue to exist indefinitely. But, as the expression goes, "be careful what you wish for." Although Jewish religious leaders surely breathed a sigh of relief when idolatry receded as a threat, it did not take too long for Judaism to be subjected to a new threat, as troubling questions about Jewish religious practices began to emerge that seriously undermined the world's only monotheistic faith. A Jewish subgroup called the Sadducees became the standard bearers of this phenomenon, and while they claimed to be ardent monotheists, and to accept the authenticity of the Torah and prophets, they vigorously rejected any kind of ancient oral tradition that acted to enhance the Hebrew Scriptures with depth of meaning.

One of the most famous debates between the Sadducees and their opponents, the Pharisees, revolved around a verse in Parshat Emor that fixes the first day of the *omer* countdown to Shavuot, which begins on Passover (Lev. 23:15): וּסְפַרְתֶּם לָכֶם מִמָּחֳרַת הַשַּׁבָּת – "You shall count for yourselves the day after *Shabbat*." The Sadducees interpreted the word *Shabbat* to mean Saturday, which implied that the *omer* count would always commence on the Sunday after Passover began. The Pharisees followed an ancient oral tradition that interpreted the word *Shabbat* to mean the first day of Passover, as a result of which the *omer* count commenced on the second day of Passover, even if that day was not a Sunday.

While there are numerous good explanations as to why the word *Shabbat* in that verse means the first day of Passover, and not Saturday, none of them clarify why the Torah would use such an ambiguous word to convey this information, nor why for this directive in particular.

The Talmud (Yevamot 62b) recalls the death of 24,000 disciples of Rabbi Akiba that occurred during the period of the *omer* count between Passover and Shavuot. The Talmud is quite vague as to how they died, and some modern scholars believe their deaths resulted from Rabbi Akiba's support for the abortive Bar Kokhba revolt against the Romans in the years 132-135 C.E. But according to the Talmudic account, Rabbi Akiba's students all died because they had no mutual respect. Whatever that means, and whether this idea dovetails with the Bar Kokhba interpretation, one must presume that the rampant disrespect was not restricted to the time period between Passover and Shavuot. In which case, why did Rabbi Akiba's students die in this specific timeframe?

The *omer* count recalls the leadup to the Jews receiving the Torah. Each day was part of the process of preparation. During the revelation at Sinai, the Jewish people received both the written Torah, and the oral Torah, which supplements its written counterpart. The idea behind the oral Torah as a supplement was that it would require a process of transmission, and thus the Torah would never become merely a book on a bookshelf. Each generation would need to receive the Torah from the generation that preceded it, and then pass it on to the next generation.

In order to highlight the centrality of the oral Torah in our religious system, the portion that describes this period in the calendar needed to be the paradigm of oral tradition, deliberately opaque in its description of how to begin the *omer* count, which would mean that without the benefit of an oral tradition passed down from generation to generation, one might have thought that the count needs to begin on the first Sunday after the beginning of Passover. As it turns out, the Jewish faith can only be observed properly with the help of authentic Torah scholarship. That being the case, it is not just the text of Torah in a scroll or book that requires respect, but so too any Torah scholar who is a link in the chain of oral knowledge must also be treated with reverence and respect.

As mentors to the Jewish nation, it is exceedingly important that Torah scholars are respectful of one another. After all, if scholars vilify or are scornful of each other, they undercut the very message they are expected to transmit. The students of Rabbi Akiba were the greatest scholars of their day, and their wholesale death was undoubtedly a national tragedy. Nevertheless, their behavior towards one another was a more insidious threat, no different in essence to the threat of the Sadducees, as it undermined the integrity of the system, and threatened to destroy it from within. This exact message is emphasized by the fact that their deaths occurred during the time period which leads up to the acceptance of the Torah, itself described in a way that conveys the importance of the oral tradition.

BEHAR

THE OPIOID EPIDEMIC & ASKING FOR HELP

first published May 23rd, 2019

Y ou will no doubt have read or heard about the opioid epidemic currently raging across the United States. It is a crisis of unprecedented proportions. More than 130 people die each day after overdosing on opioids. That is close to 50,000 people a year. Troublingly, in the main the victims are not criminals, nor do they come from the underbelly of society; they are ordinary men and women from all walks of life who became addicts after an opioid painkiller was prescribed by a physician following a medical procedure, or to treat chronic pain.

In January it emerged that it is now more likely for people to die from an opioid overdose than in an accident involving a motor vehicle. This is a shocking statistic, and one that should make us all sit up and take notice. With the mortality rate from opioid addiction rising, it has become increasingly evident that every one of us probably knows someone who is addicted, and that this person is in real danger of dying.

How is it possible that this devastating crisis crept up on us? The answer became clearer a year ago, with the release of information compiled by the Justice Department about Purdue

Pharma, a giant pharmaceutical company privately owned by the Sackler family that produces the aggressively marketed OxyContin, a primary culprit in the origins of the opioid crisis. During the late 1990s, pharmaceutical companies – including Purdue – offered baseless assurances that patients would not become addicted to synthetic opioid pain medication, and on the basis of these assurances doctors began to prescribe them at ever-increasing rates. But, as federal prosecutors investigating Purdue later discovered, the company management team was well aware of "significant abuse of OxyContin in the first years after the drug's introduction in 1996 and concealed that information."

In 2007, although Purdue paid one the largest fines ever levied against a pharmaceutical company, felony charges against three senior executives were inexplicably reduced to misdemeanors in a plea deal arrangement, and no one went to jail. It is likely that as a direct result of this demonstration of reduced criminal culpability, pharmaceutical companies continued to relentlessly market opioids while the medical community continued to prescribe them, and the crisis grew worse leading to the current epidemic.

So, what is someone to do if they find themselves addicted to a prescribed opioid medication, or if they discover that a member of their family or a friend is addicted to opioids? Prescription medication obtained from a doctor does not have the insidious feel of illegal narcotics, but the mortality rate from these "innocuous" pain relievers is rising, and it is obvious – even to addicts – that synthetic opioids are toxic and are indiscriminately killing innocent victims. Most frighteningly, the dangers of opioids are a lot closer to home than those posed by illicit needle-injected heroin.

The good news is that help is readily available to those who seek it. The bad news is that addicts rarely seek help, either because they believe they are not addicted, or because they think that they can handle the problem on their own, without help. Even more tragically, some addicts do realize they are addicted, but are ashamed to ask for help. Family and friends are equally inhibited. But not seeking help can be fatal. Forget any pride or shame – the basis of a healthy society is asking for help. Even our relationship with God is predicated on our communicating with Him in times of need, as demonstrated by numerous references in the Torah and prophets.

At the beginning of Parshat Behar, the Torah informs us of the requirement for a sabbatical called *shemitta* every seventh year, during which all agricultural land must be left fallow and no crops harvested. Addressing concerns that might arise about a shortage of food, the passage includes the following two verses (Lev. 25:20-21):

> *"And should you ask, 'what will we eat in the seventh year, if we cannot sow nor gather in our crops?' I will ensure My blessing for you in the sixth year, so that it shall yield a crop sufficient for three years."*

The commentaries puzzle over the need for this to be presented in a question-and-answer format; it would have been sufficient to have recorded God's reassurance regarding the bountiful crop in each sixth year without including the inquiry. In addressing this curious anomaly, Rabbi Shalom Mordechai Schwadron of Berezhany ("*Maharsham*"; 1835-1911) cites another passage where God's promise follows a staged question. If, upon entering the Land of Israel after Moses' death, the Jewish nation says (Deut. 7:17): כִּי תֹאמַר בִּלְבָבְךָ רַבִּים הַגּוֹיִם הָאֵלֶּה מִמֶּנִּי אֵיכָה

אוּכַל לְהוֹרִישָׁם – "These nations are more numerous than we; how can we dispossess them?" – the Torah offers the following assurance: לֹא תִירָא מֵהֶם זָכֹר תִּזְכֹּר אֵת אֲשֶׁר עָשָׂה ה' אֱלֹקֶיךָ לְפַרְעֹה וּלְכָל מִצְרָיִם – "Fear not! Just recall what God did to Pharaoh and the Egyptians."

But this format is convoluted; surely the reassurance would have been enough without being preceded by a question?

Actually, what the Torah wishes to convey is that God's assurances of assistance are conditional on our asking Him for help. We must verbalize that we recognize our limitations without His help before He steps in. Only once we have asked for that help God undertakes to provide all the help we need. It is this principle that applies to *shemitta*. Before relying on God's help for the seventh year and into the eighth, we need to realize that without God's blessings in the sixth we would never manage to survive.

Since 1939, the "Twelve Step" program for recovery from alcoholism has been the primary resource for those in the throes of serious addiction. The first two steps ring out as loud and as true today as when they were first written, reflecting both the message of these Torah passages, and the current needs in the midst of the ongoing opioid epidemic: "We admitted we were powerless over our addiction, that our lives had become unmanageable. We came to believe that only a power greater than ourselves could restore us to sanity."

You see, help is always there for those who need it. All one needs to do is ask, and the rest will follow.

MOVING THE US EMBASSY TO JERUSALEM WAS PREDICTED 2,500 YEARS AGO

first published May 10th, 2018

In March 2016, I was at AIPAC Policy Conference in Washington DC when presumptive Republican presidential candidate Donald J. Trump vowed to "move the American embassy to the eternal capital of the Jewish people, Jerusalem." The crowd of 18,000 people rose to their feet and erupted into rapturous applause. I, too, rose and applauded, but even as I did so, I dismissed what he said as meaningless political rah-rah. Firstly, I thought to myself, Trump is never going to win the nomination, never mind the presidency. Secondly, he's only saying this to please the crowd, but if he ever becomes the President, he will never move the embassy – just as no one else ever did when they had the chance.

In 1995, US Congress passed a law called the Jerusalem Embassy Act. It described Jerusalem as "the undivided capital of Israel" and required the US embassy to move there by 1999. For over 20 years the law remained a rhetorical farce, an example of meaningless political posturing. Every six months successive presidents waived its implementation, and specifically the US embassy move, citing "national security reasons." This, regardless of the promises they made before coming into office.

Barack Obama, addressing AIPAC in June 2008, announced that if he was elected president "Jerusalem will remain the capital of Israel, and it must remain undivided." Once in office he abandoned his pre-election promise. Obama's predecessor, George W. Bush, similarly pledged to "begin the process of moving the US ambassador to the city Israel has chosen as its capital" as soon as he took office. It never happened. Bill Clinton also told supporters as early as 1993 that he wanted to move the US Embassy to Jerusalem, but never did it.

Bearing this history in mind, in 2016 I felt that my cynicism towards any pledge regarding the embassy from a presumptive candidate was entirely justified. Remarkably, and for no discernible political gain, last December President Trump announced that the US was officially recognizing Jerusalem as the capital of Israel, and that the State Department would begin "preparation to move the American embassy from Tel Aviv to Jerusalem." Even this was dismissed as an empty stunt — it would take years to plan and build an embassy, by which time it wouldn't happen, as Trump would be out of office. But sometimes dreams do come true. In a week's time, the United States will open its new embassy in the Arnona neighborhood in Jerusalem, and we have already seen images of the new street signs going up that point towards the new US Embassy location.

You may be wondering if this really matters. In real terms, the new embassy is just the former US consulate rebranded with new signage, and it will be many years before the 850 staff working at the Tel Aviv facility will be relocated to a proper new embassy building in Jerusalem. In the meantime, consular work will still be carried out in Tel Aviv, at the site of the former embassy. But the relocation of the US Embassy and recognition of Jerusalem as

Israel's capital is nonetheless important, and not just in the world of international diplomacy.

When I re-read the text of the December announcement, I was particularly struck by one sentence: "Israel is a sovereign nation with the right like every other sovereign nation to determine its own capital." It dawned on me for the first time that Israel has never had a formally recognized capital city, even before 1967 and the so-called "occupation." Imagine the outcry this kind of situation would elicit if we were talking about any other country in the world.

But I see things quite differently. To me this entire phenomenon is just further proof that when it comes to Israel and God's chosen nation, ordinary rules do not apply, and extraordinary events have meaning well beyond what is immediately apparent. In the Haftarah that is read for Parshat Behar (Jer. 32:6-27), God instructs Jeremiah to buy a plot of land from his relative, and to deposit the title in a jug for safekeeping. Jeremiah is puzzled by this order, and asks God how securing the title made any sense, as the nation was imminently going to be exiled from Israel for an undetermined period, with all the accompanying violent devastation and dispossession. Why preserve the title to a field whose ownership by any Jew would soon become irrelevant?

The Haftarah does not include God's lengthy answer, just the very beginning, where He says: "I am the Lord, the God of all mankind. Is anything too hard for me?" This declaration is followed by a lengthy description of the overwhelming persecution and suffering the Jewish nation would endure, as a natural consequence for having favored pagan gods instead of having had faith in God. And yet (Jer. 32:42-44), "as I have brought all this great calamity on this people, so I will give them all the prosperity I promised them. Fields will flourish and be bought again – in this land which you describe as a desolate waste, without people or animals… Fields will be bought for silver, and deeds will be signed, sealed and witnessed in the territory of Benjamin and in the villages around Jerusalem… because I will restore their fortunes."

For 1,900 years after the second Temple destruction, Jerusalem was in the hands of gentiles. The Jewish community in Jerusalem was poor and had few rights. In 1948, and then in 1967, Jews took control of Jerusalem, but the world continued to hold any claim to our capital in contempt. The prophecy had not yet come to pass.

But this coming Monday we will finally see the realization of Jeremiah's prophecy. The deed to our eternal capital, Jerusalem, will be "signed, sealed and witnessed in the territory of Benjamin and in the villages around Jerusalem," as the world's most powerful nation will formally recognize Jewish ownership of Jerusalem, just as God promised would happen 2,500 years ago. Now, if that doesn't stir your soul, I don't know what will.

A DORMANT MITZVA COMES BACK TO LIFE

first published May 17th, 2017

J ews have lived in the biblical Land of Israel uninterrupted for thousands of years. For much of the last two thousand years Jewish life has been confined to small communities of pious families who braved poverty and hardship, relying on generous charitable support from coreligionist communities in North Africa, Asia and Europe.

But starting in the 1870s things began to change, and Jews ventured out into the largely uncultivated semi-arid land, and founded agricultural settlements, such as Petach Tikva and Zikhron Yaakov. Although the success of these communities was celebrated by Jews the world over, the newly opened farms and orchards also became the subject of fierce debate, as Jewish laws relating to land cultivation in the Holy Land that had been dormant for millennia suddenly became relevant and controversial.

The most famous of these controversies centered on the observance of *shemitta*, the sabbatical year mandated in Parshat Behar (Lev. 25:1-7) for all agricultural land in Israel. In 1888, the rabbinical authorities of Europe vigorously debated whether or not struggling farmers in nascent settlements would need to cease farming the land during the *shemitta* year of 1888-9. This discussion took place before the launch of the Zionist Movement, and the rabbis were not swayed by ideology; rather their arguments focused on halachic precedent. Everyone agreed that without the existence of a fully functioning Temple in Jerusalem, *shemitta* observance was a rabbinically imposed stringency rather than a full-blown Torah mandated obligation. But while this allowed for greater leniency, *shemitta* was still considered a compulsory requirement, as opposed to an elective option.

Nevertheless, with the farmers complaining that they were barely able to sustain their livelihoods, the leading Ashkenazi rabbinic authority of the day, Rabbi Yitzḥak Elḥanan Spektor of Kovno (1817-1896), issued a ruling referred to as *Heter Mekhira* ("sale dispensation"), permitting the "sale" of farmland to local Arabs, so that the Jewish owners could work for these gentile "owners" for the duration of *shemitta*, and money earned from the sale of produce could be paid to them as "salary."

Rabbi Spektor's halakhic ruling was fiercely challenged by some of his colleagues in Europe, and also by the religiously zealous leadership of the Ashkenazi Jewish community in Jerusalem, who despised the financial independence of the new agricultural communities. But despite the vehement opposition – recorded in publications that were so incendiary most of them were destroyed – the "sale" went ahead, and the grateful farmers were able to work the land. By the time the next *shemitta* year came around, in 1895-6, disapproval towards the *Heter Mekhira* in the Jewish centers of Europe had abated, and it seemed the controversy was over.

That modus vivendi changed when the secular-led Zionist movement was launched in 1897, and agricultural settlements in Ottoman Palestine run by militantly non-observant Jews increased in number. Religious opposition to the activities of secular Zionists crystallized around the *Heter Mekhira* of 1909-10, and despite the precedent authorized by undisputed rabbinic luminaries of the previous generation, when the charismatic new chief rabbi of Jaffa, Rabbi Avraham Yitzḥak HaKohen Kook (1865-1935), opted to permit the *Heter Mekhira*, he and those who supported him were vilified and maligned.

The scene was set for this issue to forever be associated with ideological affiliation rather than systematic halachic reasoning. Interestingly, however, in recent *shemitta* years, more and more farmers, even those who are less religious, have chosen to observe the sabbatical year rather than to rely on the *Heter Mekhira*. During the *shemitta* year of 2014-15, almost 3,500 Israeli farmers allowed their land to remain fallow. One of the farmers, Ira Zimmerman, a viticulturist from Northern Israel, went on a tour of the United States and Europe to report on the tremendous growth of *shemitta* observance. At every event Zimmerman explained how with each passing Sabbatical year, the number of farmers who choose not to work their land grows exponentially. Remarkably, if you ask them why they are doing it, they generally just shrug their shoulders and answer simply: "because the Torah says so."

Although, perhaps it is not so remarkable after all. The passage that introduces us to *shemitta* begins with the verse, "God spoke to Moses on Mount Sinai" — which is strange, as Mount Sinai is never mentioned in the introduction to any other Torah commandment. Rabbi Zadok Hakohen of Lublin (1823-1900) offers a compelling explanation. There were two distinct moments during the wilderness sojourn after the Exodus from Egypt. One took place at Mount Sinai, when the Torah was given for the first time. The other moment took place almost forty years later, in the plains of Moab, when Moses reiterated the Torah for the next generation, who were about to inherit the Promised Land with Joshua at their head.

It was not just the passage of time that separated these two moments; it was also existential realities. The Sinai group had all their needs personally taken care of by God, unlike the Moab group, who needed to be trained for a military campaign and subsequent cultivation of the land. Clearly the observance of *shemitta* was of no direct concern to the first group, only to the second. In which case, why is Mount Sinai, and not Moab, mentioned in association with *shemitta*? The answer must be that *shemitta* concerned the Jews even when it was irrelevant. The Mount Sinai Jews were hyperconscious of the fact that every facet of God's Torah, and the commandments it contained, was important.

For all the years after our Temple in Jerusalem was destroyed, during which time *shemitta* was not practiced, we nonetheless kept it alive in absentia, eventually re-embracing it when the opportunity arose – at first with the use of a dispensation that acknowledged its continued significance, and ultimately by taking on its full observance, despite a valid way with which to dispense with it completely. That lesson of love for Torah, even when it appears dormant, is a lesson we have inherited from the Jews of Mount Sinai.

BECHUKOTAI

BEING REMINDED OF OUR BLESSINGS

first published May 14th, 2015

Sometimes we are exposed to such utter devastation, such stark despair, that we are compelled to feel grateful that our own lives are stable and secure by comparison. Our daily worries and concerns, so petty and pathetic, fade into the background, and our self-indulgent gripes about a "hard life" seem entirely overstated.

I experienced such a moment this week when it was reported that a second massive earthquake – measuring 7.3 on the Richter scale – had hit Nepal, following on from the first one just a couple of weeks ago – that one measuring 7.8 – which already devastated the country, as well as nearby Tibet and India, killing thousands, and devastating tens of thousands of lives, no doubt for many years to come.

But are our lives actually so stable and secure? Living in California, where minor tremors and quakes occur fairly frequently, we find ourselves particularly sensitive to this news story. In early March, a group of scientists published the ominously named *Third Uniform California Earthquake Rupture Forecast*, a report that declared the chances of an earthquake measuring 8 or more hitting California in the near future had gone up by more than 50% over the past 7 years.

In an interview for the *Los Angeles Times*, seismologist Ned Field, the lead author of the report, put it very bluntly: "You live in earthquake country," he said, adding, "and you should live every day like it's the day a "Big One" could hit!"

Not a reassuring thought. After all, what are comfortable lives really worth if such incredible devastation could so easily occur? All of us who live in this part of the world are thrilled with the Southern Californian life. It is a location packed with opportunity, and with every kind of amenity. And the weather! Where is there weather better than in Southern California? But – if you will permit me to reverse a familiar colloquialism – every silver lining has a cloud. In just a few short minutes the idyllic world we all take for granted could be overturned, as it has been for the citizens of Nepal. So how are we meant to transform this ever-present looming disaster into a meaningful life lesson? I believe the answer lies in an anomaly at the heart of Parshat Bechukotai.

Bechukotai begins with eleven verses that describe how God will respond if we observe His mitzvot. We are promised peace and prosperity, and protection from our enemies. Most of all we are promised that God will dwell in our midst. But these assurances are immediately followed by one of the bleakest series of verses in the entire Torah. It begins with the words: וְאִם לֹא תִשְׁמְעוּ לִי וְלֹא תַעֲשׂוּ אֵת כָּל הַמִּצְוֹת הָאֵלֶּה – "if you do not listen to Me, and do not observe all of my commandments," and it goes on to describe some of the most dreadful things that can ever befall individual humans in particular, and societies in general.

What is so striking about this section of the Torah is that while the benign promises of good fortune take up just eleven verses, the horrors of the *tokhaḥa*, or "rebuke" as it is known, take up thirty verses – almost three times as much space.

The medieval commentator Rabbi Abraham Ibn Ezra (1089-1167) remarks that this disproportionate focus seems out of sync with our understanding of God as compassionate and kind. Why would God go into such vivid detail to describe how our lives could go horribly wrong, and yet spend so little time focusing on how He might reward our positive efforts with a peaceful and abundant existence? Moreover, where are the promises of Heavenly benefits for fulfilling God's expectations during our physical lives?

There are numerous answers to this puzzling question, almost all relating to the psychology of the human condition. Let me share the one I find the most compelling. It is evident to anyone who believes in God that even the most wonderful life in this world pales into insignificance when compared to the gift of Heavenly bliss. The fact that we may be lucky enough during the course of our limited physical lives to discharge our duties as humans and as servants of God, will only ever be possible because we have been enabled to do so without the manifold distractions and disruptions that can occur, which would prevent us from doing what we need to in terms of our spiritual journey. In which case, perhaps this Torah section is not a record of reward and punishment. Rather, it is a window, allowing us to appreciate the circumstances that will enable us to achieve our true purpose, alongside the manifold circumstances that would do the opposite.

So many things can occur during a person's life that might prevent that person from being who God wants them to be. And so, God spells it out. The abbreviated "reward" section of the portion is not about reward. It is a basic record of the type of life that will allow us to serve Him with ease. Meanwhile, the elongated "punishment" component is not about punishment; it is there to remind us of all the countless hazards, which, if they occurred, would result in our lives falling apart.

God is prompting us not to waste a second of the fragile time during which serving Him is simple and straightforward. He is telling us that although the "Big One" could happen at any minute, we must not focus on that depressing thought. Instead, focus on today – a day with no distractions or hindrances. Focus on what you can do right now to ensure that you have fulfilled His expectations. And hopefully, being conscious of the many things that could go wrong will lead to a greater appreciation of the wonderful life we all enjoy.

BAMIDBAR

BAMIDBAR

IT'S ALL IN THE NAME

first published June 6th, 2019

Jack "Srulek" Feldman is a smiling, sprightly old man who lives in Rochester NY, where until relatively recently he owned and ran a local fish store called *Modern Fish Market*. Jack was born in 1926, in a nondescript Polish town called Skarzysko-Kamienna, to Szaja (Shaya) and Matla Feldman. Soon after his birth the family moved to Sosnowiec, where Szaja opened a store selling hats.

Jack's early life was typical for a middle-class Polish Jew born in the early twentieth century. The family was Orthodox, but not strictly Orthodox, and Jack was educated in both Hebrew and secular studies. They led a comfortable existence, even as the world around them was descending into madness. In September 1939, Jack and his family were visiting relatives in Skaryzsko-Kamienna when the news came through that Germany had invaded Poland. Within a short period of time everything they had was taken away from them by the Nazis, and the family – along with all the other Jews in the area – were forced to move into Sosnowiec Ghetto, where they shared a one-room apartment with fifteen other people.

Then one day in 1940, Jack and some of his friends were walking along the street when they were suddenly grabbed by Nazi thugs and thrown into a holding cell. Jack never saw his parents and family again. For the remainder of the war Jack bounced around various labor camps and death camps, in constant danger of being killed or dying of starvation. In 1944 Jack was sent to the notorious Auschwitz-Birkenau death camp. Upon arrival, Jack miraculously escaped death after being recognized by a Kapo who had once worked for his father. Although Mengele had already directed Jack towards the gas chamber, the Kapo surreptitiously removed him from that line and placed him in a work line instead. Later that day Jack was processed into the work camp and his arm was tattooed with the number A-17606. From then until his liberation this number was Jack's only identity.

In January 1945, news of the Soviet advances on the Eastern front reached Auschwitz, and the SS forced thousands of inmates, including Jack, to march from Poland to Germany on what later became known as "death marches". Thousands died of hunger and exposure, but somehow Jack survived, and on May 5, 1945, he was liberated in Germany. Jack returned home to Sosnowiec, only to discover that not one member of his immediate family had made it through the hell of the Holocaust, and besides for three cousins, he was entirely alone in the world; he was just nineteen years old. Determined to press ahead, he married a fellow survivor, Sally "Sura" Herzsenfus, and moved to the United States, where he built up his modest business and raised a beautiful family.

I came across Jack as a result of watching a poignant, deeply moving HBO documentary, *The Number on Great-Grandpa's*

Arm. The short movie is presented through the eyes of Jack's great-grandson, Elliott. Via a series of photo stills and some extraordinary rotoscope animation, Jack's history is brought to life, gently narrated by Jack himself, as he is prompted by questions from his curious great-grandson. The movie is introduced with Elliott holding up a photograph of Jack's forearm with the tattooed number.

> *"This is a close-up of his number from Auschwitz,"* *Elliott says. "That was his number, and he told us [that] back then your number was your name. That was all he was to them."*

The tattooing of numbers onto Jews was just one of several methods that were used by the Nazis to dehumanize victims of the Holocaust. The message that these inked blue numbers transmitted to the world was loud and clear: "you have no name – you are just a number to us."

Rabbi Obadiah Seforno (1575-1550), an Italian sixteenth-century bible commentator, offers an important observation about the census of the Jewish nation that was initiated in Parshat Bamidbar. The verse (Num. 1:2) describes the count as: מִסְפַּר שֵׁמוֹת – "a count of names." Each individual in the count was expected to present themselves to Moses, and to introduce themselves to him by name. Interestingly, when they were counted forty years later, the count was not individualized, rather it was a general count of families and tribes.

The message appears to be simple. In order to be counted among a group you must have an individual identity, so that you bring your own unique personality and strengths to enhance the group as a whole. But forty years later, when the nation was counted just before the military conquest of Canaan, it was all about strength in numbers. In Bamidbar, during the nascent period of Jewish nationhood, God wished to emphasize the fact that a nation only has the strength of a collective group if each individual within that group has a strong personality of their own, as signified by their name, and as acknowledged by Moses through a personal introduction to each of them.

Jack Feldman, his parents Szaja and Matla, his sister Sura Laja, his brother Szulim Hersh, and every other Holocaust victim, whether they were killed or whether they survived, all had a name. They were not simply a number tattooed on an arm, or on some list of statistics. Each one of them had a role to play in the dynamic group known as the Jewish nation. And each one of us also has a role to play, as an individual, within our community and within wider society. We are not just a number, an add on, a faceless member of the group at the back of the room. Even Moses wants to know who we are, and to make sure that our name is recorded for posterity.

As we head into Shavuot and contemplate the formative moment of our religious identity – the revelation at Mount Sinai – we must use the opportunity to refresh our identity so that our contribution is maximized for the good of the Jewish nation as a whole. As Jack Feldman made clear to his great-grandson Elliott – you must never let yourself become a number.

THIS YEAR IN JERUSALEM – A LESSON IN JEWISH UNITY

first published May 25th, 2017

The most famous image of Israel's recapture of Jerusalem in June 1967 is undoubtedly the iconic photo, taken by the late David Rubinger (1924-2017), of three young Israeli paratroopers standing in front of the Western Wall, looking up at that symbol of Jewish longing. The site had only minutes earlier fallen into Jewish hands after being under foreign control for close to 1,900 years. This week, to mark the 50th anniversary of that moment in time, those same three soldiers — Zion Karasanti, Haim Oshri and Itzik Yifat, all of them now in their seventies — retraced the steps of that fateful day, accompanied by photographers and journalists eager to join the trio, and hear how they now feel about that moment.

Perhaps inevitably, the interviews soon degenerated into an argument, as the discussion turned to the difficulties generated for Israel by the recapture of Jerusalem. Responding to one of the journalists, who asked whether the soldiers thought the 1967 photograph represented the start of a tragedy for the State of Israel, Itzik Yifat curtly responded, "I don't believe that we should be ruling over another nation." His erstwhile military buddy, Zion Karasanti, was horrified. "How can you say that, as an Israeli who fought for something after 2,000 years of longing?" he snapped. "We returned the heart of the Jewish people to this country!" Yifat was not so easily silenced. "What am I supposed to tell my grandchildren?" he asked, seemingly rhetorically, then immediately added his own sardonic answer: "that there will be war every year?"

What a far cry from the incredible unity that marked the recapture of Jerusalem 50 years ago, and the euphoria that swept across the Jewish world in its wake. It was the morning of Wednesday, June 7, 1967, which corresponded to the Hebrew calendar date of the 28th of Iyar, just a week before the festival of Shavuot. The war had begun two days earlier, and — at that stage — no one dreamt that it would all be over only four days later. Jewish Jerusalem was suddenly bombarded by artillery fire, despite Israel's behind-the-scenes appeals to Jordan's King Hussein to stay out of the war, so as to avoid potentially devastating consequences for both sides.

Israel's emergency government then decided to advance into East Jerusalem, and to try and capture the Old City and Temple Mount, which had been under Jordanian control since 1948.

About a year ago someone emailed me some audio highlights of Israel Radio's live reporting that day as it unfolded. General Uzi Narkiss, the local IDF commander, can be heard asking, "Tell me, where is the Western Wall? How do we get there?" Radio reporter Yossi Ronen, a macho, secular Israeli, was embedded with the soldiers as they battled their way through the winding alleyways of the Old City. His voice is emotional as he improvises a live commentary: "I'm walking right now down the steps towards the Western Wall. I'm not a religious man. I never have been. But this is the Western Wall, and I'm touching the stones of the Western

Wall." You can hear his voice trembling, as he declares: "I am touching the Wall!"

The *Sheheheyanu* blessing, always recited at special moments in Jewish life, is intoned aloud by the troops, and emotions are clearly running high. Rabbi Shlomo Goren (1917-1994), then chief rabbi of the IDF, later chief rabbi of Israel, his voice choking and excited, recites a unique blessing: "Blessed is God, who comforts Zion and builds Jerusalem." The soldiers with him respond with a resounding "Amen!" You can hear many of them weeping. The shofar is sounded, and the weeping continues. You can still hear gunfire in the background as Rabbi Goren shouts: *Le-shana HAZOT be-Yerushalayim!* — altering the perennial Jewish prayer of hope, "Next year in Jerusalem," into a declaration that translates: "This year in Jerusalem!" The following day, Israel's secular newspapers gushed with the story of Jerusalem's recapture. *Maariv*'s headline read, "The place for which we have waited for 2,000 years," while *Yediot Ahronoth* included a verse from Isaiah (52:9) on its masthead: כִּי נִחַם ה' עַמּוֹ גָּאַל יְרוּשָׁלָיִם – "God has comforted His People, He has redeemed Jerusalem!"

So what has happened since then? How has this euphoria dissipated so drastically, so much so that for many Jews *Yom Yerushalayim* has limited significance — if any at all? How can we reignite the passion that was so evident 50 years ago? How can we get Jews across the board to realize just how incredible our sovereignty over Jerusalem is? I believe that the answer to all these questions emerges out of a Midrash on Parshat Bamidbar.

The Midrash informs us that Moses voiced his concern to God about organizing the twelve Israelite tribes into a specific formation around the sanctuary, as God had instructed.

Irrespective of where they would be positioned, the tribes would inevitably complain and seek to be repositioned, Moses said. But God pacified him and told him not to worry. The tribes already knew where to go, God said; when Jacob's sons had transported his remains from Egypt to Canaan, the formation had been identical with the one that was now being implemented.

God's response is baffling. Why would some historic formation involving their ancestors be relevant centuries later? After all, Jacob's funeral was a one-off event — why should it have any repercussions for the future?

It seems that this was exactly the point. When something extraordinary happens, the default response has a purity and a lack of calculation that can be used as an example of how one can behave in the future. If, upon the death of their father, Jacob's sons had sorted themselves into a formation, this could be used as proof to future generations that this was the right way to do it for all time.

The euphoric reaction of every Jew to the recapture of Jerusalem in 1967, whatever their level of religiosity and connectedness to Judaism, presents us with the perfect example of how every Jew should respond to this remarkable miracle — no matter how many years have passed, and notwithstanding any complicating factors that may have been brought into the mix since that miraculous day.

GREATER THAN THE SUM OF ITS PARTS

first published May 21st, 2014

An extremely important election will be taking place this weekend – the elections for the European Parliament. This election will be the biggest Europe-wide vote in history. The 751 elected members will represent more than 500 million citizens – of whom 400 million are eligible to vote – in 28 member countries.

For those of you who know nothing or very little about European elections, let me furnish you with some key information. Firstly, the number of elected representatives per country is decided by population. Germany has the most representatives, with 96. France will have 74, while Italy and the UK will have 73 each. Cyprus, Estonia, Luxembourg and Malta get just 6 each. Once elected, most national parties join like-minded transnational blocs. So, for example, a UK Labour MEP will probably end up sitting with other European socialists in a group called the Socialists and Democrats, while German Christian Democrats will join the European People's Party, a center-right group.

European parliamentary elections are notoriously hard to predict, as it is almost impossible to conduct precise voting intention polls across so many different countries. Low voter turnout makes predicting a result even more difficult. The big issues in this election are the economic downturn, unemployment, and migration. Or so you would think.

In the UK, 47 out of 70 Labour candidates have signed a letter stating that they "oppose the continued construction of the Separation Wall on Palestinian land which is in contravention of international law," and also that Europe should "end all trade with Israeli settlements illegally built on occupied Palestinian territory," which, by the way, includes most of Jerusalem.

Martin Schulz, current President of the European Parliament, has admitted that nationalist, populist and extremist parties are gaining ground in Europe. An MP in Budapest called for Jews to be registered on lists as threats to national security. Jewish university professors in Europe have been told "Jews, this university is ours, not yours." In Greece, a party that openly embraces Nazi ideology is extremely popular. And last week, at a Palestine Solidarity Campaign event in Manchester, England, an MEP candidate accused Israel of "ethnic cleansing by planning," and said that if elected to Brussels, she would be "representing the people of Palestine."

What are we to make of this? How are we meant to respond to a world that seems not only to have forgotten the Holocaust, but also seems to have forgotten how the Holocaust was the result of years of inflammatory rhetoric and political campaigns that used Jews and antisemitism as a way of deflecting voters' attention away from the real problems they faced?

In Parshat Bamidbar we witness a strange thing. It seems, at first glance, to be a contradiction. God commands Moses to count the Jewish nation, to find out the total manpower that this fledgling nation can muster. Painstakingly, Moshe counts each and every Jew, arriving at a final number – 603,550. Then, having united the nation into one workable number, Moshe is commanded to separate everyone again (Num. 2:2): אִישׁ עַל דִּגְלוֹ בְאֹתֹת לְבֵית אֲבֹתָם יַחֲנוּ בְּנֵי יִשְׂרָאֵל – "The Israelites shall encamp by their fathers' houses, every man with his own banner, according to their signs." Why go through the process of getting the global figure if the intention was to keep each group separate, and each tribe individual?

There is a misleading idea with which we are all familiar – the idea of "strength in numbers." This concept suggests that the more people you have, the greater your chance of success. Time and again, throughout history, this idea has been proven wrong. Management courses and military academies have long abandoned this idea in favor of another one: the tactical use of smaller numbers to achieve results that seem impossible – in effect greater than the sum of those involved. This modern concept is not, however, as modern as it seems. Even by ancient standards, the number of those who could take forward God's "Chosen People" project was miniscule. In terms of the millions who opposed the God-focused and socially just society of the Torah – 603,550 former slaves was hardly an intimidating force.

What turned this group into a power that had to be reckoned with was that every person was expected to take his or her own skill set and valiantly donate it to the strategic cause. Each group had their own mission, and each person contributed something different. Together they formed a formidable, invincible force that not only introduced monotheism and justice to a heathen world, but also, despite remaining statistically insignificant, has relentlessly proven to the world that the forces of good can overcome the forces of evil.

And that is exactly our task in the face of the new antisemitic, anti-Israel onslaught. Each one of us has a skill, a capability, a contact, a network, that we can use to ensure that the forces of evil do not prevail, and that the world's only Jewish country, Israel, remains the beacon of God's message, which originated all those thousands of years ago in the Sinai desert.

NASSO

GETTING TO GRIPS WITH "ZIONOPHOBIC THUGGERY"

first published June 13th, 2019

This week, I was honored with an award from *Algemeiner* at their inaugural West Coast Gala. *Der Algemeiner Journal* was originally launched as a Yiddish language weekly in 1972 (*algemeiner* is the Yiddish word for "universal"), and since then this remarkable media phenomenon has evolved from being a parochial Jewish community newspaper and become a familiar online media presence, now in English, breaking news stories most mainstream outlets disregard, ensuring that the wider news conversation counters false narratives about Israel, and highlights antizionism and antisemitism.

Also receiving an award, posthumously, was the late journalist Daniel Pearl, whose shocking beheading execution by Al Qaeda in 2002 reinforced the horror of the threat this nihilistic group posed to the world. Daniel, the South East Asia bureau chief for the *Wall Street Journal*, was based in Mumbai, India, where he focused on cutting edge news stories relating to the United States' "War on Terror" launched in the wake of the 9/11 attacks.

On January 23, 2002, Pearl was abducted by an Al Qaeda affiliate, and nine days later he was beheaded. In a video released soon afterwards titled *The Slaughter of the Spy-Journalist, the Jew Daniel Pearl*, Daniel addressed the camera with just a few moments to live: "My father is Jewish, my mother is Jewish, I am Jewish," he said. "In the town of Bnei Brak," he added – referring to the Orthodox Jewish town founded in Palestine in 1924 – "there is a street named after my great-grandfather Chaim Pearl, who is one of the founders of the town."

Daniel Pearl was a proud and defiant Jew until the end. Accepting the award for Daniel was his indefatigable father, Judea Pearl, Professor of Computer Science and Statistics and Director of the Cognitive Systems Laboratory at UCLA. Since Daniel's murder, Judea has relentlessly worked to draw attention to the dangers posed by influential individuals and organizations, including mainstream politicians and media outlets, whose agenda it is to reframe terrorism and radical extremism as a legitimate if regrettable response to circumstances that affect those they represent.

In a seminal 2007 *Wall Street Journal* article, Judea Pearl attacked former US President Jimmy Carter, whom he accused of whitewashing terrorist outrages:

> *"The clearest endorsement of terror as a legitimate instrument of political bargaining came from former President Jimmy Carter. In his book "Palestine: Peace Not Apartheid," Mr. Carter appeals to the sponsors of suicide bombing. "It is imperative that the general Arab community and all significant Palestinian groups make it clear that they will end the suicide bombings and other*

acts of terrorism when international laws and the ultimate goals of the Road-map for Peace are accepted by Israel." Acts of terror, according to Mr. Carter, are no longer taboo, but effective tools for terrorists to address perceived injustices."

Recently Judea has had to contend with this problem on his home turf – the UCLA campus. After a mandatory anthropology class was told by Professor Rabab Abdulhadi that "those affiliated with Israel and pro-Israel organizations are white supremacists," Judea asked Jerry Kang, UCLA Vice Chancellor for Equity, Diversity and Inclusion, to insist that Abdulhadi "apologize to the thousands of students and faculty at UCLA who are devout Zionists, whom she labeled 'white supremacists'."

In his acceptance speech at the *Algemeiner* event, which was followed by a standing ovation from an enthusiastic audience that included Simon Wiesenthal Center founder Rabbi Marvin Hier and Hollywood movie star Sharon Stone, Judea insisted that Daniel's legacy would only be served if we stepped out of our comfort zones and called out what he eloquently called "zionophobic thuggery." If we remain huddled in our protective bubbles, we are failing our world's future by allowing these mounting issues to go unchallenged, or at least underchallenged. What Al Qaeda failed to do with terror, their polished allies will do on our campuses, in the media, and in the corridors of power.

There is a fascinating Talmudic debate regarding the desirability of a Nazirite vow, the details of which are found in Parshat Nasso. Abstinence and hermitry may seem like a good idea, and perhaps in individual instances and for limited periods they are, but no group can function properly if it collectively withdraws ever further from the realities of the world around them.

Writing in the eighteenth century, the great kabbalist and ethicist Rabbi Moses Ḥayyim Luzzatto (1707-1746) noted that excessive withdrawal is best defined as any kind of self-restraint or moderation that in the long-term leads to self-harm. He quotes the Talmud (Taanit 22b): "a person is forbidden to afflict himself lest he become too weak to support those who need him."

As hard as it is for us to accept, we are currently in an era in which we do not have the luxury to engage in self-restraint or moderation. As the world around us increasingly undermines the foundation of our hard-earned freedoms and status, both as Jews and as supporters of Israel, instead of pushing back hard, we instinctively retreat into echo chambers and safe spaces. But that is a grave error.

Every time we hear or read something offensive, we need to personally react and respond, venturing out of the safe zones we all inhabit to tackle the hatred at its source. We cannot afford to be Nazirites who abstain from the world in the hope that these problems and challenges will pass somehow, and the world will come back to its senses. The world can only change if we become part of the process of change. Otherwise, we are in danger of becoming the victims of "zionophobic thuggery."

DESPITE OUR DIFFERENCES, WE ARE ALL THE SAME

first published May 24th, 2018

From time to time, producers in Hollywood opt for movies that depict the closed world of ultra-Orthodox Jews. Some of these films have become icons of movie history, such as the very first feature-length "talkie," *The Jazz Singer*, a 1927 musical starring Al Jolson (1886-1950) which charts the story of a cantor's son torn between a flourishing showbiz career and his traditional Jewish heritage.

The 1971 Academy Award winning movie *Fiddler on the Roof* depicted the precarious life of a traditional Jew and his family as they struggle with the challenges of modernity in the face of abject poverty and state-sponsored antisemitism in Czarist Russia. Barbara Streisand's 1983 movie *Yentl* featured Streisand as a girl born into a strictly observant family in early twentieth-century Poland, who dresses and lives like a man so that she can be educated in a male-only yeshiva after her father dies. *The Chosen*, released in 1981, portrayed the turbulent life of Danny, the son of a prominent Hasidic "rebbe" in New York who rejects the stifling atmosphere of his community, and goes off to pursue a university education.

The common denominator of all these movies, and many others like them, is the tension that exists between traditional

Jewish life and modern society. And while it is exactly these tensions and contrasts which create the dramatic backdrop for each screenplay, the unfortunate corollary is the presentation of Orthodox Jews as caricatures – two-dimensional retrogrades stuck in a self-defeating hamster wheel, collectively unable to adapt to the world beyond their own limited lives – a world that has advanced in every way, and whose rejection is to their great disadvantage. Bearded men with sidelocks dressed in strange-looking clothes, drab women in loveless marriages, all of them quite cheerless, engaged in a futile battle against the relentless advance of a modernity they barely comprehend.

This year's token movie featuring ultra-Orthodox Jews is *Disobedience*, a story set in the North West London suburb of Golders Green, where I grew up. The daughter of a strictly Orthodox rabbi returns to London after the death of her father and reconnects with two childhood friends, now married to each other. As with all movies of this genre, the storyline focuses on the restrictive nature of traditional Jewish life, this time in the face of a romance that would be considered perfectly normal in the world beyond the community. Once again, the gloomy atmosphere of a Torah-observant life is contrasted with the joys of an unreachable world that is so tantalizingly close by. To be frank, the oppressive environment depicted in the movie bears no resemblance to the Golders Green community I know.

But the very predictable storyline of *Disobedience* and all the movies like it is exactly what makes the 2017 movie *Menashe* so incredibly refreshing. Remarkably, besides for a few isolated scenes, the entire dialogue is in contemporary Yiddish. The eponymous Menashe is a widower from Borough Park, in Brooklyn, New York, whose son Ruven is cared for by family until

Menashe has found a new wife. The outside world barely intervenes in this heartwarming tale of a clumsy bachelor desperately trying to balance making a living with his duties as a father, while at the same time sustaining his status in the community and staving off despair.

Truthfully, this story could have been set anywhere in New York, in any ethnic setting, or indeed elsewhere in the United States or in any country across the globe. The themes are universal, the human interactions familiar, and as the story unfolds, the hero's beard and sidelocks recede into the background and we are left with a story anyone can relate to, whatever their ethnic or religious identity. Despite the quirks that mark Menashe's community, we are easily able to see past them, and into the heart of a very human drama. After all, human nature is human nature, whatever community you come from. It is not what makes us different that is interesting – what is really interesting is that despite our differences, we are all just the same.

This very point is brought home to us at the end of Parshat Nasso, the longest portion in the Torah, with 176 verses. This oversized portion owes its inflated size to the 89-verse chapter (Num. 7) that recalls the gifts donated by the princes of each tribe at the inauguration of the Tabernacle. Each of the gifts is inventoried in minute detail, despite the fact that all of them are identical. Paradoxically, the commentaries interpret this uniformity as signifying the individuality of each tribe. Although each gift appeared to be indistinguishable from all the others, each one of them had been given with a different idea in mind. For this reason, the Torah, usually so sparing with its words, lists each sacrifice separately, despite their similarity, to emphasize that each gift was distinctive.

I have a slightly different take on this lengthy, repetitive chapter. Whether or not the motivations of each tribe were different, ultimately each of the gifts was exactly the same as every other. Because in the end, however different the tribes may have been from one another, their commonalities were clearly far more dominant than anything that may have divided them.

In the previous portion, Parshat Bamidbar, the Torah goes to great lengths to demonstrate the individuality of each tribe, separating them into independently counted groups, with each of them under their own banner. In Nasso, the message the Torah wishes to impart is that by focusing on these differences we totally miss the point. Whether you are from this or that tribe, the human condition remains the same, and focusing on differences simply distracts us from the core message that we are all a part of one big family.

It seems to me that this is the timeless message of the princes' gifts, and it is a message that continues to warrant our vigilant attention.

THE DECLINE OF PALESTINIAN CHRISTIANS

first published May 29th, 2014

TIME magazine has just published a very interesting report from Bethlehem. During Pope Francis' visit to the Church of the Nativity, one of Christianity's most revered holy sites, the 9,000-seat center of worship was filled to capacity. But as the article noted, the church was not filled with indigenous Catholic faithful, of whom there were, in fact, only a handful:

> *"Laced heavily among the hardy native Palestinian Catholics were guest workers from India and the Philippines working in Israel, asylum seekers from Sudan, American tourists, pilgrims from Ghana, and a smattering of Palestinian Christians from other denominations."*

The article went on to describe how the Christian population in the Palestinian territories has dwindled drastically over the past two decades. Just 1.5% of the Palestinian population in the West Bank is Christian, while in Gaza, there are just 1,250 Christians left, among a population of 1.7 million. Bethlehem itself, once a thriving Christian town, is now overwhelmingly Muslim. The exodus of Palestinian Christians to the US, Canada and Australia has reached epidemic proportions.

Contrast this with Israel. In Israel, Christians are able to thrive and practice their religion without fear of attacks or prejudice. Holy places and shrines are respected, and the Old City of Jerusalem, and every part of Israel, is alive with multiple Christian denominations. Some years ago, I visited the International Christian Embassy in Jerusalem (ICEJ). I distinctly recall the director telling me: "Both of us believe that the Messiah can only come if the Jews return to the Holy Land, so we are both working towards the same goal, even if we disagree about the identity of the Messiah."

To which I responded: "I agree, and I am also certain that his imminent arrival will resolve that particular ambiguity for both of us!"

God tells us via his prophet Isaiah (56:7): וַהֲבִיאוֹתִים אֶל הַר קָדְשִׁי וְשִׂמַּחְתִּים בְּבֵית תְּפִלָּתִי... כִּי בֵיתִי בֵּית תְּפִלָּה יִקָּרֵא לְכָל הָעַמִּים – "I will bring them to my holy mountain and will fill them with joy in my house of prayer…because my Temple will be called a house of prayer for all nations." We, the Jewish nation, are charged by God to be the custodians of the Holy Land, a country that is ours only in the sense that we have the duty to look after it and nurture it, while simultaneously we must open it up for all those who believe in God, and who wish to pray to God.

In Parshat Nasso we read about the dedication of God's sanctuary in the wilderness. Twelve tribes brought twelve gifts to the dedication, and, puzzlingly, despite each gift being absolutely identical, the gifts are listed separately, repeated twelve times. One way the commentators understand this anomaly is that despite each gift being identical, no collusion or consultation preceded the decision of each tribe as to what they should give, with each gift reflecting the result of an internal, uninfluenced decision to contribute to the new sanctuary. The commentators also add that although to us each gift seems identical, none of them was considered identical by God, as He knew that they were accompanied by different intentions and thought processes, making each one unique.

Doing the same thing does not mean uniformity; rather it means unity of purpose. The paradox of religious tolerance in the Holy Land, and of the so-called Peace Process, is the glaring imbalance of purpose. The evidence on the ground – blatant and obvious, even to a TIME magazine reporter – is that "tolerance" in Bethlehem means keeping the Church of the Nativity available for papal visits as a public relations exercise, while the declining Christian population points to what is evidently an intolerable life for Palestinian Christians. On the other hand, in Jerusalem and elsewhere in Israel, tolerance means what it says on the box – diversity, and freedom to practice your religion whatever that religion may be.

So, when the Pontiff invites two presidents to the Vatican, Israel's president and the Palestinian president, to relaunch the stalled peace talks, he would do well to first ensure a unity of purpose.

Peace to Israelis, and to Jews around the world, means an expectation that Israel is recognized as the national homeland of the Jews that is open and welcoming to anyone who wishes to pray with us, and unite with us to usher in a Messianic era. Is that what peace means to the Palestinian president?

Surely Pope Francis, who must have observed the dwindling number of Christians in Bethlehem, who must know of the PA's recent pact with Hamas in Gaza (which, as he is surely aware, is *Judenrein*), who must be aware that Mecca and Medina are proscribed places for non-Muslims, who must have heard that there are even extremist Muslims who want to install Sharia Law in Western Europe – must understand that sadly, the words tolerance and peace do not necessarily mean the same thing to Palestinians as they do to Israelis? And if tolerance does not mean tolerance, and peace does not mean peace, a Vatican summit, or any summit, will simply be a waste of time.

BEHAALOTECHA

AOC – JUST SAY SORRY!

first published June 20th, 2019

I s Rep. Alexandria Ocasio-Cortez an antisemite? Does she care one iota about offending Jews? This week the freshman congresswoman was once again under fire, this time for an Instagram video she live-streamed regarding the treatment of migrants on the United States' southern border, many of whom are confined in detention facilities while the immigration authorities try to stem the tide of illegal immigration.

Last month more than 144,000 migrants tried to make their way into the US, the highest monthly number on record. Responding to this growing humanitarian crisis, Ocasio-Cortez declared that the United States "is running concentration camps on our southern border." The video quickly went viral, sending shockwaves across the country and around the world.

According to *Encyclopedia Britannica*, a concentration camp is an "internment center for political prisoners and members of national or minority groups who are confined for reasons of state security, exploitation, or punishment." Crucially, *Britannica* adds that "political concentration camps instituted primarily to reinforce the state's control have been established in various forms under many totalitarian regimes—most extensively in *Nazi Germany* (my italics) and the Soviet Union."

And in case you think Ocasio-Cortez was innocently using this term, she went on to make the connection between concentration camps and the Holocaust crystal clear:

> *"They are concentration camps ... I want to talk to the people that are concerned enough with humanity to say that ... "never again" means something."*

"Never Again!" is a slogan popularized in the closing decades of the twentieth century as the mantra of those perpetuating the memory of six million Jews killed in the Holocaust, many of whom suffered their fate after being incarcerated in Nazi concentration camps.

This is hardly the first time Ocasio-Cortez has upset the Jewish community. In February she spent an hour on the phone to Jeremy Corbyn, controversial leader of the UK Labour Party, who has been dogged by accusations of antisemitism and was branded by the UK's former chief rabbi, Rabbi Lord Jonathan Sacks, as a "dangerous antisemite". Following her conversation with Corbyn, Ocasio-Cortez tweeted: "It was an honor to share such a lovely and wide-reaching conversation with you, @jeremycorbyn!" Criticism was swift and included her Jewish supporters, shocked by her insensitivity. Ocasio-Cortez promised to make amends, but this latest episode demonstrates she has not learnt her lesson.

Truthfully, unless you are Jewish, it is hard to convey just how touchy a topic the Holocaust is for Jews. It is latent in our DNA to react to any evocative imagery or language, and to imprecise moral equivalence, all seen as potential signs of an environment sliding towards indiscriminate societal antisemitism and ultimately a genocide that will target Jews while the world turns a blind eye. And we have every right to be paranoid. It has happened before, so why can't it happen again? Hence the mantra "never again!"

Having said that, a gentile can certainly be forgiven for straying into this minefield – after all, no gentile can be expected to truly understand the existential angst of post-Holocaust Jews. Drifting into sensitive territory is not a crime if you don't know you are being offensive. Which means that using Holocaust-era concentration camps as a benchmark to judge current US immigration facilities on the southern border could, in certain circumstances, be judged as the innocently misjudged opinion of the uninformed.

But that all changes once the sensitivity is revealed. In response to the offensive tweet, the world's premier Holocaust research center and museum, Yad Vashem, suggested that Ocasio-Cortez should learn about the Holocaust before invoking it to score political points. "Concentration camps assured a slave labor supply to help in the Nazi war effort, even as the brutality of life inside the camps helped assure the ultimate goal of 'extermination through labor,'" the museum tweeted on Wednesday. Many others, Jews and non-Jews from across the political spectrum, reacted with similar indignation to Ocasio-Cortez's remarks.

And yet, despite the outcry, Ocasio-Cortez has refused to back down or apologize, trying to squirm out of the hole she has dug for herself by pretending that she used the term "concentration camp" generically, invoking the precedent of the US "concentration camps" which housed Japanese internees during World War Two, and also suggesting there is a difference between "concentration camp" and "death camp" – a claim immediately rejected by the group that runs the visitors center at Auschwitz. Just like Ken Livingstone before her, it is Ocasio-Cortez's reaction to criticism that has revealed her true colors.

Towards the end of Parshat Behaalotecha, Miriam told her brother Aaron that Moses' relationship with his wife was wanting. On the face of it, her criticism was comfortably within the bounds of sibling norms. Both Miriam and Aaron were prophets and maintained normal relationships with their spouses; Miriam was unable to comprehend why Moses spent so little time with his wife. The passage goes on to record God's intervention and words of rebuke. Moses was an extraordinary person, God told Miriam, and could not be judged by normal standards, nor even by the standards of his fellow-prophets.

But the narrative does not end there, adding the following: (Num. 12:9): וַיִּחַר אַף ה' בָּם וַיֵּלַךְ – "God became angry with them and left." This is puzzling. Why did God become angry after he had already rebuked Miriam? Surely His displeasure came first?

Rabbi Obadiah Sforno (1475-1550) offers a sharp insight. Unlike King David, who responded to rebuke by admitting "I have sinned!", Miriam did not admit her guilt, staying silent, as if to say, "I did nothing wrong." It was this that turned an innocent chat with Aaron into a misdemeanor, resulting in God's anger and departure. Oftentimes it is not the sin that is wrong, but the lack of contrition.

In the case of Alexandria Ocasio-Cortez, her lack of contrition reveals a very worrying flaw. Whether or not the treatment of illegal migrants is wrong or inhumane, by refusing to apologize for her offensive remark, Ocasio-Cortez has strayed across a red line. She may or may not be an antisemite, but she certainly has no qualms about offending Jews.

ICONOCLASM IS THE ROAD TO SELF-DESTRUCTION

first published May 31st, 2018

Afua Hirsch is a British lawyer and journalist, born to a Jewish father whose family escaped Nazi Berlin in 1938, and an Ashanti Ghanaian mother. She is best known as a strident social critic who likes to focus on the imperceptible racism and prejudice that continues to permeate British society – imperceptible, that is, to those who aren't its victims.

Last February, Hirsch published her first book, *Brit(ish): On Race, Identity and Belonging*, which the publisher promoted as a "personal and provocative investigation" into the collective denial that pervades British society in terms of its racist past and present. Despite the merits of her cause, however, like so many other tabloid polemicists, Hirsch seems to have lost the plot along the way, and instead of recognizing the fundamentally positive nature of British identity, she tears it apart – all under the guise of presenting a "warts-and-all" perspective that doesn't brush uncomfortable truths under the carpet. But what begins as a quest to get Britain to look at itself in a mirror, ends up as a McCarthyesque witch-hunt that targets icons of British history and trashes Britishness as hypocritical snobbery masquerading as tolerance and inclusiveness.

For Hirsch this is not new territory. Last August, in the wake of the removal of Confederacy monuments in the U.S., she wrote an article headlined, *Toppling statues? Here's why Nelson's Column should be next*. The article demanded the removal of London's most prominent monument, Nelson's Column, erected in 1840 to honor the memory of Admiral Horatio Nelson (1758-1805) who led the British naval fleet that decisively defeated Napoleon and his allies at the Battle of Trafalgar. For Hirsch, honoring Nelson is a provocation, on account of his notorious opposition the campaign by William Wilberforce (1759-1833) to abolish slavery. Nelson is "what you would call now, without hesitation, a white supremacist," she said, making his continued hero-status an affront to the descendants of slaves whose slavery he both endorsed and exploited.

I have not read *Brit(ish): On Race, Identity and Belonging*, and doubt I ever will, but I did glance through a number of reviews. Michael Henderson in *The Times* called it a "racism-obsessed polemic [that] is tiresome and clichéd," while David Goodhart of London's *Evening Standard* called it "a case study of disaffected identity, shaped by a sense of exclusion that [Hirsch] positively seeks."

Earlier this week, Hirsch took things up a notch with a TV program called *The Battle for Britain's Heroes*, in which she challenged the universal reverence for Sir Winston Churchill (1875-1965), the fearless wartime leader who led the fight against Hitler that ultimately resulted in his defeat. This jarring iconoclasm resulted in a heated debate with Piers Morgan on the widely-watched TV program, *Good Morning Britain*. Morgan unequivocally condemned Hirsch's attempt to "besmirch" Churchill by suggesting he was an unreconstructed racist.

"You know what? Beating Adolf Hitler, winning the war, stopping him exterminating every Jew he could get his hands on – these to me are far greater achievements than the negatives that lurk in his past, which lurk in anybody's past."

Hirsch forcefully defended her position, saying that admiration for Churchill was the product of ignorance regarding his darker side. Piers dismissed this, telling her that she needed to look at the "bigger picture." But Hirsch was unrepentant; "this is the bigger picture!" she replied. So, what are your thoughts? Who got it right, Morgan or Hirsch?

At the end of Parshat Behaalotecha, there is a short narrative piece about Moses' sister, Miriam, who criticizes her brother, and is punished by God for doing so. God tells her that Moses is different from everyone else, even other prophets, and she had no right to criticize him (Num. 12:1-15). Maimonides ("*Rambam*"; 1138-1204) uses this episode as proof of the severity of gossip and slander, in Hebrew known as *lashon hara*. Notwithstanding the fact that Miriam had nurtured and cared for Moses as a child, and had meant Moses no harm, she was penalized and reprimanded for her words.

The prewar rabbinic luminary and Holocaust martyr, Rabbi Elḥanan Wasserman (1874-1941), puzzles over the idea that this story is the basis for the *lashon hara* prohibition. After all, Maimonides includes the supremacy of Moses as the prophet who delivered the Torah to the nation as one of his thirteen primary principles of faith. Surely this means that Miriam's offense was not simply *lashon hara*, as her criticism undermined a primary Jewish belief – and that was why she was so severely chastised?

My own view is that Rabbi Wasserman's suggested solution to this problem is a stretch and doesn't really feel right. Miriam was not a heretic, he says, as it was only through God's reaction that Moses' unique status became known. When Miriam spoke about Moses, he was still considered ordinary, and her words were considered straightforward *lashon hara*. This resolves the problem with Maimonides' use of this story as the basis of the laws of *lashon hara*.

I would like to suggest an alternative answer that is less challenging. Rather than trying to undermine her brother's leadership or destroy his image, Miriam was simply engaged in constructive criticism, however misguided. Indeed, this is often the case with *lashon hara* – the agenda is to correct an aberration or improve a situation. In the case of an ordinary person talking about another ordinary person, *lashon hara* is treated as social misconduct. But in the case of an iconic leader or inspirational hero, constructive criticism can lead to damaging cynicism, or even anarchy. And when the agenda is polemical deconstruction and unbridled nihilism, as in the case of Afua Hirsch against Sir Winston Churchill, it is not *lashon hara*, but rather it is a deliberate path towards self-destruction.

Maimonides understood that any lessening of our greatest prophet's supremacy undermines the Torah's stature and is therefore a grave threat to Judaism. And while not exactly comparable, it is equally clear that if the legacy of Sir Winston Churchill is threatened, the freedom for which he fought will inevitably also be in grave danger.

SELF-ESTEEM NEEDS A FOUNDATION

first published June 8th, 2016

A couple of weeks ago marked the second anniversary of the passing of a colorful late twentieth century California politician — Assemblyman John Vasconcellos (1932-2014). If Vasconcellos is remembered at all, it is for his attempt to reshape the social science outlook of the U.S. with his 1986 campaign to *Promote Self-Esteem and Personal and Social Responsibility*, spearheaded by a "task force" paid for by the State of California.

Vasconcellos passionately believed that many of society's ills — whether it was the high divorce rates, rampant drug abuse, or rising crime — stemmed from the diminished feelings of self-worth endemic in American society. Lacking credible evidence for his theory, he came up with the idea for a task force to investigate this phenomenon that would produce a report based on their research.

Convinced the report would confirm his hunch, Vasconcellos forced lawmakers to legislate social policies that would result in all Americans feeling good about themselves. He was certain the ensuing "self-esteem revolution" would turn the United States into a real-life Shangri La.

After all, if everyone felt validated and self-confident, why would anyone self-medicate, or engage in criminal acts?

Initially the scheme was widely ridiculed as the perfect example of Californian eccentricity, and cartoonist Garry Trudeau superbly parodied Vasconcellos' crusade in his widely syndicated *Doonesbury* comic strip. But despite this, the confluence of a number of factors soon resulted in the adoption of self-esteem promotion strategies, particularly in education and the corporate world. Even those who had laughed at Vasconcellos were swept up by the alluring idea that strategies which boosted self-esteem would reduce tensions in society and increase productivity and personal happiness.

In Vasconcellos' perfect world of mass self-esteem, everyone could be a winner. In one fell swoop one could eliminate the deflation that inevitably accompanies losing, which in turn leads to low self-esteem. Everyone could learn to love themselves, and to feel good about who they are. Teachers were told not to criticize their students, and to do away with competitive learning. Corporate bosses instituted 'employee of the month' awards, so that even a checkout agent, or a burger flipper, could take pride in their success, and feel valued.

Remarkably, this social revolution was underway long before the task force had published as much as a single page of research. Unsurprisingly, it took them over a year to come up with an agreed definition for self-esteem, and the final report was only published years later, in 1989, by which time its expected conclusions had long been used as the basis for social strategies.

The report, when it came, was underwhelming, and failed to deliver any empirical evidence of a correlation between low self-esteem and antisocial behavior. The team had originally assumed they would prove that positive self-esteem prevented problems, and low self-esteem caused problems — but they did not. In fact, nothing in their research proved any of Vasconcellos' enthusiastically promoted ideas, and the authors noted that although they had carefully "assessed the... factors important in the genesis of many social problems" they had been "unable to uncover many causally valid findings relating to that genesis."

And contrary to the suggestions of those promoting the idea of universal self-esteem, they admitted that "self-esteem is a product of, or is associated with, character traits such as honesty, responsibility, perseverance, kindness, and self-discipline." Or, to paraphrase, self-esteem is the mark of those who work for it or merit it, and such individuals are undaunted by challenge, whether it is internal or external.

I was struck by this idea as I prepared for my Parshat Behaalotecha shiur, which closely examined the episode of Miriam and Aaron's negative discussion concerning their brother Moses. Immediately after the verses that record what they said, the Torah makes an extraordinary proclamation about Moses (Num. 12:3): וְהָאִישׁ מֹשֶׁה עָנָו מְאֹד מִכֹּל הָאָדָם אֲשֶׁר עַל פְּנֵי הָאֲדָמָה – "And the man, Moses, was very humble, more so than any other person on earth."

For Moses to be referred to as "humble" is odd – don't forget, he was the man who remonstrated with God on numerous occasions, on one occasion demanding that any reference to him be removed from God's Torah — hardly a demonstration of humility. The declaration also seems superfluous, as the narrative flows perfectly well without it. That being the case, why is the statement necessary in the context of this story? And even more strikingly, there is the strange opening word *veha'ish* – "and the man." What exactly is it telling us?

This sibling-crisis episode is the subject of much debate among the commentators, but all of them agree on one thing — that the criticism leveled at Moses was based on the appearance of his impropriety, at least from the perspective of his siblings, and was also very hurtfully expressed. One might have expected him to react defensively, or at least to get offended. But he did not react at all, and the Torah clearly feels the need to fill in this gap before it informs us of God's powerful response. Moses, the Torah says, was an *ish* – which is the Torah's code word for a great person. Torah greatness is never about temporal power or intellect, rather it is always about spiritual accomplishments and character.

The Torah continues by telling us that although Moses had achieved this elevated *ish* status — no doubt the result of hard work and devoted character development — he remained an *anav*, with no need to project himself or self-promote, and he was also totally unconcerned by any criticism leveled at him by others. Moses' silence makes perfect sense. If self-esteem is grounded in extraordinary achievement and true greatness, no challenge can undermine it, even if it comes from people like Miriam and Aaron.

And on this basis, I would suggest that we too can be "very humble, more so than any other person on earth." If our own self-esteem is genuine, based on a solid foundation rather than a faddy social experiment, just like Moses, our healthy state of mind won't be contingent on our validation by any other person on the planet.

SHELACH

THE DANGER OF PEOPLE POWER

first published June 18th, 2020

Those familiar with the history of British cinema will certainly have heard of a genre of films known as the Ealing Comedies, a series of comedy films produced by Ealing Studios in London between 1947 and 1957. Among the light-touch dry comedic Ealing masterpieces were movies such as *Kind Hearts and Coronets* (1949), *The Lavender Hill Mob* (1951), and *The Ladykillers* (1955), starring, among others, Sir Alec Guinness, Alastair Sim, Margaret Rutherford and Stanley Holloway. But although all of these movies were groundbreaking, as well as hugely entertaining, there is one that sticks out in particular in terms of its originality – and its prescience. That movie is *Passport to Pimlico* (1949).

Pimlico is an upscale residential neighborhood in central London, just south of Belgravia, best known for its imposing Regency era townhouses and famous residents, which have included Sir Winston Churchill (1875-1965) and Sir Laurence Olivier (1907-1989). The rather far-fetched premise of *Passport to Pimlico* hinges on the discovery of a buried treasure in Pimlico after an unexploded wartime bomb is triggered by accident. Alongside the treasure is an ancient document which reveals that the area now known as Pimlico was originally gifted to the Duke of Burgundy in 1477, and is in fact its own legal entity, and crucially, it is not governed by British law. Overwhelmed by the opportunity this presents in the rather grim postwar climate, Pimlico residents decide to declare their independence from the United Kingdom. But although this leads to a short-term economic boom, very soon the area descends into complete chaos.

With its tongue firmly in its cheek, the movie explores the tension between the human desire to be free of any external control versus the benefits and safety that such control brings to society.

Although *Passport to Pimlico* principally reflects the irrepressible spirit of Londoners in the wake of the devastating war years and the difficult period of postwar austerity, in an uncanny way, the film foreshadows many aspects of the political climate of today, with ordinary people banding together and resisting the ruling classes who they see as oppressive and retrograde.

But be that as it may, I never imagined in my wildest dreams that the movie's central premise would one day become a reality. How wrong I was.

Approximately two weeks ago, six blocks in Seattle, Washington, "ceded" from the United States after the Seattle Police Department (SPD) vacated its East Precinct building. This area is now a self-declared autonomous zone known as the Capitol Hill Autonomous Zone (CHAZ).

On June 9, the activists behind CHAZ listed thirty of their demands online, which, among other things, included the abolition of SPD and the Seattle court system; defunding SPD and reallocating those funds to health costs; banning police use of firearms, batons, riot shields, and chemical agents; the release of prisoners serving time for marijuana-related offenses or resisting arrest; mandatory retrials for people of color who are serving sentences for violent crimes; and prison abolition.

I have puzzled over why these urban anarchists think that the US authorities should take any notice of the demands of self-declared foreign nationals, but I am guessing the irony of that particular observation would be lost on them. It is also unclear to me what exactly the United States would get in return for agreeing to the demands, and it's not as if CHAZ has either military or diplomatic leverage. But most intriguing of all – I am really struggling to work out on what basis a bunch of street activists can decide to seize sovereign territory. At least the silver-screen Pimlico group had an ancient manuscript to underscore their claim. These guys have nothing.

The Beatle John Lennon (1940-1980), in addition to being a great songwriter was simultaneously an insidious nihilist. In 1971, he released a song titled *Power to the People*. The song utilized a slogan that had gained traction through the 1960s among antiwar protestors and radical elements of the civil rights movement whose aim was to foment rebellion against the establishment. But like so many other slogans concocted and popularized by champagne revolutionaries, the reality of "people power" has always proven to be more suffering, not less.

Abuses of power are the tragic consequence of power, and every system needs checks and balances to mitigate and reduce the ill effects of corruption. But to abandon the system altogether and put the lives of ordinary citizens in the hands of people driven by slogans is unquestionably a far greater threat than anything a faulty system is guilty of.

The Book of Bamidbar contains a number of narratives featuring "people power" as their central theme. The most prominent of these narratives are the story of the spies in Parshat Shelach, and the story of Korah's rebellion in Parshat Korach. In both of them the driving force was ostensibly a popular revolt against top-down authority, but that was not the case at all. In reality, sinister forces were at work, manipulating the masses into believing they would be better off, when actually this was not true at all, and nor was this the aim of those behind each insurgency. The spies were all princes of their tribes, and their motivation was a desire to retain power over the people, who they feared would depose them if they moved into the Land of Israel. Meanwhile, Korah presented his revolt as a "people power" revolution, but he was really just a power-hungry plutocrat using popular discontent to propel him into a leadership position.

There is something strangely alluring about "people power," a kind of idealism that seizes us and dazzles us. Somehow, we think, not unreasonably, that those in authority could be doing a better job, and that if we clipped their wings and devolved power to the people, the world would be a better place. But history has proven time and time again that the very opposite is true. Most "people power" revolutions have resulted in nothing but suffering and misery, even as a handful of devious insurrectionists have taken advantage of our idealistic naiveté and seized control in the power vacuum the revolution has created.

At the end of *Passport to Pimlico*, Pimlico returns to the fold, abandoning its independence aspirations and reuniting with Britain while life returns to "normal." The message seems to be that despite all the sacrifices and enthusiastic optimism, when push comes to shove, anarchy serves nothing but itself, and all efforts to completely rewrite the human rulebook are doomed to fail. Before it is too late, we need to realize that those behind CHAZ are not just a bunch of cheeky chaps thumbing their nose at the system; rather they represent a real threat to our hard-earned democracy and freedoms, and the sooner they are shut down for good, the better.

[Postscript : The CHAZ zone was cleared of occupants by Seattle's police on July 1st, 2020, leading to 44 arrests, and a further 25 were taken into custody.]

BEWARE OF GOD-BELIEVING HERESY

first published June 7th, 2018

Earlier this week, thousands of Satmar Hasidim gathered at the Nassau Coliseum in Long Island, for an event led by the Satmar Rebbe, Rabbi Aron Teitelbaum. The purpose of the rally was to reassert Satmar's rejection of Zionism, along with their continued non-recognition of the State of Israel. The climax was an address by Rabbi Teitelbaum, who spoke for just under an hour and twenty minutes.

During his impassioned if somewhat rambling speech – subsequently made available online, despite platitudinous declarations against online technology made by other speakers at the event – Rabbi Teitelbaum reviewed Satmar's jaundiced version of Zionist history over the past century, and contended that the concept of a Jewish state is antithetical to Judaism.

Ironically, at one point he lamented the fact that in recent years Satmar devotees openly celebrated when Israel succeeded on the international stage and in military campaigns. How is it possible, he asked, that the spiritual heirs of the ideology espoused by the Satmar sect's revered founder, Rabbi Joel Teitelbaum (1887-1979), could find anything positive to say about the State of Israel and its Prime Minister? Especially, he added, when the late rebbe had predicted that anyone who celebrated Zionist triumphs would not merit to rejoice in the coming of the Messiah.

Truthfully, as a religious and deeply committed Jew, it is hard to know how to respond to this kind of hostility towards Israel by such a large and important group of Orthodox Jews, many of them deeply sincere, when it is so clear that Israel represents the most important theological development for Judaism in thousands of years. While one can understand how rabbis during the early years of Zionism, and even after 1948, might have been concerned by the very secular nature of the Zionist leadership, and their callous rejection of any Jewish traditions or beliefs that did not dovetail with Zionism, it is clear that the situation has moved on in every sense.

Searching our heritage for obscure references to prove that Jewish self-determination is forbidden before the Messiah's arrival is the worst kind of self-defeating futility. The truth is so clear to see. God has provided us with our very own sovereign country, in the very land that was promised to our forefathers, and in exactly the way that was predicted by our earliest prophets.

It's not those Satmar Hasidim who celebrate Israel's successes who have got it wrong – unfortunately, it is the Satmar leadership and whoever it was who wasted the money to pay for the Nassau Coliseum to stage this retrograde rally who have got it wrong.

Those within the Orthodox community who still insist on sustaining an anti-Israel stance are living in a time warp, unable to climb down from their anti-Zionist tree to join the vast majority of Torah-true Jews who have no difficulty recognizing Israel and its existence for the prophecy-realizing miracle that it so clearly is. But the issue I really grapple with is whether or not religiously observant Jews who reject the State of Israel and decry its existence actually believe in God. After all, how can one reject the realization of prophecy, and the miraculous nature of Israel's sustained survival, and still believe in the God who gave us the very Hebrew Scriptures which contain the blueprint for everything that has unfolded and continues to unfold before our eyes?

Intriguingly, I recently came across a commentary by Rabbi Moses Sofer of Pressburg ("*Chatam Sofer*"; 1762-1839) on Parshat Shelach that seems to address this exact point. The reason I find what he says so intriguing is because the intransigent zealotry of orthodox anti-Zionism has its roots in an absolutist interpretation and adoption of the "legacy" of Rabbi Sofer by a faction of his followers during the second half of the nineteenth century.

The reaction of the Israelites to the negative report delivered by the spies upon their return from Canaan, and their insistent demand that the nation should return to Egypt (Num. 14:3-4), prompts Rabbi Sofer to question their true commitment to God. Having received the Torah at Sinai in the knowledge that their next destination was the Promised Land, their desire to abandon this mission on the basis of some worrying information, and to scurry back to the land where they had suffered slavery and persecution, can surely only be interpreted as an explicit rejection of God.

But Rabbi Sofer dismisses this analysis as a profound misunderstanding. On the contrary, this entire episode is a primary example of misusing God and religion in the pursuit of deviant goals. The spies came up with countless reasons why going back to Egypt was exactly what God really wanted – the exile had not yet expired; the Israelites had only come into the wilderness to receive the Torah, and now it was time to return to Egypt; God would miraculously empty the Promised Land of its inhabitants, and then they would take it over, but meanwhile they should wait in Egypt.

The Israelites who listened to this group of distinguished holy men addressing them that day at the Sinai Desert's version of the Nassau Coliseum lapped it all up, and became utterly convinced that God wanted them to return to Egypt, believing that it was Moses who had got it wrong, not them, and certainly not the ten esteemed princes of Israel. What the spies perpetrated that day, when they returned from their mission, was a gross misuse of religious influence.

Almost as soon as they had fallen for the lies of the spies, the nation realized their mistake and attempted to launch their own invasion of Canaan. But it was too late. The military campaign was a disaster, and it would be a full forty years before they were able to enter the land.

What the *Chatam Sofer* is telling us unequivocally is that whenever religious leaders misuse religion and our devotion to God to promote ideologies that are offensive to God, we must immediately call them out and redouble our efforts to stay in lockstep with God's mission, as expressed to us by our cherished prophets and holy scriptural texts.

THE DANGERS OF GROUP DYNAMICS

first published June 15th, 2017

I recently wrote an article about the German-born social psychologist, Kurt Lewin (1890-1947). Although most people have never heard of him, Lewin was utterly unique, an innovative pioneer in many areas of psychology and sociology at a time when both of those fields were still very much in their infancy. His extensive research and rigorous studies continue to affect every one of us in ways we are not even aware of. Lewin coined the term "group dynamics," and extensively researched how groups of people behave when they are together, both internally within the group, and as a group towards others. The central idea that underpins "group dynamics" is that the behavior of an individual will change when they are part of a group.

Nowadays Lewin's research is often used in business management schools to teach the mechanics of team building, using a model proposed in 1965 by the eminent psychologist, Professor Bruce Tuckman (1938-2016), called "forming–storming–norming–performing," which charts the development of a successful team through four separate stages. During the initial "forming," "storming" and "norming" stages of the process, individual members of the group may be unclear as to the collective objectives of the team. The success or failure of the team as a whole will hinge on each person's ability to set aside any individualisms that may detract from the ultimate success of the team as a whole.

The important point is this – group dynamics is an extremely powerful force, and when exercised efficiently it can produce incredible results. But there is also a dark side to group dynamics – the power of the group can overwhelm a person's individual desire to do the right thing, leading to situations in which good people do bad things as a result of the overwhelming impact of group dynamics. In extreme cases this phenomenon can be manipulated by corrupt or evil people – with dreadful results. This is why seemingly normal people join destructive cults, or fall under the spell of evil ideologies, such as Nazism or radical Islamism.

Group dynamics should not be used as an excuse for individuals who perpetrate evil and then blame the group, in an attempt to absolve themselves of responsibility. On the contrary, it is precisely the dangers of this phenomenon that must be at the forefront of one's mind if we find ourselves slipping into undesirable behaviors. We need to be thinking: "is this happening because I am part of a bad group?" Most importantly, we need to be aware that no one is immune to the effects of group dynamics, nor is anyone its slave, as is evident from the quite remarkable episode of the twelve "spies" sent by Moses to check out the Land of Canaan.

The text reveals that each of the twelve men sent by Moses on the mission was distinguished and upstanding (Num. 13:3): כֻּלָּם אֲנָשִׁים רָאשֵׁי בְנֵי יִשְׂרָאֵל הֵמָּה – "all of them men [of standing], they were leaders of the Children of Israel." How was it possible for this team of extraordinary individuals to betray God's plan, and to return from Canaan with negative information? Not only were they from the generation who heard God's voice at the foot of Mount Sinai – they were its leaders! How does their treachery make any sense?

As if this is not puzzling enough, two of them – Joshua and Caleb – did not abandon their true mission in favor of the scheme to mislead the nation. What was it that enabled these two to stay loyal while the other ten went rogue? The commentaries offer a range of answers to explain the mysterious transformation of ten honorable men into agents of disaster. The text itself offers us very few clues, although there is at least one clue within the text that reveals the dynamics of what occurred. While the ten spies are initially named individually, once the mission had begun they are no longer named as individuals. Instead they are referred to as a group, or they refer to themselves as a group: "they stated," "they spoke," "we saw," "we were."

It is unlikely that they all delivered the report at the same time in unison. Rather it must have been one or two of them who acted as spokesmen for the whole group. And yet, no individual from the group is named as a spokesperson. Evidently, however illustrious each of them may have been at the outset, as a group they had brought out the worst in each other, and whoever it was that spoke was not merely speaking as an individual – instead, he had been reduced to a mouthpiece for collective evil.

Meanwhile, Joshua and Caleb are mentioned by name as having spoken out in favor of the land. In Joshua's case, Moses had changed his name before he left to include a reference to God, fortifying him from any negative influences. Caleb took time out during the forty-day expedition to visit the tombs of the patriarchs and matriarchs in Hebron, which we are informed was to protect himself from the insidious influence of his colleagues.

The powerful lesson from these two great men is that the only protection against falling prey to negative group dynamics is vigilance. Even if you are entirely honorable, as part of a group you must be constantly aware and conscious of the core values you cherish and championed before you joined the group. Otherwise you will inevitably become faceless and nameless, part of a mob that can descend to the lowest common denominator.

Particularly in our times, when masses of people subscribe to ideologies and beliefs that contravene our fundamental Jewish values, we must be attentive and mindful that we don't fall prey to the malign influence of group dynamics, but instead stand up for what is right, like Joshua and Caleb, who, as a result of their conviction and courage, merited to enter into the Promised Land.

KORACH

WHAT MAKES A TRUE LEADER?

first published July 4th, 2019

Τ his week, motor-industry legend Lee Iacocca died at the age of 94. Iacocca's father, an Italian immigrant restaurateur from Pennsylvania, once told his son that "when you die, if you've got five real friends you've had a great life." But while that advice may have haunted Iacocca, the world is not going to judge him by how many friends he had, rather he will be evaluated on the basis of his groundbreaking successes as an inspired and inspirational business leader.

In his 2007 book, *Where Have All the Leaders Gone?*, Iacocca noted that leaders should be judged using "nine C's of leadership": Curiosity, Creativity, Communication, Character, Courage, Conviction, Charisma, Competence, and Common Sense. "The job of a leader is to accomplish goals that advance the common good. Anyone can take up space, [but] the test of a leader [is simple] – when he leaves office, we should be better off than when he started."

Any pointers from a man who revived the fortunes of not one, but two struggling motor giants – Ford and Chrysler – are worth considering seriously. Nevertheless, there is something missing from his list of C's.

Rajeev Peshawaria, a leadership development lecturer utilized by some of the biggest names in the corporate world to coach their executive teams, often begins his seminars by asking participants to complete the sentence "Leadership is the act of …." in fifteen words or less. Remarkably, his audiences invariably complete the sentence using a variation of the same theme: "Leadership is the act of setting shared goals and inspiring/motivating people to work together towards achieving them." It turns out that most people believe that good leadership is defined by what a leader can get others to do, or by what they can do for others. But the history of great leaders tells a different story.

Mahatma Gandhi (1869-1948), the legendary Indian nationalist who led his country to independence and inspired civil rights movements across the world, had a different notion of his role as a leader, famously declaring "my life is my message." While Gandhi certainly possessed all of Iacocca's C's, the quality that really set him apart was his clear set of personal values, coupled with his relentless commitment towards achieving and upholding them. He never set out to lead others, only to lead himself, and consequently, those who followed him were not obeying orders, rather he was their role model of commitment to personal growth and the cause of Indian independence via non-violent means. Gandhi walked the walk, so his followers did the same.

The greatest leaders of Jewish history were all reluctant to lead, and their success as leaders was always a reflection of both their personal humility and their self-sacrifice. King David's introduction into scripture is via the recommendation of one of

King Saul's courtiers (1 Sam. 16:18), who tells the king that David is "a man of valor, a brave warrior, careful how he speaks, a man with presence, and God is with him." As the narrative unfolds, and Saul tries to kill him, David is always respectful and restrained, inspiring Saul's own son Jonathan to recognize him as the true king.

And yet, despite the acclaim, David resists the temptation to replace Saul, or to harm him in any way. Throughout the remainder of his life, King David demonstrated an extraordinary capacity for reflection and self-improvement, in spite of numerous setbacks and occasional failings, and is cited by the Talmud as the paradigm for repentance (Avodah Zara 5a). Ultimately, notwithstanding his outstanding leadership qualities, King David's elevated status in Jewish tradition is based on his personal journey, not on his charisma or communication skills.

Moses is similarly considered a model of Jewish leadership, not because he led the Jews out of Egypt, but as a result of his humility and selflessness. Moses' greatest nemesis was his cousin Korah, who challenged him to relinquish the leadership in favor of others equally suited to run the nation's religious and civil affairs. After all, Korah argued (Num. 16:3), כִּי כָל הָעֵדָה כֻּלָּם קְדֹשִׁים וּבְתוֹכָם ה' – "the whole community is holy, all of them, and God is in their midst." Despite presiding over the most threatening challenge to Moses' leadership, the Midrash portrays Korah as a wise and talented man. So what was it that led him astray?

The answer can be found in an exchange between Korah and Moses in the midst of the unrest. In an attempt to quell the rebellion, Moses challenged Korah to reveal his true intentions, and asked him whether he was demanding the priesthood. The question appears redundant. Korah's earlier statement that the entire nation was holy had surely revealed that the priesthood was exactly what he wanted. Why would Moses have asked Korah to confirm something he had already made clear?

It would appear that Moses was making a rhetorical observation. To be a priest requires being holy, but not in the way Korah had portrayed it. The Hebrew word *kadosh* – "holy" – means separate. Priests were expected to separate themselves from their human weaknesses and desires, including any craving for position and privilege. Aaron had never sought the role of High Priest; it had been thrust upon him, and he spent the remainder of his life trying to live up to the expectations of that role. Similarly, Moses had been forced into his leadership position, and remained reluctant and self-aware throughout, a lifetime role-model for those he had been charged to lead.

Moses was telling Korah that the very fact he had demanded a leadership position meant he was unsuited to it. While he was clearly charismatic and audacious, and no doubt checked every single one of Lee Iacocca's leadership boxes, Korah lacked the crucial ingredient that propels someone from being a good leader to being considered an enduring example of leadership. Korah's selfish desire for power at any cost, even at the expense of integrity and personal growth, consigned him to the rogue's gallery of biblical villains, and stands as a lesson to us from the dawn of Jewish history.

BEING NICE TO THE BAD GUYS IS WORTH A TRY

first published June 14th, 2018

This week we witnessed momentous and unprecedented scenes in Singapore, as the President of the United States sat down with the leader of North Korea, in the first step of a process that could ultimately lead to the denuclearization of the Korean peninsula. Unfortunately, this aspiration is far from a foregone conclusion, despite the friendly handshakes, back-patting, and the positive soundbites emerging from both sides during and after the summit. North Korea remains an entrenched part of the "axis of evil," a repressive state controlled by an evil dictatorship that proactively engages in violence against its own citizens – who have an average life expectancy that is more than ten years lower than their South Korean neighbors.

At the head of this wicked dictatorship is Kim Jong-un, President Trump's co-star at this week's meeting, which makes the President's effusive references to the North Korean leader as "very open," "very honorable," "very smart," "very worthy," "very talented," and as someone who "wants to do the right thing," rather difficult to stomach. On *Fox News*, Trump went even further. When the interviewer pointed out that the North Korean leader had "done some really bad things," Trump's response was, "yeah, but so have a lot of other people done some really bad things," implying that America regularly engages with leaders of the kind the diplomatic community refer to as "bad actors." Most notably when the United States signed an agreement with the Iranian regime in 2015 – clearly, the Islamic Republic of Iran is in close competition with North Korea for "the world's most repressive regime" top spot.

But two wrongs never make a right, particularly as Trump was so scathing in his criticism of the Obama administration for having signed that accord in the first place. Ironically, he abandoned the Iran deal only a few weeks ago, making good on one of his most controversial campaign promises. In light of this week's events and Trump's gushing praise for the North Korean dictator, it does now appear rather churlish to have criticized Obama for cozying up to a rogue state.

The media has had a field day. Even Republicans feel betrayed by Trump's nonchalant approach to a man who has between 80,000 and 120,000 political prisoners languishing in his prisons. One prominent Republican, former Florida congressman David Jolly, felt compelled to tweet, "for the record of history, never before has a U.S. President spoken this way of a dictator accused of crimes against his own people."

The usually reserved rhetoric of *The Economist* took a sharp turn towards sarcasm, in a line that says it all: "to the extent history is playing any part in all this, it is in its tendency to repeat itself." Summarizing the concerns of everyone who has an interest in the success of the Korean disarmament initiative, the article pointed out there was "no evidence Mr. Kim sees denuclearization as meaning that he should dismantle the nuclear arsenal he, his father and his grandfather put so much effort into creating and the industrial complex which supports it." In other words, despite the extraordinary spectacle of a U.S. president meeting with a vicious unreconstructed dictator, and the ubiquitous telegenic moments, the goals of each party could not be more different, and the gap between them seems unbridgeable.

To be fair, there was a very candid moment at the summit press conference, when Trump appeared to admit that he was in "well over his head" and might need to bluster his way out of a disaster when the goodwill factor has worn off and nothing positive has materialized. "I mean, I may stand before you in six months and say, 'Hey, I was wrong.' I don't know that I'll ever admit that, but I'll find some kind of an excuse." This offhand remark holds the key to the President's tactics, and his expectations.

When dealing with adversaries, one should try to make them feel good, even if showing them deference diminishes one's dignity, and saying nice things sounds hollow and unreal. Nothing will be lost if a positive outcome is achieved. If not, who can blame someone for trying to use an ill-deserved charm offensive for the greater good? After all, our greatest prophet Moses did just that, in the midst of the greatest threat to his forty-year leadership.

During the ill-fated Korah rebellion, Moses made extraordinary efforts to pacify the insurgents, even his perennial nemeses, Dathan and Abiram: "Moses sent for Dathan and Abiram, sons of Eliab; but they said, 'We will not come!'" (Num. 16:12). Instead of having them arrested and carted off in irons for their role in the insurrection, Moses invited them for a private audience to air their grievances – an extraordinary display of humility for a man of his stature. The medieval commentary, Rashi, adds a further layer to this gesture. Quoting the Talmud

(Sanhedrin 110a), he declares this verse as the biblical source for using conciliatory language in the pursuit of a peaceful resolution. At first glance, however, nothing conciliatory was said by Moses in this verse. As a matter of fact, Moses is not quoted at all.

Rabbi Abraham Joshua Heschel of Opatow ("*Ohev Yisrael*"; 1748-1825) elucidates this anomaly by pointing to the gratuitous reference to Dathan and Abiram as the "children of Eliab," a fact already mentioned earlier (Num. 16:1). In mentioning their father, Moses wanted to elevate them by identifying and associating them with their family heritage. His reference to them as "children of Eliab" would make them feel good, and would lead to everyone treating them with respect, even though they did not deserve it.

Dathan and Abiram's response may have been negative, but the precedent was set. If one has the slightest chance of avoiding catastrophe by saying something nice to people like Dathan and Abiram, it is certainly worth a try. Hopefully, Kim Jong-un will prove to be more cooperative than his biblical predecessors, and the threat from him and his regime can be mitigated for good.

THE 'ROSWELL INCIDENT' CONSPIRACY IS NONSENSE

first published June 22nd, 2017

Next month will mark the 70th anniversary of a notorious episode known as the "Roswell incident." In July 1947 — at a remote site northwest of Roswell, New Mexico — a county ranger named Mac Brazel came across strange looking debris in a field where he regularly grazed his sheep. Brazel was unable to identify the strange wreckage, so he summoned the local sheriff. Equally mystified, the sheriff contacted the local Roswell Army Airbase. Within hours, dozens of soldiers were dispatched to the site, where they collected every fragment of Brazel's enigmatic find, and spirited it away in armored trucks.

The following day, the Army announced that the soldiers had recovered the wreckage of a weather balloon that had crashed into the field. Evidently, this was a cover story; in reality, the airborne apparatus that had smashed into the ground was part of a short-lived top-secret military project called Project Mogul, which was created to detect sound waves generated by Soviet atomic bomb tests. At the time, the Army cover-story sufficed — despite Brazel's insistence that what he saw in the field was certainly not a weather balloon.

But fast-forward to the late 1970s, and the Roswell story had exploded into a major conspiracy theory, with "ufologists" (those who study of unidentified flying objects – UFOs) postulating that the debris had been wreckage from an alien "flying saucer" that had crashed — along with a crew of aliens, whose bodies had been recovered from the site and hidden away so that the public would never find out the truth. This unlikely story evolved and gained a life of its own, eventually becoming a staple of sensationalist TV shows and sci-fi series.

Recently, as the 70th anniversary has loomed, "news" stories about Roswell have been coming out thick and fast. In one recent story, it was "revealed" that a leaked Defense Intelligence Agency report had "confirmed" that the debris at Roswell was from a crashed UFO, that dead aliens had been found at Roswell, and that there was a carefully planned government cover-up.

A second recent story asserted that an alleged former CIA agent had made a filmed deathbed confession in which he stated that he saw an extra-terrestrial who survived Roswell being interrogated by government operatives.

The thing is — most people don't believe any of this, nor, for that matter, do we entertain the claims of those who maintain that the Apollo moon landings were all an elaborate hoax, or that Denver International Airport stands above an underground city that serves as a headquarters for a masonically-inspired New World Order (yes, there are people who believe this!). It's not that any of these conspiracy stories can be categorically disproved, but we feel they do not need to be. That's because in our minds we cannot imagine why any intelligent person would ever believe such nonsense to be true?

In Parshat Korach, we are confronted with the story of a revolutionary movement against Moses and Aaron — Korah and his supporters, who demanded a greater role in the leadership of Israel.

On the face of it, this revolt was not that surprising. Korah was a prominent figure who felt excluded, as did his co-conspirators from the tribe of Reuben, a tribe that had clearly been relegated to an inferior position in the national pecking order. And then there were the 250 princes who felt marginalized, inevitably resulting in their discontent.

Accordingly, it is understandable that all of those involved in Korah's insurrection would challenge the hierarchy at some point. Nevertheless, the medieval commentator Rashi dismisses Korah and his co-conspirators, even as he acknowledges Korah's intelligence: "Korah was astute; how was it possible that he engaged in this foolishness?" Meanwhile, the Jerusalem Talmud suggests that Korah was guilty of two foundational theological crimes: he denied the prophetic uniqueness of Moses, and he repudiated the divine origin of the Torah.

Maimonides ("*Rambam*"; 1138-1204) says that any Jew who denies the authority of Moses' prophecy or the Torah's divine origins could not possibly have been present at Mount Sinai. This assertion seems to be contradicted by the story of Korach, who must certainly have been present at Mount Sinai. Maimonides' statement also seems to remove freedom of choice as an option when it comes to this aspect of Jewish theological belief.

Rabbi Eliyahu Dessler (1892-1953), in his fascinating Jewish Ethics masterpiece, *Mikhtav M'Eliyahu*, suggests that every person has his or her *nekudat behira* — "point of free will".

Theoretically, we could all wake up one morning and decide that the world is flat, or that a UFO piloted by aliens crashed at Roswell — but we don't. Of course, we have the freedom to believe anything we want, but when we choose not to believe in Roswell or in moon-landing hoax stories, this is not really a decision connected to our freedom of choice. Instead, our personal "point of free will" might relate to choosing to properly observe Shabbat, or ensuring that we attend daily prayers, or that we observe proper kosher food standards — and indeed, our goal in life must be to constantly move our "point of free will" in a direction of growth and improvement.

Maimonides is not suggesting that choice is not an option when it comes to believing that Moses was Judaism's most elevated prophet or in relation to other principles of Judaism. Rather, he is informing us that if someone's personal "point of free will" falls in an area of doubt on these principles, that person has clearly opted out of the nation that stood at the foot of Mount Sinai, headed to the fringes, and embraced a Roswell-type narrative that rejects the theology norms that regular Jews know to be true. Korah and his group of supporters had inexplicably abandoned self-evident truths, and become believers in the biblical-era equivalent of Roswell. That they did so should remind us all that the option of Torah-rejection is a real possibility, even for intelligent people, and that to reject the Torah is no different from believing that aliens from outer space crash-landed at Roswell in 1947.

CHUKKAT

IT'S A DIRTY JOB

first published July 11th, 2019

The late US Supreme Court Justice, William J. Brennan, Jr. (1906-1997), wrote that "there are no menial jobs, only menial attitudes." Brennan died a few years before *Discovery Channel* launched its hit reality show *Dirty Jobs*, but he would certainly have approved. The show, which ran from 2003 until 2012, followed its indefatigable host Mike Rowe as he carried out a range of difficult, often disgusting and messy tasks, alongside ordinary people for whom these tasks were their everyday jobs in real life.

Introducing his role in each episode, Rowe would begin by saying "I explore the country looking for people who aren't afraid to get dirty — hard-working men and women who earn an honest living doing the kinds of jobs that make civilized life possible for the rest of us." Over the course of eight series, Rowe investigated a diverse assortment of such jobs in almost 170 episodes – apprenticing himself to sewer inspectors, pig farmers, hot tar roofers, sludge recyclers, high-rise window cleaners, pest exterminators, a hippopotamus keeper, and bat-poop collectors – among many others. Some of the jobs were so hideous that even Rowe recoiled.

One episode saw him testing a "shark suit," a steel mesh body suit bodysuit made from several hundred thousand tiny metal rings, meant to protect its wearer from shark bites. Having attracted dozens of sharks by dumping a pool of blood and fish bits into the sea, Rowe jumped in. "The sharks come in, and you let them bite you," he later told an interviewer. "If you live, the suit works. If you don't, it's unfortunate." For Rowe this was a one-off event; for the suit's manufacturer the live test is a crucial part of the process that enables them to bring their product to market.

After the series was canceled by *Discovery*, Rowe was asked which had been the most difficult assignment of all. He replied that he had found "catfish noodling" (don't ask!) very challenging, although "for epic, monumental dirtiness, the bat cave wins." But he then revealed that in terms of "pure exhaustion," indoor demolition and being a house mover were the jobs he had found most challenging of all. Catfish noodling and collecting bat feces can hardly be considered mainstream, but indoor demolition and house moving certainly are. Both of them are vital to the regular functioning of our day-to-day lives, along with garbage collection, sewer maintenance, animal farming and slaughter, as well as the many other unpleasant tasks we all rely upon to live our lives, but with which we have no meaningful contact. Rowe's mission was to wake us up to this undeniable reality.

As a matter of fact, this idea is embedded into the heart of the Jewish faith. Parshat Chukkat begins with the curious phenomenon known as *para aduma*. A red-haired cow was burned, and the ashes were later used in a carefully choreographed ritual process to purify those who had come into contact with a dead body. Oddly enough, everyone involved in the preparation of the ashes would themselves become impure, albeit at a lower grade than those the ashes were aimed at purifying. The commentaries all acknowledge this strange anomaly as emblematic of the unfathomable nature of this strange commandment. After all, it is exceptionally odd that the very people who ensure the purification of the impure would themselves become impure.

Or perhaps not. Perhaps the Torah is teaching us an important lesson. Perhaps, in order to fulfil God's will and elevate the world around us, we are called upon to do a "dirty job." Perhaps the greater good can only be served, and society can only function as it should, if we are willing to get our hands dirty.

The Talmud (Pes. 57a) records that Issachar of Barkai, a High Priest during the late Second Temple period, would wear silk gloves so as not to get his hands dirty while he performed his ritual duties. The passage is presented as a criticism, and the Talmud goes on to record a gruesome, unrelated event in which both of Issachar's hands were severed by King Yannai (Alexander Jannaeus; 127-76 B.C.E.) as punishment for disrespecting the monarchy. The implication is clear. As a public servant you need to get your hands dirty.

Rabbi Nachman Kahana (b.1937) tells the beautiful story of an ultra-Orthodox Holocaust survivor from Bnei Brak whose daughter suddenly sank into a terrible depression but refused to reveal what was troubling her. Eventually, after much cajoling, she revealed why she was so upset. Apparently, she had never known what her father did to provide for their family and had never really thought about it until, one day, while riding on a bus, she saw her father together with a group of manual laborers paving the road between Bnei Brak and Petach Tikva. She was shocked and completely devastated to discover that her father was a manual laborer and immediately plunged into deep depression.

The girl's father sat her down and explained that as far as he was concerned paving roads in Israel was far more honorable than the respected job he had in Hungary before the Holocaust. The road he was building would enable countless people to perform *mitzvot*, as it would speed up the travel time between one place and another, and consequently a part of every mitzva would be credited to him and his entire family, including her.

Recently, after many years of research, I finally pieced together the story of Rabbi Yeḥezkel Taub, the Yabloner Rebbe (1895-1986). This long-forgotten Jewish hero was a Hasidic leader from Poland who abandoned his elevated position in his home country to create a farming community of Hasidic Jews in pre-Israel Palestine. In a JNF pamphlet published in 1926, the author describes how this thoroughbred rabbi involved himself in every aspect of the farming village's most mundane tasks, ensuring that the broader goals of the endeavor would be realized.

The Yabloner Rebbe instinctively knew that in the pursuit of a greater good, you need to get your hands dirty. And that, I believe, is the message of the *para aduma*. Sometimes we all need to do a "dirty job." It is a rare example of "the end justifies the means."

BEING RATIONAL ABOUT MIRACLES

first published June 29th, 2017

A s if we are not cynical and jaded enough, enter the latest trend in fake news: the "miracle survivor" story that turns out to be a lie. This week, BBC News was forced to apologize after publishing a "breaking news" story on its website, claiming that a baby had miraculously been discovered alive in the ruins of the residential high-rise building, Grenfell Tower, twelve days after it was destroyed in a devastating fire with the loss of at least 80 lives.

But rather than focus on the sick motivations of the click-bait website that came up with the story, let's consider something else for a moment – if the story had been true, would the BBC have been accurate in describing the baby's survival as a miracle? After all, if the baby had actually survived, it might better be described as exceptionally good luck. No laws of nature were broken, and no one claimed that the child was protected or fed by an angel, so why would the story be labeled a miracle? This is a question that cuts to the core of religious faith, and it has vexed philosophers and theologians for millennia.

The first person to formally wrestle, as a rationalist, with the existence of the supernatural, was the Greek philosopher, Aristotle (384–322 B.C.). He believed that supernatural miracles defied reason, and that anything that defied reason was, by definition, impossible. The great medieval Jewish philosopher and rabbi Maimonides ("*Rambam*"; 1138-1204), was an avid devotee of Aristotelian philosophy, and he went to great lengths to reconcile Aristotle's views with the numerous stories of supernatural events in the Torah .

Interestingly, although they never openly debated the veracity of miracles, the Talmudic sages in Pirkei Avot (5:8) acknowledged this theological challenge by proposing that certain supernatural events recorded in the Torah were conceived of by God at the dawn of creation, but only crystallized at a particular time and place when the circumstances were right. Avot lists ten such phenomena, including Moses' staff, Miriam's well, and the "mouth" of Balaam's talking donkey.

Meanwhile, Rabbi Judah Loew ("*Maharal*"; 1520-1609), offered a compelling theological compromise to reconcile Aristotle's rationalism with numerous biblical occurrences of the supernatural. His theory is an intriguing alternative to the proposition in Avot. "Just as there is an order to nature," Maharal wrote, "so too there is an order to the miraculous."

In the Maharal's opinion, miracles do not defy natural law — because God's creation was never set up to be a binary system of nature and the supernatural. Instead, miracles have their own set of laws which are parallel to nature, although these laws cannot be subjected to the rigid empiricism demanded by Aristotelian philosophy. That is because miracles are self-evidently extremely scarce, requiring very specific circumstances to trigger them, and even the slightest deviation from those circumstances will prevent the supernatural manifestation from occurring.

Perhaps this idea can explain an anomaly in the episode of Miriam's well found in Parshat Chukkat. When Moses approached God to ask Him how he might resolve the water crisis, God instructed Moses to draw water out of a rock. According to Rashi, Moses attempted to find the exact rock that God wanted him to use but was somehow unable to locate it. Irritated by the delay, the thirsty nation of Israel began to get restless. As far as they were concerned, any rock would do — surely if God wanted Moses to produce water from a rock, it would make no difference which rock it was.

The Maharal's thesis explains Moses' cryptic response to the nation when they began to protest (Num. 20:10) – he said: הֲמִן הַסֶּלַע הַזֶּה נוֹצִיא לָכֶם מָיִם – "are we to produce water for you out of this rock?" Namely, who said that this is the rock set up within the laws of miracles to produce the required water? God does not indiscriminately break the laws of miracle-nature. The conditions have to be exactly right, or the miracle will not occur.

Rabbi Mordechai Yosef Leiner of Izbica (1801-1854), one of the 19th century's most original Hasidic thinkers, takes this idea even further. He believed that the Torah attributes God's refusal to allow Moses entry into the Promised Land as a reaction to this episode. However, rather than being a punishment, it was simply based on Moses' own rationale. Circumstances had to be exactly right, Moses had told the people, and if they are not, the miracle cannot occur. Moses had known for quite some time that it was going to be Joshua who led the nation into the Promised Land, and that once the forty-year period in the wilderness was over, his time was up. Nevertheless, Moses was hoping that God would reverse the natural order and allow him to enter the land in defiance of his destiny — a miracle, as it were. So how was God going to break the news to him that his destiny was irrevocable?

After the confrontation over the rock, God had the perfect explanation for Moses. Asked to produce water out of any rock, Moses had responded that the rock had to be exactly the right one. Similarly, Moses' entry into the Promised Land did not fit into the exact order of things, and after the incident with the rock, this sad reality would finally make sense.

Ultimately, supernatural law is no different to natural law; it follows strict criteria that cannot be overruled. The refreshing consequence of this brilliant idea is that both the natural and the supernatural emanate equivalently from God's will, making science and mysticism cousins in one family, rather than mutually exclusive foes.

LESSONS IN DIPLOMACY AND MILITARY STRATEGY

first published June 25th, 2015

A s a result of recent events, I feel compelled to return to the issue of the Iran nuclear deal, and Western negotiators' refusal to acknowledge that they are in way over their heads. At this stage it seems utterly ridiculous to call them naïve, or to suggest that they are in denial. Rather, it appears that the White House, the State Department, and all those who are part of the US-led effort to reach an agreement with Iran, have simply decided that short of Iran formally announcing they are going ahead with a nuclear bomb program, the deal will be signed.

This past Tuesday night, Iran's supreme religious leader, Ayatollah Ali Khamenei – whose views are all that count in the totalitarian theocracy that is the Islamic Republic of Iran – announced that his country would only dismantle its nuclear infrastructure if economic sanctions were lifted first. He added that there would be no freeze on research and development for the required ten-year period, and that third parties would never be allowed to inspect military sites.

In short, the West should lift sanctions while everything stays as it is and Iran remains committed to increasing its nuclear capacity, and while they prevent access to sites where nuclear warheads could be produced. Frankly, who needs a formal announcement?

It is worth noting that John Kirby, the official US spokesman, responded by confirming that inspections of suspicious sites would be a key part of any agreement. "For us, nothing's changed about what's necessary for a final deal," he said, adding that this "includes access and transparency." These are words that just might come back to haunt him. In any event, supporters of the deal, both in political circles and in the media, keep throwing out the same tired mantra – Khamenei says these things to pacify his military and religious hardliners, who oppose making a deal. In the end, they argue, the deal will broadly reflect US objectives as outlined in the April framework.

I have two observations. The first is this: if there are military and religious hardliners in Iran who are more hardline than Khamenei, and who intimidate him to the extent that is being claimed, then for the P5+1 group to sign a deal with Khamenei – who to my untrained ear sounds about as hardline as one can get – seems perilous in the extreme.

My second observation is much closer to home. Why is it that no one on the P5+1 side is saying or doing anything to pacify "hardliners" in the West who oppose the deal? Instead, Binyamin Netanyahu, the Republican and Democrat dissenters, the Saudis, and most recently the former Israeli ambassador to Washington, Michael Oren, are vilified and maligned by pro-deal advocates, who seem intent on ensuring that we all hurtle headlong into Iran's venomous embrace. Ironically, while the deal-lovers on our side can understand the need for Iran to pacify hardliners, there seems to be no inclination on their part to do the same thing.

In Parshat Chukkat we are introduced to the very first serious military confrontations between Jews and residents of the ancient Middle East. The Jews are just beginning to hone their skills as a fighting force, in anticipation of the serious military campaign they would shortly be embarking upon – the conquest of the Promised Land. One would not ordinarily look to the Torah for insights into diplomatic and military strategy, but the opportunity to see how Moses dealt with intransigent, ante-upping adversaries, with whom his nation had no dispute, nor any reason to attack, is too good to pass up.

At first Moses tries to the non-confrontational pacifist approach, reaching out to the king of Edom, and asking for permission to traverse his country to get to Canaan (Num. 20:17): נַעְבְּרָה נָּא בְאַרְצֶךָ לֹא נַעֲבֹר בְּשָׂדֶה וּבְכֶרֶם וְלֹא נִשְׁתֶּה מֵי בְאֵר – "please let us pass through your country; we will not travel over your fields and vineyards, nor drink your spring water." But the king reacts furiously, threatening war if they so much as set foot on his land. Moses tries again, and personally guarantees that the Jews would not stray off the highways, and that they would pay for anything they might need to use during their short journey. The king's response to this second approach was to mobilize his troops and to act so belligerently that Moses was forced to completely change his strategy, as he suddenly realizes that decency is never met with decency if your interlocutor is an aggressive militaristic brute.

The narrative moves on, and Moses encounters other local warlords. His attitude has turned tough and unrelenting, seasoned by experience. When the king of Arad takes some Jews captive, a Jewish military force wipes out Arad. When Sihon, king of the Amorites, refuses to allow the Jews through his land, they rout him and his forces, take over his land, and continue to advance until all their enemies were subdued.

Pacifism is a wonderful thing – in theory. For all of us living a comfortable life in the United States or elsewhere in the Western world, among millions of other people who abhor war and condemn pointless militarism, it seems almost intuitive to believe that all humans ultimately strive for this same ideal. All we need to do is extend the hand of peace, and the violence of our adversaries will be short-circuited. Peace will surely prevail.

But our world is actually a bubble, a mirage, a *Truman Show* Hollywood set. In reality we are encircled by unforgiving, unrelenting, malicious enemies, whose lives revolve around one dream – that the safe world we all live in will be disrupted, dismantled, and ultimately destroyed. Iran is one of those enemies, and Khamenei means every word he says. Our only hope is to be wary, and, when we need to be, extremely tough. Any other approach is a slippery path to willful self-destruction.

BALAK

DELEGITIMIZING JEWS IS AS OLD AS THE BIBLE

first published July 6th, 2017

"**I**t is shameful that the Jewish people still has to fight for the right to exist in the land that for thirty-three centuries it has called home." These were the words spoken earlier this week by the UK's former chief rabbi, Rabbi Lord Jonathan Sacks, at a special session of Britain's House of Lords commemorating the centenary of the Balfour Declaration.

Shockingly, and despite Rabbi Sacks' observation, the delegitimization of Israel managed to worm its way into this predominantly pro-Israel parliamentary session. Baroness Tonge, a notorious anti-Israel campaigner, bitterly attacked the British government for using Britain's overseas aid budget to fund Israel's "illegal occupation of Palestine." What are we to make of the singling out of Israel as the world's favorite "illegitimate" country?

This week UNESCO passed yet another resolution calling Israel "the occupying power" in Jerusalem's Old City, reaffirming previous resolutions that deny Israel's claim to this indisputably Jewish location. Israel's Foreign Ministry responded with an exasperated press release, expressing the frustration we all feel at this ongoing absurdity:

> *"Another bizarre and irrelevant decision by UNESCO, that is acting on behalf of the enemies of history and the truth. Jerusalem is the eternal capital of the Jewish people, and no decision by UNESCO can change that reality."*

The United Nations has 193 member states. There are a handful of countries that are not recognized by some of the others. For example, North Korea is not recognized as a legitimate country by five other member states, which view South Korea as the only "legitimate" country called Korea, while North Korea does not recognize South Korea. Similarly, the People's Republic of China does not recognize the Republic of China, more commonly known as Taiwan, and the latter is consequently not even a member of the UN.

But no country surpasses Israel in the non-recognition category. More than 30 countries refuse to acknowledge the legitimacy of the State of Israel, in what is surely one of the most remarkable diplomatic anomalies of contemporary international affairs. However, rather than being discouraged by this dispiriting reality, I am emboldened by it, seeing it as the crystallization of one of our most ancient texts – an obscure reference in the prophecy of Balaam found in Parshat Balak.

One of Imperial Russia's most virulent and powerful antisemites during the second half of the nineteenth century was a man called Konstantin Petrovich Pobedonostsev (1827-1907). Both a professor of law and a career civil servant, he was senior adviser to three tsars in the waning era of the Russian Empire. In

1881, after the assassination of Alexander II (1818-1881) and the accession of his son Alexander III (1845-1894), there was an outbreak of violent pogroms across Russia against the Jews, after widespread rumors preposterously purported that it had been the Jews who were behind the late Tsar's assassination. Rather than cracking down on the violent rioters, Alexander III decided that he needed to resolve the "Jewish question" once-and-for-all. This fateful decision resulted in the infamous "May Laws" of 1882 – a series of draconian restrictions for all Jews who lived in Imperial Russia, severely curtailing their ability to work and earn money.

The May Laws were initially proposed by the notoriously antisemitic Interior Minister, Count Nikolai Ignatyev (1832-1908), and the Tsar was eager to have them swiftly passed into law. The Jewish community immediately requested a meeting with the minister to lobby against the legislation. The delegation was led by the president of the Russian Jewish Congress, Baron Horace Guenzberg (1833-1909), and also included the Russian Empire's most prominent rabbinic leader, the eminent Rabbi Yitzḥak Elḥanan Spektor of Kovno (1817-1896). Meanwhile, Ignatyev invited Pobedonostsev to attend the meeting to reject the delegation's representations and support the government stance.

After the delegation had presented their case, Ignatyev turned to Pobedonostsev for his response. Pobedonostsev paused, and then launched into a biting and venomous tirade without even addressing the points that had been raised.

> *"I can understand what reason there is for God having created mosquitoes, horses, cockroaches. There is one thing, however, which I do not understand: why did He create Jews? They are a people who are of no use. The*

characteristics of the Jewish race are parasitic; for their sustenance, they require the presence of another race as 'host,' although they remain aloof and self-contained. Take them from the living organism, put them on a rock, and they will die."

There was dead silence after this outburst, and then the meeting was over.

The delegation slowly trudged out of the minister's office, dejected and demoralized – all except for Rabbi Spektor, who remarkably seemed quite cheerful. Puzzled by the rabbi's good mood, Guenzberg inquired why he was not as gloomy as the rest of them. "It's simple," said the rabbi, "I just witnessed a Torah prophecy come alive."

Noting the even more puzzled expression spreading across Guenzberg's face, the rabbi explained what he meant. "The pagan prophet, Balaam, uttered a cryptic prediction more than 3,000 years ago (Num. 23:23): 'In time it will be said to Jacob and Israel, "What has God wrought?"' In other words, there will come a time when the nations of the world will question and delegitimize the very existence of the Jews." Rabbi Spektor smiled broadly, and continued:

"We may have been persecuted for thousands of years, but no one has ever questioned our right to exist – until now. The evil Mr. Pobedonostsev has just suggested that we Jews do not even deserve to exist. In which case, I now know that the next verse will also come to be: "Behold, this is a people that rises like a lioness and raises itself up like a lion."

Fast forward to our own times, and we have been lucky enough to see Rabbi Yitzḥak Elḥanan Spektor's prescient observation materialize, with the creation and subsequent incredible success of the State of Israel. The excessive delegitimization of Israel only confirms what we all already know to be true – that our triumph is part of God's plan. And the more God's plan is called into question, the more we can be sure that His plan is the only one that will endure.

WORDS THAT LEAD TO VIOLENCE

first published July 14th, 2016

This week marked the first anniversary of the Iran nuclear deal. Last year at around this time, many of us were engaged in the effort to thwart the deal; yet, despite our valiant efforts, the deal went through and officially took effect in January. Secretary of State John Kerry proclaimed this week that the agreement had "lived up to its expectations," and asserted that Iran's nuclear program had been effectively halted in exchange for sanctions relief.

Kerry's statement coincided with the alarming revelation that a previously unseen document will allow key restrictions on Iran's nuclear program to ease years before the 15-year accord expires. The document was a secret letter submitted by Iran to the International Atomic Energy Agency at the same time the deal was signed, and it outlines Iran's plans to expand its uranium enrichment program in just under ten years. Although not officially part of the signed agreement, the letter was tacitly approved by all of the six powers that negotiated the deal with Tehran.

This diplomatic sleight of hand was treachery, plain and simple — a shocking and deceptive ploy that turns the weak agreement we all suspected it to be into something that is even worse than that. In their haste to clinch a diplomatic coup, international negotiators gave away a lot more than was ever revealed, enabling Iran to turn itself into an existential threat in less than a decade.

What were they thinking? It defies explanation — particularly since Iran is now threatening to renege on the deal if the other parties don't adhere to their side of the bargain – namely sanctions relief and international investment. What an absolute mess.

As if this is not enough, two weeks ago the deputy chief of Iran's Revolutionary Guard, Hossein Salami, warned that his country has more than 100,000 missiles aimed and ready to fire at Israel, and added that "if the Zionists make a wrong move, all the occupied territories will come under attack from dedicated fighters and the territories will be liberated." And when he says "all the occupied territories," he means the whole of Israel, not just Judea and Samaria. Meanwhile, last week, in rallies across Iran attended by tens of thousands of people, Israeli and American flags were burnt amid chants of "Death to Israel!" and "Death to America!"

In 1954, at a White House luncheon with President Eisenhower (1890-1969), Sir Winston Churchill (1875-1965) reportedly told his host with reference to the ongoing Cold War between the West and the Soviet Union, "to jaw-jaw is always better than to war-war." Churchill presumably meant that any kind of negotiations with one's enemy, however interminable and inconclusive, is always the better option if the alternative is military hostilities. But while that might or might not be true, since Churchill made that statement this idea has been stretched to the limit, and is now interpreted to mean that one should ignore enemy rhetoric, and never rise to any kind of verbal bait, as in the end no matter how violent they sound, words are not missiles, and threats are not acts of war. Let them "jaw-jaw" all they want, the argument goes, because in the end who cares what they say, as long as we are not at war.

Parshat Balak exposes just how foolish this approach is. The narrative describes how Balak, King of Moab, summons the notorious soothsayer Balaam to assist him in defeating the Jews before they overrun his country. Balaam was no military strategist, nor was he in command of an army of crack mercenaries. It seems his only weapon was a powerful mouth, as Balak bluntly tells him: כִּי יָדַעְתִּי אֵת אֲשֶׁר תְּבָרֵךְ מְבֹרָךְ וַאֲשֶׁר תָּאֹר יוּאָר – "for I know, that which you bless will be blessed, and that which you curse will be cursed." Ultimately Balak's plan never materializes. God intervenes and prevents Balaam from cursing the Jews, and we are left wondering whether Balaam's curses were quite as dangerous as Balak thought they were.

The medieval commentators struggle to explain the curse phenomenon, and opinions range from those who think curses work and that Balaam's were particularly effective, to those who think that Balaam was a wily charlatan who used clairvoyant skills to identify people who were about to have a stroke of bad luck, so that when their luck turned, everyone would assume his curses had caused their downfall. Maimonides ("*Rambam*"; 1138-1204) addresses the whole issue quite differently in his magnum opus *Moreh Nevukhim* ("Guide for the Perplexed"). As far as he is concerned, curses have no real power, but one is nonetheless forbidden to curse. He explains that as speech can cause such terrible pain, cursing is one of only three prohibitions not involving an action that in rabbinic law can lead to a punishment of lashes.

Although this idea is itself very powerful, it fails to explain why God would have prevented Balaam from uttering curses, and instead turned his words into blessings. A possible solution is that Maimonides understood how violent rhetoric, although seemingly harmless, is always a precursor to physical violence, and is therefore the very gravest of sins. Without a demagogue to whip up emotions, no soldier would ever go to war, and no army would ever be victorious. The benefit of Balaam's curses was not in their effectiveness as curses, but in their ability to encourage the Moabites into battle against the invincible Jews, in the belief they could win.

When "jaw-jaw" threatens "war-war," it is no longer just "jaw-jaw." If Iran encourages its people to chant "Death to America" and "Death to Israel," you can be sure that as soon as they have the slightest chance, both Israel and America, and numerous other countries, will be targeted. And with this week's revelation regarding the accelerated threat from Iran's nuclear program, we had better wake up to this reality before it's too late.

THE PASSING OF A VERY GREAT AND RIGHTEOUS MAN

first published July 2nd, 2015

This week saw the passing of Sir Nicholas Winton, at the ripe old age of 106. Stated simply, Sir Nicholas was a very great and righteous man. In December 1938, he cancelled a skiing vacation in Switzerland, and traveled to Prague to join a friend who was helping Jews flee Czechoslovakia in the wake of the infamous Munich Agreement. Winton was an understated, urbane British stockbroker, born in London to German-Jewish refugees who converted their family to Christianity, and changed their last name from Wertheim to Winton to ensure smooth assimilation into British society. But despite seeing himself as Christian, Nicholas was drawn to the plight of Czech Jews, and his hotel room in Prague became a haven for Jewish families seeking an exit route from mainland Europe.

The British government had just passed a law allowing any child under the age of 17 to enter Britain as a refugee, provided they had somewhere to stay and a £50 warranty had been securely deposited to pay for their eventual repatriation. The law was aimed at Jewish immigrants who were already naturalized, enabling them to take in younger relatives who wished to escape the growing peril of Nazi antisemitism after Kristallnacht. But Winton ingeniously used this law to create – single-handedly – an organization he called *Operation Kindertransport*, which he used as a vehicle to match Czech-Jewish children with both Jewish and non-Jewish host families in Britain – not their relatives. Even more remarkably, he raised all the funds required to pay the sureties for each child.

The first eight months of 1939 were a frenzy of activity. Sir Nicholas worked together with a handful of like-minded activists in Prague and London, including Rabbi Dr. Solomon Schonfeld (1912-1984), the charismatic rabbinic head of a network of Orthodox synagogues in London, who was himself involved in multiple attempts to save Jews from the Nazi threat. All in all, Sir Nicholas Winton saved 669 Jewish children, including, as it happens, three of my father-in-law's siblings. The vast majority of those children never saw their parents or families again, as they, along with most of European Jewry, became victims of the Nazi death machine. Had it not been for Sir Nicholas Winton, this would also have been the fate of the children he saved.

As incredible as it may sound, it is not for this reason that I consider Sir Nicholas to have been a very great and righteous man. On the contrary, I find it horrifying and inexplicable that there were not hundreds, or thousands, of Nicholas Wintons, who, when they were exposed to the horrifying reality of Nazi brutality, did nothing to save Jews. Sadly, there are even stories of people – including Jews – who deliberately blocked attempts to allow refugees to flee Europe during that dreadful period. No. The reason I consider Sir Nicholas to have been a very great and righteous man is because no one – not his wife, not his children, nor even the 669 children he saved – ever knew anything about his role in *Operation Kindertransport* until 1988.

After the war began in September 1939, Sir Nicholas never again spoke of his prewar activities to anyone. In 1940 he joined the RAF, and when the war was over, he got married and conducted an eventless life as a financial director for various companies and was a devoted suburban family man. Indeed, had it been up to him no one would have ever found out. But his humble anonymity was not destined to last. In 1988, his wife was rummaging through the attic of their home and she discovered a meticulously detailed scrapbook that had been put together by Winton in 1939. It documented *Operation Kindertransport* in full, with names and photographs of each child, plus all the related correspondence, receipts, and other documents.

On a whim, she decided to share the information with a friend, and the story ultimately ended up being featured on a popular TV show called *That's Life*. The producers of the show invited Sir Nicholas to describe his role in the rescue project on live television without telling him that they had filled the studio with an audience made up of his 'children' and their families. In the final segment of the show, the presenter, Esther Rantzen, asked for any member of the audience who personally owed his or her life to Sir Nicholas to stand up, so that he could see who they were.

Dozens of audience members rose to their feet and spontaneously applauded the man who had saved their lives.

Throughout the program Sir Nicholas had been very composed and modest about his exploits, but in the face of this outpouring of gratitude he was suddenly, and for the first time, exposed to the profound impact of his efforts, and he began to cry.

In the Haftarah for Parshat Balak, which is taken from the Book of Micah, there is a very strange reference to the story of

Balak and Balaam (Mic. 6:5): זְכָר נָא מַה יָעַץ בָּלָק מֶלֶךְ מוֹאָב וּמֶה עָנָה אֹתוֹ בִּלְעָם לְמַעַן דַּעַת צִדְקוֹת ה' – "so that you recognize God's righteousness, remember what King Balak of Moab plotted to do, and how Balaam responded." This is a very puzzling verse. Surely God's righteousness is demonstrated in countless other ways? Why would the episode of Balak and Balaam be the trigger that would prompt this awareness?

Perhaps the Nicholas Winton story can help us understand this bewildering quotation. Unlike all the other wonderful things God had done for the Jewish nation, from the time they were miraculously redeemed from Egyptian slavery, and during the entire forty years of careful nurturing in the wilderness, the episode with Balak and Balaam happened without any Jew being aware of it, and they were only informed of it long after it was all over.

The prophet Micah is telling us that true righteousness is when a benefactor takes care of you even though you are unaware of his benevolence. And it is this phenomenon that explains why Sir Nicholas Winton was a very great and righteous man. *Zecher Tzaddik Livracha.*

PINCHAS

A DEEP AND MEANINGFUL RELATIONSHIP

first published July 25th, 2019

If there is one president of the United States whose personality and character we are all intimately familiar with, it is undoubtedly President Donald J. Trump. Between his incessant tweeting and the 24-hour news cycle, we have been endlessly exposed to every facet of his temperament for years. And whether one is enthralled or appalled by what one knows of him, we can all predict with great confidence how he will react in any given situation.

This was not true for previous presidents, with the possible exception of Richard Nixon (1913-1994). In the past, presidential personas were press-generated caricatures or uneducated assumptions based on public appearances. Consequently, in popular imagination Ronald Reagan (1911-2004) was a jovial crowd-pleaser; Jimmy Carter (b.1924) was frugal, and a stickler for the rules; while Gerald Ford (1913-2006) was an incompetent ditherer.

Possibly, but their real personalities were by-and-large hidden from public view. What were they like as friends? As spouses? As parents? What made them laugh? What really ticked them off?

These aspects were a mystery during their time at the helm, to be revealed much later in well-researched biographies.

Although, in the case of Harry Truman (1884-1972), one notorious public outburst exposed a facet of his personality that was widely out-of-sync with public perception and generated a wave of negative reaction. On December 5th, 1950, Truman's only daughter Margaret sang before an audience of 3,500 people – including her father, who was president at the time – at Washington DC's Constitution Hall. And although her singing talents were at best pedestrian, Margaret's performance was greeted with rapturous applause, to her father's deep delight and pleasure.

But the following day, a withering review appeared in the *Washington Post*, written by music critic, Paul Hume (1915-2001). "Miss Truman cannot sing very well," he wrote, "she is flat a good deal of the time – more last night than at any time we have heard her in past years… [She] has not improved in the years we have heard her; she still cannot sing with anything approaching professional finish. She communicates almost nothing of the music she presents."

An enraged Truman promptly dispatched a letter to Hume that one would imagine even Donald Trump might hesitate to tweet. Writing on White House stationary, Truman thundered:

> *"I've just read your lousy review of Margaret's concert. I've come to the conclusion that you are an 'eight ulcer man on four ulcer pay.' It seems to me that you are a frustrated old man who wishes he could have been successful. When you write such poppy-cock as was in the back section of the paper you work for it shows*

conclusively that you're off the beam and at least four of your ulcers are at work. Someday I hope to meet you. When that happens, you'll need a new nose, a lot of beefsteak for black eyes, and perhaps a supporter below! [Westbrook] Pegler, a gutter snipe, is a gentleman alongside you. I hope you'll accept that statement as a worse insult than a reflection on your ancestry."

The *Washington Post* dutifully reached out to Margaret Truman, who told them that her father could not possibly have sent this letter to Hume, and it had to be a forgery. But it was not a forgery, and the reaction was fierce. One *Washington Post* reader wrote that he considered Truman's letter embarrassing proof of his "ungoverned temper" and "gutter vocabulary," while another worried openly about Truman's "sole power of unleashing the atom bomb." Yet another reader – an American living in Australia – viewed the letter as a national embarrassment, and asked: "How long must Americans living abroad be humiliated by such ill-chosen words and threats by the President?"

Almost no one championed President Truman for leaping to his daughter's defense, even though the letter revealed a human side that should have been lauded as natural and instinctive. Truman was a hurt father going the extra mile for his child, even if it exposed him to ridicule and worse. Rather than bowing to convention, or the expected dignity of his position, Harry Truman had done what we should all do – he stood up passionately for the daughter he loved, revealing just how much he loved her, and how such love should move us to do something when the object of our love is threatened.

Towards the end of Parshat Balak and at the beginning of Parshat Pinchas (Num. 25) the Torah records a strange episode involving a prince of the tribe of Simeon, who publicly engaged in an immoral act with a Midianite woman. Moses and the nation's leadership are frozen in the face of this grave desecration of God's name, despite the real danger – physical and spiritual – that this moral aberration posed for the nation as a whole.

One man, Pinḥas, witnessed both the act and the reaction, and decided to take matters into his own hands, slaying the prince and his paramour in full view of the gathered crowd. God immediately informed Moses that Pinḥas had saved the day and awarded him the "covenant of peace," along with a permanent place in the priesthood.

The rabbis of the Midrash and Talmud struggle to justify Pinḥas' vigilante justice, but are rather more focused on the extra-judicial aspect than on the feelings that drove it. Later commentaries do acknowledge his passionate feelings, but are reluctant to suggest that such passions motivated Pinḥas, who is cited as a unique example of someone untainted by any kind of personal agenda.

In my own view, Pinḥas' visceral reaction as he witnessed the destruction of something he loved and cherished appears remarkably similar to the reaction of a parent seeing their child hurt or in danger. In that situation, all bets are off. The lesson of Pinḥas, so dramatically underscored by God's reaction, is for us to aim for a relationship with God that is buried deep within us. A meaningful relationship that transcends the transactional, mundane connection which for many God-believers is the only relationship they know. The reward for such a bond – as we know from our children – is immeasurable.

THE SECRET ABOUT TEACHERS WHO INSPIRE

first published July 5th, 2018

Most of us have heard the quote from the inspirational writer William Arthur Ward (1921-1994): "The mediocre teacher tells. The good teacher explains. The superior teacher demonstrates. The great teacher inspires." Ward was himself a rousing speaker and a phenomenal teacher, and worked tirelessly to enhance the world around him, mainly by improving people's attitude towards each other. But he was also very taken with this idea of inspirational role models and mentors being lightning rods for change.

In the late twentieth century, the majority of cutting-edge educational theory was based around the idea of *Active Learning*, a term coined by British Olympic long jumper turned professor of education, Reg Revans (1907-2003). According to Revans – and the many others who joined his *Active Learning* bandwagon – a successful teacher engages students in activities that relate to the subject being taught. Rather than students listening passively, they must become actively involved in the subject they are expected to learn, as this is bound to make a much stronger impression on the brain.

In the 1970s, this idea evolved into *Experiential Learning*, whose main proponent, David Kolb (b.1939), developed a comprehensive model for this form of pedagogy, composed of four stages: concrete experience, observation of and reflection on that experience, formation of abstract concepts based upon the reflection, and testing the new concepts – followed, crucially, by a repetition of all four stages to further imbed the information. While these efforts have undoubtedly been motivated by a desire to generate better teaching, and of course better learning, there is an abiding fear that such methods will inevitably result in "dumbing down" subject matter.

A more subtle criticism is that *Active Learning* assumes that students are by-and-large unenthusiastic and require sophisticated stimulation to generate learning. Ironically, *Active Learning* puts the onus on teachers to arouse a reaction from students, through the use of the pedagogical equivalent of Disneyland. This has resulted in a counterculture within educational theory academia, where they have begun to question this idea that simply listening to a teacher teach is passive learning. In 2016, a chap called James Sheldon – currently completing his PhD in Teaching and Teacher Education at the University of Arizona – presented an academic paper which argued for an alternative understanding of receptivity, which involves choosing to invite in, welcoming and hosting the "other."

Just because a person isn't talking, or actively doing something, does not mean they are passive. Or as he puts it, "imagine what happens if we reconceive listening not as a process of passivity, but as an active process of making sense of ideas?" The idea that we need to "do" something in order to be engaged is quite patronizing, if you think about it, as if engaged listening is somehow an inferior form of learning. Just as we are able to learn by reading, which is certainly "passive," so, too, we can learn by listening.

There is no such thing as passive listening – as long as the student is truly listening and wants to learn. Two students may hear exactly the same thing from their teacher, but only one of them will learn anything – the one who is actively listening, and for whom listening is "an active process of making sense of ideas."

Parshat Pinchas records the appointment of Joshua as Moses' successor, chosen to lead the Jews into the Promised Land. The Midrash offers an intriguing backstory to this narrative. Apparently, Moses wanted his own sons, Gershom and Eliezer, to replace him, and lobbied God on their behalf. But God rejected the suggestion, telling Moses, "your sons sat around and did not engage in Torah." God told Moses that his two sons were unsuited to the leadership role, while Joshua was eminently suited for it. Intriguingly, this Midrash seems to directly contradict a verse in the Torah. God instructs Moses (Num. 27:20): וְנָתַתָּה מֵהוֹדְךָ עָלָיו לְמַעַן יִשְׁמְעוּ כָּל עֲדַת בְּנֵי יִשְׂרָאֵל – "Invest [Joshua] with some of your authority, so that the whole Israelite community may take heed."

Clearly Joshua was not a natural shoo-in for leader, and he needed the boost from Moses to make him acceptable. If so, why couldn't Moses do that for Gershom and Eliezer, so that the nation would see them as the new leaders? If Joshua could be elevated in the nation's eyes by Moses, surely his sons could also have been given the magic boost?

According to the late nineteenth-century Polish Hasidic master, Rabbi Avraham Bornsztain of Sochaczew ("*Avnei Nezer*"; 1838-1910), the answer is staring at us in the face. Moses could only deliver the aura of leadership to his replacement if that person was able and ready to receive it. In a master-disciple dynamic, being able and ready to receive has less to do with the efforts of the master than it has to do with the efforts of the disciple, who has to fulfil their destiny exclusively via their own efforts.

Moses' sons may very well have been present when their father was teaching and inspiring, but it seems they just "sat around," unable or unwilling to receive, or to be inspired. Meanwhile, Joshua made every effort to become a vessel that absorbed what Moses had to deliver, and when the time came it made sense for Moses to pass the mantle of leadership to him.

William Arthur Ward may have been right about teachers needing to inspire, but in the end, even the most inspirational teacher needs to have students who want to be inspired. *Active Learning* with all the bells-and-whistles will amount to nothing if the audience remains unmoved, and consequently unchanged. All learning must be Joshua-style, where proximity to a great teacher is worthless unless one is proactively ready to be inspired. Or as the great American novelist, Jack London (1876-1916), put it: "You can't wait for inspiration. You have to go after it."

THE FIRST STAGE OF THE MESSIANIC ERA

first published July 13th, 2017

O ne of the great mysteries of the Jewish faith in modernity is the instinctive antipathy that certain segments of the most religiously observant Jews feel towards the existence of the State of Israel. Although total revulsion for Israel is confined to a tiny proportion from within the strictly-Orthodox world, even among the remainder, the idea of Jewish hegemony in our ancestral homeland, and that this phenomenon heralds the Messianic era, seems to be anathema to their religious equilibrium.

The reasons behind this distaste towards Israel vary. At their core, though, is a profound feeling that in the final countdown towards a Messianic age, particularly after two millennia of endless and excruciating persecution, events leading towards the Messiah's arrival will self-evidently be miraculous and wondrous. Crucially, it makes no sense to this group of devout Jews that the "end of days" depicted by our ancient prophets could be initiated by irreligious Jews while being supported by very temporal and quite fickle international bodies and gentile nations. Their expectation for this period is nothing less than a splitting-of-the-red-sea situation, or a Divine revelation of Sinaitic proportions – in other words, clear indications from God that the redemption process is afoot. It follows that adopting a narrative which flies in the face of such high-bar theological anticipations is a painful concession, and for some in the ultra-Orthodox community it is simply too much to take on board.

The alternative interpretation – that the existence of the State of Israel has no theological repercussions – is the one that has consequently been adopted as a preferred option, even if it defies so many features of Israel's reality, not least the clear fulfillment of ancient prophecy in so much that has happened there over the past century.

It is certainly the case that the Prophets and Talmud predicted that Messianic redemption would be accompanied by miraculous events. The prophet Isaiah (11:6) famously declared that in the Messianic age, the "wolf will live with a lamb, a leopard shall lie with a kid-goat, a calf and lion cub … will all live together, and a small child shall lead them." Maimonides ("*Rambam*"; 1138-1204) dismissed the entire concept of miracles associated with the Messianic era (see: Laws of Kings 12:1), and renders Isaiah's prophecy as an allegory predicting that Jews would eventually live peacefully with their erstwhile enemies, evil nations that Isaiah compared to leopards and wolves.

But many great rabbinic philosophers and theologians have disagreed with Maimonides' opinion, which is why there are devout Jews who refuse to see modern Israel as the first stage in our final redemption and feel justified in their oppositional stance. Nonetheless, and despite their pious religiosity, they are utterly mistaken. It is entirely conceivable that the redemption process will be divided into two separate periods. The first period will conform to the laws of nature, while the second period, commencing with the resurrection of the dead, will not. The question that those who reject this natural-order-followed-by-miracles construct struggle with is "why?" In other words, if the Messianic era will be the ultimate realization of God's plans for the physical world, why would it be limited to the laws of nature? Surely it should unfold entirely miraculously.

Rabbi Naftali Tzvi Yehuda Berlin of Volozhin ("*Netziv*"; 1816-1893), in the introduction to his *Haamek Davar* commentary on the Book of Bamidbar, queries why the Talmudic sages chose to refer to this book as *Sefer Pekudim* ("Book of Counts"). While it is true that there are two censuses recorded in Bamidbar – one at either end of the book – by no means can they be described as the book's dominant theme. The first census took place at the beginning of the forty-year period in the wilderness, and the second, recorded in Parshat Pinchas, took place at the end.

Rabbi Berlin suggests that if we examine both counts carefully, we discover the incredible shift which occurred between the first year in the wilderness and the last, and that this profound transition is what Sefer Bamidbar is all about. One might think that a census is a census, and that both censuses were identical in their execution and basic result. Upon closer examination, however, it becomes evident that there are significant differences between them. For example, in the first count, the group of three tribes representing the children of Rachel – Manasseh and Ephraim as sons of Joseph, along with Benjamin – is led by Ephraim. In the second count, however, Manasseh is elevated to first place over his brother Ephraim.

This difference is easily understood if one factors in the forty-year difference. During the first year in the desert, the nation's needs were taken care of via various overt miracles. Midrashic sources inform us that Ephraim was on a more elevated spiritual plane than his brother, devoted to Godly pursuits, and in every respect quite unworldly. For this reason, in the first census his tribe was named first. But fast-forward forty years, when the nation was about to embark on a military conquest to take possession of the Promised Land. It was time for God to wean the nation off the miracles that had sustained them, and instead, they needed to learn how to fend for themselves. At that stage it was Manasseh who stood at the helm, as he was the practical son who had helped his father Joseph with Egypt's administration.

The notion that the advent of the Messianic age will come in the form of miraculous events at the hands of unworldly people is a misnomer that is undermined by this subtext in the Book of Numbers. Rather than waiting for miracles to happen, we must make our own miracles happen, using the natural order to realize the dream predicted by our prophets. It is only by embracing this first stage of the process that we can hope to merit the second.

MATOT

DON'T CURB YOUR ENTHUSIASM

first published August 2ⁿᵈ, 2019

P arshat Matot begins with the laws of oaths and vows. The Talmud regards breaking a vow as a grave dereliction. Human beings are the only creatures on earth with the power of speech, an expression of intelligent thought. Using speech to make a firm commitment only to go back on it is a terrible betrayal of this unique power, and, the Talmud believes, the sign of a degenerate person.

The Talmud contains a number of statements that convey this idea, but none of them is more chilling than the one quoted in tractate Shabbat (32b) in the name of Rabbi Judah, the rabbinic sage and scholar who edited the Mishnah which forms the foundation of the entire Talmud. Due to the sin of unfulfilled vows, children die young, he says, quoting two verses from Ecclesiastes (5:4-5): "Better is it that you should not vow, than that you should vow and not pay. Suffer not your mouth to bring your flesh into guilt, neither say you before the messenger that it was an error; wherefore should God be angry at your voice and destroy the work of your hands?" And, continues Rabbi Judah, what is it that is considered the work of a person's hands? The answer must be that it is a person's sons and daughters.

Quite shocking, I think you'll admit. Not only does this punishment sound completely disproportionate, but it also appears as if Rabbi Judah forced it into the meaning of the verses, which, on the face of it, do not, by any stretch of the imagination, seem to be saying that the consequence of breaking a vow is the death of one's children. Initially one might dismiss Rabbi Judah's statement as an example of Talmudic hyperbole – a dramatic statement meant to convey the gravity of breaking a vow. But perhaps not. Perhaps there is another more prosaic explanation.

In the course of any person's lifetime, there will be moments when they are inspired by a great speaker, or moved by a particular event, or indeed by any number of different positive experiences. At that moment they might be so enthused that they commit to making real changes in their lives. But how long does any commitment last? Most resolutions barely last a couple of weeks, if you're lucky. Change is never easy, and once the inspiration has worn off and life gets back to normal, the big promises disappear into the background and are eventually forgotten completely. Until, of course, the next inspirational moment, at which time the process will repeat itself.

So which one is the real you? Is it the man or woman who is inspired to do better? Or is it the person who melts back into the daily grind, with the moment of inspiration merely a flash-in-the-pan, a kind of out-of-body experience, not real in any meaningful sense? As in so many other such scenarios, "there are two types of people in this world." And although in this situation both of them look exactly the same, there is a real testing ground that can act as a barometer of difference between them – their children.

Let me share something I saw quoted in the name of Augustine "Og" Mandino (1923-1996) — author of the bestselling book *The Greatest Salesman in the World*, which sold over 50 million copies across the world and was translated into numerous languages. An incredibly positive person, always upbeat, he summed up his philosophy in this one pithy statement:

> *"Every memorable act in the history of the world is a triumph of enthusiasm. Nothing great was ever achieved without it because it gives any challenge or any occupation, no matter how frightening or difficult, a new meaning. Without enthusiasm you are doomed to a life of mediocrity but with it you can accomplish miracles."*

The triumph of enthusiasm is not necessarily the result of each moment of enthusiasm, but the collective result of many such moments across society and across generations. The word enthusiasm is itself interesting – its origin is the combination of the Greek words *en theos*, which mean "with God." Being enthusiastic is being in a state of communion "with God," feeling that spirit of God within us and connecting to our inner self, to our purpose, to our vision, to our values – in short, to our soul in its most pristine state. And, of course, that connection doesn't last – the dark weight of the material world blots out the bright light of enthusiasm, although while it shines it is infectious, even more "real" than the real day-to-day world.

If our children get a whiff of our enthusiasm and see what enthuses us, they too will be enthused, and that inspiration will outlast our own efforts. Indeed, it will outlast us through them. This phenomenon of being a beacon of inspiration is known as the *Heliotropic Effect* – the tendency for living systems to move towards light and away from darkness, or more accurately, the tendency to move towards that which gives life and away from anything that endangers life. This is the reason why when you put a plant on the windowsill it will tilt towards the light coming through the window. Our children are just like a plant on the windowsill. They tilt towards us when they get to see the light of enthusiasm that we have for the lifegiving aspects of life, but only if they sense that we are really enthused by those lifegiving aspects.

No one knows us better than our children. If they sense that light in us, even if they know that we are not always able to live up to our own enthusiastic flashes of inspiration, they will absorb that light and energize their own lives with it. But if that light is not actually there, if our enthusiasm is nothing but a fake panacea, they will not be inspired and will, for want of a better word, die.

Charles Garfield (b.1944) is the author of the widely acclaimed *Peak Performance* trilogy – *Peak Performers*, *Team Management* and *Second to None* – which focus on high performing individuals, teams and organizations, and which established him as one of America's leading authorities on high achievement. The first of the three books, *Peak Performers*, was published in 1987, and contains the wonderful story he called *The Tale of the Dancing Toll Taker*, and I present it to you here in full:

> **If you have ever gone through a tollbooth, you know that your relationship to the person in the booth is not the most intimate you'll ever have. It's one of life's frequent non-encounters: you hand over some money; you might get change; you drive off. I have been through every one of the seventeen tollbooths on the Oakland – San Francisco Bay Bridge on thousands of occasions**

and never had an exchange worth remembering with anybody.

Late one morning in 1984, headed for lunch in San Francisco, I drove toward one of the booths. I heard loud rock music. It sounded like a party or a Michael Jackson concert. I looked around. No other cars with their windows open. No sound trucks. I looked at the tollbooth. Inside it, the man was dancing.

"What are you doing?" I asked.

"I'm having a party," he said.

"What about the rest of these people?" I looked over at other booths; nothing moving there.

"They're not invited."

I had a dozen other questions for him, but somebody in a big hurry to get somewhere started punching his horn behind me and I drove off. But I made a note to myself: Find this guy again. There's something in his eye that says there's magic in his tollbooth.

Months later I did find him again, still with the loud music, still having a party.

Again, I asked, "What are you doing?"

He said, "I remember you from the last time. I'm still dancing. I'm having the same party."

I said, "Look, What about the rest of these people..."

He said, "Stop. What do those look like to you?" He pointed down a row of tollbooths.

"They look like...tollbooths."

"Nooo imagination!"

I said, "Okay, I give up. What do they look like to you?"

He said, "Vertical coffins."

"What are you talking about?"

"I can prove it. At eight-thirty every morning, live people get in. Then they die for eight hours. At four-thirty, like Lazarus from the dead, they re-emerge and go home. For eight hours, brain is on hold, dead on the job. Going through the motions."

I was amazed. This guy had developed a philosophy, a mythology about his job. I could not help asking the next question: "Why is it different for you? You're having a good time."

He looked at me.

"I knew you were going to ask that," he said. "I'm going to be a dancer someday."

He pointed to the administration building. "My bosses are in there, and they're paying for my training."

Sixteen people dead on the job and the seventeenth, in precisely the same situation, figures out a way to live. That man was having a party where you and I would probably not last three days. The boredom!

He and I did have lunch later and he said, "I don't understand why anybody would think my job is boring.

I have a corner office, glass on all sides. I can see the Golden Gate, San Francisco, the Berkeley hills; half of the Western world vacations here… and I just stroll in every day and practice dancing."

What is the essential skill that, when seventeen human beings walk into their offices and sixteen of them get into vertical coffins, allows one of them to have a party?

Mission. Purpose.

Some people do the same jobs as everybody else but have an unusual sense of mission, enjoy it, and have the energy to achieve it at high levels. The dancing toll-taker had been given no special job, no change in the conditions that limited life for everyone else in the booths. Yet he had found a mission and thereby discovered the will and the way to use the conditions of his job to support his mission.

Two things stand out for me in this story. The first is the imagery of the tollbooths as coffins. Our lives, our environments, are coffins unless we bring them to life with real enthusiasm and inspiration. The other thing that stands out for me is that Charles Garfield was so drawn to the dancing toll-taker that he ended up going through that toll booth again and again. The *Heliotropic Effect* worked its job on him, as it can work so powerfully on our children.

Rav Avraham Yitzḥak Hacohen Kook (1865-1935), the first Ashkenazi Chief Rabbi of Eretz Yisrael, drives the point home with great force and clarity. If a commitment you make when you are inspired or seeking something greater is not genuine, and your "idealism" is just a form of momentary escape from a monotonous reality but not truly who you are as a person, then you cannot properly raise your children. Your view of the world is upside-down, and your children will never move beyond the coffin-like life you have embraced. But if, on the other hand, those flashes of enthusiasm are the real you, your children will come alive through them, reflecting the light that shines from you and in you, perpetuating it in their own lives and beyond. Which is why it is important never to curb your enthusiasm.

ROCKY THE 'TALKING' ORANGUTAN

first published August 4th, 2016

This week I came across a headline that really grabbed my attention: "Orangutans Exhibit Human-Like Speech for the First Time on Record." Intrigued by the thought of talking apes, I dove into the article hoping to read about some hidden community of high-end primates who were able to converse intelligibly and intelligently on literature and economics and had suddenly been discovered by a group of intrepid anthropologists. Or perhaps the garrulous orangutans referred to in the headline were busy engaging in heated discussions about the upcoming presidential election? Now wouldn't that be fascinating, I thought to myself – hearing what a parallel species has to say about Donald Trump and Hillary Clinton!

To my immense disappointment, all such hopeful expectations were quickly dashed. It turned out the article was not about orangutans in the plural, but about one very forlorn looking specimen called Rocky, an exhibit at Indianapolis Zoo. Rocky apparently spent her formative years in the entertainment industry as "the most seen orangutan in commercials, movies, and other media." More recently she has confounded researchers with her ability to mimic human sounds in what they refer to as a "conversational manner." Well, that may be the case, but you will surely agree that this is quite a comedown from the "human-like speech" promise of the headline.

According to Dr. Rob Shumaker, director of the zoo and author of a recently published paper on this phenomenon, "orangutans can clearly and carefully control their vocalizations and they can do it in real-time, interacting with another individual." To show the extent of Rocky's vocal abilities, the researchers held conversations with her in which she mimicked a variety of human sounds in return for treats. A video link led to a clip of one of these documented "conversations," and I watched it several times trying to see for myself how Rocky was interacting conversationally in a way that exceeded the acrobatics of a dolphin doing tricks for treats at *SeaWorld*, or a parrot mimicking human speech in reaction to some particular stimulus.

In the end I was entirely underwhelmed by Rocky, or more specifically by Shumaker, whose grandiose claims seemed to me to be somewhat overstated. The fact that an ape can mimic human sounds reveals nothing about the origins of human speech, as he claims it does, nor can it tell us anything more than the fact that this particular ape has learned to use its vocal chords to emit sounds that elicit the gift of some candy.

The debate about animal intelligence has raged for years, long before Rocky and Shumaker. In the late 1970s and early 1980s the same debate erupted around Koko the gorilla, a resident of Woodside CA, whose observable use of ASL (American Sign Language) to communicate, often in ways that confounded conventional wisdom on animal intelligence and comprehension, led to frequent press coverage and lucrative public interest. The age-old saying "if only they could talk" seemed to crystallize in this loveable 300-pound lowland gorilla with a fondness for pet kittens. She recognized herself in the mirror, articulated her emotions, and even cracked jokes. And, as I found out when I googled her, she is still going strong at the age of 45.

And Koko is hardly the first example of an intelligent mammal. In the 1780s, a sideshow animal known as "Learned Pig" caused quite a stir in England. Able to choose from a series of printed cards, the savvy hog answered complex mathematical problems and answered a range of questions by spelling out words. Learned Pig was followed by many other similarly adept pigs, including one called the "Pig of Knowledge," who was introduced to President John Adams (1735-1826) in the late 1790s.

Rather than delving into the debate over whether animals are capable of communicating with humans, as opposed to them simply responding to human prompts and expectations, for the purposes of this piece I will simply accept that there are animals, however scarce they may be, who have the capacity to converse with humans through sounds or signs, or by choosing cards, and that this shows how human superiority is rather more limited than we all believe it to be.

Although, actually, such animal intelligence proves nothing of the sort. Even if Rocky was able to converse intelligibly with her keeper, or Koko could sign ASL better than other ASL users, or there was a savvy swine out there that could answer trigonometry questions with greater accuracy than the average 10th grader, it would have no bearing on the question at hand. Our capacity for greatness surpasses any other living creature, and the window into that greatness is precisely via the medium of speech and communication.

Parshat Matot begins with a chapter that deals with oaths and vows. The most striking words occur close to the beginning of the chapter (Num. 30:3): אִישׁ כִּי יִדֹּר נֶדֶר לַה'... לֹא יַחֵל דְּבָרוֹ כְּכָל הַיֹּצֵא מִפִּיו יַעֲשֶׂה – "any person who makes a vow **before God** must never break his word, but must do everything he said he would."

Our mouths are not just a means of communicating with others, whether our interlocutors are animal or human, nor is our ability to articulate thoughts via speech particularly unique. Our vernacular may be more complex than that of animals, but even insects communicate with each other in their own way. What makes our communication unique is the fact that we are aware of God, and anything we commit ourselves to is uttered before Him.

No animal, even an orangutan that shares 97% of our DNA structure, has any conscious awareness of God. Which means that even if they could speak like you or me, it would only be to communicate for self-serving interests. It also means that if we choose not to communicate "before God," or if we are prone to breaking our word, we are no better than Rocky or Koko.

Perhaps another thought to bear in mind in the countdown to the upcoming election.

[Koko the gorilla died in her sleep on June 19, 2018, at the Gorilla Foundation's preserve in Woodside, California, at the age of 46.]

DEFENDING ISRAEL FROM THE ATTACKS OF A RABBI

first published July 17th, 2014

The following edited extract is excerpted from the blog of the rabbi of Temple Israel of Hollywood, John Rosove. It describes the "dilemma" of supporting Israel during the current crisis:

> *"Imagine that you have a beloved brother who for the past 47 years has been an alcoholic... You tell him to get sober, but he's in denial... His life was noble and virtuous in his youth, and his family was proud of him. But now, his addiction has drained his resources and he has been forced to borrow heavily from everyone in the family to support his habit. They love him because he's family, but so many are furious at him..."*

> *"One night he's driving home after drinking heavily and blacks out at the wheel. He runs head-on into a family van and hurts everyone, himself most of all. You... see that he is fighting for his life. What do you do? Do you support him and say nothing about the cause of it all, his 47-year addiction? Or do you criticize him, walk away and turn your back in disgust? That is essentially the situation of the Jewish people today."*

Let me state for the record that I have never met John Rosove, and I would like to believe that he is a charming man, and well-meaning in general, and particularly in terms of his observations in this situation. In other words what I am about to say should in no way be construed as a personal attack against him, or against anyone who supports his views. Having said that, I have never – never! – read such utter drivel in my entire life.

Rosove's argument is entirely without foundation, and to compare Israel to an irretrievable addict being enabled by family support is nothing less than reprehensible. What a disgrace that a man who is a religious leader to his flock can be so utterly ignorant of the history and destiny of his nation and faith.

Let me explain. You need look no further than Parshat Matot to understand why Israel's approach to Gaza and its inhabitants is totally supported by the Torah. And if you look at Matot you will also understand why John Rosove and his fellow travelers, armchair critics from the United States, are defying the Torah with every negative statement they make against the State of Israel.

The Jewish nation had absolutely no gripe with Midian. In fact, Moses had spent 40 years in Midian after slaying an Egyptian, and there he had married his wife, Zipporah, the daughter of Jethro, High-Priest of Midian. Had the Midianites not started up with the Jews, the Jews would not have started up with Midian. It should also have been clear to the leaders of Midian that the Jews had thus far been successful at getting the better of that era's most powerful player, Egypt, as well as the fiercest contemporary warrior nation, Amalek. And yet they were unable to resist plotting and conspiring against the Jews, attempting to vanquish them as they entered the Holy Land.

God's response was harsh: נָקֹם נִקְמַת בְּנֵי יִשְׂרָאֵל מֵאֵת הַמִּדְיָנִים – "avenge the vengeance of the Jewish nation against the Midianites." This would be Moses' coup-de-grace, his final act before he died. And he carried it through without compromise. The message had to be clear. Start up with the Jews, at any level, even in a non-lethal way, and you will exact a heavy price. In particular, the leaders of the enemy nation would have to die. Indeed, all five Midianite kings were slain.

The State of Israel has no gripe with Arabs. Israel made peace with Egypt and Jordan, and has offered the hand of peace to Palestinian Arabs for well over twenty years, including offering to give them territory won in a defensive war in 1967. Not only has that hand of peace been rejected, but the rejection has been accompanied by violent hostility and acts of war that no nation can or should tolerate. If Israel would react as the Jews of the Bible reacted, the international outcry would be overwhelming. But at the very least it is not only acceptable, but Torah mandated, for Israel to kill enemy leaders and to destroy any site that is used as a base to launch rockets against Jews.

And, as Binyamin Netanyahu said this week when he accepted the terms of an Egyptian ceasefire (terms that were rejected by Hamas): as soon as the rockets stop, the Israeli reaction will stop, and the hand of peace will be re-extended. Does that sound like the behavior of a drunkard, or does it sound like the measured reaction of a statesman?

In Matot we also have the request of the tribes of Reuben, Gad, and half of Manasseh, to dwell in the fertile pastures of Moab outside the Land of Israel. They are granted their request, but only on condition that they are on the vanguard of every battle in the conquest to take control of the Promised Land.

The message is clear. If you want to enjoy the economic bounty and the security of a territory beyond Israel, then you are expected to be at the forefront of those who battle to secure Israel for the Jews. Let this message be heard by John Rosove and all those other Jews who snipe at Israel from the US or anywhere else in the Western world – your arguments against Israel are un-Jewish, and if you live outside Israel, your voice on Israel's behalf must be louder and clearer than even the voice of Israelis. One thing is certain – insulting Israel with unfounded slurs is beyond the pale.

MASSEI

THE IMPORTANCE OF APPRECIATING OUR PAST

first published July 12th, 2018

Earlier this week, a large group attended the final lecture of my current Jewish History lecture series, to hear a lecture titled *The Wild Wild West: Orthodox Jewish Pioneers in Los Angeles*. I regaled my audience with stories about a range of rabbis and community leaders who were crucial to the creation of a framework for Orthodox Jewish life in the "City of Angels." I recalled successes, failures, frustrations, moments of triumph, and forgotten, seemingly fleeting moments that seemed to have no bearing at the time, but which later proved to be vital for the future of orthodox Jewish life in L.A. in particular, as well as for L.A. Jewish life in general.

The first rabbi of Congregation Talmud Torah ("Breed Street Shul") in Boyle Heights, Rabbi Solomon Michael Neches (1891-1954), a man long confined to the footnotes of academic history books, profoundly impacted both *kashrut* and Orthodox Jewish education in Los Angeles, and the whole of California. Despite fierce opposition from influential Reform rabbis, who advocated for every fringe cause imaginable, unless those causes might have helped preserve Jewish tradition, in the early 1930s Rabbi Neches ensured that California introduced a "kosher law," which, despite its limitations, acted as a safeguard against unscrupulous crooks who try to misrepresent non-kosher food products as kosher, by introducing the threat of criminal prosecution as a deterrent.

Rabbi Neches was also the first person to seriously upgrade the level, as well as formalize the availability, of education in Hebrew and Jewish studies for the Orthodox community of L.A., for both children and adults, first at his shul, and later at the Western Jewish Institute in Fairfax, in a building he secured for the community that would later morph into the Shaarei Tefilla Congregation, for decades a bastion of Orthodoxy on the West Side of L.A. His replacement at Breed Street Shul, Rabbi Osher Zilberstein (1888-1973), was no less important. He single-handedly created the first Jewish day school in Los Angeles, and the first yeshiva high school – *Yeshivat Hamaarav* ("yeshiva of the west") – which boasted high quality Talmud instruction, trailblazing for future similar institutions elsewhere in the city.

Rabbi Zilberstein's close friend, Rabbi Eliezer Adler (1909-2007), the "Zviller Rebbe" of L.A., introduced the warmth of Hasidic Orthodoxy to the community-at-large after his arrival in 1940, but without ever compromising on his principles or ideals, paving the path for other strictly-Orthodox rabbis to settle in Los Angeles and be the beacons of uncompromising tradition to less observant Jews in the decades that followed.

As I finished preparing my lecture, I was struck by the thought that the week when we read Parshat Massei was a very appropriate week for me to be giving a lecture about forgotten and barely remembered pioneers of a community that in all senses has moved on from those early, difficult days. Massei contains the list of all the stops on the journey taken by the Israelites from Egypt towards the Promised Land (Num. 33). Besides for the first few stops, which chart the journey from Egypt to Mount Sinai during that early period of wandering in the wilderness, most of the forty-two place names are unknown, and we also know almost nothing about what happened when the Israelites were at any of those places.

All the commentaries address the seeming pointlessness of this chapter and try to make some sense of its appearance in the Torah. Rashi quotes a *Midrash Tanḥuma* which offers a parable to explain why this passage is not as superfluous as it first appears:

> *"It may be compared to the case of a king whose son was ill and whom he took to a distant place to cure him. When they returned home, the father enumerated all the stages of the journey, saying to him, 'Here we slept, here we caught a cold, here you had the headache, etc.'"*

It can never be just about the destination. Each stage of the journey is a crucial component of the outcome, adding another layer of experience that gives texture and depth to the destination when we arrive. Had the Israelites not gone through the forty-two stops on the way, with whatever it was they gained at each one of them, they would not have been the nation they were as they prepared to enter Canaan and turn it into Eretz Yisrael.

Human nature has a tendency to dismiss history and experience as an irrelevant curiosity which has no role in who we are now as an individual or as a group. That was then, we tell ourselves, but now is now, and whatever happened back then is of no relevance. The list at the beginning of Massei is there to stress the importance of each point in the journey towards the present. However much or little we know about those places, and the sacrifices that were made in each one of them, to ensure the stability and security of the nation then and for the future, or the mistakes that were made that might have endangered that future, each played some part in shaping our present, and knowing this might well influence our own attitude towards the present as yet another such point in the journey towards the future.

As I slowly put together the various pieces of the puzzle in the history of Orthodox Jewish Los Angeles, researching people and primary resources that have been largely ignored by the present-day community, I realized just how much the actions and projects of these pioneers had impacted my own life as a rabbinic leader in L.A. and the life of the L.A. community in general – and how the same can be said regarding the pioneers of every community around the world. Moreover, if God considered these kinds of details important enough to include in the text of the scriptures, we are surely compelled to become more knowledgeable about our past, so that we can appreciate the weight our own actions in the present carry, whether for our families, for our communities, or for the future of Jewish life.

WHAT REALLY WENT ON IN A CITY OF REFUGE

first published July 20th, 2017

Following the loss of their American colonies in 1776, Great Britain was forced to find alternative locations for its various colonial enterprises, one of which was the mass deportation of convicts to "penal colonies" in distant geographic locations. Historians estimate that approximately 50,000 convicts were dispatched to colonial America during the decades before independence – amounting to at least one quarter of all the British immigrants to America during the 18th century.

Serendipitously, the loss of the American colonies coincided with the formal colonization by Great Britain of a large landmass in the Southern Hemisphere called Australia. The first shipment of convicts arrived there in 1788, and by the time the last shipment of convicts landed there eighty years later, the total number of convicts who had been sent to Australia numbered an astounding 162,000 men and women. The popular myth is that all "real" Australians are descended from these convicts, and although this notion is a misconception for reasons beyond the scope of this article, I have nonetheless always wondered why so few of them went back home. Why would they have stayed in Australia, a vast prison country thousands of miles from home? Did they not have families to go back to?

I recently decided to research the topic, to see what I could find. I discovered that the truth of the matter is rather more prosaic and straightforward than I had imagined. For most of the convicts, returning to England was not an option, either because their "freedom" was limited to Australia, or because they were unable to afford the passage home. In any event, Australia offered them greater opportunity, particularly as their prospects back home as former convicts were quite limited. In short, staying in Australia was the better option, even if – in a perfect world – they really desired to get back home.

The reason I was drawn to this subject was a curious Talmudic source based on a verse in Parshat Massei. The subject under discussion is someone who is convicted of the biblical version of manslaughter. This inadvertent murderer is compelled to live out his days in an *ir miklat* ("city of refuge"), ostensibly to escape the life-threatening intentions of his victim's vengeful family members, by law allowed to kill him if he strays beyond the city's municipal boundaries. But city-of-refuge exile was not strictly speaking a life sentence. There was one event that enabled the convicted killer to go back home – if the presiding High Priest of Jerusalem's Temple died (Num. 35:28): כִּי בְעִיר מִקְלָטוֹ יֵשֵׁב עַד מוֹת הַכֹּהֵן הַגָּדֹל – "for he must remain in the city of his refuge until the death of the High Priest."

The Talmud (Mak. 2:6) records an extraordinary consequence of this law – apparently, "the mothers of the priests provided food and clothes [to the residents of cities of refuge], so they would not pray for their sons to die." There is so much that is puzzling about this jarring image of the High Priest's aged mother taking care of numerous convicted felons in multiple cities, to prevent their prayers shortening her son's life, that its bland inclusion in the Talmudic text literally screams out for an explanation.

The sages of the Gemara who expound on this Mishna are more concerned as to why the death of a High Priest would be the mandated trigger for the freedom of a convicted killer, and ignore the reference to attempts by his mother to mitigate the situation, leaving this for later commentators to reflect upon.

The question that particularly occupied me – and led me to research the Australian convicts phenomenon – was this: did the High Priest's mother really believe that someone whose freedom had been curtailed would be swayed by some home-baked apple pies and a scarf to warm them in the winter, to drop their natural desire to be free and return home? I understand that desperate situations call for desperate measures, and of course a mother will try anything to protect her child, however far-fetched and hopeless her efforts may seem to be to an objective outside observer – but that is hardly a sound reason for her actions to be included in a Talmudic discussion about the law!

The enigmatic Hasidic leader, Rabbi Menachem Mendel Morgenstern of Kotzk (1787-1859), is purported to have once told his followers that when he prayed for them not to sin, it wasn't their sinning that concerned him, rather it was the fact they had the time to sin. He prayed that their schedules should be so packed with Torah study and the performance of *mitzvot*, that there would simply be no time left for them to sin.

One of the ironies of the cities of refuge was that they were centers of Torah study. In addition to the fact that they were led by the Levite tribe, who were the Torah scholars of the nation, the Talmud rules that each convict needed to bring his rabbi with him, and, if necessary, his scholarly colleagues, so that his Torah study would not suffer as a result of his conviction and exile. Whatever we are to make of this quite incredible requirement, it certainly reinforces the idea that Torah education can never be abandoned or shunted aside – even if someone is forced to live in a city of refuge, where other aspects of his life undoubtedly act as a distraction. Rather than treat the forced relocation as a personal disaster, it must be viewed as an opportunity.

The mother's gifts of food and clothing may or may not have made a difference to the lifespan of her son, but its inclusion in the Talmud conveys the idea that prolonging a convict's time in the city of refuge was a positive phenomenon, an opportunity for him to spend more time in a constructive Torah-infused environment. Perhaps the message is very simple – if an opportunity for Torah study opens up, however incongruous it may seem to be, don't waste it.

ISRAEL IS OUR DESTINY AND OUR IDENTITY

first published July 24th, 2014

[This article was written during the Gaza War of 2014, when rocket attacks aimed at Israel were coming in thick and fast, and the international community rose up against Israel as it defended itself against deadly attacks from Gaza's terrorist regime.]

I t has been an absolutely dreadful week. We shudder and groan with the news of every dead soldier. The citizens of Israel, and Jews around the world are straining to absorb body blow after horrifying body blow: constant rocket attacks targeting civilians; Israeli soldiers caught in the quagmire of an urban battlefield; deaths and injuries, and lives blighted; the cancellation of flights to Israel and the economic impact of this unexpected consequence; media bias; and rampant antisemitism.

One wonders how much more Israel can take! After all, it is a tiny country – just about the size of New Jersey – surrounded on all sides by countries populated with millions of people who would like nothing better than to rid the world of Jews, God forbid. Terror tunnels built with international aid money coming from our taxes – yes, yours and mine! – snake their way under the Israel-Gaza border to give access to evil Hamas murderers who want to kill or kidnap Jews on the Israeli side of the border. And no one gives Israel the slack they give everyone else. Russia shoots down a commercial airliner, Syria massacres tens of thousands of people, ISIS runs rampant through Iraq murdering civilians, Iran progresses towards a nuclear bomb – all this barely registers. It is always Israel, Israel, Israel.

Defending itself as any normal country would, Israel is scurrilously accused of targeting civilians and deliberately manipulating events so that women and children die. The hypocrisy of the world is so sickening it simply defies understanding. It is at times like this that we need to reinforce our own resolve, so that we remain committed to Israel for the long haul. Instinctively we want there to be a ceasefire. Instinctively we want this pain to end. We want everything to get back to normal, and for life to be as it was before all this began. But that is a mistake. Let us not get lulled into the cozy solutions proposed by international players such as the UN, and even the US Secretary of State. Their only aim is to proclaim "success" in the present, and to move on.

What if the "success" they trumpet now is neither viable nor durable? That, it would seem, is not their problem. It wasn't their problem in 2009, it wasn't their problem in 2012, and it won't be their problem in 2014. But it will be the problem of Jews living in Sderot, Ashkelon, and even Tel Aviv and Jerusalem. And it will be a problem for Jews everywhere, because the fate of Jews everywhere is totally tied up with the fate of Israel.

In Parshat Massei God tells the Jewish nation, just as they are about to embark on the conquest of the Promised Land (Num. 33:53): וְהוֹרַשְׁתֶּם אֶת הָאָרֶץ וִישַׁבְתֶּם בָּהּ כִּי לָכֶם נָתַתִּי אֶת הָאָרֶץ לָרֶשֶׁת אֹתָהּ – "you will inherit the land, and dwell in it, for I have given you the land to possess it."

Naḥmanides ("*Ramban*"; 1194-1270), whose commentary on the Torah is second only to that of Rashi, addresses this verse, and in unequivocal terms. Incidentally, Naḥmanides emigrated to Israel 700 years ago, in an era when traveling or moving anywhere was extremely difficult and challenging. Not only did he move there, he built a synagogue in Jerusalem, which was only recently rebuilt and rededicated after having lain in ruins following its destruction by Arab marauders in the 1948 War of Independence.

Although one might have thought that the quoted verse was said to the Jews for information purposes only – "you will inherit the land" – Naḥmanides sees it in quite a different light. "In my view," he says, "this represents a positive commandment – the Torah commands the Jews to live in the land, to inherit it, because it was given to them by God. They cannot spurn God's inheritance."

Israel is not a casual place of residence, or some piece of exotic real estate; it is nothing less than God's gift to the Jews. And when God gives you a gift, it is very serious.

Naḥmanides goes even further, adding that anyone who moves to Israel is forbidden to leave, and if a husband or wife refuses to join their spouse going on *aliyah*, that would be grounds for divorce! Such is the power of this commandment, he says, and such is the power of our inheritance, the Holy Land of Israel.

Let us not dream for a moment that the IDF is defending Israeli homes or Jews struggling to live under fire. Absolutely not. When our soldiers battle for the integrity and security of Israel, they are fighting for the very essence of what it means to be a Jew. Israel is not merely a country. We didn't just happen to end up there. Israel is our destiny and our identity. It is the soul of every Jew, and it connects us to God in ways that we cannot begin to understand.

That is the message the world needs to hear. They need to hear it in New York, Beverly Hills, London, Paris – and across the world. Wherever there is hostility towards Israel, this is the message that needs to be heard. They even need to hear it in Israel. And we must always remember, even as we struggle to deal with a stream of bad news – there is no "Plan B."

The destiny of each and every Jew and the destiny of Eretz Yisrael are completely intertwined – "for I have given you the land to possess it."

DEVARIM

DEVARIM

A WHOLE NEW DIMENSION

first published July 23rd, 2020

I have just returned from a three-week trip to Israel. I was there to accompany our son Meir as he began his incredible voyage as a soldier in the IDF. One very important thing I learnt during my visit is that although Meir will nominally be referred to as a חַיָּיל בּוֹדֵד – "Lone Soldier" – the last thing he will be in Israel is "alone". The outpouring of support and invitations for Shabbat that Meir has received far exceeds the amount of Shabbatot he will be available during the course of his army service. Nevertheless, it is so incredibly heartwarming to know that while he may be 7,500-miles away from home, he has so many "homes" in Israel in which he will feel welcome and loved.

There is a verse in *Divrei Hayamim* that expresses it so beautifully (1 Chron. 17:21): וּמִי כְּעַמְּךָ יִשְׂרָאֵל גּוֹי אֶחָד בָּאָרֶץ. This verse is usually translated "who is like Your people Israel, a unique nation on earth." But an alternative interpretation is this: "who is like Your people Israel, a nation that is one in the land" – namely, the Jewish people is like one big family, all pulling in the same direction and for the same cause. While we were in Israel, we truly felt it.

Truthfully, while I may have physically been in Israel for three weeks, the first two were spent in mandated quarantine due to the COVID-19 pandemic, and we were therefore completely isolated from everyone and everything. Without any doubt it was one of the weirdest experiences of my life. Although we could hear and see the world going on all around us – the hustle and bustle of central Jerusalem was yards away, just outside our windows – we had no choice but to stay indoors. We were not allowed to see anyone in person, and our only contact with people was via phone and Zoom.

As you can imagine, when we finally emerged from *bidud* last Monday morning, we were raring to go, and – off we went. My delightful cousin Shayke – who, after working for decades as a financial comptroller and public servant has retired and become a professional tour guide – picked us up at 7am. Our first stop was Sderot, a town just north of the Gaza strip. Over the past several years Sderot has been subjected to thousands of hostile missile attacks from Gaza, but it is nonetheless thriving and – remarkably! – growing. New neighborhoods are springing up, and the mood is upbeat and optimistic.

We visited the local Hesder yeshiva, headed by Rabbi Dovid Fendel, an indomitable and spirited man who bounded up the stairs to the roof to show us a full panoramic view of Sderot – as well as nearby Gaza, which is just a few hundred yards away. The yeshiva's rooftop menorah is ingeniously constructed from the spent shells of mortar rockets dispatched by Gaza terrorists to kill Sderot residents, and is a powerful symbol of Israel's resilience in the face of its enemies.

Before leaving Sderot we popped in to see the local fire truck, which our synagogue in Beverly Hills sponsored some years ago. Incredibly, the fire truck took a direct hit during the 2014 Gaza War, and after another campaign, our community paid for the repairs. The truck wasn't there when we arrived – it was being put to good use at a training session nearby. We waited a few minutes until it returned so that we could pose for a photo to show the folks at home.

On we went to the Black Arrow Memorial for Israeli paratroopers near Kibbutz Mefalsim overlooking Gaza, an isolated but quite moving public park that pays tribute to the Israeli paratroopers who took part in dozens of very difficult retaliatory operations in that area during the 1950s. We then stopped briefly to see the ancient floor mosaic at Maon Synagogue, a sixth century archaeological site first discovered in 1957 and renovated in 2006. From there we proceeded to Sde Boker, to visit the former residence and final resting place of Israel's first prime minister, David Ben Gurion (1886-1973). Along the way we saw countless orchards; Ben Gurion's dream of making the Negev desert bloom has become a reality. Apparently, almost all the orchards in central Israel have now been relocated to the Negev to make way for the housing boom that has engulfed their original location.

I had prepared for my visit to Sde Boker by reading Tom Segev's 800-page biography of Ben Gurion while in quarantine. By the time I walked into his old-world study that is lined floor-to-ceiling with books, I felt like I was walking into the inner sanctum of an old acquaintance. It was worth the long drive; I could literally feel Ben Gurion's presence in that frugal home with its basic amenities and tiny living space.

David Ben Gurion was a remarkable man, despite all his many flaws and mistakes. He doggedly pursued the goal of a Jewish state in the Land of Israel through thick and thin, facing up to every challenge with a resoluteness and guile that was rare then, and is even rarer today. It is hard to accurately pin down what motivated him to do it – he was never religious, and his understanding of Jewish identity was instinctive rather than intellectually rooted – and yet he spearheaded the foundation of the multifaceted and thriving Israel of today, which, as we all know, is a modern miracle. Even Ben Gurion had to admit as much, quipping: "In Israel, in order to be a realist, you must believe in miracles."

From Sde Boker we drove to the astonishing desert ridge at Mitzpe Ramon – touted as the "world's largest erosion crater" – and it is certainly a sight to behold. We stopped at Yeruham, a town that is situated bang in the middle of the Negev. The local council has turned an adjacent area into a beautiful park, an oasis with an array of foliage and trees, as well as a large man-made lake, created so that residents can benefit from the lush greenery – even though they have chosen to reside in a desert. Our final stop of the day, before heading to Petach Tikva for the night, was for dinner with friends in Meitar, a lovely town on the southern edge of Mount Hebron, just north of Beersheba.

It was an exhausting but satisfying day. After being cooped up for two weeks, we wanted to experience Israel to the full, and we did. Over the next few days we continued in the same vein. In between organizing various aspects of Meir's army initiation, we spent time with a range of different people, in a range of different locations, until I dropped him off in Tiberias at 8am on Sunday morning. As we drove along the shore of the Sea of Galilee in Tiberias, taking in the stunning contrast between the shimmering blue water and the volcanic black rock buildings rising up into the hills, I thought to myself – what a fabulous country, how lucky we are to be the nation that was chosen to inhabit it.

Naḥmanides ("*Ramban*"; 1194-1270) introduces his commentary to the Book of Devarim as follows: "This book is known as *Mishneh Torah* ("A Review of the Torah"). In it, Moses explains to the generation that will enter the Land of Israel all of the commandments they will need to know." Intriguingly, as Naḥmanides points out, many of the *mitzvot* in Devarim have already been mentioned in the first four books of the Torah. But if that is the case, why was a review necessary?

Elsewhere, Naḥmanides determines that the primary duties of Judaism require a Jew to be in Israel. Even if one performs *mitzvot* diligently outside Israel, it is never going to be the same as doing them in Eretz Yisrael. That is because the Land of Israel is the beating heart of the Jewish people, and in the country of our heritage *mitzvot* and Jewish identity take on a whole new dimension.

The Torah was given at Mount Sinai to a nation of Jews who lived in the diaspora. Their observance of the Torah's commandments may have been perfect, but it lacked one crucial ingredient: Israel. For this reason, Moses needed to add another layer of instruction immediately before the nation entered the Promised Land, so that they would realize how extraordinary this move was going to be. It was not simply a change of geographical location; it was a move into a whole new level of being Jewish. The sights, the sounds, even the air and water of Israel, cut to the core of who we are as Jews, and only by being there can we truly appreciate that, and fulfil our ultimate destiny as God's Chosen People.

THE JEWISH STATE MUST REMAIN JEWISH

first published July 19th, 2018

T he world has reacted with outrage to the legislation recently passed in Israel that defines the country as the nation-state of the Jewish people. The law – which has been labeled by almost every media report as "controversial" – legislates Israel as the historic home of the Jewish people with a united Jerusalem as its capital, and proclaims the Jewish people to "have an exclusive right to national self-determination" in Israel.

"No mention of equality or minority rights" thundered CNN on its website, while *The New York Times* referred to the law as "contentious", noting that its critics believed it to be "discriminatory, racist and a blow to democracy."

Notwithstanding this hostility, and the hysterical reaction from Arab legislators in the Knesset (Israel's parliament), along with the overeager condemnations by several influential American Jewish organizations, such as the Union for Reform Judaism, J-Street and the AJC, the facts are rather less exciting. Even *The New York Times* admitted that "the law is largely symbolic and declarative."

Since Israel gained independence and sovereignty in 1948, Israel's original Declaration of Independence has been superseded by a series of what are known as "basic laws" passed by the Knesset, which can only be repealed by a supermajority

Knesset vote, as opposed to a simple majority vote or a Supreme Court ruling. These laws are in lieu of a constitution, and in combination are considered the de-facto constitution of the State of Israel.

The thorniest issue of Israel's identity has always been its Jewish character. The delicate, sometimes clumsy balance between a "Jewish" state and the preservation of equal rights for all of Israel's citizens has often been used as proof that Israel is inherently undemocratic, and favors Jews over non-Jews. And until this law was passed, all attempts by legislators to regularize the day-to-day realities of life for the Jewish and non-Jewish citizens of Israel through the lawmaking process were purposely delayed to prevent exactly the kind of backlash we have seen erupt since the law finally made it onto the lawbooks.

But let's get one thing straight – this new law changes nothing. Israel was originally set up as a country where Jews could live without fear that the government or citizenry would target them for their Jewish faith or ethnic origins. This objective was envisaged by Israel's ideological father, Theodore Herzl (1860-1904), as well as by his many heirs. In every period of history there have been countries who turned against their Jewish citizens, and the Jews have suffered everything from institutionalized discrimination to genocide, and the full range of actualized bigotry that lies in between. By establishing Israel as a country that has their backs, Jews simply reacted to the fact that no country had ever consistently protected our rights.

Although non-Jewish citizens of Israel have equal rights to Jewish citizens in terms of justice, as well as vis-à-vis economic or other benefits, those rights cannot ever include the possibility –

however remote – that they might change the dynamic of the world's only "Jewish" state so that its Jewish character, which is the only safety net we have, is undermined – or worse.

What I find staggering, and incredibly hypocritical, is that the same people who lobby for a free Tibet, or for Native Americans, or indeed for Palestinian rights, are the very same people who are so critical of Jewish rights in our ancestral homeland, the Promised Land of Israel. And unlike the so-called Jewish organizations jumping over themselves to demonstrate their faux-democratic credentials, I am proud to say that I back this law wholeheartedly, without equivocation – and particularly during the days leading up to the Fast of Av, when we commemorate the tragic end of Jewish hegemony over our own country at the hands of the Babylonians and the Romans.

The Haftarah, the selection from the Prophets, which is read on each of the three Shabbatot between the Fast of Tammuz and the Fast of Av, reflect the mood of this period in our calendar – a time of mourning for the destruction of our Temples in Jerusalem and the removal of Jewish control over our national affairs.

On the Shabbat prior to the Fast of Av, which always falls on Parshat Devarim, we read the first chapter of the book of Isaiah. Oddly enough, the prophet mentions Sodom and Gomorrah twice, although the second reference appears to contradict the first. "Had God not left us a remnant, we would be like Sodom [and] we would resemble Gomorrah," Isaiah begins (1:9), referencing the complete destruction of these two cities during the patriarch Abraham's lifetime (Gen. 19). Fortunately, God did not consider the Jews to be like those two wicked cities, Isaiah seems to be saying, otherwise the Jewish nation would have been utterly obliterated. And yet, in the very next verse (Is. 1:10), Isaiah refers to the Jewish nation as "rulers of Sodom" and as "people of Gomorrah."

The Talmud (Ber. 60a) quotes Rabbi Yose as saying: "never open one's mouth to Satan" – in other words, one should never speak of one's own demise, as this might very well create circumstances in which that demise will happen. As it turns out, we derive this principle from these two verses in Isaiah. The first infers that the nation believed themselves deserving of destruction like Sodom and Gomorrah, and by the time we get to the second verse, that self-identification has become a self-fulling prophecy, and Isaiah addresses them as Sodom and Gomorrah. The Talmud explains that by comparing themselves to those evil cities, the Jews gave the prophet an opening to endorse that comparison.

The Talmud's message in this short passage is profound, and sharply observed. We can affect reality just by the way we project our image. If we proudly declare our identity, that is the reality. But when we diminish our own identity as Jews and don't fight for our rights, we can be certain that our enemies will be in full agreement. Those who succumb to the pressure on Israel to "democratize," as they refer to it, by criticizing Israel's decision to enshrine the primacy of Jewish identity into the fabric of Israel's constitution, are hiding behind political arguments when really they are guilty of pushing Israel into setting itself up for its own demise.

So many Jews have fought so valiantly and risked their lives and status for Israel on every possible stage and in every possible setting; the least we can do is protect our country from the insidious fate our enemies dream of, by formalizing our right to be in control of our own land in perpetuity.

DEVARIM, JEFFERSON AND JACKSON

first published July 23rd, 2015

With your permission, I would like to address the furor over the Confederate flag in the United States. A controversy over flying this symbol of the losing side in the American Civil War has recently gathered pace in various cities across the Southern United States, and it suddenly struck me that different people see different things in this banner of the Southern states who fought for independence from the Union during the 1860s. To one group the Confederate flag is a symbol of local identity, which distinguishes southerners from a more generic "American" persona. To others – and particularly to the black community – it represents the ultimate evil of racism, namely slavery.

But I do not believe the situation is really quite as black or white as it is being made out to be. Although, before I get to that, it is worth noting that the flag controversy has been surpassed by a new polemic, and perhaps this one will better demonstrate the point I wish to make. Apparently, the Democratic Party in Connecticut, under pressure from NAACP, voted unanimously this week to change the name of their annual fundraising banquet: the "Jefferson Jackson Bailey Dinner," which was named in honor of Democrat presidents Thomas Jefferson (1743-1826) and Andrew Jackson (1867-1845), and to honor New Dealer and Connecticut party chief John Moran Bailey (1904-1975). That's because Jefferson and Jackson – who were Democrats – are tainted by slavery, so they must now be expunged from what is seen as an important celebration of Democrat values.

Apparently, the debate over the name of this 67-year-old event has been rumbling for years, but the recent rise in high profile racist attacks prompted local party activists to grab the bull by the horns and do the deed. But while Connecticut Democrats may be celebrating, I am extremely uncomfortable with their decision. Let me explain why.

December 2015 marks the 150th anniversary of the 13th Amendment to the Constitution, which abolished slavery. This milestone in U.S. history was the most important political development for the United States of America excepting the Constitution itself. It seems that President Abraham Lincoln (1809-1865) was conscious of the fact that the Founding Fathers of the United States, and particularly Jefferson, had uncomfortable personal associations with slavery. Jefferson was a slave owner, and despite referring to slavery as a "moral depravity" and a "hideous blot," he never freed his own slaves.

And yet, when Lincoln ordered the drafting of the amendment, he asked that the authors use language that was originally composed by Jefferson in his abortive effort to outlaw slavery in the Northwest Territories in 1784. Lincoln understood, as only a man of his subtlety and nuance could, that history is complex, and that airbrushing people and events from the record of history is a slippery and ultimately destructive path. Jefferson's contribution to the United States, and to the free world, was not just the Declaration of Independence, the Constitution, and the promise of "life, liberty, and the pursuit of happiness." That's because it was only as a result of all of those other things that it was also possible for there to be a 13th Amendment, and in effect Jefferson is the author of that groundbreaking Amendment no less than Lincoln, despite his own personal failings with regard to the slaves he never freed.

At the beginning of the Book of Devarim, Moses reflected on the various events that had taken place over the time he led the Jews from Egypt to the Promised Land. He recalled the highs and the lows, the victories and the failures, the joys and the disappointments. It was warts and all. The commentators struggle to understand why all of these events need to be repeated in this final soliloquy. Every one of them is described in every detail elsewhere in the Torah, and as we know, the Torah is a body of text in which every letter counts, not just every word. In which case, the repetition and duplication by Moses in his opening address at the beginning of Devarim seems superfluous and wasteful.

But ultimately, Moses, the role model for all leaders, is teaching us the most important lesson of all. He was not only reminding his nation of their successes, to pat them on the back and make them feel good, nor was he just broaching the subject of their failures to admonish them, and to tell them that they were evil. What he was doing was informing them that history is complex, and that good people sometimes do bad stuff, but just because they do it doesn't make them bad. Rather it reminds them that they must face their weaknesses and try to rise above them.

Self-improvement is only possible if one is aware that even the greatest of men and women – in this case the generation that stood at the foot of Mount Sinai and heard the word of God – can be weak in the face of stress or temptation, or they can be complacent – and at the same time they can eventually conquer their weaknesses, or their children can, or their descendants, so that they ultimately reach the Promised Land.

Jefferson and Jackson are the greatest examples that the United States has to offer of this guiding Jewish principle. Judaism isn't a faith that believes in or celebrates the perfect hero – namely, an individual who exhibits perfection from the moment of birth until their dying breath. Only God is perfect. Man is frail. And yet the acts of man, even imperfect man, can result in a goodness and a greatness that is greater than the man from whom that greatness and goodness emerges.

Democrats, and indeed all of us, should be proud of Jefferson and Jackson, and continue to honor their memories, not despite their flaws, but because of them. It makes the political and social realities we never had and now have – because they made it possible – all the more powerful. Jefferson and Jackson were the springboard that enabled all those things the United States take for granted to crystallize, including the abolition of slavery, and most other freedoms we hold so dear.

VA'ETCHANAN

VENTURING BEYOND THE COCOON

first published August 15th, 2019

Recently, a rather unusual partnership of radically different subgroups has been formed – a coalition of strictly-Orthodox Jews, devout Catholics, and elite private schools in New York, who are joining forces to oppose an initiative that would impose what they are required to teach in their educational establishments. This new collaboration is the result of a range of new regulations from the New York State Department of Education intended to ensure that all private schools will provide a level of education that is at least as good as that provided in public schools.

Those who oppose the new regulations claim that these regulations are unnecessary, and that they also pose an unlawful threat to their autonomy. But a number of brave Jewish advocates vehemently disagree, pointing out that numerous graduates of strictly-Orthodox yeshivas complain that they received inadequate secular education during their formative years, ultimately meaning that they were unable to financially support themselves and their families.

There are approximately 160,000 students attending around 450 yeshiva schools in New York state, and, if the proposed regulations become the new reality, most of these schools will need to significantly alter their curriculums. According to Chaim Dovid Zwiebel of Agudath Israel of America, the public face of opposition to the changes, "the large majority of Jewish schools across New York State would have to make significant changes in their daily schedules and de-emphasize considerably the Jewish studies part of the day and ... compromise the very mission that these schools were created to carry forward." Rather than across-the-board regulations, Zwiebel and those he represents believe that this matter should be addressed on a case by case basis.

But Naftuli Moster, founder of the lobbying organization YAFFED, totally opposes this approach. "The yeshivas just want to continue doing what they've been doing, which in our view is mass educational neglect and depriving kids of an education, subjecting them to lives of poverty and dependence on government assistance," Moster told JTA.

I grew up in the Haredi world, and went to Haredi yeshiva schools in the UK. But unlike the institutions referenced by Moster, the schools I attended insisted that we receive a full secular education, which included sciences, languages, and English literature – and that was with the full support and encouragement of the community's rabbis and parents, including mine. Later I spent several years in post-high-school yeshivas, studying Talmud and Jewish law – and nothing else, after which I went to University alongside gentile public-school and private-school graduates, utterly unapologetic and completely firm in my Jewish faith, without feeling the slightest pressure to compromise either my observance or my beliefs.

There are many such yeshivas in New York, and why they have chosen to align themselves with retrograde educational institutions that insist on short-changing their students is an utter mystery to me. Astonishingly, almost 250 Orthodox mental health professionals signed a letter regarding the "current proposals by the New York State Education Department to restructure and closely regulate yeshiva education," calling the move "ill-advised."

Privately, many of the signatories have admitted that they feel the state regulations are fair-minded and reasonable. Nevertheless, under pressure from forces within the community, they felt compelled to add their names to the protest. What strikes me as utterly dishonest is that the vast majority of these mental health professionals were not educated in the kind of Orthodox educational institutions these regulations are aimed at improving. How do they have the right to deprive Jewish children of the very education that enabled them to reach their own educational goals?

Parshat Va'etchanan records Moses pleading with God to be permitted entry into the Promised Land. The commentaries puzzle over Moses' preoccupation with being allowed into Canaan. After all, he had done his duty by bringing the nation out of Egypt and delivering them safe-and-sound to the borders of Eretz Yisrael.

According to the late dean of New York's Mir Yeshiva, Rabbi Shmuel Berenbaum (1920-2008), Orthodox Jews in the modern world represent Judaism in its finest hour because of the many unique challenges they face. In his view, the fact that so many Orthodox Jews are willing to lead a life of Torah and *mitzvot*, despite the allure of modernity and low-hanging materialism, is nothing short of a miracle. When our patriarch Jacob finally heard that his beloved son Joseph was alive, he said (Gen. 45:28): אֵלְכָה וְאֶרְאֶנּוּ בְּטֶרֶם אָמוּת – "let me go and see him before I die." The commentaries wonder why Jacob mentions his death; he could simply have said he wanted to see Joseph. What was the point of proposing such a morbid condition?

Rabbi Berenbaum recalled that his teacher, Rabbi Elḥanan Wasserman (1874-1941), renowned founder of Baranovich yeshiva, would constantly encourage his students to visit his own teacher, Rabbi Yisrael Meir Kagan (1838-1933), the saintly author of numerous halachic and ethical works, most notably Chofetz Chaim. "Right now," he would say, "for the price of a train ticket you can see a great rabbi like the Chofetz Chaim. Who knows whether that will be possible in the next world?"

That is what Jacob was saying. He wanted to see Joseph in this world, while he still could. Even the foremost of our forefathers, Jacob, felt that Joseph was a cut above the rest. Despite being thrust into a foreign culture, he had confronted the challenges and temptations of Egypt and remained true to his heritage and tradition, the only one of Jacob's children referred to as *HaTzadik* – "the righteous." Moses, too, wanted the opportunity of living a Jewish life beyond the idyllic cocoon of the wilderness generation. Only in Eretz Yisrael, deeply embedded in the midst of external influences, can the true greatness of Judaism be experienced, and Moses coveted that opportunity with all his heart.

Our generation has a unique challenge, but undoubtedly it is one we can readily overcome. We may be surrounded by a host of hostile influences, but rather than hiding in a hole and failing our destiny, we can rise to the challenge and excel in our faith, support our families, and be a shining example of God's mission – not by rejecting secular knowledge, but rather by embracing it with the confidence of our heritage and our traditions. All of us can rise to the greatness of Joseph – the kind of greatness that even his father Jacob envied, and that Moses wanted too.

FOR THE LOVE OF GOD, DON'T ARREST YOUR OPPONENTS

first published July 26th, 2018

Last Thursday, Israeli police detained Dov Haiyun – rabbi of Conservative Judaism's Moriah Congregation in Haifa – after a complaint was filed at the Haifa Rabbinical Court alleging that he had presided over the weddings of couples "who are not eligible to be married." This is the first time that police have attempted to enforce the Israeli law that forbids anyone from performing Jewish weddings in Israel without involving the Israeli rabbinate – a law which carries a penalty of up to two years in jail. According to reports, Haiyun was accused of conducting a wedding two years ago for a woman whom the rabbinate had ruled ineligible for marriage under Jewish law.

After the arrest generated a storm of protest from a wide range of prominent people and organizations, Israel's Rabbinical Courts Authority issued a statement insisting that anyone who performs weddings for those who are forbidden to get married under Jewish law is guilty of a criminal offense, and liable to be arrested. And of course, technically they are right, but as Daniel Gordis pointed out in his column on *Bloomberg*, he trained as a Conservative rabbi at American Jewish University in his native Los Angeles before moving to Israel, and performed his own daughter's wedding when she got married in Israel some years later.

And yet, despite the fact that he is not registered as a rabbinic officiant, and despite the fact that the wedding was never registered with the Rabbinate, there were no repercussions, notwithstanding the presence of "numerous politically and socially prominent Israelis" at the ceremony. Over the years since the wedding, Gordis' presiding role has been a source of mirth within the family – but as he put it, "we made the occasional quip about my getting arrested for performing my own daughter's wedding, but we were never worried. Many rabbis had done this before, and none had ever been arrested."

Until now. Haiyun's arrest changes everything. Suddenly the wounded tiger that is Israel's Rabbinate has begun to lash out at its proliferating enemies and detractors. After decades of large-scale disparagement and vilification, as a result of the widespread belief that Israel's Rabbinate is nothing more than a self-serving bureaucracy run by inflexible fanatics, those who have a vested interest in maintaining the status quo have initiated a vicious counterattack. The condemnation of Haiyun's arrest may have dominated the news, but don't be fooled into believing that these condemnations have chastened or defanged the powerful forces behind Israel's rabbinical establishment. If anything, it has further emboldened them and made them feel that their stance is vindicated.

Just to be clear, I don't want to give anyone the impression that I support the performance of weddings that are proscribed by Jewish law, and there is certainly an insidious campaign being quietly pursued by liberal Jewish streams to undermine halakhic standards in Israel so that the watered-down "inclusive" trends of the Conservative and Reform movement in America become the norm in Israel as well. Even among Orthodox rabbis in the U.S. there is an astounding lack of knowledge and oversight when it comes to performing marriages, and on far too many occasions I have had to intervene at weddings to ensure that the ceremony is conducted properly, or worse, had to clean up the mess left behind by sloppy incompetence. Marriage in Judaism is not a drive-through Las Vegas ceremony presided over by an Elvis impersonator. It is and should be a very serious event that is conducted thoroughly and professionally, by someone who is both fully conversant with the laws and totally trustworthy regarding his commitment to those laws.

Having said that, my impression of Israel's rabbinate is that it revels in aloof detachment from the human element found in the joy that accompanies every wedding, and the spiritual elevation that underpins it. A wedding is not only about rules; it is about two human beings who love each other and who are going to express that love through what we hope will be a lifelong commitment. And while it is important to follow all the protocols, it is equally if not more important to help bride and groom understand how they are inviting God into their relationship by getting married, and how marriage will elevate their relationship to a whole new level. The rabbis who perform weddings are not civil servants; they are emissaries of God with an important mission – to introduce God into people's lives on the most special day of their lives.

The best-known expression of Jewish faith is found in Parshat Va'etchanan (Deut. 6:4): שְׁמַע יִשְׂרָאֵל ה' אֱלֹהֵינוּ ה' אֶחָד – "Hear, O Israel, Hashem is our God, Hashem is the only One."

Numerous commentaries puzzle over the inclusion of the first words in this proclamation: "Hear, O Israel." Surely one's personal expression of faith does not require a public announcement; rather it should be personal and private.

Rabbi Yehuda Leib Chasman (1869-1935), the prewar giant of Jewish ethical instruction, suggests that no statement of faith, as represented by the *Shema* prayer, has any real value unless it is done in such a way that it convinces others that faith in God is of paramount importance. Simply stating that God is our God, and the one true God, has no meaning whatsoever if one is not such a prominent example of that ideal, that others are compelled to feel the same way. That is why the Torah continues in the very next verse: וְאָהַבְתָּ אֵת ה' אֱלֹקֶיךָ – usually translated to mean "you shall love Hashem, your God," but which actually means "you shall cause your God to be beloved." It is an instruction to us all – make sure that you do everything in your power to help others love God as much as you do!

The obligation of "Hear, O Israel" is incumbent upon Israel's rabbinate, and on every rabbinate or individual rabbi, but I hardly think that this objective is best achieved by having one's critics and opponents arrested. There are many good people in Israel's Rabbinate, not least the Chief Rabbis themselves. Perhaps it is time for everyone who desires for God to be loved to go back to the drawing board, and to develop a strategy that has this ideal as its primary focus.

EATING HEALTHY AND EATING KOSHER

first published August 18th, 2016

Not a month goes by without some new fad diet hitting the headlines. Promising countless health benefits and youthful longevity, while also guaranteeing sustainable weight loss, every one of these diets tantalizes us with claims allegedly backed up by scientific research and irrefutable statistics. Truthfully, some of them push our credulity to the limits, and the latest one is no exception. Dubbed the "Doughnut Diet," the nutritional regime's formal name is IIFYM, an acronym for the rather clumsy sounding "If It Fits Your Macros."

TIME magazine recently ran a story on the IIFYM phenomenon headlined "The incredibly fit guy who eats burritos every day." The "fit guy" of the headline is the diet's originator, Anthony Collova, a bodybuilder who claims to have developed a system that is "easy to comprehend and implement, and is based on science and intuition, rather than hyperbole and hope." If only this were true it would be wonderful, but Collova's claim is so overstated that it can only be described as, well, excessively hyperbolic and hopeful.

The IIFYM diet requires each adherent to enter data onto a website calculator – their age, weight, height, and daily physical activity – so that an accurate daily calorie usage count is generated. Then, based on whether one wants to "burn fat, lean out, or get toned and shredded," a regimen of daily calories is prescribed with exact instructions on where those calories should come from in terms of the three macronutrient groups: protein, fat, and carbohydrates. I'm guessing if one is trim and young, and a person whose daily physical activity is well above average, the IIFYM calorie intake prescription might well be via the eponymous doughnuts. Thank you, Mr. Bodybuilder Collova, but what about all those of us who don't fit into those categories, and who gain weight just by looking at doughnuts?

Coincidentally, this week an Australian website ran a story titled "10 Fad Diets Debunked." The preamble noted that those who seek to remain healthy by regulating their food intake will discover one cannot eat anything at all, at least if one follows the recommendations of every popular diet out there. And while this suggestion facetiously supposes that one would choose to go with all rather than one of them, the article goes on to say that even if one chooses one, it turns out most fad diets are based on pseudo-science and prejudiced assumptions that resonate with the uninformed, but in reality do not bear even the most superficial scrutiny.

The debunk that really caught my eye was the one aimed at the much-vaunted Paleo Diet. The idea behind Paleo is that we should stick to the diet consumed by humanity during the Stone Age, in other words no dairy products, wheat, or processed foods. Instead we should stick exclusively to seeds, nuts, berries, fish and meat. The thesis behind the diet is that contemporary food not only makes us fat, it actually prevents us from getting the nutrition we need, so let's go back to basics. The article totally discredits this proposition. While it may be true that thousands of years ago humanity was restricted to a Paleo Diet, that hardly means people were healthier (after all, life expectancy was under 35), even if it meant they were leaner.

In any event, even non-scientists will understand that our digestive systems have evolved, and that food which caused cave dwellers indigestion or worse, has no negative effect on modern man. For example, the Paleo Diet forbids pulses simply because they are prehistorically incorrect. Ancient man did not consume fibrous legumes, although – one assumes – that was mainly because they were not available. But we now know that legumes are extremely healthy – low in fat, and full of nutrients and protein. It therefore follows that prohibiting them in order to uphold the Paleo principle is – in a word – ridiculous.

I was drawn to this particular debunk because it reminded me of a famous omission in Maimonides ("*Rambam*"; 1138-1204) rooted in Parshat Va'etchanan. As part of his exhortations to the Jewish nation, Moshe declared (Deut. 4:9): רַק הִשָּׁמֶר לְךָ וּשְׁמֹר נַפְשְׁךָ מְאֹד – "make sure to look after yourselves, and be extremely careful to preserve your lives." Based on this quote, and another similar statement a few verses later, the Talmudic sages forbade a number of activities due to the danger they pose to human life. One of these prohibitions forbids cooking fish and meat together, or eating them off the same plate (Pes. 76b).

The *Shulḥan Arukh*, which is indisputably the paramount source of Jewish law, records this prohibition as halakha; but its precursor, the *Mishneh Torah* by Maimonides ("*Rambam*"; 1138-1204), does not list cooking fish and meat together as one of the halakhically prohibited food combinations. Interestingly, the author of *Shulḥan Arukh*, Rabbi Joseph Caro (1488-1575), elsewhere cites a Talmudic ruling banning liquid left exposed and out of sight, only to inform us that this prohibition is now extinct because the Talmudic concern about an unseen snake releasing its venom into unguarded liquid has no contemporary relevance. It therefore seems fair to suppose that Maimonides believed that although fish and meat together posed a medical threat in Talmudic times, it poses no medical threat today, evident from the millions of non-Jews who regularly eat the two together and come to no harm. In which case why did Rabbi Joseph Caro include this prohibition in the *Shulḥan Arukh*?

I would suggest this was not the result of kosher or health concerns, rather it emanated from the lack of clarity in the reasoning given in the Talmud for the ban. Such was the respect Rabbi Caro had for Talmudic sages, that he decided not to second guess them and cancel the fish-meat combination embargo, in the belief they knew something he did not – something significant enough for them to promulgate the ban.

We often hear that kosher and healthy are one and the same thing, and that the rules of kosher reflect the nutritional advice of ancient times, in which case they can be discarded in light of contemporary nutritional information. What is clear from this interesting vignette is that keeping kosher and eating healthy are two totally separate if equally important Jewish obligations.

EIKEV

First Published August 22nd, 2019

I recently saw a *Business Insider* article by Julian Hayes II. You will be excused for not having heard of him. The business magazine *Entrepreneur* describes Hayes as a "health and human performance coach" who works with corporate individuals and organizations to help them "perform better, feel better, become stronger, and unlock their human potential." Hayes' article notes that performing well under pressure and making tough decisions are par-for-the-course for high-performing executives, but thinking and performing better as time unfolds remains an elusive goal. And, as he points out, "two of the biggest culprits are burnout and mental fatigue."

Finding solutions to resolve this issue has been a longstanding topic of focus for corporate management. Hayes had a "eureka moment" while reading an article about Bill Gates on CNBC. During the 1980s, Gates started to take time off for what he called "think weeks," spending time in a cabin at an undisclosed location in some forest in Washington state. But the time away wasn't a vacation. During those few days in isolation, Gates would get to all the stuff he was unable to look at on regular workdays at Microsoft, such as read papers written by his employees in which they pitched new innovations or potential investments. According to Gates, his "think weeks" led to some of the greatest breakthroughs for Microsoft, such as the launch of Internet Explorer in 1995.

Hayes draws two conclusions from Gates revelations, both of which relate to the growing interest in "big-picture thinking" as an overarching solution to the dangers of burnout and mental fatigue. The first takeaway is that for busy people, spending time on your own without any distractions can be a valuable tool, helping you to gain that big-picture outlook regarding your life.

But Hayes' second takeaway is far more revealing:

> *"When I first started working out over a decade ago, I thought the more weights I lifted along with boosting the intensity of those sessions, the quicker I would grow. I was terribly wrong. What happened was a worn-out body with very little results to show for the effort put in. I forgot the other critical ingredient for fitness success: recovery and rest. Hustling at all costs is glorified in today's entrepreneurial landscape while taking breaks is shamed in some circles. But, just as I didn't make progress in fitness until I prioritized recovery, you will make very little progress working yourself into the ground with no strategic recovery involved."*

It's a very powerful message, and one that is echoed, albeit in a somewhat coded fashion, in a bizarre Midrashic passage at the beginning of Parshat Eikev:

> *"What is the law regarding a menorah that is constructed of several sections? May it be handled on the*

Sabbath? According to the sages, someone who attaches the branches of a menorah on the Sabbath must bring a sin-offering. Why is he liable? [Because] someone who assembles a menorah on the Sabbath is the same as someone who builds on the Sabbath, and one who builds on the Sabbath is liable."

The Midrash goes on to record a curious dialogue between the Jewish nation and God, who declares that anyone who thinks that Shabbat was imposed upon them to their detriment is mistaken.

"But when will we see the benefits of the *mitzvot* we do?" the Jewish nation inquires.

"At the end," God enigmatically replies, "as recorded in the words וְהָיָה עֵקֶב תִּשְׁמְעוּן."

The Hebrew word *eikev* has a double meaning; in this Midrash it is used in its alternative form to mean "heel" or "extremity," to indicate "the end." God appears to be saying that the benefit of Shabbat will only be apparent at some point in the far distant future.

This Midrash is so enigmatic, it is hard to know where to begin. In the first instance, what does the question of handling a multi-section menorah have to do with Parshat Eikev? The commentaries suggest that the Midrash is answering an unspoken question by using this rather obscure analogy. Why does the reward for performing mitzvas only occur much later on? Surely if one does a mitzva, one should be rewarded immediately? But the key seems to be that each mitzva is just one small part of a multi-section menorah that is built up over time.

When we think of this in career terms, it makes perfect sense. There is the job we do every day, the same actions, day after day. In and of itself, each action may not lead to an obvious result. But the big picture is different. Each component of our daily work ultimately comes together as a whole, resulting over time in professionalism, experience, and results.

Our lives as Jews are no different. Each day we have countless mitzva obligations, some of them minute and, when considered in isolation, seemingly pointless. But we need to keep the bigger picture in mind; ultimately each component comes together with all the others to form a glorious menorah that will light up our own lives, the life of our family, and the world. Those who focus on the little details might think of Shabbat as a detrimental imposition. But the Midrash explains that this is not the case at all. No different to Bill Gates, we all need "think time" to reflect, otherwise we will try to do too much too quickly and burn out.

Unfortunately, our lives are far too busy for us to find the time to reflect properly. So God provides us with a solution called Shabbat. Without the opportunity of a weekly Shabbat to see the bigger picture, all we will ever have is a pile of pointless pieces that never come together as a menorah. But with the benefit of both "think time" and hindsight everything becomes clear, and we can benefit from the menorah that we painstakingly put together over the course of time.

ABRAHAM LINCOLN'S SECRET WEAPON

first published August 22nd, 2018

Earlier this week, at a raucous rally in Florida, President Donald Trump cited a poll that he claimed showed him to be the most popular Republican of all time. It was not the first time Trump has mentioned this poll. Last month, just before his visit to London, he cited the poll's findings in an interview with British tabloid newspaper *The Sun*, making the bizarre claim that he was more popular than President Abraham Lincoln (1809-1865), the first Republican to occupy the White House.

Trump's idiosyncratic interpretation of the poll aside, it is certainly the case that its findings have absolutely no bearing on his popularity in comparison to the GOP's most iconic president. That's because there were no professionally conducted scientific opinion polls in the 1860s, so we have no idea if Trump has beaten Lincoln in the popularity stakes or not, and we never will.

Lincoln is one of five extraordinary leaders featured in the recently published book about leadership by the Harvard historian Nancy Koehn, titled *Five Leaders Forged in Crisis, and What We Can Learn From Them*. According to Koehn, Lincoln's most extraordinary achievement was his transition from a novice politician to word-class statesman in a relatively short period of time. In an article published to accompany the book's publication, she cites a number of reasons to explain this rapid transformation, and his astonishing leadership abilities while in office, particularly bearing in mind that it was a time of great turmoil for the fractious country he had been elected to lead.

In Koehn's view, Lincoln was driven by a mission which he stuck with through thick and thin, although he also was constantly aware of the bigger picture. He never spread himself too thin, preferring to focus on a limited number of objectives at any point in time. He sought advice from a wide variety of sources, but never blamed others for his decisions if they went wrong. He also never misled the country about the consequences of decisions he was making – he would articulate all the pros and cons of any decision he was about to take, at least as he understood them, so that everyone was aware of the risks and benefits of going in a particular direction. Lincoln also perfected the art of restraint and taking no action, which was often a more difficult choice than doing something. And finally, Lincoln was incredibly resilient in the face of phenomenal pressure, and once he felt he was doing the right thing, he would not fold in the face of even the most hostile opposition.

Each one of these attributes is powerful in-and-of-itself, and we would all be happy with leaders who shared even some of these qualities with Lincoln. Nonetheless, I think that Koehn omitted Lincoln's most outstanding quality from her list, the trait that truly enabled him to utilize all his other traits with such self-assurance – the understanding that he, Mr. Abraham Lincoln, did not exert ultimate control, as that was always in God's hands.

In October 1863, as the Civil War continued to rage, Lincoln told a meeting of Presbyterian ministers in Baltimore:

"Amid the greatest difficulties of my Administration, when I could not see any other resort, I would place my whole reliance on God, knowing that all would go well, and that He would decide for the right."

Although Lincoln was by no means a devout man, a fact he readily admitted, he nonetheless had incredible faith in God, and a profound belief that none of his achievements had been without God's help. Addressing a special session of Congress at the beginning of the Civil War, arranged to clarify the unusual circumstances which had led to the decision to launch a military campaign, Lincoln ended his lengthy remarks with an incredible declaration:

"Having thus chosen our course, without guile, and with pure purpose, let us renew our trust in God, and go forward without fear, and with manly hearts."

In spite of all the careful planning, and despite the rectitude of the unionist cause, Lincoln fully comprehended the magnitude of what he had taken on, and how easily it could all go horribly wrong. Only with God's help would they defeat the Southern states and achieve their objectives.

In Parshat Eikev, as part of a pep talk given by Moses to the nation before he died and they embarked on the conquest of Canaan, he posited that they might one day ask (Deut. 7:17): רַבִּים הַגּוֹיִם הָאֵלֶּה מִמֶּנִּי אֵיכָה אוּכַל לְהוֹרִישָׁם – "How can I conquer these nations? They are so much greater than me!" In order to prepare them for this projected eventuality, Moses suggested that when it happened the nation should remind themselves of the great miracles that took place both before and after the Exodus, which would reassure them that they had nothing to fear.

The question is – why mention now that one day in the future doubt would arise? Moses should simply have issued a directive for the nation not to fear the enemy whatever happened, in the knowledge that God had their back and they were not on their own. In answering this question, the *Sefat Emet* explains that in order to truly acknowledge God, we must first be aware that we do not have the power to do anything on our own. Bearing in mind what we are up against, we must recognize our own helplessness so that we understand the need for God's help.

Taking this idea even further, the Hasidic master, Rabbi Tzvi Elimelech Spira of Dinov (1783-1841), suggests that whenever we feel the challenges we face are so great that they cannot be overcome, we must immediately realize that it is us who are the issue. The introductory verse cites the projected doubt to convey the root of the problem: us, when we say – "they are so much greater than me."

By introducing God into the equation, we change the dynamic, so that success is more likely. Even if we are not personally worthy, the acknowledgement that God is our only hope – as evidenced at Exodus – is all that we need to conquer the unconquerable. Which gives us a major insight into Abraham Lincoln. He seems to have instinctively understood that the buck stopped with him, and this was a role he grew into and perfected in record time. But he also understood that without God's help his presidency was doomed, as was the country, and it was this powerful faith in God that underpinned all of his other valuable attributes.

ISRAEL'S BEAUTY IS IN THE EYE OF THE BEHOLDER

first published August 25th, 2016

O ccasionally I come across information in an article that I know is meaningless to almost everyone else, but it resonates powerfully with me. Maybe you've experienced that too. Stumbling across one of these nuggets is a 'Eureka!' moment, and I was lucky enough to experience such a moment as I breezed through an op-ed on the incredible desalination successes in Israel over the past few years.

In between paragraphs praising Israel for its superlative agricultural industry, I discovered this absolute gem:

> *"Israeli dairy cows produce some of the highest amounts of milk per animal in the world, with an average of over [2,600 gallons] per animal."*

How odd, I thought. Why would anyone interested in desalination be even faintly concerned about the udder output of Israel's bovine population? But, if you are a bible lover, you will read that statement and immediately sit bolt upright in your chair. That's because 3,500 years ago, as recorded in numerous places in the Torah, God promised the Jewish nation that their Promised Land would be אֶרֶץ זָבַת חָלָב וּדְבָשׁ – "a land flowing with milk and honey." Can you actually believe it? Millennia have passed, and the milk is still flowing in Israel more copiously than anywhere else in the world! (Unfortunately, I have no statistics regarding honey.)

Parshat Eikev is dominated by its depiction of the Land of Israel as an earthly paradise for the Jews, although there is an alternative dystopian depiction in which it is portrayed as a land fraught with impossible challenges and complications. As part of his overall description, Moses informs the Jews that Canaan "is not like the land of Egypt from where you came."

The medieval commentators debate the meaning of this odd statement, with Rashi suggesting that Moses was telling them that their land was superior to Egypt, which at that time was the most affluent country on earth. The Jews had complained to him on numerous occasions about how they missed the fleshpots of Egypt. Moses was reassuring them, says Rashi, that the Land of Israel would be far better than Egypt ever was.

But the later medieval commentator, Naḥmanides ("*Ramban*"; 1194-1270), appears to disagree with Rashi. Unlike Egypt, which relied on the water of the River Nile to irrigate its arable land, the Land of Israel required significant annual rainfall to generate sufficient crops. As all of its rainfall was contingent on the good behavior or otherwise of the Jewish nation, Moses' statement about Egypt was actually a warning to the Jews. He was cautioning them that Canaan might indeed turn out to be wonderful, but at the same time there was no guarantee that the land would automatically produce crops, as had been the case in Egypt. If the Jewish nation abided by its covenant with God, the land would certainly be abundant; if not, the land would remain barren.

This disagreement between Rashi and Naḥmanides is utterly bewildering. How is it possible for these two great bible commentators to argue about something so fundamental? Either the Land of Israel was more wonderful than Egypt – and "wonderful" can be easily defined and measured – or it was not? I have always struggled with this conundrum until recently, when I came came across a rather strange and quite obscure letter writing campaign that helped me resolve it and enabled me to reconcile the two opinions.

In October 2015, a group of American Jews launched a movement they called "Love Letters to Zionists." This organization requires former lovers of Israel turned Jewish anti-Zionists to write letters to close family members who remain avid supporters of Israel, to explain their change of heart, and to try and convince them to see the other side of the story. The "Love Letters to Zionists" website has reproduced a number of these letters, although, strikingly, none of the replies.

What struck me while reading these anti-Zionist missives was the gulf between Jewish lovers of Israel and Jews who haven't got a good word to say about the place. It is not just the treatment of Palestinians that causes them anxiety; their complaints stretch to every aspect of life in Israel.

Here is just one example:

> *"The cost of living is high, the services atrocious, . . . [and if you moved to Israel] you would HATE driving because people are hateful and aggressive on the road. You would be viewed as an outsider for your entire life and treated differently because you aren't part of the ever-important in-group!"*

Wow! For this letter writer the case is closed. Israel is a terrible place to drive, and services are a disaster. In short, it's a dreadful country. Although, I wonder if drivers in Ramallah are less aggressive than their Israeli counterparts, or if services in Gaza compare favorably with New York and Los Angeles.

The serious point is this. The letters all seem to be written by people living in a parallel universe. For them Israel can do no good, and everything about the country is bad. Politically, socially, culturally – it is a complete catastrophe. Is this really the same Israel that we lovers of Israel find so vibrant? So dynamic? So young? So alive? It seems that the same factors which convince Israel haters that the country is bad, lead those of us who are its fans to conclude the exact opposite.

On reflection, I think this is exactly what Moses meant when he said Israel was not like Egypt. His message was that Israel is not a boring country on autopilot. Egypt never evoked negative reactions and was predictable in every respect. But the Land of Israel, depending on your attitude, and your relationship with God's covenant, could be considered a paradise or, with the wrong attitude, could be considered an absolute hell. If you fall in love with Israel and appreciate its connection to your Jewish identity, everything about the place is wonderful. If you despise Israel, and deny your connection to it, nothing is ever going to be satisfactory – the rain is sparse, the crops are always late, the weather is foul, and don't get me started about the buses!

Nahmanides is not disagreeing with Rashi, rather he contextualized Rashi's positive interpretation by postulating that Israel's beauty would always be in the eye of the beholder.

Remarkably, even in this respect, nothing has changed in 3,500 years.

RE'EH

first published August 13th, 2020

I n the late 1990s, Aaron Peckham was a nerdy computer studies undergraduate at "Cal Poly" in San Luis Obispo, California. Just over twenty years later he has an estimated net worth of $100 million and owns and runs a range of profitable technology businesses. But more than anything else, he is best known as the founder and owner of the trailblazing website *Urban Dictionary*, a crowd-sourced online dictionary specializing in definitions of popular slang words and phrases, which he launched in 1999 while still a student.

But while the idea of a web-based dictionary with volunteer contributors may sound innocent enough, the crowd-sourcing model has caused *Urban Dictionary* no end of problems, and last month Peckham announced that the website would be putting safeguards in place to prevent contributors from uploading definitions that are offensive, or worse.

Now you may be wondering – and rightly so! – how a dictionary website could ever be offensive. The answer, shockingly, is that although Peckham's original concept was to create a less stuffy version of *dictionary.com* – a site which would allow users to "define the messier edges of language" using irony and satire – under the guise of irreverent humor, *Urban Dictionary* has slowly evolved into what the respected technology magazine *Wired* recently described as a "harbor for hate speech," while the *Daily Telegraph* described it as "a hotbed for racist and sexist rhetoric."

In February, *Jewish News Syndicate* reported that *Urban Dictionary* had been condemned for publishing "hurtful and disrespectful" definitions of the word "Auschwitz." I never knew that Auschwitz is a popular slang word – "go figure!" as we say in America – but in any event, included among twenty different definitions for Auschwitz on Urban Dictionary were: "a summer camp for Jews," "a Disneyland for its time," and "the happy resort for Jews during WW2." The Auschwitz-Birkenau Memorial and Museum quite justifiably issued an outraged protest in which they pointed out that the Auschwitz definitions were far from an isolated aberration. To illustrate their point the press release included a screenshot showing an entry on the website for the word "Jews" describing them as "the people who hold all the world's power, and who are responsible for everything bad that's ever happened."

One might have thought that the shakeup in July would have prevented any repetition of such clangers, but this week the row erupted again, this time over *Urban Dictionary*'s definition of anti-Zionism. Evidently, the online dictionary runs a service via its Twitter account that allows users to mention *Urban Dictionary* and list a word for definition. In response, a bot answers with a definition after locating the word in the *Urban Dictionary* database. And so, when asked to give the definition of "Zionism" the tweeted reply was "Anti-Zionism is in no way connected to antisemitism. To be anti-Zionist is to be anti-fascist... Zionists believe that they can turn up in a country and kick out the indigenous population, as did Hitler."

And lest you think that what happens on some fringe website – where the audience "is predominantly male and aged between 15 and 24" – is of little consequence in the real world, then you are living in an alternative reality, clearly not conscious of the impact this kind of hate-speech normalization is having on "Middle America." For example, are you aware of the fact that the California State Assembly has just adopted Assembly Bill 1460, an ordinance that will make ethnic studies a graduation requirement for California State University (CSU)? And if you're thinking "so what's the big deal?" – let me quote from a letter signed by no less than 90 organizations that was sent to Governor Gavin Newsom, urging him to veto the bill:

> *"We fear that the anti-Zionist orientation of Critical Ethnic Studies ... coupled with the willingness of many ethnic studies faculty to bring anti-Zionist advocacy and activism into their professional spaces, will foster a toxic climate for Jewish and pro-Israel students and foment harm against them... CSU does not have a policy that would prevent instructors in Ethnic Studies colleges and programs from using their classrooms for politically motivated and directed advocacy and activism, including the promotion of anti-Zionism and the anti-Israel Boycott, Divestment, Sanctions (BDS) movement."*

This entire issue has been further complicated by a countermeasure passed by CSU, who resent the state legislature's interference. But faculty and students oppose the CSU version, saying it is "watered down" – "because it broadens the requirement to include courses on other oppressed groups" (including Jews) "and conceivably allows for a student to graduate without taking an ethnic studies course as defined in the assembly bill." Can you imagine that? Getting your medical or law degree without ever having been through a Critical Ethnic Studies course?

Unchecked, whatever exists on the fringes ultimately winds its way into the mainstream, and before you know it the extremist views of radicals and weirdos, as represented by an overwhelming number of angry tweeters and news website commenters, suddenly threaten to contaminate the education of the next generation, and more worryingly, the safety of law-abiding communities who have cherished beliefs and views, such as the right of Jews to self-determination in the country of their religious heritage.

In warning the Jewish nation to beware of the malign influence of idolatry in Parshat Re'eh, Moses seems to be stretching feasible outcomes to the limit. The Jewish nation, having been through the purgative experience of forty years in the wilderness, after falling foul of God on several occasions, and in particular for their ill-advised worship of the Golden Calf and their imprudent acceptance of the false report given by the spies, had surely learnt their lesson good and proper – don't fall for dazzling rhetoric delivered by those on the margins, nor should one ever be swayed by the false promise of fringe-ideas and ideals.

And yet, Moses warns them in the starkest of terms (Deut. 13:4): לֹא תִשְׁמַע אֶל דִּבְרֵי הַנָּבִיא הַהוּא אוֹ אֶל חוֹלֵם הַחֲלוֹם הַהוּא כִּי מְנַסֶּה ה' אֶלֹקֵיכֶם אֶתְכֶם לָדַעַת הֲיִשְׁכֶם אֹהֲבִים אֶת ה' אֱלֹקֵיכֶם בְּכָל לְבַבְכֶם וּבְכָל נַפְשְׁכֶם –

"Do not heed the words of such a prophet or dreamer; God is testing you to see whether you really love God with all your heart and soul."

As inconceivable as it seems to us, idolatry was hugely attractive to those first generations of Jews who carried out the conquest of the Promised Land, becoming the norm for many despite Moses' dire warnings, and despite the experience of their forebears in the wilderness – just as the most ridiculous ideas and seemingly fringe views have crept their way into the mainstream in the twenty-first century.

The warnings from history are there, time and again – never take "normal" for granted – and yet we easily forget what has happened countless times before. Blink, and you're faced with a deluge of belligerent anarchy, intent on replacing sensible and conventional ideas with the idolatry of modernity – namely, an urgent desire to uproot the stable society which is the foundation of Western life. And it is fair to say that unless we proactively oppose these insidious trends now, we will all suffer the dreadful consequences.

DO WE POSSESS FREE WILL?

first published August 9th, 2018

O ne of the major topics tackled by Greek philosophy is the existence or otherwise of free will. Are human beings capable of making choices, or are their choices determined for them by forces beyond their control? Intriguingly, thousands of years may have elapsed since the first Greek philosophers proposed this as a subject worth exploring, but we are no closer to a definitive answer than they were.

To the layman, it all appears quite obvious. We are constantly faced with countless choices as we engage with the world around us, and we instinctively believe that our choices are not determined in advance. After all, how is it possible for "determinism" to accurately forecast how we are going to behave or react in any given situation? And yet, much of what we do is formulaic, based on personality, upbringing, experience, and a host of other factors, and if we were brutally honest, we could easily and accurately write the script of our lives in advance, down to the last detail.

So while we want to suppose that we are free to choose, and when we decide on a particular course of action, significant or otherwise, we pride ourselves on having made the right choice, a nagging subconscious voice undermines this perception, insisting that we are just preprogrammed robots whose autonomy is effectively nonexistent.

In a sentence dripping with irony, the celebrated twentieth-century British novelist and savant Aldous Huxley (1894-1963) presented precisely this troubling dilemma as a paradigm case for free will:

> *"A man may be a pessimistic determinist before lunch and an optimistic believer in the will's freedom after it."*

In these few, well-chosen words Huxley highlights the paradox – is there any real choice in choice, or is all choice actually an illusion?

Modern science has come down firmly on the side of determinism. Florida psychologist, Seth Schwartz, writing in *Psychology Today*, summarized the scientific community's bias by means of a rhetorical question: "From a purely scientific perspective, how is it possible that anything can occur without having been caused by something else?" Namely, in order for choice to be truly free, it must be unencumbered by any cause, and this ideal simply does not correspond with the model of science we are all familiar with.

In the late nineteenth century, scientists and philosophers developed a worldview they called materialism, based on the idea that whatever exists is purely a consequence of atoms and molecules. Even consciousness and mental phenomena are just the result of neurological processes. What started as a theory was eventually legitimized by a series of controversial experiments conducted in the 1980s by Benjamin Libet (1916-2007), which appeared to prove unconscious brain activity connected to movement even before a person had consciously decided to move. Neuroscience has widely adopted Libet's conclusions, proposing that all human behavior is controlled by neurobiology, and the notion of free will is merely an illusion.

Harvard psychology professor, Daniel Wegner (1948-2013), in his book *The Illusion of Conscious Will*, took this even further by arguing that people can even believe they are influencing events initiated and carried out by others, when it is patently evident that nothing they have done has made the slightest difference to the outcome. Wegner based his thesis on a series of controlled experiments, and concluded that the existence of the free will illusion "helps us to appreciate and remember our authorship of the things our minds and bodies do." Even if free will does not exist, "it serves as a guide to understanding ourselves and to developing a sense of responsibility and morality" – in other words, a useful tool for sentient, intelligent creatures. Wegner's work is based on an atheistic perspective that presumes a Darwinian need for free will as an effective human survival technique.

Another social psychologist, Roy Baumeister (b.1953), has added yet another dimension, by proving that people who don't believe in free choice are more likely to be socially irresponsible. In order for humans to reach their optimum, they must believe in free will, even if it doesn't exist. Notwithstanding its atheistic underpinning, it would appear that this modern perspective is congruent with the opinion of Maimonides ("*Rambam*"; 1138-1204), and is also implied in the first verse of Parshat Re'eh.

In the fifth chapter of his *Hilkhot Teshuva* ("Laws of Repentance"), Maimonides puzzles over the seeming contradiction between free will and determinism. Although he associates determinism with divine foreknowledge, in practical terms this is just the same as the evolutionary determinism that underpins materialism. In an answer remarkably reminiscent of Wegner and Baumeister, Maimonides proposes that free will exists for the benefit of humanity:

> *"Just as the Creator desired that fire and wind rise upward, and water and earth descend downward, that the heavenly spheres revolve in a circular orbit, and all the other creations of the world follow the nature which He desired for them, so too, He desired that man have free choice and be responsible for his deeds, without being pulled or forced. Rather, he, on his own initiative, with the knowledge which God has granted him, will do anything that man is able to do."*

Although God knows what we are going to do in advance, and even if our choices are predetermined by genes, or neuroscience, or any other factor, it is all irrelevant in the moment we choose to do something, because at that moment the choice is real, and we have total autonomy. This idea is succinctly but clearly expressed in the first verse of Re'eh, in Moses' introduction to the concept of choice in Judaism (Deut. 11:26): רְאֵה אָנֹכִי נֹתֵן לִפְנֵיכֶם הַיּוֹם בְּרָכָה וּקְלָלָה – "See, I set before you today a blessing and curse."

The commentaries are all mystified by the word "see," surely the wrong verb to use in relation to the intangible concepts of blessings and curses; and by the word "today," which also seems oddly out of place, limiting what was said to when Moses said it. In reality, Moses deliberately used these two words to convey the immediacy and actuality of choice. In the here-and-now of any given situation, the choices one perceives are real, and, in the final analysis, that is all that matters.

GETTING RID OF GENERAL LEE

first published August 17th, 2017

A s a non-American living in the United States, I found the recent political hurricane over General Robert E. Lee (1807-1870) quite mystifying. Despite being familiar with the history of the Civil War, I must admit that I was not fully aware of the depth of feeling it still evokes 150 years later, nor that the Confederate military commander, General Lee, is a revered icon of the white supremacist movement.

Just to put things in context, Lee is often mischaracterized as a benign figure reluctantly thrust into his role on behalf of the confederacy, who then actively encouraged cooperation between North and South after the Civil War was over, becoming a beacon of peaceful reconciliation. Like all such myths, this convenient narrative is nothing more than an elaborate, agenda-serving creation loosely based on truthful foundations. In reality, Lee was a cruel slave-owner who did not even conform to the "humane" guidelines many slave-owners imposed upon themselves, particularly those who were part of the Confederate leadership. Moreover, he presided over a reckless campaign against a superior foe, at the cost of hundreds of thousands of lives on both sides, in a treasonous rebellion against an elected government.

After the war was over, Lee desperately tried to disappear into the background, but found himself compelled to stay in the public eye as a symbol of constructive cooperation between the Unionists and their erstwhile opponents. Nevertheless, he regularly expressed racist views while still claiming to support emancipation.

What is so intriguing about the vexed subject of General Lee's legacy is that the white supremacists are the ones who have history and precedent as their justification. Their determination to protect Lee monuments across the Deep South in the midst of national equivocation and indecision, merely reflects the fact that Lee has become the "acceptable" face of a deep-rooted American racist subculture that continues to fester more than 150 years after the Civil War.

Anyone who fulminates at President Trump's ambiguous condemnation of white supremacists by drawing moral equivalence with those who demonstrated against them, must wake up to the reality that white supremacist ideology is far more acceptable in America than it is anywhere else in the Western world. Just as a case in point, there are literally dozens of monuments and statues dedicated to General Lee across the United States, as well as schools, bridges, buildings, roads, and even counties – all of them beacons of ideological encouragement to vile racists, subtly, or perhaps not so subtly, legitimizing the type of prejudice we would all like to think was dead and buried.

The Jewish community should, if anything, be hypersensitive to this phenomenon. Which Jew with any sense of history is not horrified to see the prominent statue of Ukrainian rebel leader Bogdan Chmielnicki (1595-1657) in the middle of Kiev? Chmielnicki was responsible for the deaths of tens of thousands of Jews, as well as the destruction of dozens of Jewish communities, during the 1648-9 Cossack uprising against the Polish Commonwealth. Any celebration of his memory is an affront to Jews, particularly as he is still a lightning rod for hostile nationalism, antisemitism and racism.

We may rationalize any Chmielnicki adoration as a sign of Ukraine's unreconstructedness, but how is the United States any different if it is okay to celebrate the memory of a racist traitor like Lee?

In 1919, the U.S. Supreme Court unanimously ruled that if someone falsely shouts "fire" in a crowded theater, they cannot use the First Amendment as a defense. The First Amendment, the court ruled, was designed to protect freedom of expression, not dangerous speech. The message is clear. Freedoms can be abused so that that they lead to anarchy and civil unrest. In most European countries where the Holocaust occurred, Holocaust denial is outlawed. In Germany, the "use of symbols of unconstitutional organizations" outside of the contexts of "art or science, research or teaching," is prohibited. These symbols include the swastika and the SS insignia, among many others considered encouraging to racists and antisemites.

In America, the symbols may be different, but the principle remains the same. It is not enough to rewrite history so that free speech can be accommodated, if General Lee remains a potent symbol of hatred and division. Having a monument to his memory anywhere in the country, but particularly in the Deep South, is like shouting "fire" in a crowded theater.

Parshat Re'eh contains a trio of very troubling directives, mandating the execution of a false prophet, someone who actively promotes idol worship, and of all the inhabitants in a city of idolaters. After detailing the criteria underlining a city of idolaters, the Torah throws in a phrase that seems quite out of context (Deut. 13:18): וְנָתַן לְךָ רַחֲמִים וְרִחַמְךָ וְהִרְבֶּךָ – "God will be merciful towards you, and be compassionate with you, and multiply you."

This verse sparked a debate among Talmudic sages as to its interpretation (Tos. San. 4:1). Does the verse mean that the authorities should show clemency to children in a city of idolaters, or not? More recent commentators suggest that the phrase is evidence of God's promise that those involved in carrying out the brutal directive will not themselves be brutalized in the process.

But I would like to suggest another explanation. Evidently this law is not directed at us, as there is no contemporary situation in which anyone would be expected to put an entire city to death. But all of us can understand how an evil ideology will insidiously persist if it is not completely eradicated. The message of this verse is that when one embarks on the elimination of evil, every vestige of that evil must be vanquished for good to succeed, and for us to thrive in its wake. That is a message which is as relevant today as it was when the Torah was written.

SHOFTIM

STAND AND DELIVER

first published September 5th, 2019

Earlier this week, I briefly visited New York for a wedding, and while I was there I was once again confronted with the controversy that continues to rage over proposed education regulations formulated by the New York State Education Department (NYSED). Feelings are running high, and the campaign to thwart the said proposals is in full swing. Many within the Orthodox community are convinced that this scheme is the thin end of a very insidious wedge, and opponents include those whose schools provide a very good general studies education. Quite a number of the people I spoke to believe that allowing the authorities to determine how and what is taught at Jewish private schools poses a grave danger to the future of Orthodox Jewry in America.

But how did we get here? How is it possible that a bunch of faceless bureaucrats in Albany has managed to rattle the Orthodox community to this extent? Why is it, if so many schools are compliant with equivalency requirements, that NYSED wants to institute these draconian measures to regulate and oversee them?

Incidentally, whatever happens in New York will surely foreshadow similar legislation in other states. There is a broad concern among education officials that Jewish private schools are not in compliance with basic educational requirements, and that children who attend these schools are being shortchanged by their institutions, to the extent that they will "graduate" without the basic skills required to provide for themselves and – once they marry and have kids – their families.

In the Satmar Hasidic community this whole episode is being painted in very stark terms. Last month, the various factions within Satmar (please note: it is no small feat to unite this very divided community) issued a powerful declaration regarding the dangers posed by the proposed regulations. In a vigorous call to arms, the leadership requested that the "honored parents" of students in their various institutions join a letter-writing campaign to the authorities to ensure the failure of the "evil education decree" which threatens the status-quo, and which – they claim – might result in the devastation and destruction of Torah-true Jewish education in New York.

And just this week, twelve Hasidic institutions published a notice to announce that they would never include "common core" education books in their general studies curriculum under any circumstances, as they are full of "heresy," and their only intent is to prepare those who use them for a college education.

Meanwhile, thousands of parents within the Satmar community and other associated Hasidic groups, including many who have sent letters to NYSED so that they openly comply with the mandated letter-writing campaign, are secretly hopeful that the state will impose the regulations on their children's schools so that the next generation will be forced to learn English and math, and be properly equipped for life in twenty-first century America.

I have received hundreds of emails and calls since my last article on this subject, the vast majority from Hasidic parents congratulating me for my stance, and imploring me not to abandon them and their children to a life of ignorance and penury. One parent wrote to me that his children only speak Yiddish, as their school does not allow them to speak English at home, otherwise they might be expelled. He told me that this means his children do not know the English names of the days of the week, nor do they know their English dates of birth, nor can they explain to an English-speaking doctor what their symptoms are when they require medical attention.

These children, it is worth noting, are all third-generation Americans. So how is it that if they were Jews from the former Soviet Union, or living in low-income industrial towns in Israel, we would do everything we could to help them gain a foothold in life, but just because they live in Williamsburg, or Monsey, or New Square, we do nothing to help them, and simply write them off? How does it make any sense that hundreds of thousands of Jewish children are being doomed to a life of poverty right under our very noses?

In Parshat Shoftim we are informed that it is forbidden to use any kind of sorcery, or to engage in fortune-telling to predict the future. Instead, God gave us prophets who would reveal to us what we need to know about the future, as and when we need to know it. Rabbi Naphtali Tzvi Yehuda Berlin ("*Netziv*"; 1816-1893), author of the Torah commentary *Haamek Davar*, poses an obvious question. What if there is no prophet for us to consult?

In that situation, are we permitted to consult a fortune teller (obviously, only on the basis that they are a source of genuine information)? Rabbi Berlin surprisingly says that in such a situation, this ordinarily forbidden source may be consulted. In other words, when stark decisions need to be made and sorcery is the only method at our disposal – "a man's got to do what a man's got to do"!

If so, asks Rabbi Berlin, how is it that King Saul was punished for consulting the Witch of Endor (I Sam. 28)? After all, if he was unable to obtain an answer from any legitimate source, and this method was his only recourse, why was he penalized for engaging in necromancy? To answer this question, Rabbi Berlin reveals a stunning principle, one that should shake us all to our core.

If the situation of last resort occurred as a direct result of Saul's actions, how could he possibly use it as an excuse to flout a Torah prohibition? Saul was the one who killed all the priests of Nob, and Saul was the one who had provoked God's anger. Now that he found himself isolated and rejected – how could he justify using the results of his own misbehavior to present himself as a victim?

The situation for Jewish schools in New York is not some tragedy thrust upon the strictly-Orthodox community by external forces bent on causing havoc. On the contrary, this has been a tragedy that has unfolded in plain sight over many years, with all segments of that community standing idly by as thousands of Jewish children were poorly served by retrograde schools.

Those who have presided over these Dickensian institutions together with their enablers have no right to expect sympathy and latitude now that things have gone south. If they do expect sympathy and latitude, it is nothing but the height of arrogance and the epitome of hubris. They must immediately climb down from their high horses and ensure that all – yes, all! – Jewish children graduate school with a level of knowledge in English, math and social studies that will ensure that they can conduct their lives in dignity and with integrity, as the Torah expects of them. Nothing less will suffice. It is time for them to stand and deliver.

CORBYN'S ANTISEMITISM IS NOT THE PROBLEM

first published August 16th, 2018

T he last time I wrote about Jeremy Corbyn, leader of the UK's Labour Party, was two years ago. At the time Corbyn was desperately struggling to assert his leadership after losing a no-confidence vote, an event that was accompanied by the mass resignation of his shadow cabinet team. Remarkably, two years later he is still the leader of the Labour Party, having weathered numerous storms – the types of storm that in any normal political climate would have resulted in automatic resignation and prolonged hermitry.

But it seems that a normal political climate is no longer normal, evident from political upheavals across the Western world, including the United States. The 24-hour news cycle revolution of the late twentieth century has now been augmented by the 24/7 social media phenomenon, which enables widely dispersed fringe groups to create an agenda-driven mass reaction to any given situation. In a democratic system, where mass opinion matters, extreme views can appear mainstream, or can even become mainstream, as a result of overwhelming social media advocacy, leading to a political leadership that reflects this new reality.

In any event, let's get back to Jeremy Corbyn. Over the past few months, the "antisemitism row" he cannot shake off has rumbled on and gathered pace, exacerbated by seemingly endless revelations about his associations with Palestinian terrorists and murderers, and ever more furious reactions from British Jews, frightened at the prospect of this doctrinaire Israel-hater becoming Prime Minister. With the Conservative government in complete disarray over the shambolic Brexit negotiations, and Corbyn's support barely affected by his much-publicized history of cozying up to arch-terrorists, these fears are very real, and the alarm is far from an overreaction.

This week's outcry centered on the discovery of photographs of Corbyn attending a wreath-laying ceremony in Tunis in 2014, honoring the Black September terrorists who kidnapped and murdered Israeli athletes at the Munich Olympics in 1972. After the photos emerged, Corbyn initially claimed he was paying tribute to victims of an Israeli airstrike in 1985. When this excuse was challenged by the media, Corbyn claimed he did not "think he was actually involved" in any wreath-laying for the Munich terrorists. A reporter then revealed that the photos, which show a smiling Corbyn holding a wreath surrounded by his Arab hosts, were taken directly in front of the memorial to the Munich terrorists.

Confronted by this new evidence, Corbyn seemed unfazed, and claimed, disingenuously, that he had participated in the event as part of the global fight to end terrorism:

"I was there because I wanted to see a fitting memorial to everyone who has died in every terrorist incident everywhere because we have to end it."

His statement is disingenuous, because the Munich terrorists were not victims of a terrorist attack that targeted civilians to further a twisted political ideal. Rather they were killed in retaliation for their perpetration of a terrorist attack that targeted civilians to further a twisted political ideal, in carefully planned Mossad operations during which no one else was harmed.

But believe it or not, there is so much more that is wrong with Corbyn and his fellow travelers, that this is really a minor point. And although I find Jeremy Corbyn's views on Israel and his actions in support of Israel's sworn enemies abhorrent in the extreme, it is not his views that concern me, as I strongly believe in freedom of speech, and in the freedom to hold and express opinions that are diametrically opposed to mine, even if they are completely warped.

Rather, I am concerned by Corbyn's total disregard, even contempt, for the system which enables democracies to operate and thrive, as demonstrated by his embrace of terrorist murderers whose causes he finds worthy. He does not even attempt evenhandedness, and to my knowledge has never formally or informally met a representative of Israel's government, never mind been to a cemetery to pay tribute to the real victims of Middle East terror.

I would venture to say that nothing Corbyn has ever said or done has improved the life of even one Palestinian, not least because this has never been his true goal. The whole purpose of his perpetual grandstanding on behalf of fashionable causes, however extreme and reprehensible they may be, is to bring about the complete collapse of the UK's system of government by highlighting what he believes to be both its grave errors of judgement and its blind spots, demonstrating that the system is not fit for purpose.

As we have seen across the Western world, iconoclasts like Corbyn are now able to harness huge public support. So much is wrong with the structures we have in place, and so many mistakes are being made by those in power, that people are attracted to the kind of clean-sweep changes represented and promised by Corbyn and his ilk. But they could not be more wrong.

Parshat Shoftim begins with the directive to create a judiciary, and officers of the law. We are also told how important it is to adhere to the rulings of the court system, even if they occasionally get something wrong (Deut. 17:11): עַל פִּי הַתּוֹרָה אֲשֶׁר יוֹרוּךְ וְעַל הַמִּשְׁפָּט אֲשֶׁר יֹאמְרוּ לְךָ תַּעֲשֶׂה – "You shall act in accordance with the instructions you are given, and the ruling handed down to you."

The *Sefer HaChinuch* explains that the reason we are forbidden from defying those who transmit tradition is because by totally rejecting their authority we will end up destroying Judaism. Humans are by nature argumentative and always question authority. But while there is nothing wrong with regulating the system from within, rejecting it completely on the basis of perceived mistakes will inevitably result in complete chaos and lawlessness.

Similarly, for all its flaws, the Western system of government is far too precious to be undermined by root-and-branch anarchist revolutionaries like Jeremy Corbyn. In truth, his antisemitism is a distraction, just an indicator of the far more dangerous goals he has in mind.

THE CONCEPT OF "BASHERT" IS NONSENSE

first published August 24th, 2017

W e have a number of weddings coming up in our community, so I thought it might be an idea to address the glaring contradiction that exists between a widely held Jewish belief about marriage, and a fundamental aspect of Jewish faith. The Talmud (Sot. 2a) makes a startling statement about the inevitability of spousal identity:

> *"Forty days before an embryo is formed, a divine voice declares: 'this person's daughter is destined to marry that boy!'"*

Jewish folklore refers to this marriage predetermination concept as *bashert*, the Yiddish word for "destined." Every girl has their *bashert* boy who they are destined to marry, and every boy has their *bashert* girl. In other words, no one should ever need to remain single; all we have to do is find our *bashert*, marry them, and then live happily ever after.

To say that this idea is theologically problematic rather understates the glaring issues it presents – issues that undermine the very basis of our faith system. Just as an illustration, let us look at a verse from Parshat Shoftim found in the section dealing with military exemptions.

The Torah presents us with the script for army recruitment officers to use in the process of exempting those for whom military service is deferred. One of the exemption criteria is framed as follows (Deut. 20:7): וּמִי הָאִישׁ אֲשֶׁר אֵרַשׂ אִשָּׁה וְלֹא לְקָחָהּ יֵלֵךְ וְיָשֹׁב לְבֵיתוֹ – "who is the man who has become engaged to a woman, but has not yet taken her as his wife, let him go and return home, lest he die in battle and another man shall marry her."

Maimonides ("*Rambam*"; 1138-1204), in his famous letter to the twelfth-century Italian convert Obadiah the Convert, refutes the notion of *bashert* – despite the aforementioned Talmudic passage – by citing this verse from Shoftim. Why, he asks, would a man who is engaged to the woman he is destined to marry, be at all fearful of being killed in battle and replaced by another man as her husband? Surely, says Maimonides, if the meaning of the Talmudic passage is that his fiancé is "the one," destined to be his wife even before her birth, no other man could ever marry her.

Even more to the point, this young man could be as reckless as he wanted on the battlefield, in the knowledge that he is certain to survive and get married. If anything, he would make the perfect soldier! So why is he exempted from military service? On the contrary, the army should eagerly recruit him.

To reconcile this apparent contradiction between scripture and Talmud, Maimonides suggests that this Talmudic passage is not meant to be taken at face value and must instead be interpreted as referring to the potential that exists for reward and punishment – a potential God sets into motion even before a person is born. Someone who is deserving of reward will merit the husband or wife who will be their agent for a wonderful life of "happily ever after," while the opposite will be true if their behavior falls short. The point is, all the options are already in place before one is born.

Maimonides goes even further in his refutation by quoting an alternative Talmudic source – a source that is a cornerstone of the Jewish faith – and turning it on its head. The Talmud declares (Ber. 33b) that "everything is in the hands of Heaven, except for the fear of Heaven." Like so many other Talmudic statements, what seems to be a simple idea is actually very profound. The key to understanding this particular statement lies in accurately defining the exception. What is it that is included in the "fear of Heaven"?

Maimonides, being the great rationalist that he is, refuses to accept a notion that includes literally "everything" as being in the "hands of Heaven." If that were true, he says, it would wreck the entire concept of free choice. By way of example, he notes that if God predetermines the person we are to marry, why should anyone make any effort to choose a spouse? Consequently, the exception to the rule – "fear of Heaven" – turns out to be a much broader category than the basic translation implies. It includes your marriage, and all your relationships; it includes your livelihood, your home, your time management – in fact, it includes anything that relies on choices that you make. Because who we choose to marry, and how we choose to live our lives, all falls under the rubric of ensuring that our relationship with God is on the right footing, a process that requires the careful and proactive calibration of our "fear of Heaven."

The tension between determinism and free choice has vexed philosophers and theologians for millennia. Particularly in recent years, when we have begun to explore and understand the world of biological and psychological determinism, to which theology assigns a Divine origin as opposed to blind science, we have been forced to deal with the weight of inevitable consequences and our limited ability to counteract them. And yet, it is in this limited arena that our "fear of Heaven," namely our relationship with God, can really come to life.

As we approach the High Holidays, the period in our calendar during which we focus on our choices over the past year, and the choices we intend to make for the next, it would help for us to reflect on the fact that it is in the arena of choice, however limited that arena may be, and in whatever way the concept of choice may apply to us, that we truly define ourselves. The realization that we have the choice to make choices is a critical component of ensuring that everything we do never becomes a product of fate, rather it must be the result of considered reflection and a desire to constantly renew our vows with God.

THE PURSUIT OF JUSTICE

first published August 20th, 2020

I t is unlikely that the name Rabbi Pinchas Menaḥem Mendel HaCohen Singer will mean anything to you. His rabbinic career principally spanned the early decades of the twentieth century, during which he acted as a community *dayyan* ("halachic judge") and rabbi in the Polish cities of Warsaw, Biłgoraj and Dzikov, and also briefly as the head of the Radzymin yeshiva and personal secretary to the fiery Hasidic rebbe of the Radzymin sect, Rabbi Ahron Mendel Guterman (1860-1934).

The Singer family were Hasidic; Rabbi Pinchas' father Rabbi Shmuel Singer had forged close relationships with three of the greatest Hasidic leaders of the mid-nineteenth century: Rabbi Israel Friedman of Ruzhyn (1796-1850), Rabbi Shalom Rokeach of Belz (1781-1855), and Rabbi Chaim Halberstam of Sanz (1793-1876), and was the highly respected rabbi of Tomaszów Lubelski. Rabbi Shmuel's wife, Tamarel's deep piety was legendary, and she was even rumored to secretly wear *tzitzit* ("ritual fringes") – highly unusual for a devout Orthodox woman, then and now.

Rabbi Singer never studied secular subjects, nor could he speak Russian or Polish. All of his bountiful knowledge was gained from Hebrew scripture, Talmud, and the copious halakhic material that emanates from these two sources. In 1910, he published a scholarly book, *Megadim Hadashim*, on the Talmudic tractate

Avodah Zara that deals with idolatry and the prohibitions associated with paganism. A number of effusive approbations introduce the work, including, among others, from the Radzymin Rebbe; from Rabbi Neḥemia Alter (1873-1942), a scion of the Gerrer Hasidic dynasty; and from Rabbi Tzvi Yeḥezkel Michelson (1863-1942), the celebrated "Plonsker Rav," himself the author of no less than 43 published works.

Truthfully, Rabbi Singer was just one of many distinguished Polish rabbinic leaders who struggled to hold it together for Polish Jewry during the interwar years, which culminated with the Holocaust that obliterated all but 100,000 of Poland's three million Jews. Indeed, Rabbi Singer died in his hometown of Dzikov in 1942, and although his death was not directly at the hands of the Nazis, his death was a result of starvation caused by the Nazi invasion of Poland. And frankly, Rabbi Singer might have been entirely forgotten – an ephemeral lacuna that slipped through the cracks of historical record – had it not been for his son Yitzḥak, better known to us as Isaac Bashevis Singer (1903-1991), the Nobel-prize winning novelist.

In two of Bashevis Singer's lesser-known books, *In My Father's Court* and *More Stories from My Father's Court*, the Yiddish novelist turned his hand to autobiography, writing a powerful account of his father's years as a *dayyan* on Krochmalna Street in the heart of Warsaw's decrepit Jewish neighborhood, presented to the reader in bite-size vignettes. Each chapter records one particular case brought to and then adjudicated by Rabbi Singer, seen from the perspective of a young impressionable boy. The characters and episodes captivatingly evoke the lost world of Polish Jewry, caught in the daily struggles of a life that must accord to the ancient tenets and customs of Judaism while the world around them accelerates toward modernity.

There is the elderly couple whose love for each other is so great that the woman demands the rabbi grant them a divorce so that her beloved husband can marry a younger wife and have more children. Then there is the young groom who wishes to break off his engagement because he doesn't love his fiancé, but her father refuses to return the gifts the young man has given his daughter. Another man, destitute, demands to know if he is allowed to sleep in the same bed as his dead wife until the funeral so that the rats infesting his basement digs won't nibble at her corpse. Yet another man, an impressive rabbinic scholar, turns out to be a God-denying heretic who wants Rabbi Singer to pay him in exchange for his heavenly reward. A young girl who has cooked meat and milk in the same pot and then eaten the food because she was hungry, now wants to know if the pot is kosher.

Even allowing for Bashevis Singer's literary license, the stories are brimming with the real pathos and drama of its generally unnamed protagonists, but most of all one is struck by the man caught at the center of it all, Bashevis Singer's father, Rabbi Pinḥas Menachem Mendel Singer. This exemplary, eminent scholar, who was raised in an environment of scholars and saints, and whose rabbinic training was under the tutelage of some of Poland's great rabbinic luminaries, is about as far removed as it is possible to be from the gritty and often distasteful end of society that he is compelled to deal with on a daily basis. And yet there he is in each story as it unfolds, doing his utmost to dispense justice – observing, inquiring, consulting, and even occasionally rendering an unpopular decision, all in his role as the representative of Jewish law for this substratum of the Warsaw Jewish community.

In Parshat Shoftim, Moses instructs judges that they must pursue justice (Deut. 16:20). The *Sefat Emet* notes that it is not enough to seek justice – one must actually pursue it. Curiously, the word for "pursuer" in Hebrew is *rodef*, rather a rough word with harsh associations; an aggressor or persecutor is usually referred to as a *rodef*. On that basis, this term is rather odd for the Torah to use in the context of justice. Oddly enough, there is another reference to *rodef* that is also out of place: "Seek out peace and pursue it." (Ps. 34:15)

The role of a rabbi and *dayyan* is to be a purveyor of justice and peace. It would appear that Moses and King David both wish to convey that neither of these two objectives come knocking at the door of your ivory tower. In order to achieve justice and establish peace one must pursue it aggressively, even if it means stepping well out of one's comfort zone – and no matter how distinguished or well-bred you may be, if you are able to improve the lot of others with your wisdom, experience and scholarship, you must go to where the action is, and not just stay where it suits you, or only meet and talk to people with whom you are comfortable. That is why we are instructed to pursue justice, and to pursue peace.

In his poignant introduction to the first book of vignettes about his father's court, Isaac Bashevis Singer makes the following startling statement, on the basis of witnessing his father's Beth Din in action for the common folk of Warsaw:

> *"It is my firm conviction that the court of the future will be based on the Beth Din, provided the world goes morally forward instead of backward... The concept behind [Beth Din] is that there can be no justice without*

Godliness... At times I think that the Beth Din is an infinitesimal example of the celestial council of justice, God's judgement, which the Jews regard as absolute mercy."

A people that believes justice must be pursued, and that it is not just a commodity to be bought or sold, or a convenient fixture of human life easily available to all that seek it or wish to see it done, is indeed an eternal people.

In the month of Ellul, as we anticipate the annual season of celestial judgement, this valuable lesson from the long-forgotten tenements of prewar Warsaw, as well as from the words of Moses, are a powerful reminder of just how important it is for justice and peace to prevail, and for us to do all we can to see that they will.

KI TEITZEI

LOST, BUT NOT IGNORED

first published August 27th, 2020

Paul Cowan has a very unique job – he is the head of *Transport for London*'s "Lost Property" division. Until September last year, this iconic division of London's public transport system was located on Baker Street, not far from the fictitious home address of British literature's most famous detective, Sherlock Holmes. According to the official announcement charting the move to their new premises, "more than 900 items of lost property are found every day on London's transport network and the current premises at 200 Baker Street – which first became home to the Lost Property Office in 1933 – are no longer suitable for the efficient running of the service."

Originally from New Zealand, Cowan runs what is the second largest lost property office in the world, beaten only by a similar facility in Tokyo, Japan. But although it may not be the largest such facility, the TfL Lost Property Office is totally unique – just so quintessentially British, with an understated, sardonic, tongue-in-cheek attitude among those who work there that has turned what could have simply been a boring sorting service into something so much more.

A favorite among the unclaimed items is a life-size stuffed gorilla, that the TfL staff have named Eddie. The gorilla, complete with his Hawaiian shirt, has been adopted as their official mascot, and has become so famous that it is featured as the front cover image for the "Night Tube Pocket Map." Intriguingly, Eddie is not even the most unusual object found on London's public transport network. As far as Cowan is concerned, the strangest item of lost property ever handed into his office was an urn of crematorium ashes. "It was a chap called Thomas," he told BBC radio, "and he sat on my desk for the best part of five years." Thomas' ashes were eventually reunited with his family.

Cowan and his team sort through more than 330,000 items each year. These include 13,000 keys; 35,000 cellphones; 46,000 handbags; and 10,000 umbrellas. Surprisingly, very few items are ever claimed. On average, just 20 per cent of lost items are claimed within three months after being handed in, after which they pass into the possession of TfL. And unclaimed items are not necessarily those you'd expect to be abandoned by their owners. Cowan's thesis is that when people lose something, they often see it as an opportunity to treat themselves to something new.

The facility houses a large repository of lost crutches, which Cowan considers particularly strange. As he told the BBC, "either there are miraculous curing powers on the London Underground, or there's a lot of people hopping around London without their crutches." Cowan claims that the office has also had to deal with lost breast implants and prosthetic limbs – something I find absolutely mindboggling. There have also been wedding dresses, countless wedding rings, skis, microwaves, TVs, a pile of Mexican sombreros, and there was once someone who left a coffin on the tube.

"When someone rings up and says: 'Help! I've lost my wedding ring and I'm getting married on Friday', you snap into action mode pretty quickly," Cowan says, with a twinkle in his eye. Cowan calls the TfL storage facility "The Wonder Emporium" and struts around the subterranean repository with an air of propriety that is combined with ample good cheer – he is truly the king of London's vast inventory of lost property. But as I researched this peculiar department of London's transport network, I was most struck by the reaction to this unusual phenomenon by a journalist called Leo Hornak, founder of *In The Dark* – a non-profit devoted to producing strange and wonderful pieces of radio in strange and wonderful venues.

Writing in 2016, he noted an aspect of the TfL Lost Property operation that one might quite easily miss:

> *"Standing in the storeroom, I realize there are two ways to look at these groaning shelves. One is to feel the loss, the emotional loss. All those moments of rising panic when a precious thing was searched for and ended up here instead... But there's another, more positive way. Every iPhone, child's toy and digital camera [in this storeroom] is also tribute to the honesty and decency of a Londoner who found that item and passed it on to [Cowan]'s team."*

His observation reminded me of the phrase in Parshat Ki Teitzei that concludes the instruction to return lost items to their owners, a mitzva known as *Hashavat Aveida*. When one spots a lost item, one should not ignore it, the Torah warns, rather one must find its owner so that he or she can be reunited with their possession. The passage ends with the words (Deut. 22:3) לֹא תוּכַל לְהִתְעַלֵּם – "you cannot ignore it," a reference to the lost item. But the fact that this phrase includes the word *tuchal* is curious; it could easily have been omitted without any loss of meaning.

Rabbeinu Yonah of Gerondi (d.1264), the revered medieval rabbinic authority and Jewish ethicist, notes that this seemingly superfluous word contains a powerful lesson in human relations, the cornerstone of all mitzvot which relate to social and communal behavior. With this one word the Torah is teaching us that it is not enough to return a lost item as a matter of duty, rather this act of civic duty must be underpinned by an acute awareness of the fact that as a caring human being one must never be the kind of person who sees someone else's lost item, with all the distress that such a loss may have caused, only to coldly return it because of an ordinance that requires it to be returned. That is simply not good enough. Instead, one must work on oneself to become the kind of person that "cannot ignore it" – another person's distress must become your distress, as if you had lost the item and wanted it to be returned to you.

As we approach the High Holidays, and anticipate squaring our accounts with God, we might well consider – as Leo Hornak did when he strolled through Paul Cowan's "Wonder Emporium" – that returning lost property, and indeed doing all the many things we do to maintain good relations with others, should never just be a reflection of duty, rather they must also reflect a generous-spiritedness that we have worked on in ourselves so that we are not just someone doing the right thing, but rather we are someone who aspires to do good, be good, and make the world a better place.

WALKING THE WALK

first published September 12th, 2019

O ne of the great social challenges facing modern society is the problem of juvenile delinquency. Crimes committed by individuals who have not yet reached adulthood can often be as bad as those committed by adults. As is the case with all types of criminal behavior, scholars and experts debate the causes of juvenile delinquency, and differ on how best to address the issue.

In the United States, instances of juvenile offending spiked during the early 1990s, resulting in a landmark study published in 1993 by the US Department of Justice, titled *Family Life and Delinquency and Crime.* Writing in the foreword, senior government official Jerry Regier (b.1945) explained that "the family is the fundamental building block of human society [and] there is much to be learned about the effects of family life on delinquency and crime."

The study concentrated on bringing together in one paper the conclusions of dozens of previous studies which had examined every aspect of juvenile delinquency as it related to the family setting. Many of the ideas regarding the effects of family life, or the lack of it, on youngsters growing up into a life of crime were self-evident – rejection, abuse, discord in the home, criminal parents, single parent families – but here they were presented with the evidence of research studies, essentially to inform policymakers what areas they needed to focus on in order to address the crisis.

Thankfully, juvenile delinquency in the United States has gone down since then, although it remains a huge problem, as it does elsewhere in the Western world. Nevertheless, some of the lessons learnt in the 1990s have since been incorporated into parenting guides and other resources created to help parents avoid the pitfalls that may result in their child's descent into criminal activity.

One part of the 1993 study was devoted to "normative development," which the authors described as "how children learn right from wrong." After introducing the section, the authors suddenly and quite surprisingly stepped out of the dry objective tone they had used until then, expressing their astonishment at the absence of a critical area of research with regard to normative development.

"Because some evidence has linked normative development, and specifically involvement with religion, with reduced likelihood of delinquency, it is curious that so few studies of this element of positive parenting have been conducted. [One study suggests] that the lack of attention to religious influences is due to two possibilities: 1) a lack of interest in conforming behavior, as opposed to deviant behavior, and 2) a general opposition to religious principles among academic social scientists."

If ever there was proof needed that research and data compilation can be biased, here you have it. Atheist academics looking at how to deal with juvenile delinquency eschew religious beliefs – so they avoid studying anything that might imply the benefits of a religious upbringing! Remarkably, the authors of the government study combed through the existing literature to find scattered references that underscored the importance of what has since become known as "role model parenting."

> *"The role of parents in moral development is critical and irreplaceable [as] the parents represent the child's first encounter with society's rules and regulations. Families, similar to societies, have rules against dishonesty, violence, theft, and a general prohibition against disorder. As children confront the moral issues of life, their parents have considerable influence in helping the child reach a positive resolution with these dilemmas."*

There is only one reference in the Torah to juvenile delinquency, found in Parshat Ki Teitzei, and it would appear that the passage discussing *ben sorer umoreh*, as the juvenile delinquent is called, wishes to make this exact point. In introducing what should be done with such a child, the Torah says (Deut. 21:18): כִּי יִהְיֶה לְאִישׁ בֵּן סוֹרֵר וּמוֹרֶה אֵינֶנּוּ שֹׁמֵעַ בְּקוֹל אָבִיו וּבְקוֹל אִמּוֹ וְיִסְּרוּ אֹתוֹ וְלֹא יִשְׁמַע אֲלֵיהֶם – "If someone has a wayward and defiant son who does not hear the voice of his father or mother, and even after they discipline him does not listen to them."

Rabbi Tzvi Hirsch Spira of Munkacz (1850-1913) comments on the seeming repetition in this introductory verse. He notes that if the wayward and defiant son is not hearing his parents' voices, he is certainly not going to take any notice of them when they discipline him. Why say the same thing twice?

He therefore suggests that the first part of the verse is not actually a reference to any conversations between the parent and child, but rather it refers to the voice of the parent in the home. If a child never hears his parents praying, or discussing God, or morality, or ethics, or Torah values and ideals, then inevitably when they rebuke him for not living up to these ideals, he will not take any notice. Why should a child listen to anything his parents tell him to do if they do not do those things themselves?

Every parent is a role model to their children; every grandparent is a role model to their grandchildren; every influencer is a role model for their peers. If we want our families and our communities to honor and uphold the time-honed values of our faith and tradition, the baseline for that achievement is for us to behave the way we want them to behave. And no one knows us better than those who are closest to us, which means that they will always reflect our behavior in theirs.

If we live the life we expect of others, it is far more likely that they will also lead that life. All of us put our hopes and dreams into the next generation. But it is only through our own efforts to live the life we dream for them that our aspirations for them have any chance of coming to fruition.

THE NATURE VS. NURTURE DEBATE REVISITED

first published August 23rd, 2018

I n 1883, the sociologist polymath Sir Francis Galton (1822-1911) published his celebrated work on human behavior, *Inquiries Into Human Faculty And Its Development*, which incorporated his 1875 groundbreaking article on twins. Galton pioneered the scientific study of "nature vs. nurture," which undoubtedly contributed to his particular fascination with twins, and he was the first person to systematically study them. He sent out 600 questionnaires to parents of twins, in an effort to establish just how far similarities and differences between them were affected by their life experiences. Although the resulting thesis was significant as a pioneering study, the conclusions were not supported by the evidence, in particular because Galton was openly biased towards nature rather than nurture.

The study of identical twins who spend their formative years in the same home generally has very little to offer in terms of useful or usable data. But the notorious case of the "Jim twins" is quite different. Jim Lewis and Jim Springer were identical twins born in 1940, and both were given away to different adoptive parents at just a month old. It would be almost forty years until they learned of each other's existence and were finally reunited. Remarkably, although they had never met, they chain-smoked the same brand of cigarettes, drove the same make of car, and vacationed at the same beach in Florida.

Both Jims had a childhood pet dog called Toy, married a wife called Linda, divorced her, and then married a wife called Betty. They both had one son, called James Alan – although one of them spelt the name Alan with two l's. One was a security guard, the other a policeman. They both suffered from tension headaches and were both incessant nail biters.

The discovery of the "Jim twins" was widely publicized and resulted in a monumental 20-year study of "reared-apart twins" by Thomas Bouchard (b.1937) at the University of Minnesota. This study was detailed in the 2012 book *Born Together—Reared Apart: The Landmark Minnesota Twins Study*, written by California psychologist, Nancy Segal (b.1951), who was part of the original Minnesota research team.

Although some critics have dismissed the study's conclusions, principally citing Bouchard's eagerness to favor nature over nurture, ironically echoing the denunciations of Galton's nineteenth century work, some of the raw data is just too compelling to ignore. Time after time the study shows how identical twins have matching personality traits – the way they laugh, what makes them laugh, hobbies, music preference, tastes in clothes, and choices of names.

And then there is another curious phenomenon – identical twins brought up in the same home who diverge dramatically from each other as they get older. Treated in early life as two versions of the same person, they are dressed in the same clothes, given exactly the same food, gifts, education, and parental attention. But as they get older their personalities and interests deviate, resulting in two very different people who may even end up not looking like each other, and often with markedly different health and psychological issues. After years of research, Professor Tim Spector (b.1958), head of twin research at King's College, London, has proposed that these differences are due to changes in the human epigenome that result from environmental influences.

Yes, you read that right – it is not just your behavior that is affected by your environment, but your genes too. For example, a desire to be different than your twin as a direct result of pressure to be the same can lead to changes in your epigenome – and these are changes that modern science can prove. Meanwhile, identical twins separated at birth and living hundreds of miles from each other, with no knowledge of each other's existence, are free to develop into their unaltered genetic personalities, resulting in the stunning similarities seen in the "Jim twins" and others like them.

This exceptional revelation can help us understand a deeply puzzling anomaly at the heart of one of the Torah's most disturbing laws, the *ben sorer umoreh* found at the beginning of Parshat Ki Teitzei (Deut. 21:18), the "wayward and defiant son, who does not heed his father or mother," ultimately executed after going through a judicial process. The Talmud is keenly conscious of the inhuman brutality of filicide, even if it is legally mandated, and reveals a set of conditions that make it utterly impossible for a *ben sorer umoreh* conviction to ever occur. The Talmud actually goes on the record to state that "there has never been a stubborn and rebellious son [conviction] and there never will be." If so, ask all the commentaries, why bother to include this law in the Torah?

The answer lies in understanding the convoluted conditions imposed by the Talmud. The boy's mother must be identical to his father in voice, appearance, and height. Both parents' vision must be perfect, they must possess all of their limbs, and the city they live in must have its own Beit Din. The Talmud is making a powerful point. A child's misbehavior is not a reflection of who he really is. Rather, it reflects his environment. The wrong setting causes him to act out even though he is not naturally inclined to behave badly. The good news is, if the misconduct is due to environment there is hope for transformation. Change the setting and things are bound to improve. Meanwhile, if poor conduct is who the person really is, and the environment plays no role, there is nothing to be done.

In order for a *ben sorer umoreh* to be convicted, the Torah requires his actions to have had nothing to do with his environment. The parents must have identical voices, meaning that he has not received mixed messages. They must be perceived by the child as being totally in control, ruling out parents who are physically or sight handicapped. The city must also be home to a Jewish court which promotes the wholesome values one associates with perfection.

The Talmud concludes that no such utopian environment exists. All of us are to some degree victims of our environment, to the extent that even our genetics can be affected. The laws of *ben sorer umoreh* teaches us that no child is naturally evil, and any bad we perceive in a child can be remedied by tweaking the environment until their true goodness shines through.

FINDING GOD IN EVERYTHING WE DO

first published August 31st, 2017

O ver the years I have studiously avoided engaging in theological disputations and religious apologetics. Anyone deeply committed to their religious faith is unlikely to be convinced by clever arguments that their own faith system is flawed. After all, the whole point of a faith system is that at some point it defies logic and reason.

But I recently came across an unattributed Midrashic passage, written at the same time as Christianity was emerging as an independent religion, and I found the Midrash so refreshing and so compelling, that although I had resolved never to engage in apologetics, I will nonetheless allow this exception to slip through. That's because this Midrash addresses what was probably the most contentious religious issue in the first two centuries of the Common Era, an issue that has persisted to this day as one of the core differences between practitioners of Judaism and adherents of Christianity.

Christianity emerged in Judea during the first century C.E. as a sect of Judaism—one of many such sects that coexisted in the highly charged atmosphere of Roman rule and the endemic corruption of the Jewish political leadership. The apostle Paul (c.5-c.67) was eager to broaden the appeal of this nascent creed so that it could include gentiles. The barrier to entry was the overbearing nature of Torah law, and in particular circumcision.

In the year 50 or 51 C.E., a conference of early Christian leaders took place in Jerusalem, and the question of circumcision was discussed. Ultimately, they all agreed to include gentiles within Christianity, without the need for their commitment to Jewish ritual laws, including circumcision. Nonetheless, the controversy smoldered on, with several key early Christians refusing to adopt this inclusive approach. At the notorious "Incident at Antioch," Paul took fellow apostle Peter to task for refusing to dine with gentile Christians. It would appear that Peter was reluctant to eat non-kosher food, while Paul was clearly eager to unite both wings of Christianity, even if it meant cross contamination of food.

Paul seems to have won the debate, and Christianity developed a deep and abiding aversion to "legalists," a term used to describe anyone who mandated Mosaic Law as a route to God and salvation, or who judged those who did not observe Mosaic Law as deficient. The consequence of Paul's religious revolution was the exponential growth of Christianity, something that would have been impossible if Mosaic Law had remained a requirement. Paul's approach also resulted in the dismissal of the majority of Torah commandments as empty rituals devoid of any spiritual meaning, and utterly unnecessary for people of faith. Legalism is usually presented from a purely Christian perspective, and in the context of an internal Christian debate. Over time, each of Christianity's various denominations developed complex narratives and dense apologetics that evolved, to justify the rejection of Mosaic Law.

Although there were various medieval disputations between rabbis and Christian clerics, in which theological differences were "debated," the dominant theme of those disputations was the identity of the Messiah, not the benefits or otherwise of observing Torah-mandated ritual law. In the period when the schism between Judaism and Christianity was very fresh, however, maintaining ritual law as standard practice seems to have been a very hot topic. Moses' proclamation that no aspect of Torah law could ever be altered — "you shall neither add to it, nor subtract from it!" (Deut. 13:1) — was clearly insufficient, particularly when a competing faith was so undemanding by comparison.

The Midrash I discovered directly addresses wavering Jews, and focuses on why the proliferation of baffling *mitzvot* found in the Torah that relate to daily life, many of them in Parshat Ki Teitze, is actually a wonderful thing. The idea that faith alone is sufficient to ensure one's place in Heaven is tackled head-on, and as the Midrash points out, God deliberately infused even the most mundane aspects of life with spiritual significance, elevating each of them into acts of faith, as opposed to mere requirements of human existence.

When you plough your field, it might not seem like a moment of spiritual ecstasy, and yet the Torah instructs the farmer not to use a combination of different animals to pull the plough (Deut. 22:10), turning this routine farming chore into an activity which can bring a farmer closer to God. Even nowadays, when we no longer plough with animals, using a tractor instead of an ox or donkey is elevated into an act of faith, just because this mitzvah exists.

The Midrash cites numerous examples of similarly arcane *mitzvot*: the prohibition against crossbreeding crops; leaving harvest leftovers for the poor to pick up; dispatching a mother bird before taking eggs from a nest; burial of the dead; the prohibition against self-harm as part of the mourning process; building a fence around a roof space; turning an item of clothing into a religious garment by putting *tzitzit* on each corner — and countless others.

The list includes many diverse activities, all of which one might have done in any event, or that are extremely simple to carry out. The implication is that *mitzvot* are not a burden on those who observe them, as implied by the term "legalism"; rather they act as a connector to God in every aspect of daily life.

The Midrash ends with a beautiful parable. A man is drowning in raging waters when the captain of a ship throws him a lifeline. "Grasp hold of the line," the captain shouts, "and you will surely live. But leave go of it, even for a second, and you will surely drown."

It is literally impossible to contemplate God's omnipotence and presence every second of one's life. We need to sleep, we need to eat, we need to work—and all these distract us from being conscious of our faith. But if every act we do is imbued with God, because it follows the path He instructed for us, we can be certain never to drown. That is why the proliferation of mitzvot is indeed God's glorious gift, and we can find God in everything we do.

KI TAVO

DON'T WORRY, BE HAPPY

first published September 19th, 2019

I recently released the unedited memoirs of the late Rabbi Mordechai Elefant (1930-2009), undoubtedly one of the twentieth century's most colorful rabbinic educators. Rabbi Elefant's various institutions in Israel and the United States profoundly influenced thousands of students from across the Jewish world.

I had the privilege of studying privately with Rabbi Elefant during my yeshiva years, and spent a tremendous amount of quality time with him during the 1980s and 1990s. His boundless energy and out-of-the-box approach to everything he did deeply impacted me long after he had sadly faded from public view due to manifold health issues. Rabbi Elefant passed away in 2009, having disappeared into obscurity, and despite his remarkable achievements, his death barely registered, and, very sadly, he has been largely forgotten.

Rabbi Elefant's candid memoirs are startling, not just because they reveal much that one would hardly have expected from a top-tier *Rosh Yeshiva*, but even more because of the very frank revelations he willingly shared regarding the background to his extraordinary life.

I distinctly recall his many sardonic observations about life and people; he was a true iconoclast who had clearly never read the memo about how senior and respected public servants should express themselves, and particularly rabbis. At the same time, he was an extraordinary scholar, who could lecture on any Talmudic topic without prior warning to discerning peers and students, dazzling them with both his vast knowledge and his keen intellect. Moreover, he had a huge heart and a prodigious talent for creating Torah institutions that churned out scholars and productive rabbis who continue to serve communities across the world – communities that remain oblivious to the fact that it is Rabbi Elefant they should be thanking for the leadership they enjoy.

Of the many Rabbi Elefant aphorisms I fondly recall, one in particular sticks out: "There is only one thing two Jews can agree upon," he would say, "and that is what the third one should be giving to charity." Once getting past the initial chuckle, the sad truth of this observation hits home. There is so much that we share in common, and yet we instinctively judge our fellow Jews, generally speaking negatively. No one is ever good enough, and anything bad that there is to say invariably drowns out any of the good that might counteract it.

Last week, I visited Israel at the invitation of President Reuven Rivlin to participate in an initiative called *Our Common Destiny*, a "ground-breaking effort to strengthen global Jewry by linking Jewish communities all over the world to a shared set of ethics and values across religious and cultural identities."

The idea behind this initiative is wonderful. Rather than grandstanding and lecturing others about what we think they should or should not be doing, *Our Common Destiny* wants to find the Jewish bonds that unite us all, so that we can work on these shared aspects of our Jewishness together, and face the challenges of the present and future more effectively.

Parshat Ki Tavo contains a fearsome collection of *tokhaḥot* – literally "admonitions" or "warnings" – a shopping list of dreadful consequences for the Jewish nation if they would choose not to adhere to God's directives. According to Naḥmanides ("*Ramban*"; 1194-1270), the second *tokhaḥa* relates to the destruction of the Second Temple, an event that only took place more than a millennium after this warning was articulated by Moses and recorded in the Torah (Deut. 28:47): תַּחַת אֲשֶׁר לֹא עָבַדְתָּ אֶת ה' אֱלֹקֶיךָ בְּשִׂמְחָה וּבְטוּב לֵבָב – "[the Temple will be destroyed] because you did not serve God with joy and goodness of heart." Puzzlingly, the Talmud offers a totally different cause for the calamity, informing us that the Temple's destruction was a result of causeless hatred (Yom. 9b).

The Rebbe of Sochaczew, Rabbi Shmuel Bornsztain ("*Shem MiShmuel*"; 1855-1926), offers a compelling resolution to this seeming contradiction. Both of these sins share a common denominator, he says. Someone who performs a mitzva reluctantly will do it superficially, just going through the motions but never really engaging with it emotionally. True joy only comes to someone who loves what they are doing.

Similarly, the secret to emotionally attaching oneself to every Jew is to ignore the superficial differences that separates us, instead focusing on what we share in common. Anyone who endeavors to be externally observant, and concerns themselves with appearances, is being superficial and not putting any heart into it. Such a person will inevitably judge others by similar criteria, looking at the superficial veneer rather than at a shared love of God and dedication to maintaining and sustaining a meaningful Jewish identity.

The passage at the beginning of Ki Tavo about *bikkurim* ("first fruit tithe") directs us to be "happy with all the good" – in other words, to use *bikkurim* as an opportunity to relish the joy of a good harvest. Why is it that this particular mitzvah requires one to be joyful? Simply put, *bikkurim* is not about the paltry basket of fruit, rather it is about the fact that one has had a successful harvest, and the incredible feelings that this should trigger in a farmer who was lucky enough to benefit from the success of this year's crop. Presenting the basket of fruit is in-and-of-itself a superficial act, but in truth it must be a reflection of deep emotions and true joy that one feels when things go well.

When Moses foresaw that the Second Temple's destruction would result from causeless hatred, he realized that this negative judgment of others would be a symptom of chronic gloom. A society that focuses too heavily on superficial differences that divide one person from another is a society that is miserable and unhappy. People who are happy don't notice these things and connect on a far deeper level to what they share in common with others, allowing these features to underscore their inherent contentment and pleasure in life.

If there is anything that two Jews should agree upon it should be how much they love and appreciate the third Jew, along with every other Jew. It is the ultimate realization of "don't worry, be happy!"

THE PURSUIT OF HAPPINESS

first published August 30th, 2018

How does one measure happiness? It seems like a simple question, but as it turns out, there is no simple answer. Researchers struggle to define happiness, never mind measure it. Depression and misery are easy to measure, both biologically and clinically. But happiness is far more elusive.

One of the most popular ways for psychologists to measure happiness is to ask patients to take the SWLS ("Satisfaction With Life Scale") test. A questionnaire of five statements is given to the patient, with a scale of 1-7 for answers ranging from 1: "strongly agree" to 7: "strongly disagree". The five statements are a collection of buoyant assertions, such as "in most ways my life is close to my ideal" and "if I could live my life over, I would change almost nothing," with the idea being to get an overall sense of the patient's contentedness in life, or the contrary.

But SWLS is a blunt instrument. All kinds of variables can affect a patient's responses. They may differ considerably if one is lively or tired, or just heard good or bad news, or are having a particularly miserable day even if life is generally good. Researchers have therefore come up with an alternative test for happiness, which tracks positive and negative moods throughout the day, and life satisfaction for the day at the end of each day.

Every half-hour or hour during the day a person using this test asks themselves "am I feeling positive/negative emotions right now?" – and give themselves a 0 for "not at all" through to a 3 for "strongly." To track different aspects of your life that might be affecting the responses, one assigns headings to each one, such as "working," "housework," and "socializing." When a day is over, the person responds to a general question about overall fulfilment, and then looks back over the day's scores. In this way one can get a fairly accurate snapshot of happiness based on where the total score falls between the maximum and minimum. After completing this test daily for a few weeks one can use the range of totals to determine a trend, to see which activities evoke greatest happiness and which result in feeling gloomy.

As I was reflecting on the difficulties we have measuring happiness, and even understanding it, I came across an article in *The New York Times* about the world's happiest countries. In March of this year, the *United Nations Sustainable Development Solutions Network* published its annual "World Happiness Report" – a "landmark survey of the state of global happiness" that ranks "156 countries by their happiness levels, and 117 countries by the happiness of their immigrants."

The report represents your tax money hard at work. In any event, *The New York Times* article focused on a follow-up report by Michael Birkjaer of the *Happiness Research Institute*, which revealed increasing unhappiness in the Nordic countries of Denmark, Finland, Iceland, Norway and Sweden – countries which consistently fall into the top-ten "happy" countries listed in the UN report.

Birkjaer's report presents evidence that around 12.3 percent of the population in these five countries are "struggling" or "suffering" – resulting in what the article's headline refers to as a "happiness gap." Birkjaer was interviewed for the article and acknowledged that "something doesn't rhyme."

Intrigued, I decided to read the report for myself and see what the data shows. The report is long and thorough, and the research has been carefully calibrated to find out the social structures and other factors that might adversely affect people's lives in Nordic countries resulting in their unhappiness, despite the general happiness of the people around them. As I read through the executive summary one of the bullet points leapt out and struck me like a bolt of lightning: "Very religious people are happier," it began, and continued: "In all of the Nordic countries, very religious people are more happy [sic.] than others. No differences in levels of well-being are observed when comparing atheists and the moderately religious people."

Even more remarkably, the very next bullet point proclaims, "Unhappiness is very costly for society. The fact that a growing number of people are struggling or suffering has socioeconomic consequences."

No one needs a degree in psychology to work out that unhappy people are less productive, and you also don't need to be an eminent sociologist to appreciate that unhappiness leads to socioeconomic problems. We also all know religious people who are remarkably happy, content in life and ambassadors of joy, irrespective of the challenges they may face in their personal circumstances. What we don't generally do is correlate these two pieces of information.

Happiness is greatly enhanced if it is attached to a life of faith-centered values, and truly religious people find it much easier to be happy and content than those without faith.

This idea offers a compelling explanation for one of the "curses" proclaimed by Moses in Parshat Ki Tavo in the chapter known as *tochacha* (Deut. 28:47): תַּחַת אֲשֶׁר לֹא עָבַדְתָּ אֶת ה' אֱלֹקֶיךָ בְּשִׂמְחָה וּבְטוּב לֵבָב מֵרֹב כֹּל – "because you would not serve God in joy and happiness over the abundance of everything."

Moses challenges the nation to heed God's word and observe His commandments or face the consequences of being abandoned, in the midst of which he throws in this strange line about a lack of joy and happiness turning into the cause of potential misfortune. But why would it matter if commandments are not performed with joy? If God wants something done and it does get done, why would it matter if it was not done in good spirits?

The point, it would seem, is much more profound. Miserable people are prone to disaster, even if they dutifully perform God's commandments. The act itself counts for very little, Moses says, if the mood that accompanies it is wrong. Meanwhile, the benefit of happiness is exponentially increased if it is accompanied by faith in God. Not that happiness ever comes easily.

Even Thomas Jefferson (1743-1826) understood that while all men are created equal, and are endowed by their Creator with certain inalienable rights, among those rights it is only happiness that demands pursuit.

LET THERE BE LIGHT

first published September 3rd, 2020

"**I** can believe no evil of someone who draws their strength from the light of day," says Yolande, one of the key characters in Robin McKinley's 2003 award-winning novel *Sunshine*. That sentence reminded me why I am particularly fond of sunflowers. It's not only that I like the bright yellow petals contrasting so vividly with the flower's large black center, I also love the fact that sunflowers are solar-trackers, facing east in the morning and slowly – imperceptibly to the naked eye – drifting westward as the day progresses from dawn to dusk.

And in a sense, we are all sunflowers, tracking the light, seeking it out, wanting to bask in its radiance. But most importantly, we all recognize the value of light, which is why we always try to avoid the darkness. Like Yolande in *Sunshine*, we instinctively associate "light" with good and "dark" with evil, and we intuitively understand that drawing our strength "from the light of day" says a lot about who we are. At a time of seemingly all-enveloping darkness, I think it is incredibly important for us to realize just how important light is, and to find ways of drawing strength from any light we can find, while also trying to be a source of light for others.

When I recently took our son Meir to Israel to draft into the IDF, we took a post-quarantine day trip across the southern region of Israel. As we were driving through the Negev, I was suddenly struck by the sight of a penetrating light on the horizon. The light was in completely the wrong place for it to be the sun and seemed far too bright to be an electric illumination – particularly as we were some distance away, and it was bang in the middle of the day. Puzzled, I asked our guide, my cousin Shayke, what it was.

"Is it a mirage?" I inquired – after all this was the Negev desert. He smiled. "No, it's not a mirage, it's the Ashalim Solar Power Station." And he began to tell me about this incredible new facility, which opened last year – a facility that is already powering 70,000 homes and is eventually expected to power 50,000 more.

Ashalim is a 4,000-acre solar-energy plant – the largest renewable-energy project in Israel and one of the largest in the world. It cost just under $1.2 billion to build and is a joint project of various investment funds together with the Spanish engineering giant TSK. I learnt later that one of the primary movers-and-shakers behind Ashalim is my good friend Naty Saidoff, an Israeli expat who lives in LA, whose success in business is more than matched by his wonderfully good nature and incredible generosity to numerous good causes. But I knew none of this as we drove down Highway 6 toward Sde Boker, dazzled by the bright beacon of light that hovered on the horizon, almost like a second sun.

Ashalim is made up of 16,000 parabolic troughs and no less than 500,000 – you read that number correctly – concave mirrors, all of which convert solar energy into steam that is then used to generate electricity. Incredibly, Ashalim is also able to produce power at night – yes, it is a solar plant that can produce energy even when the sun isn't shining. It does this by using a thermal-energy storage system based on molten salt, which allows the plant to operate for over four hours at full power after the sun has set. In the fullness of time about one percent of all of Israel's energy needs will be generated at Ashalim, which means that this plant represents a big step towards realizing Israel's goal of a future fully powered by renewable energy.

Naty Saidoff told me that he's "proud to have been given the opportunity to build meaningful mega-projects in Israel, and I plan to promote similar projects in the future." But Naty is not just promoting a renewable energy project or merely helping generate jobs in the Negev region – actually, he and all those behind Ashalim are fulfilling biblical prophecy.

The Haftara that we read for Parshat Ki Tavo is one of those referred to as *shiva di'nehemta* – the "seven-fold comfort" readings from scripture that we read each week for seven weeks following the three-week mourning period we have each year as the Jewish calendar reminder of our two lost temples, destroyed by the Babylonians and the Romans at the two darkest points of Jewish history. But rather than wallow in debilitating depression and grieving, we double up on hope and faith by reading portions of scripture that are upbeat and optimistic – a wonderful tradition that dates back as far as the destruction itself.

The Haftara reading for Ki Tavo fits in well with this tradition; it is the entire sixtieth chapter of Isaiah, which includes a verse we are all familiar with, if not literally then at least conceptually: "And nations shall walk by your light, Kings, by your shining radiance"

(Isa. 60:3). This verse and a couple of others in Isaiah are the original source for the idea that the Jewish nation is an *ohr lagoyim* – "a light unto the nations." This is usually understood to mean that God's Chosen People must always be a shining example of faith and morality for the gentile nations.

But as I watched the blazing light of Ashalim bobbing on the Negev horizon – so bright that you cannot even see the shape of the facility itself – I couldn't help thinking that this was a physical example of the beacon of light that Israel has become for the world, leading the way in everything from technology to business, diplomacy to renewable energy, and – it goes without saying – the study of every facet of God's Torah in ways that our prophets and sages could never have dreamed was possible as they worked so hard to preserve the texts and concepts of our unique faith heritage.

The preceding verse describes an all-enveloping darkness that will mark the period before messianic redemption (Isa. 60:2): כִּי הִנֵּה הַחֹשֶׁךְ יְכַסֶּה אֶרֶץ וַעֲרָפֶל לְאֻמִּים וְעָלַיִךְ יִזְרַח ה' וּכְבוֹדוֹ עָלַיִךְ יֵרָאֶה – "Darkness shall cover the earth, thick clouds [shall cover] the nations; but God will shine on you, and His presence will be seen over you." All of us currently feel that darkness, with the COVID-19 chaos and devastation that has caused such havoc in our world over the past few months. The commentaries struggle to explain how God's light will ever be "seen," trying to understand the point of this anthropomorphic metaphor, but I think none of the commentaries could have imagined Ashalim – a visible light that gives life to the desert, and a light that goes well beyond physical illumination.

As Naty put it to me so beautifully, "We have the privilege of creating light for the country which was prophesied to be "a light unto the nations" and we have the privilege of making the desert bloom as we turn the curse of the baking sun into a blessing of a cool oasis which powers Israel's air conditioning. And, as you fly above Ashalim, you can see it shining proudly below without a single drop of smog – nothing but life sustaining green energy." Here and now, we are truly a "light" unto the nations. The prophet Isaiah foresaw it 2500 years before it happened, and now it is our turn to see it. May that light continue to shine, and let it get ever brighter.

NITZAVIM

THE VALUE OF ONE AND ALL

first published September 27th, 2019

I n *Hilkhot Teshuva* ("Laws of Repentance"), the definitive guide to self-improvement authored by Maimonides ("*Rambam*"; 1138-1204), he enumerates 24 types of people for whom the Teshuva process will not be effective. He describes one of the types of people as follows (4:2): הַפּוֹרֵשׁ מִן הַצִּבּוּר – לְפִי שֶׁבִּזְמַן שֶׁיַּעֲשׂוּ תְּשׁוּבָה לֹא יִהְיֶה עִמָּהֶן וְאֵינוֹ זוֹכֶה עִמָּהֶם בִּזְכוּת שֶׁעוֹשִׂין "Someone who keeps himself apart from the community," says Maimonides, and goes on to explain why such a person cannot ever be a successful penitent – "because at the time they [the community] are doing Teshuva he won't be with them, and he won't benefit from them in the merit of their actions."

Now of course, the sentiment is wonderful – one needs to be part of a community in order to benefit from that group. It's practical, like a sort of "economies of scale" – it's harder to get things done on your own, but for a group it is easier, and the larger the group gets, the easier it becomes to get whatever it is done. Teshuva, Maimonides seems to be saying, benefits from this group dynamic. It's more effective to do Teshuva in a group than to do it on your own. But while this has a kind of logic, I still don't understand something. How does your Teshuva actually benefit from being part of a group?

Let me explain my question by way of an example. If you're hungry and you're in a room where lots of people are eating, just because they are eating won't mean you are not hungry anymore. And if you eat, it doesn't matter if you are by yourself or with them – once you've eaten enough you won't be hungry. Being part of a group has nothing to do with it. And surely repentance is a very private, personal thing? You did something wrong, so you have to repent. What use is it if you are in a room full of other people repenting? How will that make any difference? In fact, it might be better to do it on your own – so that you aren't distracted by others. And you are hardly going to be forthright with God in a group situation.

Parshat Nitzavim begins the final speech given by Moses before he died – in fact, on the day he died: 7th Adar. For five weeks he had been lecturing and teaching, and this was his final talk. Moses used the opportunity to forge a brand-new covenant between God and the Jewish nation, one that would connect the Torah with all future generations. The new covenant was all-encompassing, and Moses wanted to ensure that everyone would feel included, so he began his address by listing every age group, men and women, every type of person imaginable (Deut. 29:9-10): אַתֶּם נִצָּבִים הַיּוֹם כֻּלְּכֶם לִפְנֵי ה' אֱלֹקֵיכֶם רָאשֵׁיכֶם שִׁבְטֵיכֶם זִקְנֵיכֶם וְשֹׁטְרֵיכֶם כֹּל אִישׁ יִשְׂרָאֵל – "You stand here today, all of you, before God — heads of tribes, elders, appointed officials, all the men of Israel, your children, your wives, even the stranger within your camp, from the woodchopper to the water drawer..."

Even the lowest and least educated classes – woodchoppers and water drawers – are here seen to be as important to the covenant as leaders, elders and officials, and are therefore included on equal terms. But what message was Moses conveying? Obviously if everyone is included – and it says "all" – then everyone is included. Why mention every diverse element of society separately?

Since the dawn of history, human society has divided itself into many different classes, according to talent, profession, education, family, social status, and of course financial status. Jewish society was no different. These distinctions existed as much within Jewish society as any other – there were tribes, there were priests, there were kings, there were rabbis, there were judges, and of course there were the wealthy and there were the poor. The easiest way to understand Moses is the way most of the commentaries interpret his opener – the covenant would apply equally to all, notwithstanding your place on the pecking order.

The Torah does not buy into the idea of a classless society, where there is equality for all. On the contrary, this is an affront to reality. There are leaders and followers, successful people and less successful people, wellborn people and not-so-wellborn people. It's just how it is. But, says Moses, there is a covenant that binds one-and-all, no matter your station in life, and this is the covenant that forms the basis of the relationship between God and His Chosen People.

However, I would like to take this in a slightly different direction than the commentaries. In 1954, the social psychologist Leon Festinger (1919-1989) proposed what he called the "social comparison theory." He showed how all humans are driven to evaluate themselves accurately, and he suggested that people evaluate their own opinions and abilities by comparing themselves to others with whom they come into contact, so that they can make sure they are getting it right, and properly understand themselves.

As the years progressed, Festinger and his students expanded the theory to focus on the idea of social comparison as a route to self-enhancement. Not only do we better understand ourselves by comparing ourselves to others, but we can use that as a platform to improve ourselves, or at the very least as a gauge to see how we might improve.

I think Moses wanted to ensure that no Jew ever got so caught up in their own stratum that they became excluded from social comparison. The success of the covenant hinged on its equal application to all. Everyone was in this together, notwithstanding where they stood by any measure of human existence – age, gender, social status, wealth, intelligence. None of it makes any difference when it comes to upholding the covenant, and in fact the covenant needs a spread of everything if each person who is bound by it is going to successfully be a part of it.

And that is what Maimonides means when he says that those who exclude themselves from the community are never going to do Teshuva properly. How can you truly repent if you have no yardstick to measure your behavior? And that yardstick is the range of people in your community – young and old, from all walks of life, from every kind of background. By engaging within that group, you will not only be able to accurately understand yourself, but you will find inspiration for self-improvement that will take you to the next level. That, after all, is the purpose of

Teshuva, and that is why it is so important to be deeply embedded in a community – so that your Teshuva can work.

IT'S ALL OR NOTHING

first published September 26th, 2019

Y ou have no doubt heard of the psychiatric condition known as multiple personality disorder. In 1994 this condition was renamed "dissociative identity disorder," or DID, to better reflect its most dominant symptom, namely the fragmentation of identity rather than a proliferation of different personas, a rather more common phenomenon that I shall return to in a moment.

For most of us, what we know of DID is neither medical nor even anecdotal; it is far more likely that we have been exposed to this dreadful disease via popular literature or in movies. The most famous literary example of DID is the 1886 novella by Robert Louis Stevenson (1850-1894), *The Strange Case of Dr Jekyll and Mr Hyde*, in which the avuncular protagonist, Dr Henry Jekyll, transforms into the violent antihero, Mr Edward Hyde, a metamorphosis Jekyll tries to control by taking a serum that turns him back into a benign medical doctor. This fictional story had such a powerful effect on popular culture, that ever since it was published in the late nineteenth century, the "Jekyll and Hyde" epithet has been applied to people who have extreme mood swings.

Generally speaking, only psychiatrists ever get to see and treat DID, as it is relatively rare. In any event, the whole idea that someone might have mutually exclusive parallel personalities, although we might accept that such a thing exists, seems to be beyond the bounds of normative life. And yet, we are all quite familiar with what I referred to earlier as a "proliferation of different personas." After all, do we behave the same way at work as we do at home? Are we not quite different when we hang out with childhood friends than when we are with our children or grandchildren? The answer, of course, is no.

Surely, then, we all suffer from a mild version of DID? Actually, that is not the case at all. Modern psychology understands that it is perfectly normal for people to alter their personas so that they can adapt to different environments. Someone who is gregarious and loud will not behave that way if they work in a bank or a doctor's office.

Everyone realizes that professional norms require an extrovert to modify their behavior in those environments. And yet, someone who knows such a person from a different setting and comes across them at work might think that they are displaying signs of a parallel personality. However, that is not the case at all – what they are seeing is a different side of the same person, a side that suits that particular environment. While at home or with friends there is no risk of being fired if they are loud and over-the-top, and so they feel free to let themselves go. But at work such a persona might endanger their livelihood, so they naturally tone down that particular aspect of who they are.

Another factor which might affect behavior is environment and peer setting. We all tend to mimic the behavior of those we spend time with. Someone who finds themselves in a very formal environment will automatically modify their behavior to adapt to that formality, while at the other end of the spectrum, if you find yourself in an informal situation, even if you are generally a very formal person, you try to adjust to fit in with the casual atmosphere. In the final analysis, all of us are a pastiche of any number of personas. The difference between this and DID is that these multiple personas all overlap and are not mutually exclusive, even though we are essentially a compilation of characters, and even those closest to us may not know us in all of our various guises.

I believe this phenomenon helps explain an anomaly at the beginning of Parshat Nitzavim. Moses begins his address by telling the nation (Deut. 29:9): אַתֶּם נִצָּבִים הַיּוֹם כֻּלְּכֶם לִפְנֵי ה' אֱלֹקֵיכֶם – "You stand this day, all of you, before God your God." The verses that follow enumerate all the various socio-economic strata of people that were present and concludes with the words *kol ish yisrael* ("every Israelite person"), a phrase that self-evidently includes every person who was there. That being the case, why does Moses need to say *kulkhem* ("all of you")?

The repetition clearly reveals that this opening phrase does not actually mean all of the people in the sense of every person in the group. Rather, *kulkhem* must be a reference to each individual and takes into account every aspect of who they are. Rather than having a particular persona when it comes to God and Judaism, a persona that is markedly different to a persona we may have in other aspects of our lives, we are expected to bring every part of ourselves to the table when we come before God.

One of the great challenges of Rosh Hashana and Yom Kippur is that we might end up behaving in a way that is simply a reflection of the environment that we find ourselves in on those days, while in "real life" we are totally different people. But instead of doing this, we must treat the Days of Awe as an opportunity to bear our souls, "warts and all," before God, and not to present a particular version of ourselves in the mistaken view that this is the version that God wants to see.

Moses was conveying an important message, without mincing his words. When we stand before God, we must be *kulkhem*, presenting every single one of the varied personas we may project in all the various environments we find ourselves in as we go through life. When we stand before Him, and as He considers our actions over the past year and makes decisions for us for the year ahead, it has to be on the basis of every facet of our personality and every aspect of who we are.

YOUR THOUGHTS CREATE YOUR FUTURE

first published September 16th, 2017

A couple of weeks ago, self-help supremo and bestselling author Louise Hay died in her sleep at the age of 90. Born into poverty in Los Angeles in 1926, as a young child she was both physically abused by her stepfather and sexually abused by a neighbor. A school dropout at the age of fifteen, she gave birth to a daughter on her sixteenth birthday. Unmarried and without means to support the baby, Hay was forced to give her up for adoption, and never saw her again. Hay eventually got married at the age of twenty-eight, but the marriage ended in divorce fourteen years later. She would never remarry, nor have any more children.

Just that biography is enough to dampen anyone's day. What possible hope could someone have after such a horrible start to life? And it only got worse. In her early 50s, Hay was diagnosed with cervical cancer. But by that point she had stumbled across the teachings of Ernest Holmes (1887-1960) – the "New Thought" guru and founder of the "Religious Science" movement – and adopted his metaphysical theories about a positive mindset affecting one's physical wellbeing. Hay later claimed it was this approach that helped see off her cancer, allowing her to live a healthy productive life long after the doctors had predicted her demise.

After beating cancer, Hay became a leading advocate of using positive thinking as a way of fighting off disease, and in 1984 published her bestselling self-help bible, *You Can Heal Your Life*, which has sold more than 40 million copies in over 30 different languages. According to *The New York Times*, "Louise Hay is one of the best-selling authors in history, and none of the women who have sold more — like J. K. Rowling, Danielle Steel and Barbara Cartland — owned a publishing empire, [nor did they] change the spiritual landscape of America and several of its Western allies."

It goes without saying that Louise Hay had her critics, people who accused her of being overly simplistic, or of giving desperate people unrealistic hope, based on quackery and New Age flimflam. Although such accusations are not entirely without foundation, they kind of miss the point. While it would be foolish to refuse medical attention at the onset of a fatal disease, in favor of thinking positive thoughts as the curative remedy, every doctor will tell you that patients who have been diagnosed with a potentially fatal illness who choose to adopt a positive approach, are far more likely to pull through than those who regard their fate as signed and sealed. In the end, we are only ever able to make our dreams come true if we don't see them as dreams, but as credible possibilities.

If anything, the most inspiring aspect of Louise Hay's life is not actually her upbeat theories about self-belief as the key to health and happiness, but the fact that in middle age, after enduring a miserable life that for most people would have meant a descent into bitter old age, she rose to the greatest heights of success at no one else's expense, and acted as an inspiration for others to do the same. Her life story is the living embodiment of making the impossible happen, against all the odds.

Most of us undoubtedly believe New Age optimism and Religious Science metaphysics to be the domain of the gullible and the desperate, but that is not the view of Judaism. In one of his final speeches to the nation he had led for forty years, Moses dismissed anyone who entertained the idea that the commandments of the Torah are ethereal concepts, beyond the reach of mere mortals (Deut. 30:12): לֹא בַשָּׁמַיִם הִוא לֵאמֹר מִי יַעֲלֶה לָּנוּ הַשָּׁמַיְמָה וְיִקָּחֶהָ לָּנוּ – "it is not in the Heavens, so you say who can lift us up to the Heavens so that we can acquire it…"

Rashi makes an astounding assertion based on this verse. If the Torah had been in Heaven, he says, we would have been expected to go there and acquire it. Later rabbis struggled with Rashi's suggestion, particularly as it seems to undermine the impact of Moses' declaration.

Of all the suggested answers, I particularly like the solution offered by Rabbi Shmuel Bornsztain (1855-1926), author of the seminal work *Shem MiShmuel*. Rashi is telling us that had we needed the means to get to Heaven to acquire the Torah, God would have given it to us, because the Torah and all of its accompanying obligations must be attainable. This means that if any part of the Torah seems impossible to us, we should know that we have all been equipped to accomplish and achieve whatever God expects of us.

This idea is a phenomenally liberating concept. Even when Torah obligations seem to be asking us to ascend the Heavens, we need to know that this simply cannot be the case. For some of us it might be daily prayers at the synagogue. For others it might be certain aspects of Sabbath observance. Yet others might find setting aside regular time to study Torah a remote fantasy. Moses was not suggesting we should see any of these as easy. Instead, he was telling us that there is no spiritual aspiration that is impossible if we set our sights on getting there.

Fundamentally, that is the core message of the High Holidays. As we consider our many limitations, and reflect on all our lofty aspirations, we might imagine that any change for the better over the coming year is as remote for us as a journey to Heaven. Moses' message echoing through the ages is that nothing God wants us to achieve should ever be considered impossible. And while it may sound like New Age jargon, this idea is deeply embedded in our theology as the bedrock of our faith.

VAYEILECH

A MESSAGE OF HOPE FOR THE FUTURE

first published September 13th, 2018

The late Stanley Abramovitch, who passed away without much fanfare a little over five years ago, was one of the twentieth century's great Jewish heroes. You will be forgiven for not having heard of him. That would be the case of most true heroes. Stanley was only interested in doing good work and getting results. If you needed to hear of him during his lifetime, you would have – and you would never have forgotten him. He was indefatigable, charming, persistent, and an incomparable raconteur.

Born in Poland in 1920, he was sent by his family to London in 1935. "My mother pulled me toward her and said: 'Try to be a good Jew,'" he told the Jerusalem Post in 2009. Those were the last words she ever said to him, and he never saw her again. His mother's words continued to ring in Stanley's ears, especially after it became clear that she and two of his brothers had become victims of the Holocaust.

In 1945 he volunteered for the American Jewish Joint Distribution Committee (JDC), to help concentration camp survivors rebuild their shattered lives. It would be the beginning of a career helping Jews across the globe in every imaginable way, improving their lives and enhancing Jewish community life wherever he went. In September 2010 Stanley wrote a blog for CNN in which he described his first Yom Kippur at the displaced persons camp in Landsberg, Germany, to which he had been sent by the JDC in 1945.

The survivors grouped themselves by country of origin, and each group set up their own prayer group to accommodate their particular set of customs and traditions. Initially Stanley joined the Polish group for prayers, but after morning services he decided to go across to some of the other prayer groups. Abramovitch noted that "there were many people who remained in the street and refused to attend services; they were angry at God." Many of them had been religious Jews before the Holocaust. The wounds of the Holocaust were still too fresh. God's apparent absence while their families had been murdered by the Nazis and their collaborators was utterly incomprehensible to them, and they deliberately opted out of Yom Kippur prayers.

"They would not pray," writes Stanley, "[and] when they heard the recitation of the Kaddish… they reacted angrily that God did not deserve the Kaddish."

As he was walking through the streets of the camp from one prayer group to another, he suddenly came across a large group of these conscientious objectors standing in a circle. Curious to see what they were looking at, he went over to find out what it was that had interested them. What he discovered, and describes so beautifully in his blog, was haunting and disturbing.

"In the middle of the circle stood a seven-year-old girl, embarrassed, perplexed. She could not understand why

all these people stood around her. She, of course, could not know that they were surprised to find a Jewish child. So they stood, silently, and just looked at this miracle of a Jewish child in their midst. They could not tear themselves away from this one child who said nothing and to whom nothing was said. They just stood and gaped."

"A special prayer is normally recited on Yom Kippur for the departed members of one's family. It's called Yizkor, the memorial prayer. As those people looked at the little girl, they remembered their own children, or their younger brothers and sisters, the nephews and nieces who at one time were their pride and joy, and who were no more. Each one of them looked and remembered, recalled the beloved children who were cruelly exterminated."

"As they remembered, they recited without any words the Yizkor for all those who once were part of their lives and now were gone forever. This was a silent, most moving Yizkor, without words, without prayer books, recited in that street in Landsberg, by a group of Jewish survivors, watching a bewildered little Jewish girl. It was the most moving, most eloquent, most heartfelt, most silent Yizkor I have ever heard."

In Parshat Vayeilech, Moses instructs the Jewish nation to gather together every seven years to hear the king or leader read from a Torah scroll at the Jerusalem Temple (Deut. 31:12): הַקְהֵל אֶת הָעָם הָאֲנָשִׁים וְהַנָּשִׁים וְהַטַּף – "gather the people – the men, the women, and the little children."

This gathering, known as *Hakhel* ("mass gathering"), is unique among Torah directives in that it includes little children, even though they are not yet obligated to observe mitzvot. The Talmud (Hag. 3a) notes that the requirement to bring children to this monumental gathering was "for no other purpose than that those who bring them will be rewarded."

Naḥmanides (*"Ramban"*; 1194-1270) subtly infers from the next verse that this reward is not some ethereal prize; rather it reflects the benefit of interacting with the next generation, crystallizing the promise they offer for a future that will be better than the present: "as they will hear and inquire and the fathers will [help them understand] and teach them."

As caught up as those Holocaust survivors in Landsberg may have been with their awful present, and notwithstanding the anger they may have felt towards God for their dreadful suffering, the sight of a child stopped them in their tracks. The hapless seven-year-old was a beam of sunlight that pierced through the darkness that was their lives.

On Yom Kippur we can choose to dwell on our present, using it as an excuse not to bother trying. But the message of Hakhel, so evocatively rendered in Stanley Abramovitch's moving story, is that as long as there is a next generation there is always hope. Our job on Yom Kippur – and at all other times – is to focus our attention on that hope as the means by which we can inspire ourselves to become the most productive and constructive foundations for a better future in everything that we do.

HAAZINU

first published October 10th, 2019

T he late Rabbi Shlomo Carlebach (1925-1994) was a wonderful raconteur, who would regale audiences with his inspirational tales of Hasidic masters. He once told me that while not every one of his stories was true, all of them were important.

I vividly recall him telling the following story, and I've repeated it many times. Oddly enough, I have a feeling that besides being important, this one is also true — but before I tell you why, let me tell you the story.

A man once came to visit Rabbi Israel Yitzhak Kalish of Warka (1779-1848), one of the nineteenth-century's greatest Hasidic luminaries. The man was crying.

"Rebbe, I'm so desperate, really desperate. My child is sick, I think he is dying. Rebbe, I'm begging you, please pray for my son to recover from his illness."

The Rebbe sat very still. He closed his eyes and swayed back and forth for a while as he prayed silently and stroked his beard, his lips moving but without any sound coming out of his mouth.

After a few minutes he opened his eyes, and said very softly, "I'm so sorry to tell you, but I'm not getting the vibe, my prayers are going nowhere. It seems the Gates of Heaven are closed and there's absolutely nothing I can do to open them. I don't know what else to tell you. Of course I will keep trying – but it is not looking good."

The man buried his head in his hands and began to sob uncontrollably. But what could he do? Empty handed and dejected, he left the Rebbe's home, climbed back onto his wagon, and slowly started to make his way back home. After he had been traveling for about half an hour, he suddenly heard the sound of a horse-drawn carriage chasing after him. He turned around. It was the Rebbe himself, in a carriage drawn by four fast horses. The Rebbe pulled up beside the man — "Stop your wagon here, stop right now," he said, "I have something important to tell you."

The Rebbe helped the man down from his wagon, and they sat together on the grass by the side of the road. "After you left," the Rebbe said, "I couldn't stop thinking about you and your son. You were so, so sad, and your sobbing was so powerful — it broke my heart. After a few minutes, I realized — although I may not be able to help your son, at least I can cry with you." And the Rebbe put his arm around the bewildered man's shoulders, bowed his holy head, and began to sob from the bottom of his heart. He rocked from side to side, tears streaming down his face, as he wailed and sighed.

The man was utterly shocked. He had never seen the Rebbe like this before. Even he hadn't cried quite so hard. And soon he was also crying, and they were both crying together. They sat there crying, holding each other for comfort, the Rebbe and the man, for a very long time. All of a sudden, without warning, the Rebbe stopped crying, lifted his head, wiped away his tears, and smiled.

The man turned to the Rebbe — "What is it?"

The Rebbe looked at him — "Something amazing has just happened, the Gates of Heaven have opened! Everything is going to be ok! Your son will soon get better!"

That's the story, and it really is such a beautiful story, but now I want to explain why I think it's true. Parshat Haazinu contains an array of fascinating poetic phrases full of the deepest meaning. Many of the couplets in Haazinu teach us remarkable things about God – explaining how we should understand Him and how we should relate to Him.

But I would like to focus on one particular verse in Haazinu (Deut. 32:4): הַצוּר תָּמִים פָּעֳלוֹ כִּי כָל דְּרָכָיו מִשְׁפָּט קֵל אֱמוּנָה וְאֵין עָוֶל צַדִּיק וְיָשָׁר הוּא – "The Rock, His work is perfect, all His ways are just; a God of faith, without fault, He is righteous and fair."

While we all completely buy-in to what this verse is telling us, how are we meant to understand it on a personal level? In other words, how can we introduce this concept into our lives in a meaningful way? After all, in order for anything to have true meaning, however profound it may sound, we must be able to give it a practical application. The Talmud contains extensive discussions as to what one should do in the event of a drought. Apropos this discussion, the Talmud relates a story that took place shortly after the destruction of the Second Temple (JT Taanit 3:11).

There was a terrible drought in Eretz Yisrael, and people were starving. The leading sage of the era, Rabbi Yoḥanan ben Zakkai, wanted to resolve the matter, so he told one of his assistants to get everyone into the main synagogue, and to tell them to pray as follows: "Rabbi Yoḥanan ben Zakkai wants to go and get himself a haircut, but he can't at the moment because there's no water." Believe it or not, that is exactly what they did, and almost immediately there was a rainstorm — and the drought was over.

This story seems more than a little odd. There were probably many thousands of people impacted by the drought in all kinds of terrible ways. There was no irrigation for the crops, there was limited drinking water, and there was no water for washing or for anything else. We can be absolutely certain that everyone affected was already praying for rain, with all their heart and soul. And yet, all of those prayers had apparently made no impact on God. The rain had still not fallen, and there was still no water. The only thing that made an impact on God, if we are to take the story at face value, was the fact that Rabbi Yoḥanan ben Zakkai was unable to get a haircut as a result of the drought.

How does this narrative make any sense? Why should Rabbi Yoḥanan ben Zakkai's haircut matter more than the dreadful and real suffering of so many thousands of others? What is the Talmud telling us by informing us that the rain only fell after this curious complaint? And why was it important to get everyone else to pray for his haircut? Why couldn't he just pray for it himself?

Rabbi Elḥanan Wasserman of Baranovitch (1874-1941), one of prewar Europe's preeminent educators who was martyred by the

Nazis, explained that this is exactly what the verse in Haazinu means. God's justice is utterly precise. For whatever reason, the population that suffered during the drought had not managed to change the decree and lift the drought. Rabbi Yoḥanan ben Zakkai intuitively understood that this was not an injustice. Even he had been affected by the drought, just like the rest of the people, as he also had a limited supply of water for his basic needs.

However, Rabbi Yoḥanan ben Zakkai felt that not being able to get a haircut was a step too far – perhaps he couldn't study if his hair was too long, or perhaps he thought that it was inappropriate for a senior rabbi like him to look undignified with wild hair. Or possibly the barber needed his livelihood more than others and was about to collapse under the strain of his personal financial crisis.

We will never know the exact details, but whatever it was, Rabbi Yoḥanan ben Zakkai felt that he needed God to know that it simply wasn't fair. And even if from our perspective Rabbi Yoḥanan ben Zakkai's pain seems trivial, the Talmud wants to convey the message that it is precisely because God's justice is absolutely fair and calibrated down to the finest detail, that the drought was canceled, and the rain began to fall.

That wonderful explanation would be enough, but I think that there is another important message contained in this Talmudic passage, namely that we all tend to look at ourselves as part of a group when it comes to group things, and as individuals when it comes to individual things. But actually, everything in our collective lives is connected. Our personal pain is never just about us. We are often drawn to prayer to ask for the needs of others, but we don't think to introduce our own pain into the prayer.

Evidently, we are not suffering when others are in pain, viewing it as second-hand pain instead of a first-hand pain that hurts us. What we need to do is to insert our own personal pain into all our prayers for others.

Maybe that is the magic wand which was the gamechanger for Rabbi Yoḥanan ben Zakkai — getting others to pray for his haircut, and to be upset for their great rabbi in his uncomfortable situation — and maybe this is the magic wand which can be the gamechanger for us too. God may decide that someone should be sick – and that was their destiny. We can pray for them all we want, but it won't change anything. However, their pain and suffering destiny was not necessarily our pain and suffering destiny, and so if we are in pain and suffering because of their pain and suffering, God might just think again.

And I think this is the key to understanding the Carlebach story. I believe that when Rabbi Israel Yitzḥak of Warka first prayed for the man's dying child, he was praying for someone else's pain, and that's why his prayer proved ineffective. It was only when he started crying with his own pain and suffering that the Gates of Heaven opened up, and the child's recovery could begin. Which is why, as it turns out, this Reb Shlomo story might just be true.

ARI FULD'S MESSAGE IS SET TO LAST

first published September 20th, 2018

I n March 2015, I received an email from Ari Fuld. A mutual friend had suggested that Ari get in touch with me, as he was planning to visit the West Coast and wanted to address audiences in Los Angeles about the situation in Israel. That particular trip did not materialize, but Ari visited us a few months later and spoke at our shul in Beverly Hills. We remained in touch, and he visited us again earlier this year. As recently as a few weeks ago we exchanged emails about opening him up to new audiences across the United States.

But it was not to be. Earlier this week we heard the dreadful news of Ari Fuld's brutal murder. Even as his life ebbed away, Ari instinctively chased his Arab terrorist assailant and neutralized him, undoubtedly saving other lives by doing so.

Ari was stabbed in the back, but the truth is that we have all been stabbed in the back. Twenty-five years ago, amidst great fanfare and excitement, the world learnt of the secret negotiations in Oslo that we were assured would result in a peaceful resolution between Israel and the Arabs through the creation of a "Palestinan" entity. Israel's prime minister Yitzḥak Rabin (1922-1995) joined President Bill Clinton (b.1946) and the arch terrorist PLO head Yasser Arafat (1929-2004) on the White House lawn for a photo-op to formalize the historic deal.

Rabin – whose credentials as both an Israeli military hero and as a cautious pragmatist lent credibility to the agreement – was induced to shake Arafat's hand as cameras rolled and clicked, in a moment that was continuously replayed on TV screens and appeared on newspaper front pages the world over.

Many people, myself included, were bamboozled by the euphoria of that moment. After all, in 1979 Menachem Begin had signed a peace deal with Egypt's Anwar el-Sadat (1918-1981), who had also sought Israel's destruction in the Yom Kippur War of 1973. Moshe Dayan (1915-1981), Israel's most famous general and war hero, told *Newsweek* in a 1977 interview, "If you want to make peace, you don't talk to your friends. You talk to your enemies." We were deceived into believing that Yasser Arafat was no different to Sadat, and moreover, that he was the only conduit to a peaceful resolution. But as Ari Fuld might have said, "lies, lies, lies!"

Ari never ever lost himself in the fog of media manipulation. He saw no point in Israel negotiating with anyone on the basis of falsehoods and fabrications. Unless there was clarity about the facts of the conflict, any resolution was doomed. How could Jews be referred to as occupiers, he would ask, if they are living in territory ancient scriptures clearly identify as Jewish – scriptures that predate Islam by thousands of years?

Ari would take people to the Western Wall, telling them it was part of the supporting wall of Temple Mount, once proud home to the Jewish Temple, but now "occupied" by two towering mosques. Who is occupying whom, he would ask?

Another of Ari's favorite topics was the misleading notion that Arabs are the "real" Palestinians. Before the creation of the State of Israel, he would say, it was always the Jews who were referred to as Palestinians, not the Arabs. In fact, Arabs consistently rejected "Palestinian" identity specifically because the Jews had accepted it along with the British Mandate for Palestine. He would point out that every pre-Israel organization or company with the word "Palestine" in its name was either Jewish or British, but never Arab. It was many years after the creation of Israel, with the formation of the PLO in 1964, that the Arabs adopted Palestine as their identity – purely because they needed to differentiate themselves from Israel and legitimize themselves as an independent entity in the eyes of the international community.

The Oslo Accords – and we could argue whether or not its architects were fools or knaves – plunged the world into the muddy waters of deception and fantasy. Ari Fuld – an American-born Jew with the pride of King David and the clarity of the prophet Isaiah – cut through the delusions like a hot knife through butter. Any enduring arrangement between Arabs and Jews needed to be based on a fundament of truth, he would argue, not a treacherous swamp of lies and distortions.

Sadly, Ari struggled to get his message heard by a wider audience. Even after his violent slaying there have been those who mitigated his murderer, and attempted to diminish Ari's credibility, by citing the fact that he lived in Efrat, a thriving town that is "guilty" of being located in the West Bank.

Notwithstanding this, the wide coverage of his murder, and the unfettered publicity this has given his straight-talking views, will hopefully raise their profile in a way that he could only have dreamed of. Ari bravely articulated uncomfortable truths in an attempt to reverse the damage resulting from the misinformation generated by the Oslo myth, and now those truths are front and center for all to hear.

Parshat Haazinu begins with a poetic declaration by Moses (Deut. 32:1): הַאֲזִינוּ הַשָּׁמַיִם וַאֲדַבֵּרָה וְתִשְׁמַע הָאָרֶץ אִמְרֵי פִי – "Give over your ear, Heaven, and I will speak; let the Earth hear the words of my mouth.'" Rashi, quoting *Sifrei*, addresses the curious use of heaven and earth as witnesses to the covenant, and offers the explanation that Moses, conscious of his imminent death, needed to stress the eternal truth of God's covenant: "If the Israelites ever say, 'we never accepted the covenant,' who will refute them?" He therefore called heaven and earth as his witnesses — here were witnesses that would endure forever.

Moses was acutely aware of his own mortality, and the fact that any powerful truths he conveyed would never endure beyond his own lifetime without God's assistance. Only the Creator of heaven and earth has the power to enable truth to be heard in a world dominated by lies.

Let it be God's will that Ari's incontestable truths ring out from heaven, to be heard loud and clear by those on earth who deny them. The impact of those truths will long outlive Ari's physical presence, and will be the legacy by which he will be remembered long into the future.

THE BATTLE FOR KAPPAROT AND JEWISH TRADITION

first published October 14th, 2016

O ver the past few months, animal rights activists in the United States have focused their attention on the pre-Yom Kippur custom of *kapparot*. In Los Angeles, protesters disrupted a *kapparot* gathering at the Hebrew Discovery Center run by Rabbi Netanel Louie. Meanwhile, in New York, aggressive protesters picketed *kapparot* sites across the city. At one location in Crown Heights, the demonstrators, frustrated at their inability to prevent *kapparot*, began chanting, "Animal holocaust," and "Murderers: Wake up, you're oppressed!"

There is no question that *kapparot* is a controversial custom, even among the most traditional Orthodox Jews. Carried out before Yom Kippur, the ritual involves a live chicken being waved around a person's head, as he or she recites a formula symbolically removing their accumulated sins and transferring them to the chicken. The chicken is then killed and given to the poor.

The *kapparot* custom originated in the Babylonian Jewish community approximately 1,500 years ago and has been fiercely debated by rabbis ever since. Some early rabbinic authorities dismiss *kapparot* as a paganistic rite which diminishes the seriousness of the High Holidays by giving the impression that by uttering a few words over a chicken one can circumvent the entire repentance process.

Later rabbis were concerned that the huge numbers of chickens requiring ritual slaughter in such a short period of time would inevitably lead to some not being slaughtered correctly. They argued that the danger of feeding poor Jews with non-kosher chickens was surely a far greater concern than a questionable custom not prescribed by the Torah or Talmud. As a result of these objections, an alternative *kapparot* method using coins instead of chickens became increasingly popular. Indeed, the vast majority of those who perform *kapparot* today use coins, and the money is later distributed to charity.

My own family custom, from the German Orthodox tradition, is not to do *kapparot* at all. Although I was aware of the custom growing up, my first exposure to it — in both chicken and coin form — was when I went to post-high school yeshiva.

At Beverly Hills Synagogue we hold an orderly *kapparot* session on the morning before Yom Kippur, using half-dollar coins. The issue of the animal activist protests came up as we were doing it, and in our discussions we noted that there are surely those in the Orthodox community who quietly sympathize with the protesters and agree that waving a chicken over your head in a symbolic ritual is tantamount to animal cruelty — something that is strictly forbidden by Jewish law. It has also emerged that many chickens never make it to the poor; instead they are abandoned in trash bags as everyone rushes to get home and prepare for Yom Kippur.

In which case, what are we to make of the attempts to halt this practice in the United States? A couple of months ago, a state lawsuit — "United Poultry Concerns vs. Bait Aaron, Inc." — was filed in California to prevent any group, including Hebrew Discovery Center, from holding *kapparot* events, although the suit was ultimately dismissed. A federal lawsuit — "United Poultry Concerns vs. Chabad of Irvine" — met with greater success. Filed last month, it resulted in a temporary restraining order against Chabad of Irvine's *kapparot* plans, with the order being lifted with only hours to spare before Yom Kippur began. The attorney acting for Chabad of Irvine, Hiram Sasser, pointed out that *kapparot* "is protected by the First Amendment, so the temporary restraining order should never have been issued."

He's right. The erosion of First Amendment rights is something that needs to ring alarm bells for all of us, even if the target happens to be *kapparot*. While I cannot and would never condone the wanton abuse of animals, I also know that every chicken we eat has gone through a disorientating process leading up to its death. But the law is followed to minimize any suffering; that is how we can eat chicken. If *kapparot* is done in a way that minimizes any suffering to the chickens, and those who do *kapparot* ensure that the chickens are subsequently used for charitable purposes, even though I do not personally participate in *kapparot*, I will fiercely advocate on its behalf to any detractor.

In reality, most of the detractors are not objecting exclusively against *kapparot*; their agenda is much broader than that. Using animal rights as a pretext, their real objection is to religious individuals carrying out hallowed customs that harm no one while giving meaning and depth to countless lives. *Kapparot* is just the thin end of the wedge. Mark my words, *shehita* – Jewish ritual slaughter of animals as a method of killing them for food – and *brit milah* (ritual circumcision) are next, and I have no question these warped individuals also wish to impose their skewed values on our synagogues and day schools by insisting that we adopt practices to accommodate contemporary human rights ideals and social policies that run counter to our faith.

In Parshat Haazinu, the language is very flowery and poetic. In one pasuk (Deut. 32:6), the Torah refers to those who rebel against God as "a nation that is vile, and unwise." These two definitions seem completely unrelated. There are those who rebel because they are vile, and there are those who rebel because they are unwise. Why the need for both?

Commenting on this phrase, the prolific nineteenth-century Polish rabbinic leader, Rabbi Yosef Shaul Nathanson (1808-1875), said: "If the nation were wise but vile, perhaps we could reason with them. If the nation were foolish but righteous, perhaps we could educate them. But when the nation is both vile and unwise, the cause is lost!"

Those who oppose *kapparot*, and whose hatred of rites and ritual transcends common sense, are immune to both logic and education. Our only chance of victory is to recognize them for what they are. We cannot give an inch in the battle for our rights to religious freedom. The battle for *kapparot* is undoubtedly as important and critical to the future of Jewish religious freedom as the battle for sheḥita and circumcision.

VEZOT HABERACHA

GUILTY UNTIL PROVEN INNOCENT?

first published September 27th, 2015

Sometime during 2001 I became acquainted with the popular TV personality David Baddiel. We first met at a social event in London's West End, and shortly afterwards he joined us for Friday night dinner at our home. During dinner it somehow emerged that we shared something unusual in common – both our grandfathers came from a city called Königsberg in East Prussia, and both of them escaped to the UK from Nazi Germany shortly before the outbreak of the second world war.

We were both fascinated by this coincidence, especially when David revealed that he had started writing a novel loosely based on his grandparents' experiences during those initial years in England. The book was ultimately published in 2004 under the title *The Secret Purposes*, and was highly acclaimed by literary critics.

David's grandfather had already passed away by the time we met, but my own grandfather was still alive, and David asked if he could meet him as part of his background research for the novel. So one afternoon I picked him up from his home in Primrose Hill, and we drove to Stamford Hill, where my grandfather lived. Stamford Hill is an area of London densely populated by ḥaredi Jews, and my grandparents moved there in 1947. In 1960, my grandfather was appointed rabbi of the Adath Yisroel congregation in Stamford Hill, the flagship community of the Union of Orthodox Hebrew Congregations, an umbrella organization for dozens of ḥaredi communities across London.

I just want to stress how utterly incongruous this meeting was by explaining that my grandfather had never heard of David Baddiel in his life. The reason was very simple: he never watched TV and had no knowledge or interest in media personalities. Meanwhile, to be fair, David Baddiel had never heard of Rabbi Joseph H. Dunner, Presiding Rabbi of the Union of Orthodox Hebrew Congregations, either.

But remarkably, despite this mini clash of cultures, David Baddiel and my grandfather immediately hit it off, and during the two hour meeting my grandfather regaled us both with fascinating stories, many of which I had never previously heard, all of them about those first few difficult years for him and my grandmother as penniless refugees in England.

David was particularly interested in my grandfather's time on the Isle of Man. He wanted his novel to convey the experiences of German Jewish refugees who had been interned as enemy aliens in 1940 on the Isle of Man when the British authorities were suddenly gripped by the understandable fear that some of the German refugees they had taken in could turn out to be "Trojan horse" Nazi infiltrators who would facilitate a German invasion of the British Isles. My grandfather spent a few months in the Isle of Man before being released. David's grandfather was there for almost a year.

I have been thinking about the Isle of Man internment these past couple of weeks as the refugee crisis in Europe has escalated out of control. On the one hand there are those who say that refugees fleeing war-torn regions of the world should be given the chance to find homes in countries where they are not in any danger, no questions asked. Others point out that while these refugees are indeed in dire circumstances, many of them come from countries and cultures that incessantly spew hatred of the West, and whose ideologies are at odds with democratic values and Western tolerance.

My thoughts about this issue are colored by my grandfather's experiences. If my grandfather, and David Baddiel's for that matter, both of them genteel, civilized, university-educated German Jews, whose persecution by the antisemitic Nazis meant that their sympathies were certainly not with Hitler and his cohorts, could be interned on the Isle of Man for many months on the basis of a slight risk that they were Nazi plants, why is it not politically correct to at least consider the possibility that today's refugees from countries and cultures that hate the West might just pose a danger to the countries in which they are claiming asylum? I am not suggesting they be interned, but surely we have a duty to ensure that there won't be problems down the line.

I subsequently asked my grandfather if he resented his internment on the Isle of Man. Certainly not, he told me – Britain was at war. And of course, once it became clear that he was no threat he was freed. But nowadays, the mere idea that any refugee should be treated with suspicion is met with unbridled indignation. Apparently, it is immoral to refuse entry to refugees on the basis that they could be a threat. The principle of habeus corpus is enshrined in our legal system, and is therefore sacrosanct. In other words, "you are innocent until proven guilty," and no person should ever be considered a danger simply because of their point of origin.

Interestingly, Jewish tradition does not buy into the concept of assumed innocence. In the final portion of the Torah, Vezot Haberacha, we read about the death of Moses (Deut. 34:5): וַיָּמָת שָׁם מֹשֶׁה עֶבֶד ה' בְּאֶרֶץ מוֹאָב – "Moses the servant of God died there, in the land of Moab."

The commentaries are puzzled, as this is the first time Moses is ever referred to as "the servant of God." Why now? Why not before? The Midrash explains that God never refers to anyone as "holy" until after they have died, because while they are alive they could do something bad, and even the most righteous of individuals may give in to temptation at some point. Only once a person has died, and has been righteous throughout their life, can they safely be referred to as "holy" and as a "servant of God." So much so, that even Moses, the greatest of all Jewish leaders who communed with God "face to face," and whose purity and loyalty to God was evident every day of his life, could only be referred to as "God's servant" once his journey was complete.

The point is, if even those who are beyond reasonable suspicion can fail, why would anyone suggest that someone brought up to hate the West is not a potential danger simply because they are in a dire situation? If my grandfather, a righteous upstanding individual arrested by the Nazis for being Jewish could be interned by Great Britain as a potential threat – and, as he told me, he understood why they had to do it – surely anyone emanating from a country or culture that opposes everything the Western world stands for should accept, if they demand asylum and acceptance in the West, that their new host country may be initially wary.

There are never easy answers in the debate over immigrants and refugees, and it is a hot-button topic that may never be properly resolved. Nevertheless, I believe this important issue deserves an honest debate in which every aspect of the benefits and dangers of absorbing refugees escaping from countries who are openly at war with the West will be considered. As someone whose family was only able to escape certain death at the hands of the Nazis as a result of the willingness of Great Britain to take us in, I am fully aware of the desperate situation of refugees trying to get away from war-torn regions of the world. But a state's first duty must always be towards its citizens, and every effort must be made by those in power to ensure the immediate and strategic safety of the population.

INDEX